Reading Digital Culture

Edited by

David Trend

BLACKWELL
Publishers

Copyright © Blackwell Publishers Ltd 2001; editorial matter and organization copyright
© David Trend 2001

First published 2001

2 4 6 8 10 9 7 5 3 1

Blackwell Publishers Inc.
350 Main Street
Malden, Massachusetts 02148
USA

Blackwell Publishers Ltd
108 Cowley Road
Oxford OX4 1JF
UK

Library of Congress Cataloging-in-Publication Data

Reading digital culture / edited by David Trend.
    p. cm.—(Keywords in cultural studies; 4)
    Includes bibliographical references and index.
    ISBN 0–631–22301–0 (alk. paper)—ISBN 0–631–22302–9 (pb.: alk. paper)
    1. Information society. 2. Information technology—Social aspects. I. Trend, David. II.
Series.

HM851 .R43 2001
303.48′33—dc21   00-057914

British Library Cataloguing in Publication Data
A CIP catalogue record for this book is available from the British Library.

Typeset in Galliard 10 on 12.5pt
by Kolam Information Services Pvt. Ltd, Pondicherry, India
Printed in Great Britain by TJ International, Padstow, Cornwall

This book is printed on acid-free paper.

Contents

Acknowledgments

Preparing a book like this takes time and requires intellectual support. In 1999 the University of California, Irvine granted me a sabbatical to work on this anthology and my forthcoming book of essays, *Welcome to Cyberschool*. During the same period, the Getty Research Institute provided sustenance through its Visiting Scholars Program. Crucial perspectives about digital media and network culture came through my association with University of California's Digital Arts Research Network (DARNet). Timothy Allen Jackson contributed substantial insight in the preparation of this collection, providing articles and authors drawn from his research in the area of new media. This book was initiated in concept and supported throughout its development by Blackwell Cultural Studies Editor Jayne Fargnoli.

Introduction

To say that we inhabit a digital world is an understatement. In recent years the Internet and other information technologies have transformed many fundamental parts of life: how we work and play, how we communicate and consume, how we create knowledge and learn, even how we understand politics and participate in public life. Smart machines, smart houses, and smart cards exist in a world of cyberbodies, cybercities, and cybercash. It is nearly impossible to make it through a day without encountering a computer, a digitally mediated image, or a news report about the current "digital revolution." The ubiquity of digital data storage, computation, and telecommunication have made us profoundly dependent on computer networks (whether we realize it or not), enveloping society in what might be termed a "digital culture." Indeed, mediation and invisibility have become defining characteristics of an age in which cyberspace has transformed much of material culture into a vaporous cloud of signal and code.

Reading Digital Culture addresses the changes evinced by emerging communication technologies and the way we think about them. The use of the term "reading" in the title is intended to suggest a critical approach to the rapidly growing digital media field. Such scrutiny is needed at a time when novel technological phenomena frequently are accepted without question or naturalized as neutral occurrences. The term "culture" is meant to accent the human dimension of this anthology. It is a book primarily about people, not technology in isolation. If *Reading Digital Culture* has a point to make, it is that technologies emerge from specific contexts and serve particular interests. Yet the interrogation of these contexts and interests remains a blind spot in most discussions of cyberspace and digital media.

Celebrating the new computer era is a massive discourse in both mainstream media and academic literature in which the figure of utopia looms large. Evoking traditions of technological determinism and free-market boosterism, the denizens of information technology have promoted digital culture as the culmination of the Enlightenment project and the economic panacea of the post-industrial world. All of this is equated with a narrative of humankind's ever advancing march of progress, as information technology is touted as the ultimate vehicle of mastery and transcendence. Indeed, to some this technology is seen as the key to overcoming the limits of material existence – an "extension of man" through which we become "posthistorical" and "posthuman."

In mainstream media, this cyberenthusiasm becomes manifest in tendencies to periodize the digital era as a radical break from anything that came before it, or to exceptionalize it as a moment in which the logic of mathematics has enabled society to overcome human irrationality and failed communication. This overwhelmingly positive view of the information age is driven in a narrow sense by the very computer and software industries that have created the wealthiest and most powerful corporate infrastructure in human history, and more broadly supported by the enormous "information economy" of content producers, merchandisers, and other ancillary services of the digital industrial complex.

This utopian enthusiasm has been met by a less ubiquitous, but frequently vociferous, measure of resistance from a myriad assortment of critics, skeptics, and conspiracy theorists – ranging from those who despair the threats of genetic engineering, computer surveillance, and cybercapitalism, to the countless peoples and nations who stand on the wrong side of the "digital divide." As Bill Gates and Steve Case proclaim the global omnipresence of the Internet, the majority of non-Western nations and nearly 97 percent of the world's population remain unconnected to the net for lack of money, access, or knowledge. This exclusion of so vast a share of the global population from the Internet sharply contradicts the claims of those who posit the World Wide Web as a "universal" medium of egalitarian communication.

In the context of such disagreements and intellectual cul-de-sacs, digital culture finds itself without a unifying set of principles or an overarching sense of purpose. The "consensual hallucination" of cyberspace has proven as difficult to explain as an acid trip – in large part due to the growing ability of technological tools to enable human subjectivity and expression in unfamiliar ways. In cyberspace considerably more is at stake than the mere representation of a putative reality, as regimes of communication that "reproduce" data, images, and cognition are supplanted by systems that "simulate" consciousness, agency, and desire. Hard-edged certainties of industrialization, Enlightenment empiricism, and modernity have given way to more malleable concepts of postindustrialism, technoscience, and postmodernity.

Despite the exponential growth of web sites, magazine articles, journal issues, books, and television programs about computer media, readers of digital culture find themselves confounded by a destabilizing war of positions that often exhibits more contradiction than coherence. Discussions in academic circles have fragmented into a myriad of camps that all too frequently privilege hyperbole and polemic over complexity and dialogue. Writers and theorists have situated themselves on one side or another of the utopian divide, or they have analyzed a particular aspect of digital culture. Books with optimistic titles like *e-topia*, *Internet Dreams*, and *The Road Ahead* are answered by less sanguine works like *Flame Wars*, *Data Trash*, and *Cyberspace Divide*. Lacking a stable language to describe this seemingly new world, writers reach for neologisms or cling to tired metaphors like the nervous system, the highway or the post office.

Only recently have commentators come to acknowledge the history of such technological discussions or the vast diversity of approaches to them. *Reading Digital Culture* presents a collection of texts that offer a critical conversation about these issues. While acknowledging various debates surrounding digital media, *Reading Digital Culture* does not seek to ameliorate such disagreements. Deferring this impulse for closure is difficult at a time when unresolved tensions in the discourse of information technology seem to demand foundational principles and groundrules. In resisting these tendencies, *Reading Digital Culture* seeks to promote a multiplicity of avenues for addressing this interdisciplinary field. In this spirit, *Reading Digital Culture* is organized into six overlapping sections.

I. *The Machine in the Garden.* Digital culture did not emerge from a vacuum. Like any historical phenomenon, it is the product of past and present thinking, material relations, and social contexts. And like other moments, the information age is brimming with speculation about future possibilities. This section contains essays from a range of humanists, artists, and scientists, who have grappled with the implications of digital media inside and outside of their disciplines. While referencing major debates in the history and philosophy of technology, these writings focus on the particular questions posed by digital media.

II. *Knowledge and Communication in a Digital Age.* Digital culture is distinguished by the myriad definitions, interpretations, and metaphors it has evoked in the minds of futurists, scholars, netsurfers, audiophiles, e-merchants, communitarians, voyeurs, and pioneers of the "electronic frontier," among countless others. Variously seen as a catalyst for innovation, a doorway to human spirit, or a shortcut to the stock exchange, digital media have become a veritable "rosetta stone" for translating the desires of speakers into prescriptions for the good life. This section engages that process of translation in the various ways that digital media organize, store, transmit, and transform meaning into digits and code.

III. *Living in the Immaterial World.* Digital culture inhabits an existing world of physical objects, economies, and geopolitical institutions. It also creates a "virtual world" in its relationship to what others perceive as "real." As elsewhere in this anthology, considerable disagreement exists over the extent to which computers, software, and network technologies contribute to the world as it exists or that they enable changes in that world. Essays in this section address topics ranging from globalization, commercialization, and militarism, to issues of education, labor, and research.

IV. *Performing Identity in Cyberspace.* How digital media change the way we think about our personal and collective identities is of central importance to cyberculture. This section examines how engagement with computers affects subjectivity and agency, as well as the ways digital media highlight or obscure identities and social groupings. Of special importance in this section is the way the body is produced, replicated, and inscribed by literal and figurative technologies. Equally significant are the circuits of power that inhere in technologies of identification and social ritual. These issues are profoundly important, since they will shape the very character of what it means to be human in the twenty-first century.

V. *Searching for Community Online.* Benedict Anderson's now-famous formulation of the "imagined community" holds special significance in digital culture, as a means for people dislocated in space and time to form groups and engage each other.[1] Again the relationship of "virtual" to "real" worlds becomes an issue in debating the efficacy of computer-mediated social relations. Similarly, the much-celebrated assertions that the Internet will instill new forms of democracy and global unity cry out for critical scrutiny. Topics in this section include access to technology, designations of social class, demarcations of public and private space, education and information policy, community organizing, and democratic practice.

VI. *Reading Digital Culture.* Given the youth of the discourse surrounding digital culture, much of the writing that emerges shares a certain unselfconsciousness. This becomes apparent in tendencies toward ahistoricity, a lack of context, or simply an entrenched determination to say something "new." During the last decade cultural critics have begun to comment on this discourse itself as a form of meta-analysis. *Reading Digital Culture* concludes with some representative examples of these "readings" of digital discourse.

Reading Digital Culture is intended to speak to many audiences. Written by an eclectic assortment of the field's most widely read commentators, *Reading Digital Culture* addresses topics ranging from virtual reality, Internet commerce, and computer art to the effects of new technology on work, leisure, and community. In stressing a multiplicity of perspectives, *Reading Digital Culture* seeks to move beyond the tired dualisms and polemics that have characterized so much thinking of the past millennium – and that have dogged the more recent discourse on digital media. As William Mitchell has stated, "we will do far better to sidestep the well-known trap of technological determinism, to renounce the symmetrical form of fatalism proposed by booster-technocrats and curmudgeonly techno-scoffers," and to move forward with whatever degree of criticality and self-consciousness is possible in a postmodern age. "Our job is to design the future we want, not to predict its predetermined path."[2]

While acknowledging the problems often entailed in canon-building and the impossibility of authoritatively mapping such a rapidly changing field, *Reading Digital Culture* presumes a measure of prescription in emphasizing the imbrication of technological and social relations. As cyborg consciousness erodes the boundaries between human and machine, it becomes all the more important to bring an element of awareness – and ethics – to digital culture. No one could have predicted the speed and ferocity with which an obscure network for exchanging research findings could have evolved into the most powerful economic force in human history. We are only beginning to understand the consequences of this phenomenon, and the responsibilities it has brought with it.

Notes

1   Benedict Anderson, *Imagined Communities: Reflections on the Origins and Spread of Nationalism* (London: Verso, 1983).

2   William J Mitchell, *E-topia: Urban Life, Jim – But Not as We Know It* (Cambridge, MA: MIT Press, 1999), p. 12.

Part I

The Machine in the Garden

Any analysis of contemporary technology needs to acknowledge the historical patterns of ideology, production, and social organization that invariably reproduce themselves from generation to generation. At the same time, digital technologies enable certain distinctive ways of conceiving ideas and understanding the world. Current controversies over the role of digital media in contemporary life have their roots in unresolved contradictions in the history of technology itself, an area of study largely ignored through much of Western history. The aristocratic culture of ancient Greece rarely considered the everyday banalities of technology, electing instead to focus on social, political, and theoretical concerns. In a mindset that endured for centuries, the reluctance to critically scrutinize technology in the eighteenth and nineteenth centuries enabled a romanticization of machines as "natural" manifestations of human agency – an organic and unremittingly positive "extension of man."

With the rise of science and the mechanization of work in the late-nineteenth and early twentieth centuries came the development of large-scale integrated "technological systems" to make industrialization possible. The mass production and distribution of commodities like automobiles called into existence a complex constellation of workers, suppliers, clerks, managers, transporters, dealers, and service people. The legacy of these early technological systems and their ideological underpinnings are still with us today but they no longer go unchallenged.

In the years following World War II, a range of counter arguments arose to question unproblematized premises of technological progress. With Hiroshima, the nuclear arms race, and the US involvement in the Vietnam War, public anxieties began to erode the unquestioned role of technology as an instrument of social good. Technology was no longer seen as neutral, but instead an embodiment of often-contested social values. Materialist analysts addressed the overarching linkage of technology to markets. Feminists critiqued the patriarchal biases of science. Postcolonial scholars linked advances in technology to the expansionist paradigm of the West. Poststructuralist theorists questioned technology's universal definitions of progress and rationality. Ironically, it was during this period of growing skepticism that the science of computational systems was nurtured and developed. Over time, the nascent field of information science would breathe new life into the dream of a world made perfect by the machine.

The essays in this section approach digital culture from historical and philosophical perspectives, linking contemporary discussions of information technology and virtual environments to broader questions of epistemology, agency, and ethics. How can society grapple with the seemingly infinite capacities of computational devices? What are the implications of geometrically accelerating rates of obsolescence? What are the problems and promises inherent as machines assume the functions of human bodies and minds? As recently as a decade ago, no one would have predicted the ubiquitous role the Internet would play in society. So pervasive has the Net become that is difficult to overstate its role in the popular imaginary.

From different perspectives Vannevar Bush, Sadie Plant, and Paul Virilio discuss ways that digital culture has altered fundamental understandings of knowledge, invention, and temporality. The contributions by Félix Guattari, Donna Haraway, and Slavoj Žižek extend these discussions by exploring the confluence of human and computer intelligence. Indeed, how do we grapple with the machine in the garden? As an ensemble, these writings illustrate the paradoxical character of technology described by Martin Heidegger as something with which we struggle, yet ultimately must rely upon. As a substance existing throughout human history, "It is impossible," Heidegger wrote, "for man to imagine a position outside of technology."[1]

Note

1 Martin Heidegger, *Being and Time*, trans. John Macquarrie and Edward Robinson (New York: Harper and Row, 1962), p. 41.

1

As We May Think

Vannevar Bush

Vannevar Bush, "As We May Think," *Atlantic Monthly* (July 1945), pp. 47–61.

Vannevar Bush (1890–1974) was director of the Federal Office of Scientific Research and Development. In this famous essay published in the *Atlantic Monthly* in 1945, Bush presents his "memex" model of a computational "thinking machine" as a means for scientists to make stored knowledge more accessible. "As We May Think" also appears in Bush's book *Endless Horizons* (Ayer Co., 1975).

This has not been a scientist's war; it has been a war in which all have had a part. The scientists, burying their old professional competition in the demand of a common cause, have shared greatly and learned much. It has been exhilarating to work in effective partnership. Now, for many, this appears to be approaching an end. What are the scientists to do next?

For the biologists, and particularly for the medical scientists, there can be little indecision, for their war work has hardly required them to leave the old paths. Many indeed have been able to carry on their war research in their familiar peacetime laboratories. Their objectives remain much the same.

It is the physicists who have been thrown most violently off stride, who have left academic pursuits for the making of strange destructive gadgets, who have had to devise new methods for their unanticipated assignments. They have done their part on the devices that made it possible to turn back the enemy. They have worked in combined effort with the physicists of our allies. They have felt within themselves the stir of achievement. They have been part of a great team. Now, as peace approaches, one asks where they will find objectives worthy of their best.

1

Of what lasting benefit has been man's use of science and of the new instruments which his research brought into existence? First, they have increased his control of his material environment. They have improved his food, his clothing, his shelter;

they have increased his security and released him partly from the bondage of bare existence. They have given him increased knowledge of his own biological processes so that he has had a progressive freedom from disease and an increased span of life. They are illuminating the interactions of his physiological and psychological functions, giving the promise of an improved mental health.

Science has provided the swiftest communication between individuals; it has provided a record of ideas and has enabled man to manipulate and to make extracts from that record so that knowledge evolves and endures throughout the life of a race rather than that of an individual.

There is a growing mountain of research. But there is increased evidence that we are being bogged down today as specialization extends. The investigator is staggered by the findings and conclusions of thousands of other workers – conclusions which he cannot find time to grasp, much less to remember, as they appear. Yet specialization becomes increasingly necessary for progress, and the effort to bridge between disciplines is correspondingly superficial.

Professionally our methods of transmitting and reviewing the results of research are generations old and by now are totally inadequate for their purpose. If the aggregate time spent in writing scholarly works and in reading them could be evaluated, the ratio between these amounts of time might well be startling. Those who conscientiously attempt to keep abreast of current thought, even in restricted fields, by close and continuous reading might well shy away from an examination calculated to show how much of the previous month's efforts could be produced on call. Mendel's concept of the laws of genetics was lost to the world for a generation because his publication did not reach the few who were capable of grasping and extending it; and this sort of catastrophe is undoubtedly being repeated all about us, as truly significant attainments become lost in the mass of the inconsequential.

The difficulty seems to be, not so much that we publish unduly in view of the extent and variety of present-day interests, but rather that publication has been extended far beyond our present ability to make real use of the record. The summation of human experience is being expanded at a prodigious rate, and the means we use for threading through the consequent maze to the momentarily important item is the same as was used in the days of square-rigged ships.

[...]

Our ineptitude in getting at the record is largely caused by the artificiality of systems of indexing. When data of any sort are placed in storage, they are filed alphabetically or numerically, and information is found (when it is) by tracing it down from subclass to subclass. It can be in only one place, unless duplicates are used; one has to have rules as to which path will locate it, and the rules are cumbersome. Having found one item, moreover, one has to emerge from the system and re-enter on a new path.

The human mind does not work that way. It operates by association. With one item in its grasp, it snaps instantly to the next that is suggested by the association of thoughts, in accordance with some intricate web of trails carried by the cells of the brain. It has other characteristics, of course: trails that are not frequently followed are prone to fade, items are not fully permanent, memory is transitory. Yet the speed of action, the intricacy of trails, the detail of mental pictures, is awe-inspiring beyond all else in nature.

Man cannot hope fully to duplicate this mental process artificially, but he certainly ought to be able to learn from it. In minor ways he may even improve, for his records have relative permanency. The first idea, however, to be drawn from the analogy concerns selection. Selection by association, rather than by indexing, may yet be mechanized. One cannot hope thus to equal the speed and flexibility with which the mind follows an associative trail, but it should be possible to beat the mind decisively in regard to the permanence and clarity of the items resurrected from storage.

Consider a future device for individual use, which is a sort of mechanized private file and library. It needs a name, and to coin one at random, "memex" will do. A memex is a device in which an individual stores all his books, records, and communications, and which is mechanized so that it may be consulted with exceeding speed and flexibility. It is an enlarged intimate supplement to his memory.

It consists of a desk, and while it can presumably be operated from a distance, it is primarily the piece of furniture at which he works. On the top are slanting translucent screens, on which material can be projected for convenient reading. There is a keyboard, and sets of buttons and levers. Otherwise it looks like an ordinary desk.

In one end is the stored material. The matter of bulk is well taken care of by improved microfilm. Only a small part of the interior of the memex is devoted to storage, the rest to mechanism. Yet if the user inserted 5,000 pages of material a day it would take him hundreds of years to fill the repository, so he can be profligate and enter material freely.

Most of the memex contents are purchased on microfilm ready for insertion. Books of all sorts, pictures, current periodicals, newspapers, are thus obtained and dropped into place. Business correspondence takes the same path. And there is provision for direct entry. On the top of the memex is a transparent platen. On this are placed longhand notes, photographs, memoranda, all sort of things. When one is in place, the depression of a lever causes it to be photographed onto the next blank space in a section of the memex film, dry photography being employed.

There is, of course, provision for consultation of the record by the usual scheme of indexing. If the user wishes to consult a certain book, he taps its code on the keyboard, and the title page of the book promptly appears before him, projected onto one of his viewing positions. Frequently-used codes are mnemonic, so that he seldom consults his code book; but when he does, a single tap of a key projects it for his use. Moreover, he has supplemental levers. On deflecting one of these levers to the right he runs through the book before him, each page in turn being projected at a speed which just allows a recognizing glance at each. If he deflects it further to the right, he steps through the book 10 pages at a time; still further at 100 pages at a time. Deflection to the left gives him the same control backwards.

A special button transfers him immediately to the first page of the index. Any given book of his library can thus be called up and consulted with far greater facility than if it were taken from a shelf. As he has several projection positions, he can leave one item in position while he calls up another. He can add marginal notes and comments, taking advantage of one possible type of dry photography, and it could even be arranged so that he can do this by a stylus scheme, such as is now employed in the telautograph seen in railroad waiting rooms, just as though he had the physical page before him.

7

All this is conventional, except for the projection forward of present-day mechanisms and gadgetry. It affords an immediate step, however, to associative indexing, the basic idea of which is a provision whereby any item may be caused at will to select immediately and automatically another. This is the essential feature of the memex. The process of tying two items together is the important thing.

When the user is building a trail, he names it, inserts the name in his code book, and taps it out on his keyboard. Before him are the two items to be joined, projected onto adjacent viewing positions. At the bottom of each there are a number of blank code spaces, and a pointer is set to indicate one of these on each item. The user taps a single key, and the items are permanently joined. In each code space appears the code word. Out of view, but also in the code space, is inserted a set of dots for photocell viewing; and on each item these dots by their positions designate the index number of the other item.

Thereafter, at any time, when one of these items is in view, the other can be instantly recalled merely by tapping a button below the corresponding code space. Moreover, when numerous items have been thus joined together to form a trail, they can be reviewed in turn, rapidly or slowly, by deflecting a lever like that used for turning the pages of a book. It is exactly as though the physical items had been gathered together to form a new book. It is more than this, for any item can be joined into numerous trails.

The owner of the memex, let us say, is interested in the origin and properties of the bow and arrow. Specifically he is studying why the short Turkish bow was apparently superior to the English long bow in the skirmishes of the Crusades. He has dozens of possibly pertinent books and articles in his memex. First he runs through an encyclopedia, finds an interesting but sketchy article, leaves it projected. Next, in a history, he finds another pertinent item, and ties the two together. Thus he goes, building a trail of many items. Occasionally he inserts a comment of his own, either linking it into the main trail or joining it by a side trail to a particular item. When it becomes evident that the elastic properties of available materials had a great deal to do with the bow, he branches off on a side trail which takes him through textbooks on elasticity and tables of physical constants. He inserts a page of longhand analysis of his own. Thus he builds a trail of his interest through the maze of materials available to him.

And his trails do not fade. Several years later, his talk with a friend turns to the queer ways in which a people resist innovations, even of vital interest. He has an example, in the fact that the outranged Europeans still failed to adopt the Turkish bow. In fact he has a trail on it. A touch brings up the code book. Tapping a few keys projects the head of the trail. A lever runs through it at will, stopping at interesting items, going off on side excursions. It is an interesting trail, pertinent to the discussion. So he sets a reproducer in action, photographs the whole trail out, and passes it to his friend for insertion in his own memex, there to be linked into the more general trail.

8

Wholly new forms of encyclopedias will appear, ready-made with a mesh of associative trails running through them, ready to be dropped into the memex and there amplified. The lawyer has at his touch the associated opinions and decisions of his whole experience, and of the experience of friends and authorities. The patent attorney has on call the millions of issued patents, with familiar trails to every point of his client's interest. The physician, puzzled by its patient's reactions, strikes the trial established in studying an earlier similar case, and runs rapidly through analogous case histories, with side references to the classics for the pertinent anatomy and histology. The chemist, struggling with the synthesis of an organic compound, has all the chemical literature before him in his laboratory, with trails following the analogies of compounds, and side trails to their physical and chemical behavior.

The historian, with a vast chronological account of a people, parallels it with a skip trail which stops only at the salient items, and can follow at any time contemporary trails which lead him all over civilization at a particular epoch. There is a new profession of trailblazers, those who find delight in the task of establishing useful trails through the enormous mass of the common record. The inheritance from the master becomes, not only his additions to the world's record, but for his disciples the entire scaffolding by which they were erected.

2

"ada"

Sadie Plant

Sadie Plant is the author of *Zeros and Ones: Digital Women + The New Technoculture* (Doubleday, 1997). In this essay, Plant discusses the dilemma faced by nineteenth-century mathematician Charles Babbage, who developed his computational device called the "Difference Engine," only to then develop a newer version which rendered the original obsolete.

In 1833, a teenage girl met a machine which she came to regard "as a friend." It was a futuristic device which seemed to have dropped into her world at least a century before its time.

Later to be known as Ada Lovelace, she was then Ada Byron, the only child of Annabella, a mathematician who had herself been dubbed Princess of Parallelograms by her husband, Lord Byron. The machine was the Difference Engine, a calculating system on which the engineer Charles Babbage had been working for many years. "We both went to see the thinking machine (for such it seems) last Monday," Annabella wrote in her diary. To the amazement of its onlookers, it "raised several Nos. to the 2nd & 3rd powers, and extracted the root of a quadratic Equation." While most of the audience gazed in astonishment at the machine, Ada "young as she was, understood its working, and saw the great beauty of the invention."

When Babbage had begun work on the Difference Engine, he was interested in the possibility of "making machinery to compute arithmetical tables." Although he struggled to persuade the British government to fund his work, he had no doubt about the feasibility and the value of such a machine. Isolating common mathematical differences between tabulated numbers, Babbage was convinced that this "method of differences supplied a general principle by which *all* tables might be computed through limited intervals, by one uniform process." By 1822 he had made a small but functional machine, and "in the year 1833, an event of great importance in the history of the engine occurred. Mr. Babbage had directed a portion of it, consisting of sixteen figures, to be put together. It was capable of calculating tables having two or three orders of differences; and, to some extent, of forming other tables. The action of this portion completely justified the expectations raised, and gave a most satisfactory assurance of its final success."

Shortly after this part of his machine went on public display, Babbage was struck by the thought that the Difference Engine, still incomplete, had already superseded itself. "Having, in the meanwhile, naturally speculated upon the general principles on which machinery for calculation might be constructed, *a principle of an entirely new kind* occurred to him, the power of which over the most complicated arithmetical operations seemed nearly unbounded. On reexamining his drawings . . . the new principle appeared to be limited only by the extent of the mechanism it might require." If the simplicity of the mechanisms which allowed the Difference Engine to perform addition could be extended to thousands rather than hundreds of components, a machine could be built which would "execute more rapidly the calculations for which the *Difference* Engine was intended; or, that the *Difference* Engine would itself be superseded by a far simpler mode of construction." The government officials who had funded Babbage's work on the first machine were not pleased to learn that it was now to be abandoned in favor of a new set of mechanical processes which "were essentially different from those of the Difference Engine." While Babbage did his best to persuade them that the "fact of a new superseding an old machine, in a very few years, is one of constant occurrence in our manufactories; and instances might be pointed out in which the advance of invention has been so rapid, and the demand for machinery so great, that half-finished machines have been thrown aside as useless before their completion," Babbage's decision to proceed with his new machine was also his break with the bodies which had funded his previous work. Babbage lost the support of the state, but he had already gained assistance of a very different kind.

"You are a brave man," Ada told Babbage, "to give yourself wholly up to Fairy-Guidance! – I advise you to allow yourself to be unresistingly bewitched . . ." No one, she added, "knows what almost *awful* energy & power lie yet undevelopped in that *wiry* little system of mine."

In 1842 Louis Menabrea, an Italian military engineer, had deposited his *Sketch of the Analytical Engine Invented by Charles Babbage* in the Bibliothèque Universelle de Génève. Shortly after its appearance, Babbage later wrote, the "Countess of Lovelace informed me that she had translated the memoir of Menabrea." Enormously impressed by this work, Babbage invited her to join him in the development of the machine. "I asked why she had not herself written an original paper on a subject with which she was so intimately acquainted? To this Lady Lovelace replied that the thought had not occurred to her. I then suggested that she should add some notes to Menabrea's memoir; an idea which was immediately adopted."

Babbage and Ada developed an intense relationship. "We discussed together the various illustrations that might be introduced," wrote Babbage. "I suggested several, but the selection was entirely her own. So also was the algebraic working out of the different problems, except, indeed, that relating to the numbers of

Bernoulli, which I had offered to do to save Lady Lovelace the trouble. This she sent back to me for an amendment, having detected a grave mistake which I had made in the process."

> "A strong-minded woman! Much like her mother, eh? Wears green spectacles and writes learned books...She wants to upset the universe, and play dice with the hemispheres. Women never know when to stop..."
>
> William Gibson and Bruce Sterling, *The Difference Engine*

Babbage's mathematical errors, and many of his attitudes, greatly irritated Ada. While his tendency to blame other bodies for the slow progress of his work was sometimes well founded, when he insisted on prefacing the publication of the memoir and her notes with a complaint about the attitude of the British authorities to his work, Ada refused to endorse him. "I never *can* or *will* support you in acting on principles which I consider not only wrong in themselves, but suicidal." She declared Babbage "one of the most impracticable, selfish, & intemperate persons one can have to do with," and laid down several severe conditions for the continuation of their collaboration. "Can you," she asked, with undisguised impatience, "undertake to give your mind *wholly and undividedly*, as a primary object that no engagement is to interfere with, to the consideration of all those matters in which I shall at times require your intellectual *assistance & supervision; &* can you promise not to *slur & hurry* things over; or to mislay & allow confusion & mistakes to enter into documents &c?"

Ada was, she said, "very much *afraid* as yet of exciting the powers I *know I have over others*, & the *evidence* of which I have certainly been *most unwilling to admit*, in fact for a long time considered quite fanciful and absurd...I therefore carefully refrain from all attempts *intentionally* to exercise unusual powers." Perhaps this was why her work was simply attributed to A.A.L. "It is not my wish to *proclaim* who has written it," she wrote. These were just a few afterthoughts, a mere commentary on someone else's work. But Ada did want them to bear some name: "I rather wish to append anything that may tend hereafter to *individualize it & identify* it, with other productions of the said A.A.L." And for all her apparent modesty, Ada knew how important her notes really were. "To say the truth, I am rather *amazed* at them; & cannot help being struck quite *malgré moi*, with the really masterly nature of the style, & its Superiority to that of the Memoir itself." Her work was indeed vastly more influential – and three times longer – than the text to which they were supposed to be mere adjuncts. A hundred years before the hardware had been built, Ada had produced the first example of what was later called computer programming.

[...]

3

From Virtual Reality to the Virtualization of Reality

Slavoj Žižek

Slavoj Žižek, "From Virtual Reality to the Virtualization of Reality," in Timothy Druckery, ed., *Electronic Culture: Technology and Visual Representation* (New York: Aperture, 1996), pp. 290–5.

Slavoj Žižek is a senior researcher at the Institute for Social Sciences at the University of Ljubljana, Slovenia. He has written extensively on social and aesthetic theory in such books as *Writing on Drugs* (Farrar, Straus & Giroux, 2000) and *The Sublime Object of Ideology* (Verso, 1989). This essay discusses the notion of machine intelligence as a simulation of "real" human thinking.

How are we to approach "virtual reality" from the psychoanalytical perspective? Let us take as our starting point Freud's most famous dream, that of Irma's injection;[1] the first part of the dream, Freud's dialogue with Irma, this exemplary case of a dual, specular relationship, culminates in a look into her open mouth:

> There's a horrendous discovery here, that of the flesh one never sees, the foundation of things, the other side of the head, of the face, the secretory glands par excellence, the flesh from which everything exudes, at the very heart of the mystery, the flesh in as much as it is suffering, is formless, in as much as its form in itself is something which provokes anxiety. Spectre of anxiety, identification of anxiety, the final revelation of you are this – You are this, which is so far from you, this which is the ultimate formlessness.[2]

Suddenly, this horror changes miraculously into "a sort of ataraxia" defined by Lacan precisely as "the coming into operation of the symbolic function"[3] exemplified by the production of the formula of trimethylamin, the subject floats freely in symbolic bliss. The trap to be avoided here, of course, is to contrast this symbolic bliss with "hard reality." The fundamental thesis of Lacanian psychoanalysis is, on the contrary, that what we call "reality" constitutes itself against the background of such a "bliss"; i.e., of such an exclusion of some traumatic Real (epitomized here by a *woman's* throat). This is precisely what Lacan has in mind when he says that fantasy is the ultimate support of reality: "reality" stabilizes itself when some fantasy-frame of a "symbolic bliss" forecloses the view into the abyss of the Real. Far from being a kind of figment of our dreams that prevents us from "seeing reality as it effectively is," fantasy is constitutive of what we call reality: the most common bodily "reality" is constituted via a detour through the maze of imagination. In other words, the price we pay for our access to "reality" is that something – the reality of the trauma – must be "repressed."

What strikes you here is the parallel between the dream of Irma's injection and another famous Freudian dream, that of the dead son who appears to his father and addresses him with the reproach, "Father, can't you see that I'm burning?" In his interpretation of the dream of Irma's injection, Lacan draws our attention to the appropriate remark by Eric Ericson that after the look into Irma's throat, after his encounter of the Real, *Freud should have awakened* like the dreamer of the dream of the burning son who wakes up when he encounters this horrifying apparition: when confronted with the Real in all its unbearable horror, the dreamer wakes up; i.e., escapes into "reality." One has to draw a radical conclusion from this parallel between the two dreams: what we call "reality" is constituted exactly upon the model of the asinine "symbolic bliss" that enables Freud to continue to sleep after the horrifying look into Irma's throat. The anonymous dreamer who awakens into reality in order to avoid the traumatic Real of the burning son's reproach proceeds the same way as Freud who, after the look into Irma's throat, "changes the register"; i.e., escapes into the fantasy which veils the Real. What has this to do with the computer? As early as 1954 Lacan pointed out that in today's world, the world of the machine proper, the paradigmatic case for "symbolic bliss" is the computer,[4] as one can ascertain when one enacts a kind of phenomenological investigation, leaving aside (technological) questions of how the computer works, and confining oneself to its symbolic impact, to how the computer inscribes itself into our symbolic universe.

In other words, one must conceive the computer as a *machine à penser* (a thinking machine) in the sense that Levi-Strauss talks about food as an *objet à penser* (to think about) and not just an *objet à manger* (to eat); because of its "incomprehensibility," its almost uncanny nature, the computer is an "evocatory object,"[5] an object which, beyond its instrumental function, raises a whole series of basic questions about the specificity of human thought, about the differences between animate and inanimate, etc. – no wonder that the computer metaphor is reproduced in miscellaneous fields and achieves universal range (we "program" our activities; we do away with a deadlock via "debugging," etc.). The computer is a third, new stage in Marx's scheme of development, which goes from tool (an extension of the human body) to machine (which works automatically and imposes its rhythm on man). On the one hand, it is closer to a tool in that it does not work automatically, man provides the rhythm, etc.; on the other hand, it is more independently active than a machine, since it works as a partner in a dialogue in which it raises questions itself, etc. In contrast to a mechanical machine, its internal action is "nontransparent," *stricto sensu* unrepresentable (we can "illustrate" its workings, as with a clutch or a gear box), and it operates on the basis of a dialogue with the user; for that reason, it triggers in the subject-user a split of the type "I know, but nevertheless. . . ." Of course, we know that it is "inanimate," that it is only a machine; nevertheless, in practice we act toward it as if it were living and thinking. . . .

How then does one "think with a computer" beyond its instrumental use? A computer is not unequivocal in its socio-symbolic effect but operates as some kind of "projective test," a fantasy screen on which is projected the field of miscellaneous social reactions. Two of the main reactions are "Orwellian" (the computer as an incarnation of Big Brother, an example of centralized totalitarian control) and "anarchistic," which in contrast sees in the computer the possibility for a new self-managing society, "a cooperative of knowledge" which will enable anyone to control "from below," and thus make social life transparent and controllable. The common axis of this contrast is the computer as a means of control and mastery, except that in one case it is control "from above" and in the other "from below"; on the level of individual impact, this experience of the computer as a medium of mastery and control (the computer universe as a transparent, organized, and controlled universe in contrast to "irrational" social life) is countered by wonderment and magic: when we successfully produce an intricate effect with simple program means, this creates in the observer – who of course in the final analysis is identical to the user himself – the impression that the achieved effect is out of proportion to the modest means, the impression of a hiatus between means and effect. It is of particular interest how on the level of programming itself, this opposition repeats the male/female difference in the form of the difference between "hard" (obsessional) and "soft" (hysterical) programming – the first aims at complete control and mastery, transparency, analytical dismemberment of the whole into parts; the second proceeds intuitively: it improvises, it works by trial and thus uncovers the new, it leaves the result itself "to amaze," its relations to the object are more of "dialog."

The computer works most effectively of course as an "evocatory object" in the question of "artificial intelligence" – here, an inversion has already taken place which is the fate of every successful metaphor: one first tries to simulate human thought as far as possible with the computer, bringing the model as close as possible to the human "original," until at a certain point matters reverse and it raises the questions: *what if this "model" is already a model of the "original" itself, what if human intelligence itself operates like a computer, is "programmed,"* etc? The computer raises in pure form the question of semblance, a discourse which would not be a simulacrum: it is clear that the computer in some sense only "simulates" thought; *yet how does the total simulation of thought differ from "real" thought?* No wonder, then, that the specter of artificial intelligence summons the paradoxes of the prohibition of incest – "artificial intelligence" appears as an entity which is simultaneously prohibited and considered impossible: one asserts that it is not possible for a machine to think, at the same time being occupied in prohibiting research in these directions, on the grounds that it is dangerous, ethically dubious, and so on.

The usual objection to "artificial intelligence" is that in the final analysis, the computer is only "programmed," that it cannot in a real sense "understand," while man's activities are spontaneous and creative. The first answer of the advocates of "artificial intelligence": are not man's creativity, "spontaneity," "unpredictibility," etc., an appearance which is created by the simultaneous activity of a number of programs? So the path toward "artificial intelligence" leads *via* the construction of a system with multiple processors. . . . But the main answer of advocates of "artificial intelligence" is above all that the computer is far from obeying a simple linear-mechanical logic: its logic follows Gödel's, the logic of self-reference, recursive functions, paradoxes, where the whole is its own part, self-applicable. The idea of a computer as a closed, consistent, linear machine is a mechanical, precomputer age concept: the computer is an inconsistent machine which, caught in a snare of self-reference, can never be totalized. Here the proponents of the computer culture seek the link between science and art: in the principled, not just empirical, nontotality, and inconsistency of the computer – is not such self-reflective activity of the computer homologous to a Bach fugue which constantly takes up the same theme?[6]

These ideas form the basis of the hacker subculture. Hackers operate as a circle of initiates who exclude themselves from everyday "normality" in order to devote themselves to programming as an end in itself. Their enemy is the "normal," bureaucratic, instrumental, consistent, totalizing use of the computer, which does not take into account its "aesthetic dimension." Their "master-signifier," their manna, the aim, trick, of the hack is when one succeeds in beating the system (for example, when one breaks into a protected, closed circuit of information). The hacker consequently attacks the system at the point of its inconsistency – to perform a hack means to know how to exploit the fault, the symptom of the system. The universalized metaphorical range of the hack corresponds exactly to this dimension: so, for example, in the subculture of the hacker, Gödel's theorem is understood as "Gödel's hack," that subverted the totalitarian logic of the Russell-Whitehead system. . . .

Yet in contrast to this search for the point of inconsistency of the system, the hacker's aesthetic is the aesthetic of a "regulated universe." It is a universe that excludes intersubjectivity, a relation to the other *qua* subject: notwithstanding all the danger, tension, amazement which we experience when immersed in a video game, there is a basic difference between that tension and the tension in our relation to the "real world" – a difference which is not that the computer-generated video world is "just a game," a simulation; the point is rather that in such games, even if the computer cheats, it cheats consistently – the problem is only a matter of cracking the rules which govern its activities. So, for the hackers, the struggle with the computer is "straightforward": the attack is clean, the rules are laid down, although it is necessary to discover them, nothing inconsistent can interfere with them as in "real life."

Therein consists the link of the computer world with the universe of science fiction: we conceive of a world in which all is possible, we can arrange the rules arbitrarily, the only predetermined thing is that these rules must then apply; i.e., that world must be consistent in itself. Or, as Sherry Turkle puts it: all is possible, yet nothing is contingent – what is thereby excluded, is precisely the real. Impossible *qua* contingent encounter. . . . This reality, the reality of the other which is excluded here, is, of course, woman: the inconsistent other par excellence. The computer as partner is the means by which we evade the impossibility of the sexual relationship: a relationship with the computer is possible. *Das Unheimliche* (the eeriness) of the computer is exactly in that it is a machine, a consistent other, stepping into the structural position of an intersubjective partner, the computer is an "inhuman partner" (as Lacan says of the lady in courtly love).[7] One can also explain from this the feeling of something unnatural, obscene, almost terrible when we see children talking with a computer and obsessed with the game, oblivious of everything around them: with the computer, childhood loses the last appearance of innocence.

How then to resolve the discrepancy between the computer universe as a consistent "regulated universe" and the fact that the hacker tries to catch the system precisely at the point of its inconsistency? The solution is elementary, almost self-evident. We simply have to distinguish between two levels, two modes of inconsistency or self-reference: the hacker's finding of the point of nonconsistency, the point at which the system is caught in the trap of its own self-referentiality and starts to turn in a circle, always leaves untouched some basic consistency of the "regulated universe" – the self-reference at which the hacker arrives is, if we can put it thus, a consistent self-reference. The difference between the two levels of self-reference with which we are concerned is contained in Hegel's distinction between "bad" and "proper" infinity – the computer's self-referentiality remains on the level of "bad infinity." We can clarify this distinction with two different paradoxes of self-reference which were both developed along the same subject, a map of England.

First there was an accurate map of England, on which were marked all the objects in England, including the map itself, in diminished scale, on which they again had to mark the map, etc., in bad infinity. This type of self-reference (which is today mainly familiar in the form of television pictures which are reflected by television) is an example of Hegel's bad infinity; the giddiness triggered by this vicious circle is far removed from "proper" infinity which is only approached by the other version of the paradox, which we encounter – where else – in Lewis Carroll: the English decided to make an exact map of their country, but they were never completely successful in this endeavor. The map grew ever more enlarged and complicated, until someone proposed that England itself could be used as its own map – and it still serves this purpose well today. . . . This is Hegel's "proper infinity": the land itself is its own map, its own other – the flight into bad infinity does not come to an end when we reach the unattainable final link in the chain but when we recognize instead that the first link is its own other. From there we could also derive the position of the subject (in the sense of the subject of the signifier): if the land is its own map, if the original is its own model, if the thing is its own sign, then there is no positive, actual difference between them, though there must be some blank space which distinguishes the thing from itself as its own sign, some nonentity, which produces from the thing its sign – that "nonentity," that "pure" difference, is the subject. . . . Here we have the difference between the order of sign and the order of signifier: from the sign we may obtain the signifier by including in the chain of signs "at least one" sign which is not simply removed from the designated thing, but marks the point at which the designated thing becomes its own sign. The computer's self-referentiality remains on the level of bad infinity in that it cannot reach any position of turnaround where it begins to change into its own other. And perhaps we could find in this – beyond any kind of obscurantism – the argument for the claim that "the computer doesn't think."

The reason why the computer "doesn't think" thus keeps to the above-mentioned logic of the reverse metaphor where, instead of the computer as model for the human brain, we conceive of the brain itself as a "computer made of flesh and blood"; where, instead of defining the robot as the artificial man, we conceive of man proper as a "natural robot," a reversal that could be further exemplified in a crucial case-in-point from the domain of sexuality. One usually considers masturbation an imaginary sexual act, i.e., an act where bodily contact with a partner is only imagined; would it not be possible to reverse the terms and to think of the sexual act proper, the act with an actual partner, as a kind of "masturbation with a real (instead of only imagined) partner"? The whole point of Lacan's insistence on the "impossibility of a sexual relationship" is that this, precisely, is what the "actual" sexual act is (let us just recall his definition of phallic enjoyment as essentially masturbatory)! And, as we have already seen, this refer-ence to sexuality is far from being a simple analogy: the Real whose exclusion is constitutive of what we call "reality," virtual or not, is ultimately that of woman. Our point is thus a very elementary one: true, the computer-generated "virtual reality" is a semblance; it does foreclose the Real in precisely the same way that, in the dream of Irma's injection, the Real is excluded by the dreamer's entry into the symbolic bliss – yet what we experience as the "true, hard, external reality" is based upon exactly the same exclusion. The ultimate lesson of virtual reality is the virtualization of the very true reality. By the mirage of "virtual reality," the "true" reality itself is posited as a semblance of itself, as a pure symbolic construct. The fact that "the computer doesn't think" means that the price for our access to "reality" is also that something must remain unthought.

Notes

1   See Sigmund Freud, *Interpretation of Dreams* (Harmondsworth: Penguin Books, 1977), Chapter 11.
2   "The Seminar of Jacques Lacan," *Book 11: The Ego in Freud's Theory and in the Technique of Psychoanalysis* (Cambridge: Cambridge University Press, 1988), pp. 154–5.
3   Ibid., p. 168.
4   Ibid., Chapter XXIII.
5   See Sherry Turkle, *The Second Self: Computers and the Human Spirit* (New York: Simon & Schuster, 1984).
6   See Douglas R. Hofstader's cult book *Gödel, Escher, Bach: An Eternal Golden Braid* (New York: Basic Books, 1978).
7   Turkle offers here a rather naive psychological interpretation: the subculture of the hacker is a culture of male adolescents who are running away from sexual tensions into a world of formalized "adventure," in order to avoid "burning their fingers" with a real woman. Their attitude is inconsistent: they fear loneliness, at the same time being afraid of the approach of the other woman, who because of her inconsistency is undependable; she can cheat, betray trust. The computer is a salvation from this dilemma: it is a partner; we are no longer alone, and at the same time it is not threatening, it is dependable and consistent.

4

Speed and Information: Cyberspace Alarm!

Paul Virilio

Paul Virilio, "Speed and Information: Cyberspace Alarm!," originally published in *Le Monde Diplomatique*, August 1995. Translated by Patrice Riemens, University of Amsterdam.

Paul Virilio has written many works on digital media and representation, including such books as *The Information Bomb* (Verso, 2000) and *Open Sky* (Verso, 1997). This article states that the technologically created "twin phenomena of immediacy and instantaneity" present serious problems for contemporary society.

The twin phenomena of immediacy and of instantaneity are presently one of the most pressing problems confronting political and military strategists alike. Real time now prevails above both real space and the geosphere. The primacy of real time, of immediacy, over and above space and surface is a *fait accompli* and has inaugural value (ushers a new epoch). Something nicely conjured up in a (French) advertisement praising cellular phones with the words: "Planet Earth has never been this small." This is a very dramatic moment in our relation with the world and for our vision of the world.

Three physical barriers are given: sound, heat, and light. The first two have already been felled. The sound barrier has been cut across by the super- and hypersonic aircraft, while the heat barrier is penetrated by the rocket taking human beings outside the Earth's orbit in order to land them on the moon. But the third barrier, that of light, is not something one can cross: you crash into it. It is precisely this barrier of time which confronts history in the present day. To have reached the light barrier, to have reached the speed of light, is a historical event which throws history in disarray and jumbles up the relation of the living being towards the world. The polity that does not make this explicit, misinforms and cheats its citizenry. We have to acknowledge here a major shift which affects geopolitics, geostrategy, but of course also democracy, since the latter is so much dependent upon a concrete place, the "city."

The big event looming upon the 21st century in connection with this absolute speed, is the invention of a perspective of real time, that will supersede the perspective of real space, which in its turn was invented by Italian artists in the

Quattrocento. It has still not been emphasized enough how profoundly the city, the politics, the war, and the economy of the medieval world were revolutionized by the invention of perspective.

Cyberspace is a new form of perspective. It does not coincide with the audio-visual perspective which we already know. It is a fully new perspective, free of any previous reference: it is a *tactile perspective*. To see at a distance, to hear at a distance: that was the essence of the audio-visual perspective of old. But to reach at a distance, to feel at a distance, that amounts to shifting the perspective towards a domain it did not yet encompass: that of contact, of contact-at-a-distance: tele-contact.

A Fundamental Loss of Orientation

Together with the build-up of information superhighways we are facing a new phenomenon: loss of orientation. A fundamental loss of orientation complementing and concluding the societal liberalization and the deregulation of financial markets whose nefarious effects are well-known. A duplication of sensible reality, into reality and virtuality, is in the making. A stereo-reality of sorts threatens. A total loss of the bearings of the individual looms large. To exist, is to exist *in situ*, here and now, *hic et nunc*. This is precisely what is being threatened by cyberspace and instantaneous, globalized information flows.

What lies ahead is a disturbance in the perception of what reality is; it is a shock, a mental concussion. And this outcome ought to interest us. Why? Because never has any progress in a technique been achieved without addressing its specific negative aspects. The specific negative aspect of these information superhighways is precisely this loss of orientation regarding alterity (the other), this disturbance in the relationship with the other and with the world. It is obvious that this loss of orientation, this non-situation, is going to usher in a deep crisis which will affect society and hence, democracy.

The dictatorship of speed at the limit will increasingly clash with representative democracy. When some essayists address us in terms of "cyber-democracy," of virtual democracy; when others state that "opinion democracy" is going to replace "political parties democracy," one cannot fail to see anything but this loss of orientation in matters political, of which the March 1994 "media-coup" by Mr. Silvio Berlusconi was an Italian-style prefiguration. The advent of the age of viewer-counts and opinion polls reigning supreme will necessarily be advanced by this type of technology.

The very word "globalization" is a fake. There is no such thing as globalization, there is only virtualization. What is being effectively globalized by instantaneity is time. Everything now happens within the perspective of real time: henceforth we are deemed to live in a "one-time-system."[1]

For the first time, history is going to unfold within a one-time-system: global time. Up to now, history has taken place within local times, local frames, regions and nations. But now, in a certain way, globalization and virtualization are inaugurating a global time that prefigures a new form of tyranny. If history is so rich, it is because it was local, it was thanks to the existence of spatially bounded times which overrode something that up to now occurred only in astronomy: universal time. But in the very near future, our history will happen in universal time, itself the outcome of instantaneity – and there only.

Thus we see on one side real time superseding real space. A phenomenon that is making both distances and surfaces irrelevant in favor of the time-span, and an extremely short time-span at that. And on the other hand, we have global time, belonging to the multimedia, to cyberspace, increasingly dominating the local time-frame of our cities, our neighborhoods. So much so, that there is talk of substituting the term "global" by "glocal," a concatenation of the words local and global. This emerges from the idea that the local has, by definition, become global, and the global, local. Such a deconstruction of the relationship with the world is not without consequences for the relationship among the citizens themselves.

Nothing is ever obtained without a loss of something else. What will be gained from electronic information and electronic communication will necessarily result in a loss somewhere else. If we are not aware of this loss, and do not account for it, our gain will be of no value. This is the lesson to be had from the previous development of transport technologies. The realization of high velocity railway service has been possible only because engineers of the 19th century had invented the block system, that is a method to regulate traffic so that trains are speeded up without risk of railway catastrophes.[2] But so far, traffic control engineering on the information (super)highways is conspicuous by its absence.

There is something else of great importance here: no information exists without dis-information. And now a new type of dis-information is raising its head, and it is totally different than voluntary censorship. It has to do with some kind of choking of the senses, a loss of control over reason of sorts. Here lies a new and major risk for humanity stemming from multimedia and computers.

Albert Einstein, in fact, had already prophesized as much in the 1950s, when talking about "the second bomb." The electronic bomb, after the atomic one. A bomb whereby real-time interaction would be to information what radioactivity is to energy. The disintegration then will not merely affect the particles of matter, but also the very people of which our societies consist. This is precisely what can be seen at work with mass unemployment, wired jobs, and the rash of delocalizations of enterprises.

One may surmise that, just as the emergence of the atomic bomb made very quickly the elaboration of a policy of military dissuasion imperative in order to avoid a nuclear catastrophe, the information bomb will also need a new form of dissuasion adapted to the 21st century. This shall be a societal form of dissuasion to counter the damage caused by the explosion of unlimited information. This will be the great accident of the future, the one that comes after the succession of accidents that was specific to the industrial age (as ships, trains, planes or nuclear power plants were invented, shipwrecks, derailments, plane crashes and the melt-down at Chernobyl were invented at the same time too . . .)

After the globalization of telecommunications, one should expect a generalized kind of accident, a never-seen-before accident. It would be just as astonishing as global time is, this never-seen-before kind of time. A generalized accident would be something like what Epicurus called "the accident of accidents" [and Saddam Hussein surely would call the "mother of all accidents" -trans.]. The stock-market collapse is merely a slight prefiguration of it. Nobody has seen this generalized accident yet. But then watch out as you hear talk about the "financial bubble" in the economy: a very significant metaphor is used here, and it conjures up visions of some kind of cloud, reminding us of other clouds just as frightening as those of Chernobyl...

When one raises the question about the risks of accidents on the information (super)highways, the point is not about the information in itself, the point is about the absolute velocity of electronic data. The problem here is interactivity. Computer science is not the problem, but computer communication, or rather the (not yet fully known) potential of computer communication. In the United States, the Pentagon, the very originator of the Internet, is even talking in terms of a "revolution in the military" along with a "war of knowledge," which might supersede the war of movement in the same way as the latter had superseded the war of siege, of which Sarajevo is such a tragic and outdated reminder.

Upon leaving the White House in 1961, Dwight Eisenhower dubbed the military-industrial complex "a threat to democracy." He sure knew what he was talking about, since he helped build it up in the first place. But comes 1995, at the very moment that a military-informational complex is taking shape with some American political leaders, most prominently Ross Perot and Newt Gingrich, talking about "virtual democracy"[3] in a spirit reminiscent of fundamentalist mysticism, how not to feel alarmed? How not to see the outlines of cybernetics turned into a social policy?

The Narco-Capitalism of the Wired World

The suggestive power of virtual technologies is without parallel. Next to the illicit drugs-based narco-capitalism which is currently destabilizing the world economy, a computer-communication narco-economy is building up fast. The question may even be raised whether the developed countries are not pushing ahead with virtual technologies in order to turn the tables on the under-developed countries, which are, in Latin America especially, living off, or rather barely scraping by, the production of illicit chemical drugs. When one observes how much research effort in advanced technologies has been channeled into the field of amusement (viz. video-games, real virtuality goggles, etc.), should this instantaneous subjugating potential – and it has been applied successfully in history before – which is being unleashed on the populations by these new techniques remain concealed?

Something is hovering over our heads which looks like a "cybercult." We have to acknowledge that the new communication technologies will only further democracy if, and only if, we oppose from the beginning the caricature of global society being hatched for us by big multinational corporations throwing themselves at a breakneck pace on the information superhighways.

Translator's Notes

1 "Le temps unique" in French. This is an obvious reference to Ignacio Ramonet's now quasi-paradigmatic editorial "La pensée unique" – the one-idea-system, in *Le Monde Diplomatique*, January 1995 (cf. *CTHEORY, Event-Scene 12, "The One Idea System"*).

2 The automatic block system consists in splitting up a railway line into segments, each "protected" by an entry signal. A train running on one segment automatically closes it off (while the previous segment can only be approached at reduced speed). This system enables a string of trains to run at very high speed within a controlled distance (2 blocks, i.e., typically $3\frac{1}{2}$ miles) of each other. In its pure form, this system cannot entirely prevent frontal collisions, and is hence best used on multi-track railway lines. The block system was an improvement over the – still widely used – Anglo-American "token" system, whereby the line is also divided in segments, each of which can only be used by the train holding the "token." This is an almost fail-safe but cumbersome procedure. Virilio is in error in that modern (i.e. computerized) railway traffic control techniques, though originating from the 19th century block system, have altered those practices beyond recognition. [This lengthy and technical note is motivated both by the translator's railway mania and by the paradigmatic importance Virilio attaches to the block system (cf. especially "L'horizon negatif".)]

3 *En anglais dans le texte.* On this subject, see for example *Esther Dyson's interview with "Newt" in Wired* 3.08, August 1995.

5

A Manifesto for Cyborgs: Science, Technology, and Socialist Feminism in the 1980s

Donna Haraway

Donna Haraway, excerpt from "A Manifesto for Cyborgs: Science, Technology, and Socialist Feminism for the 1980s," *Socialist Review* 80, vol. 15, 2 (March–April, 1985) pp. 65–107. This version published in Socialist Review Collective, eds., *Unfinished Business: 20 Years of Socialist Review* (London: Verso, 1991).

Donna Haraway is a professor in the History of Consciousness program at the University of California, Santa Cruz. She is the author of *Primate Visions: Gender, Race, and Nature in the World of Modern Science* (Routledge, 1990) and *Simians, Cyborgs, and Women: The Reinvention of Nature* (Routledge, 1991). Originally appearing in *Socialist Review*, this classic feminist essay presents the theoretical idea of the human/machine confluence in the persona of the cyborg.

An Ironic Dream of a Common Language for Women in the Integrated Circuit

This essay is an effort to build an ironic political myth faithful to feminism, socialism, and materialism. Perhaps more faithful as blasphemy is faithful, than as reverent worship and identification. Irony is about contradictions that do not resolve into larger wholes, even dialectically, about the tension of holding incompatible things together because both or all are necessary and true. Irony is about humor and serious play. It is also a rhetorical strategy and a political method, one I would like to see more honored within socialist-feminism. At the center of my ironic faith, my blasphemy, is the image of the cyborg. A cyborg is a cybernetic organism, a hybrid of machine and organism, a creature of social reality as well as a creature of fiction.

By the late twentieth century, our time, a mythic time, we are all chimeras, theorized and fabricated hybrids of machine and organism; in short, we are cyborgs. The cyborg is our ontology; it gives us our politics. The cyborg is a condensed image of both imagination and material reality, the two joined centers structuring any possibility of historical transformation. In the traditions of "Western" science and politics – the tradition of racist, male-dominant capitalism; the tradition of progress; the tradition of the appropriation of nature as resource for the productions of culture; the tradition of reproduction of the self from the reflections of the other – the relation between organism and machine has been a border war. The stakes in the border war have been the territories of production, reproduction, and imagination. This essay is an argument for *pleasure* in the confusion of boundaries and for *responsibility* in their construction. It is also an effort to contribute to socialist-feminist culture and theory in a postmodernist, nonnaturalist mode and in the utopian tradition of imagining a world without gender, which is perhaps a world without genesis, but maybe also a world without end. The cyborg incarnation is outside salvation history.

The cyborg is resolutely committed to partiality, irony, intimacy, and perversity. It is oppositional, utopian, and completely without innocence. No longer structured by the polarity of public and private, the cyborg defines a technological polis based partly on a revolution of social relations in the *oikos*, the household. Nature and culture are reworked; the one can no longer be the resource for appropriation or incorporation by the other. The relationships for forming wholes from parts, including those of polarity and hierarchical domination, are at issue in the cyborg world. Unlike the hopes of Frankenstein's monster, the cyborg does not expect its father to save it through a restoration of the garden; i.e., through the fabrication of a heterosexual mate, through its completion in a finished whole, a city and cosmos. The cyborg does not dream of community on the model of the organic family, this time without the Oedipal project. The cyborg would not recognize the Garden of Eden; it is not made of mud and cannot dream of returning to dust. Perhaps that is why I want to see if cyborgs can subvert the apocalypse of returning to nuclear dust in the manic compulsion to name the Enemy. Cyborgs are not reverent; they do not remember the cosmos. They are wary of holism, but needy for connection – they seem to have a natural feel for united front politics, but without the vanguard party. The main trouble with cyborgs, of course, is that they are the illegitimate offspring of militarism and patriarchal capitalism, not to mention state socialism. But illegitimate offspring are often exceedingly unfaithful to their origins. Their fathers, after all, are inessential.

I want to signal three crucial boundary breakdowns that make the following political fictional (political scientific) analysis possible. By the late twentieth century in United States scientific culture, the boundary between human and animal is thoroughly breached. The last beachheads of uniqueness have been polluted if not turned into amusement parks – language, tool use, social behavior, mental events, nothing really convincingly settles the separation of human and animal. And many people no longer feel the need of such a separation; indeed, many branches of feminist culture affirm the pleasure of connection of human and other living creatures. Movements for animal rights are not irrational denials of human uniqueness; they are a clearsighted recognition of connection across the discredited breach of nature and culture. Biology and evolutionary theory over the last two centuries have simultaneously produced modern organisms as objects of knowledge and reduced the line between humans and animals to a faint trace re-etched in ideological struggle or professional disputes between life and social sciences. Within this framework, teaching modern Christian creationism should be fought as a form of child abuse.

The second leaky distinction is between animal-human (organism) and machine. Precybernetic machines could be haunted; there was always the specter of the ghost in the machine. This dualism structured the dialogue between materialism and idealism that was settled by a dialectical progeny, called spirit or history, according to taste. But basically machines were not self-moving, self-designing, autonomous. They could not achieve man's dream, only mock it. They were not man, an author to himself, but only a caricature of that masculinist reproductive dream. To think they were otherwise was paranoid. Now we are not so sure. Late-twentieth-century machines have made thoroughly ambiguous the difference between natural and artificial, mind and body, self-developing and externally designed, and many other distinctions that used to apply to organisms and machines. Our machines are disturbingly lively, and we ourselves frighteningly inert.

Technological determinism is only one ideological space opened up by the reconceptions of machine and organism as coded texts through which we engage in the play of writing and reading the world. "Textualization" of everything in poststructuralist, postmodernist theory has been damned by Marxists and socialist-feminists for its utopian disregard for lived relations of domination that ground the "play" of arbitrary reading. It is certainly true that postmodernist strategies, like my cyborg myth, subvert myriad organic wholes (e.g., the poem, the primitive culture, the biological organism). In short, the certainty of what counts as nature – a source of insight and a promise of innocence – is undermined, probably fatally. The transcendent authorization of interpretation is lost, and with it the ontology grounding "Western" epistemology. But the alternative is not cynicism or faith-lessness, i.e., some version of abstract existence, like the accounts of technological determinism destroying "man" by the "machine" or "meaningful political action" by the "text." Who cyborgs will be is a radical question; the answers are a matter of survival. Both chimpanzees and artifacts have politics, so why shouldn't we?

The silicon chip is a surface for writing; it is etched in molecular scales disturbed only by atomic noise, the ultimate interference for nuclear scores. Writing, power, and technology are old partners in Western stories of the origin of civilization, but miniaturization has changed our experience of mechanism. Miniaturization has turned out to be about power; small is not so much beautiful as preeminently dangerous, as in cruise missiles. Contrast the TV sets of the 1950s or the news cameras of the 1970s with the TV wristbands or hand-sized video cameras now advertised. Our best machines are made of sunshine; they are all light and clean because they are nothing but signals, electro-magnetic waves, a section of a spectrum.

The ubiquity and invisibility of cyborgs is precisely why these sunshine belt machines are so deadly. They are as hard to see politically as materially. They are about consciousness – or its simulation. They are floating signifiers moving in pickup trucks across Europe, blocked more effectively by the witchweavings of the displaced and so unnatural Greenham women who read the cyborg webs of power very well, than by the militant labor of older masculinist politics, whose natural constituency needs defense jobs. Ultimately the "hardest" science is about the realm of greatest boundary confusion, the realm of pure number, pure spirit, C^3I, cryptography, and the preservation of potent secrets. The new machines are so clean and light. Their engineers are sun worshipers mediating a new scientific revolution associated with the night dream of postindustrial society. The diseases evoked by these clean machines are "no more" than the experience of stress. The nimble little fingers of "Oriental" women, the old fascination of little Anglo-Saxon Victorian girls with doll houses, women's enforced attention to the small take on quite new dimensions in this world. There might be a cyborg Alice taking account of these new dimensions. Ironically, it might be the unnatural cyborg women making chips in Asia and spiral dancing in Santa Rita whose constructed unities will guide effective oppositional strategies.

One of my premises is that most American socialists and feminists see deepened dualisms of mind and body, animal and machine, idealism and materialism in the social practices, symbolic formulations, and physical artifacts associated with "high technology" and scientific culture. The analytic resources developed by progressives have insisted on the necessary domination of technics and have recalled us to an imagined organic body to integrate our resistance. Another of my premises is that the need for unity of people trying to resist worldwide intensification of domination has never been more acute. But a slightly perverse shift of perspective might better enable us to contest for meanings, as well as for other forms of power and pleasure in technologically mediated societies.

Fractured Identities

It has become difficult to name one's feminism by a single adjective – or even to insist in every circumstance upon the noun. Consciousness of exclusion through naming is acute. Identities seem contradictory, partial, and strategic. With the hard-won recognition of their social and historical constitution, gender, race, and class cannot provide the basis for belief in "essential" unity. There is nothing about being "female" that naturally binds women. There is not even such a state as "being" female, itself a highly complex category constructed in contested sexual scientific discourses and other social practices. Gender, race, or class consciousness is an achievement forced on us by the terrible historical experience of the contradictory social realities of patriarchy, colonialism, and capitalism. And who counts as "us" in my own rhetoric? Which identities are available to ground such a potent political myth called "us," and what could motivate enlistment in this collectivity? Painful fragmentation among feminists (not to mention among women) along every possible fault line has made the concept of *woman* elusive, an excuse for the matrix of women's dominations of each other. For me – and for many who share a similar historical location in white, professional middle class, female, radical, North American, mid-adult bodies – the sources of a crisis in political identity are legion. The recent history for much of the US Left and US feminism has been a response to this kind of crisis by endless splitting and searches for a new essential unity. But there has also been a growing recognition of another response through coalition – affinity, not identity.

"Women of color," a name contested at its origins by those whom it would incorporate, as well as a historical consciousness marking systematic breakdown of all the signs of Man in "Western" traditions, constructs a kind of postmodernist identity out of otherness and difference. This postmodernist identity is fully political, whatever might be said about other possible postmodernisms. This identity marks out a self-consciously constructed space that cannot affirm the capacity to act on the basis of natural identification, but only on the basis of conscious coalition, of affinity, of political kinship. Unlike the "woman" of some streams of the white women's movement in the United States, there is no natur-alization of the matrix.

[. . .]

Women in the Integrated Circuit

If it was ever possible ideologically to characterize women's lives by the distinction of public and private domains – suggested by images of the division of working-class life into factory and home, of bourgeois life into market and home, and of gender existence into personal and political realms – it is now a totally misleading ideology, even to show how both terms of these dichotomies construct each other in practice and in theory. I prefer a network ideological image, suggesting the profusion of spaces and identities and the permeability of boundaries in the personal body and in the body politic. "Networking" is both a feminist practice and a multinational corporate strategy – weaving is for oppositional cyborgs.

The only way to characterize the informatics of domination is as a massive intensification of insecurity and cultural impoverishment, with common failure of subsistence networks for the most vulnerable. Since much of this picture interweaves with the social relations of science and technology, the urgency of a socialist-feminist politics addressed to science and technology is plain. There is much now being done, and the grounds for political work are rich. For example, the efforts to develop forms of collective struggle for women in paid work, like SEIU's District 925, should be a high priority for all of us. These efforts are profoundly tied to technical restructuring of labor processes and reformations of working classes. These efforts are also providing understanding of a more com-prehensive kind of labor organization, involving community, sexuality, and family issues never privileged in the largely white male industrial unions.

The structural rearrangements related to the social relations of science and technology evoke strong ambivalence. But it is not necessary to be ultimately depressed by the implications of late-twentieth-century women's relation to all aspects of work, culture, production of knowledge, sexuality, and reproduction. For excellent reasons, most Marxisms see domination best and have trouble understanding what can only look like false consciousness and people's complicity in their own domination in late capitalism. It is crucial to remember that what is lost, perhaps especially from women's points of view, is often virulent forms of oppression, nostalgically naturalized in the face of current violation. Ambivalence toward the disrupted unities mediated by high-tech culture requires not sorting consciousness into categories of "clearsighted critique grounding a solid political epistemology" versus "manipulated false consciousness," but subtle understanding of emerging pleasures, experiences, and powers with serious potential for changing the rules of the game.

There are grounds for hope in the emerging bases for new kinds of unity across race, gender, and class, as these elementary units of socialist-feminist analysis themselves suffer protean transformations. Intensifications of hardship experienced worldwide in connection with the social relations of science and technology are severe. But what people are experiencing is not transparently clear, and we lack sufficiently subtle connections for collectively building effective theories of experience. Present efforts – Marxist, psychoanalytic, feminist, anthropological – to clarify even "our" experience are rudimentary.

I am conscious of the odd perspective provided by my historical position – a PhD in biology for an Irish Catholic girl was made possible by Sputnik's impact on US national science education policy. I have a body and mind as much constructed by the post-World War II arms race and Cold War as by the women's movements. There are more grounds for hope by focusing on the contradictory effects of politics designed to produce loyal American technocrats, which as well produced large numbers of dissidents, rather than by focusing on the present defeats.

The permanent partiality of feminist points of view has consequences for our expectations of forms of political organization and participation. We do not need a totality in order to work well. The feminist dream of a common language, like all dreams for a perfectly true language, of perfectly faithful naming of experience, is a totalizing and imperialist one. In that sense, dialectics too is a dream language, longing to resolve contradiction. Perhaps, ironically, we can learn from our fusions with animals and machines how not to be Man, the embodiment of Western logos. From the point of view of pleasure in these potent and taboo fusions, made inevitable by the social relations of science and technology, there might indeed be a feminist science.

Cyborgs: A Myth of Political Identity

Earlier I suggested that "women of color" might be understood as a cyborg identity, a potent subjectivity synthesized from fusions of outsider identities. There are material and cultural grids mapping this potential. Audre Lorde captures the tone in the title of her *Sister Outsider*. In my political myth, Sister Outsider is the offshore woman, whom US workers, female and feminized, are supposed to regard as the enemy preventing their solidarity, threatening their security. Onshore, inside the boundary of the United States, Sister Outsider is a potential amidst the races and ethnic identities of women manipulated for division, competition, and exploitation in the same industries. "Women of color" are the preferred labor force for the science-based industries, the real women for whom the worldwide sexual market, labor market, and politics of reproduction kaleidoscope into daily life. Young Korean women hired in the sex industry and in electronics assembly are recruited from high schools, educated for the integrated circuit. Literacy, especially in English, distinguishes the "cheap" female labor so attractive to the multinationals.

Contrary to orientalist stereotypes of the "oral primitive," literacy is a special mark of women of color, acquired by US black women as well as men through a history of risking death to learn and to teach reading and writing. Writing has a special significance for all colonized groups. Writing has been crucial to the Western myth of the distinction of oral and written cultures, primitive and civilized mentalities, and more recently to the erosion of that distinction in "postmodernist" theories attacking the phallogocentrism of the West with its worship of the monotheistic, phallic, authoritative, and singular word, the unique and perfect name. Contests for the meanings of writing are a major form of contemporary political struggle. Releasing the play of writing is deadly serious. The poetry and stories of US women of color are repeatedly about writing, about access to the power to signify; but this time that power must be neither phallic nor innocent. Cyborg writing must not be about the Fall, the imagination of a once-upon-a-time wholeness before language, before writing, before Man. Cyborg writing is about the power to survive, not on the basis of original innocence, but on the basis of seizing the tools to mark the world that marked them as other.

The tools are often stories, retold stories, versions that reverse and displace the hierarchical dualisms of naturalized identities. In retelling origin stories, cyborg authors subvert the central myths of origin of Western culture. We have all been colonized by those origin myths, with their longing for fulfillment in apocalypse. The phallogocentric origin stories most crucial for feminist cyborgs are built into the literal technologies – technologies that write the world, biotechnology and microelectronics – that have recently textualized our bodies as code problems on the grid of C^3I. Feminist cyborg stories have the task of recoding communication and intelligence to subvert command and control.

Figuratively and literally, language politics pervade the struggles of women of color; and stories about language have a special power in the rich contemporary writing by US women of color. For example, retellings of the story of the indigenous woman Malinche, mother of the mestizo "bastard" race of the new world, master of languages, and mistress of Cortes, carry special meaning for Chicana constructions of identity. Cherríe Moraga, in *Loving in the War Years*, explores the themes of identity when one never possessed the original language, never told the original story, never resided in the harmony of legitimate heterosexuality in the garden of culture, and so cannot base identity on a myth or a fall from innocence and right to natural names, mother's or father's. Moraga's writing, her superb literacy, is presented in her poetry as the same kind of violation as Malinche's mastery of the conqueror's language – a violation, an illegitimate production, that allows survival. Moraga's language is not "whole"; it is self-consciously spliced, a chimera of English and Spanish, both conqueror's languages. But it is this chimeric monster, without claim to an original language before violation, that crafts the erotic, competent, potent identities of women of color. Sister Outsider hints at the possibility of world survival not because of her innocence, but because of her ability to live on the boundaries, to write without the founding myth of original wholeness, with its inescapable apocalypse of final return to a deathly oneness that Man has imagined to be the innocent and all-powerful Mother, freed at the End from another spiral of appropriation by her son. Writing marks Moraga's body, affirms it as the body of a woman of color, against the possibility of passing into the unmarked category of the Anglo father or into the orientalist myth of "original illiteracy" of a mother that never was. Malinche was mother here, not Eve before eating the forbidden fruit. Writing affirms Sister Outsider, not the Woman-before-the-Fall-into-Writing needed by the phallogocentric Family of Man.

Writing is pre-eminently the technology of cyborgs, etched surfaces of the late twentieth century. Cyborg politics is the struggle for language and the struggle against perfect communication, against the one code that translates all meaning perfectly, the central dogma of phallogocentrism. That is why cyborg politics insist on noise and advocate pollution, rejoicing in the illegitimate fusions of animal and machine. These are the couplings which make Man and Woman so problematic, subverting the structure of desire, the force imagined to generate language and gender and so subverting the structure and modes of reproduction of "Western" identity, of nature and culture, of mirror and eye, slave and master, body and mind. "We" did not originally choose to be cyborgs, but choice grounds a liberal politics and epistemology that imagines the reproduction of individuals before the wider replications of "texts."

From the perspective of cyborgs, freed of the need to ground politics in "our" privileged position of the oppression that incorporates all other dominations, the innocence of the merely violated, the ground of those closer to nature, we can see powerful possibilities. Feminisms and Marxisms have run aground on Western epistemological imperatives to construct a revolutionary subject from the perspective of a hierarchy of oppressions and/or a latent position of moral superiority, innocence, and greater closeness to nature. With no available original dream of a common language or original symbiosis promising protection from hostile "masculine" separation, but written into the play of a text that has no finally privileged reading or salvation history, to recognize "oneself" as fully implicated in the world, frees us of the need to root politics in identification, vanguard parties, purity, and mothering. Stripped of identity, the bastard race teaches about the power of the margins and the importance of a mother like Malinche. Women of color have transformed her from the evil mother of masculinist fear into the originally literate mother who teaches survival.

To recapitulate, certain dualisms have been persistent in Western traditions; they have all been systemic to the logics and practices of domination of women, people of color, nature, workers, animals – in short, domination of all constituted as *others*, whose task is to mirror the self. Chief among these troubling dualisms are self/other, mind/body, culture/nature, male/female, civilized/primitive, reality/appearance, whole/part, agent/resource, maker/made, active/passive, right/wrong, truth/illusion, total/partial, God/man. The self is the One who is not dominated, who knows that by the service of the other; the other is the one who holds the future, who knows that by the experience of domination, which gives the lie to the autonomy of the self. To be One is to be autonomous, to be powerful, to be God; but to be One is to be an illusion, and so to be involved in a dialectic of apocalypse with the other. Yet to be other is to be multiple, without clear boundary, frayed, insubstantial. One is too few, but two are too many.

High-tech culture challenges these dualisms in intriguing ways. It is not clear who makes and who is made in the relation between human and machine. It is not clear what is mind and what body in machines that resolve into coding practices. Insofar as we know ourselves in both formal discourse (e.g., biology) and in daily practice (e.g., the homework economy in the integrated circuit), we find ourselves to be cyborgs, hybrids, mosaics, chimeras. Biological organisms have become biotic systems, communications devices like others. There is no fundamental, ontological separation in our formal knowledge of machine and organism, of technical and organic.

One consequence is that our sense of connection to our tools is heightened. The trance state experienced by many computer users has become a staple of science fiction film and cultural jokes. Perhaps paraplegics and other severely handicapped people can (and sometimes do) have the most intense experiences of complex hybridization with other communications devices. Why should our bodies end at the skin, or include at best other beings encapsulated by skin? From the seventeenth century till now, machines could be animated – given ghostly souls to make them speak or move or to account for their orderly development and mental capacities. Or organisms could be mechanized – reduced to body understood as resource of mind. These machine/organism relationships are obsolete, unnecessary. For us, in imagination and in other practice, machines can be prosthetic devices, intimate components, friendly selves. We don't need organic holism to give impermeable wholeness, the total woman and her feminist variants (mutants?).

There are several consequences to taking seriously the imagery of cyborgs as other than our enemies. Our bodies, ourselves; bodies are maps of power and identity. Cyborgs are no exceptions. A cyborg body is not innocent; it was not born in a garden; it does not seek unitary identity and so generate antagonistic dualisms without end (or until the world ends); it takes irony for granted. One is too few, and two is only one possibility. Intense pleasure in skill, machine skill, ceases to be a sin, but an aspect of embodiment. The machine is not an *it* to be animated, worshiped and dominated. The machine is us, our processes, an aspect of our embodiment. We can be responsible for machines; *they* do not dominate or threaten us. We are responsible for boundaries, we are they. Up till now (once upon a time), female embodiment seemed to be given, organic, necessary; and female embodiment seemed to mean skill in mothering and its metaphoric extensions. Only by being out of place could we take intense pleasure in machines, and then with excuses that this was organic activity after all, appropriate to females. Cyborgs might consider more seriously the partial, fluid, sometimes aspect of sex and sexual embodiment. Gender might not be global identity after all.

Cyborg gender is a local possibility taking a global vengeance. Race, gender, and capital require a cyborg theory of wholes and parts. There is no drive in cyborgs to produce total theory, but there is an intimate experience of boundaries, their construction and deconstruction. There is a myth system waiting to become a political language to ground one way of looking at science and technology and challenging the informatics of domination.

Cyborg imagery can help express two crucial arguments in this essay: 1) the production of universal, totalizing theory is a major mistake that misses most of reality, probably always, but certainly now; 2) taking responsibility for the social relations of science and technology means refusing an anti-science metaphysics, a demonology of technology, and so means embracing the skillful task of reconstructing the boundaries of daily life, in partial connection with others, in communication with all of our parts. It is not just that science and technology are possible means of great human satisfaction, as well as a matrix of complex dominations. Cyborg imagery can suggest a way out of the maze of dualisms in which we have explained our bodies and our tools to ourselves. This is a dream not of a common language, but of a powerful infidel heteroglossia. It is an imagination of a feminist speaking in tongues to strike fear into the circuits of the super-savers of the new right. It means both building and destroying machines, identities, categories, relationships, spaces, stories. Though both are bound in the spiral dance, I would rather be a cyborg than a goddess.

Notes

Socialist Review regrets that all the references that originally appeared in this article had to be cut due to space restraints. Many of the ideas in the piece emerged in relations to others, including several graduate students at the History of Consciousness program at the University of California, Santa Cruz.

6

Machinic Heterogenesis

Félix Guattari

Félix Guattari, "Machinic Heterogenesis," translated by James Creech, in Verena Andermatt Conley, et al. eds., *Rethinking Technologies* (Minneapolis: University of Minnesota Press, 1993), pp. 13–28.

Félix Guattari (1930–1992) wrote extensively about language and technology in such works as *Anti-Oedipus: Capitalism and Schizophrenia* (Minnesota, 1985), *What is Philosophy?* (Columbia, 1994), and *Chaosmosis: An Ethnio-Aesthetic Paradigm* (Indiana, 1995). In this essay Guattari offers philosophical ruminations on what is gained and lost when machines assume the human function of thought.

Machinism

Although machines are usually treated as a subheading of "technics," I have long thought that it was the problematic of technics that remained dependent on the questions posed by machines. "Machinism" is an object of fascination, sometimes of delirium. There exists a whole historical "bestiary" of things relating to machines. The relation between human and machine has been a source of reflection since the beginning of philosophy. Aristotle considers that the goal of *techné* is to create what nature finds it impossible to achieve so that *techné* sets itself up between nature and humanity as a creative mediation. But the status of this "intercession" is a source of ambiguity. While mechanistic conceptions of the machine rob it of anything that can differentiate it from a simple construction *partes extra partes*, vitalist conceptions assimilate it to living beings, unless the living beings are assimilated to the machine. This was the path taken by Norbert Wiener as he opened up the cybernetic perspective in *Cybernetics*.[1] On the other hand, more recent systemist conceptions reserve the category of autopoiesis (or self-production) for living machines (in Francisco Varela's *Autonomie et connaissance*),[2] whereas an older Heideggerian mode of philosophy entrusts *techné*, in its opposition to modern technicity, with the mission of "unveiling the truth," thus setting it solidly on an ontological pedestal – on a *Grund* – that compromises its definition as a process of opening. It is by navigating between these two obstacles that we will attempt to discern the thresholds of ontological intensity that will allow us to grasp "machinism" [*le machinisme*] all of a piece in its various forms, be they technical, social, semiotic, or axiological. With respect to each type of machine, the question will be raised not of its vital autonomy according to an animal model, but of its specific enunciative consistency.

The first type of machine that comes to mind is that of material assemblages [*dispositifs*], put together artificially by the human hand and by the intermediary of other machines, according to diagrammatic schemas whose end is the production of effects, of products, or of particular services. From the outset, through this artificial montage and its teleology [*finalisation*] it becomes necessary to go beyond the delimitation of machines in the strict sense to include the functional ensemble that associates them with humankind through multiple components:

material and energy components;

semiotic components that are diagrammatic and algorithmic;

social components relative to the search, the formation, the organization of work, the ergonomics, the circulation, and the distribution of goods and services produced;

the organ, nerve impulse, and humoral components of the human body;

individual and collective information and mental representation;

investments by "desiring machines" producing a subjectivity in adjacency with its components;

abstract machines setting themselves up transversally to the machinic, cognitive, affective, and social levels considered above.

In the context of such a functional ensemble, which henceforth will be qualified as *machinic ordering* [*agencement machinique*], the utensils, the instruments, the simplest tools, and, as we shall see, the slightest structured parts of a machinery will acquire the status of a protomachine. Let us deconstruct, for example, a hammer by removing its handle. It remains a hammer but in a "mutilated" state. The "head" of the hammer, another zoomorphic metaphor, can be reduced by fusion. It will then cross the threshold of formal consistency, causing it to lose its form, its machinic gestalt, which works on a technological as well as on an imaginary level (as, for example, when we evoke the obsolete memory of the hammer and sickle). From then on, we are confronted with nothing more than a metallic mass that has been returned to its smooth state – to deterritorialization – preceding its entrance into that mechanical form. But we will not settle for this experiment, similar to Descartes's experiment with a piece of wax. In effect, we can move in the opposite direction of this deconstruction and its limit threshold, toward the association of the hammer and the arm, the nail, the anvil, which maintain among each other relationships that we can call syntagmatic. Their collective dance even expands to include the defunct corporation of blacksmiths, the sinister epoch of the old iron mines, ancestral use of iron-rimmed wheels. As Leroi-Gourhan pointed out, the technological object is nothing outside of the technological ensemble to which it belongs. But is it any different with sophisticated machines such as robots, which we suspect – probably with good reason – will soon be engendered exclusively by other robots in a gestation involving virtually no human action until some glitch requires our residual, direct intervention? But doesn't all that sound like a kind of dated science fiction? In order to acquire more and more life, machines require more and more abstract human vitality as they make their way along their evolutive phyla. Thus, conception by computer – expert systems and artificial intelligence – gives us back at least as much as it takes away from thought, because in the final analysis it only subtracts inertial schemas. Computer-assisted forms of thought are thus mutant and arise from other kinds of music, from other universes of reference.

It is thus impossible to refuse human thought its part in the essence of machinism. But how long can we continue to characterize the thought put to work here as human? Doesn't technicoscientific thought emerge from a certain type of mental and semiotic machinism? Here it becomes necessary to establish a distinction between, on the one hand, semiologies producing significations that are the common currency of social groups and, on the other, asignifying semiotics that, despite the significations they can foster, manipulate figures of expression that work as diagrammatic machines in direct contact with technical-experimental configurations. Semiologies of signification play on distinctive oppositions of a phonemic or scriptural order that transcribe enunciations [*énoncés*] into expressive materials that signify. The structuralists liked to make the Signifier a unifying category for all expressive economies of whatever order, be it language, icon, gesture, urbanism, or cinema. They postulated a general translatability able to signify all forms of discursivity. But in doing that, did they not miss the mark of a machinistic autopoiesis that does not derive from repetition or from mimesis of significations and their figures of expression, but that is linked instead to the emergence of meaning and of effects that are no less singular for being indefinitely reproducible?

Ontological Reconversions

This autopoeitic nexus of the machine is what wrests it from structure. Structural retroactions, their input and output, are called upon to function according to a principle of eternal return; they are inhabited by a desire for eternity. The machine, on the contrary, is haunted by a desire for abolition. Its emergence is accompanied by breakdown, by catastrophe, by the threat of death. Later on we will have to examine the different relations of alterity thus developed, relations that constitute differences from structure and its homeomorphic principle. The principle of difference proper to machinistic autopoiesis is based on disequilibrium, on prospecting for virtual universes far from equilibrium. And it is not just a question of a formal rupture of equilibrium, but a radical ontological reconversion. And that is what definitively denies any far-reaching importance to the concept of Signifier. The various mutations of ontological referent that shunt us from the universe of molecular chemistry to the universe of biological chemistry, or from the world of acoustics to the world of polyphonic and harmonic music, are not brought about by the same signifying entities. Of course, lines of signifying decipherability, composed as they are of discrete figures subject to being converted into binary oppositions, syntagmatic and paradigmatic chains, can be linked from one universe to another so as to give the illusion that all phenomenological regions are woven together in the same fabric. But things change completely when we turn to the texture of these universes of reference, which are, each time, singularized by a specific constellation of expressive intensities, given through a pathic relationship, and delivering irreducibly heterogeneous ontological consistencies. We thus discover as many types of deterritorialization as we do characteristics of expressive matter. The signifying articulation that looms above them – in its superb indifference and neutrality – is unable to impose itself upon machine intensities as a relation of immanence. In other words, it cannot preside over what constitutes the nondiscursive and self-enunciating nexus of the machine. The diverse modalities of machine autopoiesis essentially escape from signifying mediation and refuse to submit to any general syntax describing the procedures of deterritorialization. No binary couple such as being/entity [*être/étant*], being/nothingness, being/other can claim to be the "binary digit" of ontology. Machinic propositions escape the ordinary game of energetic/spatial/temporal discursivity. Even so, there nevertheless exists an ontological "transversality." What happens at a particle/cosmic level is not without relationship to what happens at the level of the socius or the human soul, but not according to universal harmonics of a platonic nature (as in "The Sophist"). The composition of deterritorializing intensities is incarnated in machines that are abstract and singularized, machines that have the effect of rendering things irreversible, heterogeneous, and necessary. On this score, the Lacanian signifier is doubly inadequate. It is too abstract in that it renders too easily translatable the materials of heterogeneous expressions; it falls short of ontological heterogenesis; it gratuitously renders uniform and syntactic the diverse regions of being. At the same time, it is not abstract enough because it is incapable of accounting for the specificity of these autopoietic nexes, to which we must now return.

Autopoietic Nexus

Francisco Varela characterizes a machine as "the ensemble of the interrelations of its components, independent of the components themselves."[3] The organization of a machine thus has nothing to do with its materiality. From there Varela goes on to distinguish two types of machines: allopoietic machines which produce something besides themselves, and autopoietic machines, which continually engender and specify their own organization and their own limits. They carry out an incessant process of replacing their components because they are subject to external perturbations for which they are constantly forced to compensate. In fact, Varela reserves the qualification "autopoietic" for the biological domain. Social systems, technical machines, crystalline systems, and so forth are excluded from the category. That is the sense of his distinction between allopoiesis and autopoiesis. But autopoiesis, which thus encompasses only autonomous, individuated, and unitary entities that escape relations of input and output, lacks characteristics essential to living organisms, such as being born, dying, and surviving through genetic phyla. It seems to me, however, that autopoiesis deserves to be rethought in relation to entities that are evolutive and collective, and that sustain diverse kinds of relations of alterity, rather than being implacably closed in upon themselves. Thus institutions, like technical machines, which, in appearance, depend on allopoiesis, become ipso facto autopoietic when they are seen in the framework of machinic orderings that they constitute along with human beings. We can thus envision autopoiesis under the heading of an ontogenesis and phylogenesis specific to a mecanosphere that superimposes itself on the biosphere.

The phylogenetic evolution of machinism can be construed, at a first level, in the fact that machines arise by "generations"; they supersede each other as they become obsolete. The filiation of past generations is continued into the future by lines of virtuality and by their implied genealogical descendancy [*arbres d'implication*]. But we are not talking about a univocal historical causality. Evolutive lineages present themselves as rhizomes; datings are not synchronic but heterochronic. For example, the industrial ascendancy of steam engines took place centuries after the Chinese empire had used them as children's toys. In fact, these evolutive rhizomes traverse technical civilizations by blocks. A technological mutation can know periods of long stagnation or regression, but it is rare for it not to resurface at a later time. That is particularly clear with technological innovations of a military nature, which frequently punctuate large-scale historical sequences that they stamp with a seal of irreversibility, wiping out empires in favor of new geopolitical configurations. But, I repeat, the same was already true of the humblest instruments, utensils, and tools that are part of the same phylogenesis. One could, for example, mount an exposition on the subject of the evolution of the hammer since the stone age, and produce conjectures about what it might become in the context of new materials and new technologies. The hammer we buy today at the hardware store is, in some ways, "appropriated" from a phylogenetic lineage with virtual possibilities for the future that are undefined.

The movement of history is singularized at the crossroads of heterogeneous machinic universes, of differing dimension, of foreign ontological texture, with radical innovations, with benchmarks of ancestral machinisms previously forgotten and then reactivated. The neolithic machine associates, among other components, the machine of spoken language, the machines of cut stone, the agrarian machines founded on the selection of seeds and a protovillage economy. The scriptural machine, on the other hand, will see its emergence only with the birth of urban megamachines (compare Lewis Mumford) correlated to the implantation of archaic empires. In a parallel fashion, great nomadic machines will be constituted from the collusion between the metallurgical machine and new war machines. As for the great capitalistic machines, their basic machinisms were proliferative: first urban, then royal state machines, commercial and banking machines, navigational machines, monotheistic religious machines, deterritorialized musical and plastic machines, scientific and technical machines, and so forth.

The question of the reproducibility of machines on an ontogenetic level is more complex. The maintenance of a machine is never fail-safe for the presumed duration of its life. Its functional identity is never absolutely guaranteed. Wear and tear, precariousness, breakdowns, and entropy, as well as normal functioning, require a certain renovation of a machine's material, energetic, and informational components, the last of which is susceptible to disappearing in "noise." At the same time, maintenance of the consistency of machinic ordering requires that the quotient of human gesture and intelligence that figures in its composition must also be renewed. Man-machine alterity is thus inextricably linked to a machine-machine alterity that plays itself out in relations of complementarity or agonistics (between war machines) or else in the relations of parts or assemblages [*pièces ou dispositifs*]. In fact, wear and tear, accident, death, and resurrection of a machine in a new "example" or model are part of its destiny and can be foregrounded as the essence of certain aesthetic machines (Cesar's "compressions," "Metamechanics," happening machines, Jean Tinguely's machines of delirium). The reproducibility of machines is thus not a pure, programmed repetition. Its rhythms of rupture and fusion, which disconnect its model from all grounding, introduce a certain quotient of difference that is as ontogenetic as it is phylogenetic. On the occasion of these phases of transformation into diagrams, into abstract and disincarnated machines, the "soul supplement" of the machine nexus is granted its difference relative to simple material agglomerate. A pile of stones is not a machine, whereas a wall is already a static protomachine, manifesting virtual polarities, an inside and an outside, a high and a low, a right and a left. These diagrammatic virtualities lead us away from Varela's characterization of machinic autopoiesis as unitary individuation, without input or output, and prompts us to emphasize a more collective machinism, without delimited unity and whose autonomy meshes with diverse bases for alterity. The reproducibility of the technical machine, unlike that of living beings, does not rely upon perfectly circumscribed sequences of coding in a territorialized genome. Each technological machine has indeed its own plans of conception and assemblage, but, on the one hand, these are not conflated with the machine, and on the other hand, they get sent from one machine to another so as to constitute a diagrammatic rhizome that tends to cover the mecanosphere globally. The relations of technological machines among themselves, and adjustments of their respective parts, presuppose a formal serialization and a certain loss of their singularity – more so than in living machines – that is correlative to the distance assumed between the machine (manifested in the coordinates of energy/space/time) and the diagrammatic machine that develops in coordinates that are more numerous and more deterritorialized.

This deterritorializing distance and this loss of singularity must be attributed to a stronger smoothing out of the materials constitutive of the technical machine. Of course, the irregularities particular to these materials can never be completely smoothed out, but they should not interfere in the "freeplay" [*jeu*] of the machine unless required to by its diagrammatic function. Using a seemingly simple machinic ordering [*agencement machinique*], let us look closer at the couple formed by a lock and its key, at these two aspects of machinic separation and smoothing out. Two types of form, characterized by heterogeneous ontological textures, are at work here:

1. Materialized forms, which are contingent, concrete, and discrete, forms whose singularity is closed on itself, incarnated in profile F(L) of the lock and profile

F(K) of the key. F(L) and F(K) never coincide completely. They evolve in the course of time as a result of wear and oxidation. But both are obliged to remain within the framework of a delimiting standard deviation beyond which the key would no longer be operational.

2. Diagrammatic, "formal" forms, subsumed by this standard deviation, which are presented as a continuum including the whole gamut of profiles F(K) and F(L) compatible with the effective unlatching of the lock.

We notice right away that the effect, the possible act of opening the lock, is located altogether in the second (diagrammatic) type of form. Although they are graduated according to the most restricted possible standard deviation, these diagrammatic forms appear in infinite number. In fact, we are dealing with an integal of forms F(K) and F(L).

This integral, "infinitary" form doubles and smooths out the contingent forms F(K) and F(L), which have machinic value only to the extent that they belong to it. A bridge is thus established "over" the authorized concrete forms. This is the operation that I am qualifying as deterritorialized smoothing out, an operation that has just as much bearing upon the normalization of constitutive materials of the machine as it does upon their "digital" and functional qualification. An iron mineral that had not been sufficiently laminated and deterritorialized would show unevenness from pounding that would falsify the ideal profiles of the key and the lock. The smoothing out of the material must remove the aspects of its excessive singularity and ensure that it behaves in a way that will take the molding of formal imprints exterior to it. We should add that this molding, in this sense comparable to photography, must not be too evanescent, and must keep a consistency that is its own and that is sufficient. There again we encounter a phenomenon of standard deviation, bringing into play both a material consistency and a theoretical diagrammatic consistency. A key made of lead or of gold might bend in a steel lock. A key brought to a liquid state or to a gaseous state immediately loses its pragmatic efficiency and falls outside the category of technical machine.

This phenomenon of formal threshold will recur at every level of intra- and extramachinic relations, particularly with the existence of spare parts. The components of technical machines are thus like the coins of a formal money, a similarity that has become even more manifest because computers have been used both to conceive and to execute such machines.

These machinic forms, this smoothing out of material, of standard deviation between the parts and of functional adjustments would tend to make us think that form takes precedence over consistency and material singularity, since the reproducibility of technological machines seems to require that each of its elements be inserted into a preestablished definition of a diagrammatic sort. Charles Sanders Pierce, who characterized the diagram as an "icon of relation" and attributed to it the algorithmic function, suggested an expanded vision that is still adaptable to the present perspective. Pierce's diagram is in effect conceptualized as an autopoietic machine, thus not only granting it a functional consistency and a material consistency, but also requiring it to deploy its various registers of alterity that remove what I call the machinic nexus from a closed identity based on simple structural relations. The subjectivity of the machine is set up in universes of virtuality that everywhere exceed its existential territoriality. Thus do we refuse to postulate a subjectivity intrinsic to diagrammatic semiotization, for example, a subjectivity "nestled" in signifying chains according to the famous Lacanian principle: "A signifier represents the subject for another signifier." There does not exist, for the various machine registers, a univocal subjectivity based on rupture, lack, and suture, but rather, ontologically heterogeneous modes of subjectivity, constellations of incorporeal universes of reference that take a position of a partial enunciator in domains of multiple alterity that it would be better to call domains of "alterification." We have already encountered certain of these registers of alterity:

the alterity of proximity among different machines and among parts of the same machine;
the alterity of internal material consistency;
the alterity of formal diagrammatic consistency;
the alterity of evolutive phyla;
the agonistic alterity among war machines, which we could expand to include the "autoagonistic" alterity of desiring machines that tend to their own collapse, their own abolition, and, in a more general way, the alterity of a machinic finitude.

Another form of alterity has been taken up only very indirectly, one we could call the alterity of scale, or fractal alterity, which sets up a play of systematic correspondence among machines belonging to different levels.[4] Even so, we are not establishing a universal table of forms of mechanical alterity because, in truth, their ontological modalities are infinite. Such forms are organized by constellations of reference universes that are incorporeal and whose combinatories and creativity are unlimited.

Archaic societies are better armed than white, male, capitalistic subjectivities to map this multivalence of alterity. In this regard I would refer the reader to the exposé by Marc Augé showing the heterogeneous registers to which the Legba fetish in the African Fon society refers. The Legba is set up transversally in:

a dimension of destiny;
a universe of life principle;
an ancestral filiation;
a materialized good;
a sign of appropriation;
an entity of individuation; and
a fetish at the entrance to the village, another on the door of the house, and then at the entrance to the bedroom after initiation, and so forth.

The Legba is a handful of sand, a receptacle but at the same time the expression of the relation to others. It is found at the door, at the market, on the village square, at the crossroads. It can transmit messages, questions, answers. It is also the instrument of relation to the dead or to ancestors. It is at the same time an individual and a class of individuals, a proper name and a common name. "Its existence corresponds to the evidence of the fact that the social is not only a matter of relation, but a matter of being." Augé underscores the impossible transparency and translatability of symbolic systems. "The Legba apparatus...is constructed according to two axes. One seen from the outside on the inside, the other from identity to alterity."[5] Thus, being, identity, and relationship to the other are constructed, through fetishist practice, not only as symbolic, but also as ontologically open.

Contemporary machinic orderings, even more than the subjectivity of archaic societies, lack a univocal standard referent. But we are much less used to irreducible heterogeneity – or "heterogenicity" – of their referential components. Capital, Energy, Information, the Signifier are so many categories that make us believe in the ontological homogeneity of referents – biological, ethnological, economic, phonological, scriptural, or musical referents, to mention only a few.

In the context of a reductionist modernity, it is up to us to rediscover that a specific constellation of reference universes corresponds to each emergence of a machinic crossroads, and that from that constellation a nonhuman enunciation is instituted. Biological machines advance the universes of the living, which differentiate themselves into vegetal becomings and animal becomings. Musical machines are founded on the basis of sonoric universes that have constantly been reworked since the great polyphonic mutation. Technical machines are founded at the crossroads of the most complex and the most heterogeneous enunciative components. Heidegger, who well understood that it was not only a means, came to consider technics as a mode of unveiling of the domain of truth. He took the example of a commercial airplane waiting on a runway: the visible object hides "what it is and the way in which it is." It does not unveil its "grounds" except "insofar that it is commissioned to assure the possibility of a transportation," and, to that end, "it must be commissionable, that is, ready to take off, and it must be so in all its construction."[6] This interpellation, this "commission," that reveals the real as a "ground" is essentially operated by man and is translated in terms of universal operation, travel, flying. But does this "ground" of the machine really reside in an "already there," in the guise of eternal truths, revealed to the being of man? Machines speak to machines before speaking to man, and the ontological domains that they reveal and secrete are, at each occurrence, singular and precarious.

Let us return to this example of a commercial airplane, no longer in a generic sense, but through the technologically dated model that was christened the Concorde. The ontological consistency of this object is essentially composite; it is at the crossroads, at the pathic point of constellation and agglomeration of universes, each of which has its own ontological consistency, marks of intensity, particular organization and coordination: its specific machines. The Concorde arises at the same time:

from a diagrammatic universe, with its theoretical "feasibility" plans;
from technological universes that transpose this "feasibility" in terms of materials;

from an industrial universe capable of producing it effectively;

from a collective, imaginary universe corresponding to a desire sufficient to bring the project to term; and

from political and economic universes allowing, among other things, the earmarking of funds for its production.

But the ensemble of these final, material, formal, and efficient causes, in the final analysis, don't make the grade! The object Concorde travels between Paris and New York, but it has remained bolted to the economic ground. This lack of economic consistency has definitively imperiled its global ontological consistency. The Concorde exists only within the limits of a reproducibility of twelve copies and at the root of the possibilist phylum of supersonics yet to come. That is already no small feat!

Why am I insisting so much on the impossibility of establishing solid grounds for a general translatability of various components of reference and for the partial enunciation of ordering? Why this lack of reverence toward the Lacanian conception of the signifier? It is precisely because this theorization, coming out of linguistic structuralism, does not get us out of structure, and prohibits us from entering the real world of the machine. The structuralist signifier is always synonymous with linear discursivity. From one symbol to another, the subjective effect emerges with no other ontological guarantee. As against that, heterogeneous machines, such as those envisioned in our schizoanalytic perspective, yield no standard being orchestrated by a universal temporalization. In order to illuminate this point I must establish distinctions among the different forms of semiological, semiotic, and encoding linearity:

1. encodings of the "natural" world, which operate in several spatial dimensions (those of crystallography, for example), and which do not imply extraction of autonomized encoding operators;
2. the relative linearity of biological encodings, for example, the double helix of DNA, which, based on four basic chemicals, develops equally in three dimensions;
3. the linearity of presignifying semiologies, which is developed in relatively autonomous parallel lines, even if phonological lines of spoken language always seem to overcode all the others;
4. the semiological linearity of the scriptural signifier, which imposes itself in a despotic manner upon all other modes of semiotization, which expropriates them and even tends to make them disappear in the framework of a communicational economy dominated by data processing (or, to be more precise, data processing at its current state of development, as this state of affairs is in no way definitive!); and
5. the superlinearity of asignifying substances of expression, where the signifier sheds its despotism, where informational lines can retrieve a certain parallelism and work in direct contact with referent universes that are in no way linear and that tend, moreover, to escape any logic of spatialized ensembles.

The signs of asignifying semiotic machines are "sign-points." Partly they are of a semiotic order, partly they intervene directly in a series of material machinic processes (for example, the code number of a credit card that makes a cash machine work).

Asignifying semiotic figures do not secrete only significations. They issue starting and stopping orders and, above all, they provoke the "setting into being" of ontological universes. An example may be found at present, in pentatonic musical ritornelli that, after a few notes, catalyze the Debussyan universe, with its multiple components:

the Wagnerian universe around Parsifal, which is linked to the existential territory constituted by Bayreuth;
the universe of Gregorian chant;
the universe of French music, with the rehabilitation of Rameau and Couperin for contemporary taste;
the universe of Chopin, thanks to a nationalist transposition (Ravel, for his part, having appropriated Lizst);
Javanese music that Debussy discovered at the 1889 World's Fair; and the world of Manet and Mallarmé, which is linked to his stay at the Villa Medici.

And to these present and past influences should be added the prospective resonances constituted by the reinvention of polyphony since L'Ars Nova, its repercussions on the French musical phylum of Ravel, Duparc, and Messiaen, and on the sonic mutation unleashed by Stravinsky, its presence in the work of Proust, and so forth.

Clearly there exists no biunivocal correspondence between, on the one hand, signifying linear links or links of *arché-écriture*, according to authors, and, on the other hand, this machinic, multidisciplinary, multireferential catalyst. The symmetry of the scale, transversality, the pathic and nondiscursive character of their expansion, all these dimensions get us out of the logic of the excluded third term and comfort us by the ontological binarism that we had previously denounced. A machine ordering, through its various components, tears away its consistency by crossing ontological thresholds, thresholds of nonlinear irreversibility, ontogenetic and philogenetic thresholds, thresholds of creative heterogenesis and autopoiesis.

It is the notion of scale that we should expand upon here in order to think fractal symmetries in terms of ontology. Substantial scales are traversed by fractal machines. They traverse them as they engender them. But it must be admitted that these existential orderings that they "invent" have already been there forever. How can we defend such a paradox? The reason is that everything becomes possible, including the recessive smoothing out of time described by René Thom, as soon as we allow for an escape from ordering outside of energy/space/time coordinates.

And there again, it falls to us to rediscover being's way of being – before, after, here and everywhere else, without however being identical to itself – of being eternal, of being processual, polyphonic, singularizable with textures that can become infinitely complex, at the whim of infinite speeds that animate its virtual compositions.

Ontological relativity sanctioned here is inseparable from an enunciative relativity. Knowledge of a universe in the astrophysical sense or in the axiological sense is possible only through the mediation of autopoietic machines. It is fitting that a foyer of self-belonging should exist somewhere so that whatever entity or whatever modality of being might be able to come into cognitive existence. Beyond this coupling of machine and universe, beings have only the pure status of virtual entities. The same goes for their enunciative coordinates. The biosphere and the mecanosphere, clinging to this planet, bring into focus a spatial, temporal, and energetic point of view. They make up an angle of constitution of our galaxy. Outside this particularized point of view, the rest of the universe exists – in the sense that we apprehend existence here below – only through the virtuality of the existence of other autopoietic machines at the heart of other biomecanospheres sprinkled about the cosmos. Even so, the relativity of spatial, temporal, and energetic points of view does not cause the real to dissolve into a dream. The category time dissolves in cosmological reflections about the big bang, while the category of irreversibility is affirmed. The residual object is the object that resists being swept away by the infinite variability of the points of view by which it can be perceived. Let us imagine an autopoietic object whose particles might be built on the basis of our galaxies. Or, in the opposite sense, a cognitivity constituting itself on the scale of quarks. Another panorama, another ontological consistency. The mecanosphere appropriates and actualizes configurations that exist among an infinity of others in fields of virtuality. Existential machines are on the same level as being in its intrinsic multiplicity. They are not mediated by transcendent signifiers subsumed by a univocal ontological foundation. They are themselves their own material of semiotic expression. Existence, insofar as it is a process of deterritorialization, is a specific intermachinic operation that is superimposed onto the advancement of singularized existential intensities. And, I repeat, there exists no generalized syntax of these deterritorializations. Existence is not dialectic. It is not representable. It is hardly even livable!

Desiring machines, which break with the great social and personal organic balances and turn commands upside down, play the game of the other upon encountering a politics of ego self-centering. For example, the partial drives and the polymorphously perverse investments of psychoanalysis do not constitute an exceptional and deviant race of machines. All machinic orderings contain within them, even if only in an embryonic state, enunciative nuclei [*foyers*] that are so many protomachines of desire. To circumscribe this point we must further enlarge our transmachinic bridge in order to understand the smoothing out of the onto-logical texture of machinic material and diagrammatic feedback as so many dimensions of intensification that get us beyond the linear causalities of capitalistic apprehension of machinic universes. We must also surpass logic based on the principle of the third excluded term and on sufficient reason. Through smoothing out, a being beyond comes into play, a being-for-the-other, which makes an existing being take consistency outside of its strict delimitation in the here and now. The machine is always synonymous with a constitutive threshold of existential territory against a background of incorporeal reference universes. The "mecan-ism" of this reversal of being consists in the fact that certain discursive segments of the machine begin to play a game that is no longer only functional or significa-tional, but assumes an existentializing function of pure intensive repetition, what I have elsewhere called a ritornello function. Smoothing out is like an ontological ritornello and, thus, far from apprehending a univocal truth of Being through *techné*, as Heideggerian ontology would have it, it is a plurality of beings as machines that give themselves to us once we acquire the pathic and cartographic means of access to them. Manifestations not of Being, but of multitudes of ontological components are of the order as machines – without semiological mediation, without transcendent coding, directly, as "given-to-being" – as Donor [*Donnant*]. To accede to such a giving is already to participate in it ontologically, by rights [*de plein droit*]. This term of "right" does not crop up here by chance, so true is it that, at this proto-ontological level, it is already necessary to affirm a protoethical dimension. The play of intensity within the ontological constellation is, in a way, a choice of being not only for itself [*pour soi*], but for all the alterity of the cosmos and for the infinity of time.

If there must be choice and freedom at certain "superior" anthropological stages, it is because we shall also have to find them at the most elementary levels of machinic concatenation. But notions such as element and complexity are here susceptible to brutal reversal. The most differentiated and the most undifferen-tiated coexist amid the same chaos that, with infinite speed, plays its virtual registers one against the other, and one with the other. The machinic-technical world, at whose "terminal" today's humanity is constituting itself, is barricaded by horizons formed by a mathematical constant and by a limitation of the infinite speeds of chaos (speed of light, cosmological horizon of the big bang, Planck's distance and elementary quantum of action of quantum physics, the impossibility of crossing absolute zero). But this same world of semiotic constraint is doubled, tripled, infinitized by other worlds that, under certain conditions, ask only to bifurcate outside of their universes of virtuality and to engender new fields of the possible.

Desire machines, aesthetic creation machines, are constantly revising our cosmic frontiers. As such, they have a place of eminence in the orderings of subjectivation, which are themselves called upon to relay our old social machines that are unable to follow the efflorescence of machinic revolutions that are causing our time to burst apart at every point.

Notes

1   Norbert Wiener, *Cybernetics; or, Control and Communication in the Animal and the Machine* (Cambridge, MA: Massachusetts Institute of Technology Press, 1948).
2   Francisco Varela, *Autonomie et connaissance* (Paris: Seuil, 1989).
3   Varela, *Autonomie et connaissance*; translation by James Creech.
4   Leibniz, in his concern to homogenize the infinitely large, and the infinitely small, thinks that the living machine, which he assimilates to a divine machine, continues to be a

machine even in its smallest parts. This would not be the case for a machine made by human art. See, for example, Gilles Deleuze, *Le Pli* (Paris: Minuit, 1988); translated by Tom Conley as *The Fold* (Minneapolis: University of Minnesota Press, 1993).

5   Marc Augé, "Le Fétiche et son objet," in *L'Objet en psychanalyse*, ed. Maud Mannoni (Paris: Denoël, 1986).

6   Martin Heidegger, *Essais et conférences* (Paris: Gallimard, 1988), 1, pp. 9, 48.

Part II

Knowledge and Communication in a Digital Age

Marshall McLuhan argued that the content of any new medium is frequently the old medium that it replaces.[1] Hence digital culture finds itself haunted by analog-style images and endless written texts. While recognizing that semiotic continuities exist across languages and other communicative forms, including those in the digital realm, it would be imprudent to assert a set of foundational principles for all cultures and all media. The best one can do is to map the linkages and ruptures from one "mode of information" to another.[2] This is all the more important in digital culture, which seems especially conducive to exceptionalist claims.

The most common representation of cyberspace is that of a radically new medium born of the confluence of network technology and the rise of the personal computer. Proponents of this view argue that cyberspace offers an essential break from past systems of communication, commerce, or social interaction. Frequently emphasis is placed on the formal aspects of the medium: the ability of information technology to atomize or synthesize data, its capacity to process large volumes of information at increasing speeds, or its ways of linking users across space and time. Following the thinking of early modernist aestheticians, this brand of cyberexceptionalism argues that new communicative structures enable new modes of creative expression and foster novel forms of subjectivity.

A different approach is taken by those who view cyberspace as a doorway to the human spirit. Whether the goal is insight or adventure, the overriding ethos evokes a traditional Platonic metaphysics in which ideal forms are privileged over material objects. For some writers this focus on the "poetry" of cyberspace is its central premise. Digital technology becomes the means of achieving the transcendent and unified subjectivity that has been the desire of Western philosophy for centuries. Often this translates into an inexplicable mysticism, a belief in the ability of digital technology to locate hidden territories of knowledge and consciousness, detached from the material world by virtue of immersion in a virtual computer environment. This embrace of a machine as an instrument of spirituality is notable in the separation it makes between the virtual space of the computer world and the material space of the world outside of it.

A similar romanticism is evoked in assertions that cyberspace fulfills the dream of a universal language in its ability to combine disparate audio and visual material in a uniform digital format. This "perfect medium" is credited with the ability to link all peoples of the world through its global networking capabilities. Proponents of this view see cyberspace as a great social leveler, bringing users of all media and speakers of all languages together in what McLuhan termed a "unified public field of awareness." But not everyone subscribes to such ecumenical beliefs. Aside from the empirical fallacy of such universalist claims lies the ethical dilemma of asserting one language over all others. This is hardly an issue restricted to metaphysics at a time when so much of the world's population, especially people in developing nations, remains unconnected to the "perfect medium."

Taking a nearly opposite position are those who locate the Internet's greatest benefits in its decentralized structure and user diversity. This perspective asserts a fundamental correspondence between the architecture of computer networks and certain strains of contemporary social theory. These writers latch onto the notion that the Internet – specifically its form of writing known as hypertext – constitutes a long-sought physical embodiment of the anti-hierarchical principles of postmodernism. Within this scheme, the decentered character of hypertext links from one Internet site to another enables systems of nodes, links, and networks to replace regimes founded upon center, hierarchy, and linearity. Similar critiques of foundationalism derived from theories of representation suggest that the artificial experience of virtual environments eclipses our knowledge of the "real" world. This claim of the primacy of representations over their referents, the replacement of things with images, is widely embraced because of the way it matches the experience of people spending long hours staring at televisions or computer screens.

As one might expect from a field with such conceptual diversity, the writings in this part take varying – and at times contradictory – approaches to knowledge and communication. From the expressive strategies illuminated by William Gibson and Brenda Laurel, to the theoretical exegetics of Hakim Bey, Michael Heim, George Landow, and Margaret Morse, the contributions engage the various ways that digital media organize, store, transmit, and transform meaning as ideas are translated into digits, signals, and code. How is one to make sense of this often confusing and seemingly contradictory range of opinions? Perhaps by refusing to settle on any simple or singular explanation for a phenomenon as complex and multidimensional as digital culture. Like any important moment in human history, the current era requires a variety of theoretical tools and analytical strategies to make sense of it. This moment asks from us the patience and intellectual generosity to listen to the many voices that struggle with its questions.

Notes

1 Marshall McLuhan, *Understanding Media: Extensions of Man* (New York: McGraw-Hill, 1964).
2 Mark Poster, *The Mode of Information: Poststructuralism and Social Context* (Cambridge, MA: Polity Press, 1990).

Johnny Mnemonic

William Gibson

William Gibson is a journalist and science fiction writer, who is best known for his dystopian novel *Neuromancer* (Bantam, 1984) which introduced the term "cyberspace." This selection first appeared in *Omni* magazine in 1981 and later in Gibson's book *Burning Chrome* (Arbor House, 1986). In 1995, "Johnny Mnemonic" became a feature film directed by Robert Longo.

I put the shotgun in an Adidas bag and padded it out with four pairs of tennis socks, not my style at all, but that was what I was aiming for: If they think you're crude, go technical; if they think you're technical, go crude. I'm a very technical boy. So I decided to get as crude as possible. These days, though, you have to be pretty technical before you can even aspire to crudeness. I'd had to turn both these twelve-gauge shells from brass stock, on a lathe, and then load them myself; I'd had to dig up an old microfiche with instructions for hand-loading cartridges; I'd had to build a lever-action press to seat the primers – all very tricky. But I knew they'd work.

The meet was set for the Drome at 2300, but I rode the tube three stops past the closest platform and walked back. Immaculate procedure.

I checked myself out in the chrome siding of a coffee kiosk, your basic sharp-faced Caucasoid with a ruff of stiff, dark hair. The girls at Under the Knife were big on Sony Mao, and it was getting harder to keep them from adding the chic suggestion of epicanthic folds. It probably wouldn't fool Ralfi Face, but it might get me next to his table.

The Drome is a single narrow space with a bar down one side and tables along the other, thick with pimps and handlers and an arcane array of dealers. The Magnetic Dog Sisters were on the door that night, and I didn't relish trying to get out past them if things didn't work out. They were two meters tall and thin as greyhounds. One was black and the other white, but aside from that they were as nearly identical as cosmetic surgery could make them. They'd been lovers for years and were bad news in a tussle. I was never quite sure which one had originally been male.

Ralfi was sitting at his usual table. Owing me a lot of money. I had hundreds of megabytes stashed in my head on an idiot/savant basis, information I had no conscious access to. Ralfi had left it there. He hadn't, however, come back for it. Only Ralfi could retrieve the data, with a code phrase of his own invention. I'm not cheap to begin with, but my overtime on storage is astronomical. And Ralfi had been very scarce.

Then I'd heard that Ralfi Face wanted to put out a contract on me. So I'd arranged to meet him in the Drome, but I'd arranged it as Edward Bax, clandestine importer, late of Rio and Peking.

The Drome stank of biz, a metallic tang of nervous tension. Muscle-boys scattered through the crowd were flexing stock parts at one another and trying on thin, cold grins, some of them so lost under superstructures of muscle graft that their outlines weren't really human.

Pardon me. Pardon me, friends. Just Eddie Bax here, Fast Eddie the Importer, with his professionally nondescript gym bag, and please ignore this slit, just wide enough to admit his right hand.

Ralfi wasn't alone. Eighty kilos of blond California beef perched alertly in the chair next to his, martial arts written all over him.

Fast Eddie Bax was in the chair opposite them before the beef's hands were off the table. "You black belt?" I asked eagerly. He nodded, blue eyes running an automatic scanning pattern between my eyes and my hands. "Me, too," I said. "Got mine here in the bag." And I shoved my hand through the slit and thumbed the safety off. Click. "Double twelve-gauge with the triggers wired together."

"That's a gun," Ralfi said, putting a plump, restraining hand on his boy's taut blue nylon chest. "Johnny has an antique firearm in his bag." So much for Edward Bax.

I guess he'd always been Ralfi Something or Other, but he owed his acquired surname to a singular vanity. Built something like an overripe pear, he'd worn the once-famous face of Christian White for twenty years – Christian White of the Aryan Reggae Band, Sony Mao to his generation, and final champion of race rock. I'm a whiz at trivia.

Christian White: classic pop face with a singer's high-definition muscles, chiseled cheekbones. Angelic in one light, handsomely depraved in another. But Ralfi's eyes lived behind that face, and they were small and cold and black.

"Please," he said, "let's work this out like businessmen." His voice was marked by a horrible prehensile sincerity, and the corners of his beautiful Christian White mouth were always wet. "Lewis here," nodding in the beefboy's direction, "is a meatball." Lewis took this impassively, looking like something built from a kit. "You aren't a meatball, Johnny."

"Sure I am, Ralfi, a nice meatball chock-full of implants where you can store your dirty laundry while you go off shopping for people to kill me. From my end of this bag, Ralfi, it looks like you've got some explaining to do."

"It's this last batch of product, Johnny." He sighed deeply. "In my role as broker —"

"Fence," I corrected.

"As broker, I'm usually very careful as to sources."

"You buy only from those who steal the best. Got it."

He sighed again. "I try," he said wearily, "not to buy from fools. This time, I'm afraid, I've done that." Third sigh was the cue for Lewis to trigger the neural disruptor they'd taped under my side of the table.

I put everything I had into curling the index finger of my right hand, but I no longer seemed to be connected to it. I could feel the metal of the gun and the foam-pad tape I'd wrapped around the stubby grip, but my hands were cool wax, distant and inert. I was hoping Lewis was a true meatball, thick enough to go for the gym bag and snag my rigid trigger finger, but he wasn't.

"We've been very worried about you, Johnny. Very worried. You see, that's Yakuza property you have there. A fool took it from them, Johnny. A dead fool."

Lewis giggled.

It all made sense then, an ugly kind of sense, like bags of wet sand settling around my head. Killing wasn't Ralfi's style. Lewis wasn't even Ralfi's style. But he'd got himself stuck between the Sons of the Neon Chrysanthemum and something that belonged to them – or, more likely, something of theirs that belonged to someone else. Ralfi, of course, could use the code phrase to throw me into idiot/ savant, and I'd spill their hot program without remembering a single quarter tone. For a fence like Ralfi, that would ordinarily have been enough. But not for the Yakuza. The Yakuza would know about Squids, for one thing, and they wouldn't want to worry about one lifting those dim and permanent traces of their program out of my head. I didn't know very much about Squids, but I'd heard stories, and I made it a point never to repeat them to my clients. No, the Yakuza wouldn't like that; it looked too much like evidence. They hadn't got where they were by leaving evidence around. Or alive.

Lewis was grinning. I think he was visualizing a point just behind my forehead and imagining how he could get there the hard way.

"Hey," said a low voice, feminine, from somewhere behind my right shoulder, "you cowboys sure aren't having too lively a time."

"Pack it, bitch," Lewis said, his tanned face very still. Ralfi looked blank.

"Lighten up. You want to buy some good free base?" She pulled up a chair and quickly sat before either of them could stop her. She was barely inside my fixed field of vision, a thin girl with mirrored glasses, her dark hair cut in a rough shag. She wore black leather, open over a T-shirt slashed diagonally with stripes of red and black. "Eight thou a gram weight."

Lewis snorted his exasperation and tried to slap her out of the chair. Somehow he didn't quite connect, and her hand came up and seemed to brush his wrist as it passed. Bright blood sprayed the table. He was clutching his wrist white-knuckle tight, blood trickling from between his fingers.

But hadn't her hand been empty?

He was going to need a tendon stapler. He stood up carefully, without bothering to push his chair back. The chair toppled backward, and he stepped out of my line of sight without a word.

"He better get a medic to look at that," she said. "That's a nasty cut."

"You have no idea," said Ralfi, suddenly sounding very tired, "the depths of shit you have just gotten yourself into."

"No kidding? Mystery. I get real excited by mysteries. Like why your friend here's so quiet. Frozen, like. Or what this thing here is for," and she held up the little control unit that she'd somehow taken from Lewis. Ralfi looked ill.

"You, ah, want maybe a quarter-million to give me that and take a walk?" A fat hand came up to stroke his pale, lean face nervously.

"What I want," she said, snapping her fingers so that the unit spun and glittered, "is work. A job. Your boy hurt his wrist. But a quarter'll do for a retainer."

Ralfi let his breath out explosively and began to laugh, exposing teeth that hadn't been kept up to the Christian White standard. Then she turned the disruptor off.

"Two million," I said.

"My kind of man," she said, and laughed. "What's in the bag?"

"A shotgun."

"Crude." It might have been a compliment.

Ralfi said nothing at all.

"Name's Millions. Molly Millions. You want to get out of here, boss? People are starting to stare." She stood up. She was wearing leather jeans the color of dried blood.

And I saw for the first time that the mirrored lenses were surgical inlays, the silver rising smoothly from her high cheekbones, sealing her eyes in their sockets. I saw my new face twinned there.

"I'm Johnny," I said. "We're taking Mr. Face with us."

He was outside, waiting. Looking like your standard tourist tech, in plastic zoris and a silly Hawaiian shirt printed with blowups of his firm's most popular microprocessor; a mild little guy, the kind most likely to wind up drunk on sake in a bar that puts out miniature rice crackers with seaweed garnish. He looked like the kind who sing the corporate anthem and cry, who shake hands endlessly with the bartender. And the pimps and the dealers would leave him alone, pegging him as innately conservative. Not up for much, and careful with his credit when he was.

The way I figured it later, they must have amputated part of his left thumb, somewhere behind the first joint, replacing it with a prosthetic tip, and cored the stump, fitting it with a spool and socket molded from one of the Ono-Sendai diamond analogs. Then they'd carefully wound the spool with three meters of monomolecular filament.

Molly got into some kind of exchange with the Magnetic Dog Sisters, giving me a chance to usher Ralfi through the door with the gym bag pressed lightly against the base of his spine. She seemed to know them. I heard the black one laugh.

I glanced up, out of some passing reflex, maybe because I've never got used to it, to the soaring arcs of light and the shadows of the geodesics above them. Maybe that saved me.

Ralfi kept walking, but I don't think he was trying to escape. I think he'd already given up. Probably he already had an idea of what we were up against.

I looked back down in time to see him explode.

Playback on full recall shows Ralfi stepping forward as the little tech sidles out of nowhere, smiling. Just a suggestion of a bow, and his left thumb falls off. It's a conjuring trick. The thumb hangs suspended. Mirrors? Wires? And Ralfi stops, his back to us, dark crescents of sweat under the armpits of his pale summer suit. He knows. He must have known. And then the joke-shop thumbtip, heavy as lead, arcs out in a lightning yo-yo trick, and the invisible thread connecting it to the killer's hand passes laterally through Ralfi's skull, just above his eyebrows, whips up, and descends, slicing the pear-shaped torso diagonally from shoulder to rib cage. Cuts so fine that no blood flows until synapses misfire and the first tremors surrender the body to gravity.

Ralfi tumbled apart in a pink cloud of fluids, the three mismatched sections rolling forward onto the tiled pavement. In total silence.

I brought the gym bag up, and my hand convulsed. The recoil nearly broke my wrist.

It must have been raining; ribbons of water cascaded from a ruptured geodesic and spattered on the tile behind us. We crouched in the narrow gap between a surgical boutique and an antique shop. She'd just edged one mirrored eye around the corner to report a single Volks module in front of the Drome, red lights flashing. They were sweeping Ralfi up. Asking questions.

I was covered in scorched white fluff. The tennis socks. The gym bag was a ragged plastic cuff around my wrist. "I don't see how the hell I missed him."

"'Cause he's fast, so fast." She hugged her knees and rocked back and forth on her bootheels. "His nervous system's jacked up. He's factory custom." She grinned and gave a little squeal of delight. "I'm gonna get that boy. Tonight. He's the best, number one, top dollar, state of the art."

"What you're going to get, for this boy's two million, is my ass out of here. Your boyfriend back there was mostly grown in a vat in Chiba City. He's a Yakuza assassin."

"Chiba. Yeah. See, Molly's been Chiba, too." And she showed me her hands, fingers slightly spread. Her fingers were slender, tapered, very white against the polished burgundy nails. Ten blades snicked straight out from their recesses beneath her nails, each one a narrow, double-edged scalpel in pale blue steel.

I'd never spent much time in Nighttown. Nobody there had anything to pay me to remember, and most of them had a lot they paid regularly to forget. Generations of sharpshooters had chipped away at the neon until the maintenance crews gave up. Even at noon the arcs were soot-black against faintest pearl.

Where do you go when the world's wealthiest criminal order is feeling for you with calm, distant fingers? Where do you hide from the Yakuza, so powerful that it owns comsats and at least three shuttles? The Yakuza is a true multinational, like ITT and Ono-Sendai. Fifty years before I was born the Yakuza had already absorbed the Triads, the Mafia, the Union Corse.

Molly had an answer: you hide in the Pit, in the lowest circle, where any outside influence generates swift, concentric ripples of raw menace. You hide in

Nighttown. Better yet, you hide *above* Nighttown, because the Pit's inverted, and the bottom of its bowl touches the sky, the sky that Nighttown never sees, sweating under its own firmament of acrylic resin, up where the Lo Teks crouch in the dark like gargoyles, black-market cigarettes dangling from their lips.

She had another answer, too.

"So you're locked up good and tight, Johnny-san? No way to get that program without the password?" She led me into the shadows that waited beyond the bright tube platform. The concrete walls were overlaid with graffiti, years of them twisting into a single metascrawl of rage and frustration.

"The stored data are fed in through a modified series of microsurgical contra-autism prostheses." I reeled off a numb version of my standard sales pitch. "Client's code is stored in a special chip; barring Squids, which we in the trade don't like to talk about, there's no way to recover your phrase. Can't drug it out, cut it out, torture it. I don't *know* it, never did."

"Squids? Crawly things with arms?" We emerged into a deserted street market. Shadowy figures watched us from across a makeshift square littered with fish heads and rotting fruit.

"Superconducting quantum interference detectors. Used them in the war to find submarines, suss out enemy cyber systems."

"Yeah? Navy stuff? From the war? Squid'll read that chip of yours?" She'd stopped walking, and I felt her eyes on me behind those twin mirrors.

"Even the primitive models could measure a magnetic field a billionth the strength of geomagnetic force; it's like pulling a whisper out of a cheering stadium."

"Cops can do that already, with parabolic microphones and lasers."

"But your data's still secure." Pride in profession. "No government'll let their cops have Squids, not even the security heavies. Too much chance of interdepartmental funnies; they're too likely to watergate you."

"Navy stuff," she said, and her grin gleamed in the shadows. "Navy stuff. I got a friend down here who was in the navy, name's Jones. I think you'd better meet him. He's a junkie, though. So we'll have to take him something."

"A junkie?"

"A dolphin."

He was more than a dolphin, but from another dolphin's point of view he might have seemed like something less. I watched him swirling sluggishly in his galvanized tank. Water slopped over the side, wetting my shoes. He was surplus from the last war. A cyborg.

He rose out of the water, showing us the crusted plates along his sides, a kind of visual pun, his grace nearly lost under articulated armor, clumsy and prehistoric. Twin deformities on either side of his skull had been engineered to house sensor units. Silver lesions gleamed on exposed sections of his gray-white hide.

Molly whistled. Jones thrashed his tail, and more water cascaded down the side of the tank.

"What is this place?" I peered at vague shapes in the dark, rusting chain link and things under tarps. Above the tank hung a clumsy wooden framework, crossed and recrossed by rows of dusty Christmas lights.

"Funland. Zoo and carnival rides. 'Talk with the War Whale.' All that. Some whale Jones is . . . ."

Jones reared again and fixed me with a sad and ancient eye.

"How's he talk?" Suddenly I was anxious to go.

"That's the catch. Say 'hi,' Jones."

And all the bulbs lit simultaneously. They were flashing red, white, and blue.

* * *

RWBRWBRWB
RWBRWBRWB
RWBRWBRWB
RWBRWBRWB
RWBRWBRWB

"Good with symbols, see, but the code's restricted. In the navy they had him wired into an audiovisual display." She drew the narrow package from a jacket pocket. "Pure shit, Jones. Want it?" He froze in the water and started to sink. I felt a strange panic, remembering that he wasn't a fish, that he could drown. "We want the key to Johnny's bank, Jones. We want it fast."

The lights flickered, died.

"Go for it, Jones!"

B
BBBBBBBBB
B
B
B

Blue bulbs, cruciform.
Darkness.
"Pure! It's *clean*. Come on, Jones."

WWWWWWWWW
WWWWWWWWW
WWWWWWWWW
WWWWWWWWW
WWWWWWWWW

White sodium glare washed her features, stark monochrome, shadows cleaving from her cheekbones.

* * *

```
R     RRRRR
R     R
RRRRRRRRR
        R   R
RRRRR    R
```

The arms of the red swastika were twisted in her silver glasses. "Give it to him," I said. "We've got it."

Ralfi Face. No imagination.

Jones heaved half his armored bulk over the edge of his tank, and I thought the metal would give way. Molly stabbed him overhand with the Syrette, driving the needle between two plates. Propellant hissed. Patterns of light exploded, spasming across the frame and then fading to black.

We left him drifting, rolling languorously in the dark water. Maybe he was dreaming of his war in the Pacific, of the cyber mines he'd swept, nosing gently into their circuitry with the Squid he'd used to pick Ralfi's pathetic password from the chip buried in my head.

"I can see them slipping up when he was demobbed, letting him out of the navy with that gear intact, but how does a cybernetic dolphin get wired to smack?"

"The war," she said. "They all were. Navy did it. How else you get 'em working for you?"

"I'm not sure this profiles as good business," the pirate said, angling for better money. "Target specs on a comsat that isn't in the book—"

"Waste my time and you won't profile at all," said Molly, leaning across his scarred plastic desk to prod him with her forefinger.

"So maybe you want to buy your microwaves somewhere else?" He was a tough kid, behind his Mao-job. A Nighttowner by birth, probably.

Her hand blurred down the front of his jacket, completely severing a lapel without even rumpling the fabric.

"So we got a deal or not?"

"Deal," he said, staring at his ruined lapel with what he must have hoped was only polite interest. "Deal."

While I checked the two recorders we'd bought, she extracted the slip of paper I'd given her from the zippered wrist pocket of her jacket. She unfolded it and read silently, moving her lips. She shrugged. "This is it?"

"Shoot," I said, punching the RECORD studs of the two decks simultaneously.

"Christian White," she recited, "and his Aryan Reggae Band."

Faithful Ralfi, a fan to his dying day.

Transition to idiot/savant mode is always less abrupt than I expect it to be. The pirate broadcaster's front was a failing travel agency in a pastel cube that boasted a desk, three chairs, and a faded poster of a Swiss orbital spa. A pair of toy birds with blown-glass bodies and tin legs were sipping monotonously from a Styrofoam cup of water on a ledge beside Molly's shoulder. As I phased into mode, they accelerated gradually until their Day-Glo-feathered crowns became solid arcs of color. The LEDs that told seconds on the plastic wall clock had become meaningless pulsing grids, and Molly and the Mao-faced boy grew hazy, their arms blurring occasionally in insect-quick ghosts of gesture. And then it all faded to cool gray static and an endless tone poem in an artificial language.

I sat and sang dead Ralfi's stolen program for three hours.

The mall runs forty kilometers from end to end, a ragged overlap of Fuller domes roofing what was once a suburban artery. If they turn off the arcs on a clear day, a gray approximation of sunlight filters through layers of acrylic, a view like the prison sketches of Giovanni Piranesi. The three southernmost kilometers roof Nighttown. Nighttown pays no taxes, no utilities. The neon arcs are dead, and the geodesics have been smoked black by decades of cooking fires. In the nearly total darkness of a Nighttown noon, who notices a few dozen mad children lost in the rafters?

We'd been climbing for two hours, up concrete stairs and steel ladders with perforated rungs, past abandoned gantries and dust-covered tools. We'd started in what looked like a disused maintenance yard, stacked with triangular roofing segments. Everything there had been covered with that same uniform layer of spraybomb graffiti: gang names, initials, dates back to the turn of the century. The graffiti followed us up, gradually thinning until a single name was repeated at intervals. LO TEK. In dripping black capitals.

"Who's Lo Tek?"

"Not us, boss." She climbed a shivering aluminum ladder and vanished through a hole in a sheet of corrugated plastic. " 'Low technique, low technology.' " The plastic muffled her voice. I followed her up, nursing my aching wrist. "Lo Teks, they'd think that shotgun trick of yours was effete."

An hour later I dragged myself up through another hole, this one sawed crookedly in a sagging sheet of plywood, and met my first Lo Tek.

" 'S okay," Molly said, her hand brushing my shoulder. "It's just Dog. Hey, Dog."

In the narrow beam of her taped flash, he regarded us with his one eye and slowly extruded a thick length of grayish tongue, licking huge canines. I wondered how they wrote off tooth-bud transplants from Dobermans as low technology. Immunosuppressives don't exactly grow on trees.

"Moll." Dental augmentation impeded his speech. A string of saliva dangled from his twisted lower lip. "Heard ya comin'. Long time." He might have been fifteen, but the fangs and a bright mosaic of scars combined with the gaping socket to present a mask of total bestiality. It had taken time and a certain kind of creativity to assemble that face, and his posture told me he enjoyed living behind it. He wore a pair of decaying jeans, black with grime and shiny along the creases. His chest and feet were bare. He did something with his mouth that approximated a grin. "Bein' followed, you."

Far off, down in Nighttown, a water vendor cried his trade.

"Strings jumping, Dog?" She swung her flash to the side, and I saw thin cords tied to eyebolts, cords that ran to the edge and vanished.

"Kill the fuckin' light!"

She snapped it off.

"How come the one who's followin' you's got no light?"

"Doesn't need it. That one's bad news, Dog. Your sentries give him a tumble, they'll come home in easy-to-carry sections."

"This a *friend* friend, Moll?" He sounded uneasy. I heard his feet shift on the worn plywood.

"No. But he's mine. And this one," slapping my shoulder, "he's a friend. Got that?"

"Sure," he said, without much enthusiasm, padding to the platform's edge, where the eyebolts were. He began to pluck out some kind of message on the taut cords.

Nighttown spread beneath us like a toy village for rats; tiny windows showed candlelight, with only a few harsh, bright squares lit by battery lanterns and carbide lamps. I imagined the old men at their endless games of dominoes, under warm, fat drops of water that fell from wet wash hung out on poles between the plywood shanties. Then I tried to imagine him climbing patiently up through the darkness in his zoris and ugly tourist shirt, bland and unhurried. How was he tracking us?

"Good," said Molly. "He smells us."

"Smoke?" Dog dragged a crumpled pack from his pocket and prized out a flattened cigarette. I squinted at the trademark while he lit it for me with a kitchen match. Yiheyuan filters. Beijing Cigarette Factory. I decided that the Lo Teks were black marketeers. Dog and Molly went back to their argument, which seemed to revolve around Molly's desire to use some particular piece of Lo Tek real estate.

"I've done you a lot of favors, man. I want that floor. And I want the music."

"You're not Lo Tek. . . ."

This must have been going on for the better part of a twisted kilometer, Dog leading us along swaying catwalks and up rope ladders. The Lo Teks leech their webs and huddling places to the city's fabric with thick gobs of epoxy and sleep above the abyss in mesh hammocks. Their country is so attenuated that in places it consists of little more than holds for hands and feet, sawed into geodesic struts.

The Killing Floor, she called it. Scrambling after her, my new Eddie Bax shoes slipping on worn metal and damp plywood, I wondered how it could be any more lethal than the rest of the territory. At the same time I sensed that Dog's protests were ritual and that she already expected to get whatever it was she wanted.

Somewhere beneath us, Jones would be circling his tank, feeling the first twinges of junk sickness. The police would be boring the Drome regulars with questions about Ralfi. What did he do? Who was he with before he stepped outside? And the Yakuza would be settling its ghostly bulk over the city's data banks, probing for faint images of me reflected in numbered accounts, securities transactions, bills for utilities. We're an information economy. They teach you that in school. What they don't tell you is that it's impossible to move, to live, to operate at any level without leaving traces, bits, seemingly meaningless fragments of personal information. Fragments that can be retrieved, amplified . . .

But by now the pirate would have shuttled our message into line for blackbox transmission to the Yakuza comsat. A simple message: Call off the dogs or we wideband your program.

The program. I had no idea what it contained. I still don't. I only sing the song, with zero comprehension. It was probably research data, the Yakuza being given to advanced forms of industrial espionage. A genteel business, stealing from Ono-Sendai as a matter of course and politely holding their data for ransom, threatening to blunt the conglomerate's research edge by making the product public.

But why couldn't any number play? Wouldn't they be happier with something to sell back to Ono-Sendai, happier than they'd be with one dead Johnny from Memory Lane?

Their program was on its way to an address in Sydney, to a place that held letters for clients and didn't ask questions once you'd paid a small retainer. Fourth-class surface mail. I'd erased most of the other copy and recorded our message in the resulting gap, leaving just enough of the program to identify it as the real thing.

My wrist hurt. I wanted to stop, to lie down, to sleep. I knew that I'd lose my grip and fall soon, knew that the sharp black shoes I'd bought for my evening as Eddie Bax would lose their purchase and carry me down to Nighttown. But he rose in my mind like a cheap religious hologram, glowing, the enlarged chip on his Hawaiian shirt looming like a reconnaissance shot of some doomed urban nucleus.

So I followed Dog and Molly through Lo Tek heaven, jury-rigged and jerry-built from scraps that even Nighttown didn't want.

The Killing Floor was eight meters on a side. A giant had threaded steel cable back and forth through a junkyard and drawn it all taut. It creaked when it moved, and it moved constantly, swaying and bucking as the gathering Lo Teks arranged themselves on the self of plywood surrounding it. The wood was silver with age, polished with long use and deeply etched with initials, threats, declarations of passion. This was suspended from a separate set of cables, which lost themselves in darkness beyond the raw white glare of the two ancient floods suspended above the Floor.

A girl with teeth like Dog's hit the Floor on all fours. Her breasts were tattooed with indigo spirals. Then she was across the Floor, laughing, grappling with a boy who was drinking dark liquid from a liter flask.

Lo Tek fashion ran to scars and tattoos. And teeth. The electricity they were tapping to light the Killing Floor seemed to be an exception to their overall aesthetic, made in the name of . . . ritual, sport, art? I didn't know, but I could see that the Floor was something special. It had the look of having been assembled over generations.

I held the useless shotgun under my jacket. Its hardness and heft were comforting, even though I had no more shells. And it came to me that I had no idea at all of what was really happening, or of what was supposed to happen. And that was the nature of my game, because I'd spent most of my life as a blind receptacle to be filled with other people's knowledge and then drained, spouting synthetic languages I'd never understand. A very technical boy. Sure.

And then I noticed just how quiet the Lo Teks had become.

He was there, at the edge of the light, taking in the Killing Floor and the gallery of silent Lo Teks with a tourist's calm. And as our eyes met for the first time with mutual recognition, a memory clicked into place for me, of Paris, and the long Mercedes electrics gliding through the rain to Notre Dame; mobile greenhouses,

Japanese faces behind the glass, and a hundred Nikons rising in blind phototropism, flowers of steel and crystal. Behind his eyes, as they found me, those same shutters whirring.

I looked for Molly Millions, but she was gone.

The Lo Teks parted to let him step up onto the bench. He bowed, smiling, and stepped smoothly out of his sandals, leaving them side by side, perfectly aligned, and then he stepped down onto the Killing Floor. He came for me, across that shifting trampoline of scrap, as easily as any tourist padding across synthetic pile in any featureless hotel.

Molly hit the Floor, moving.

The Floor screamed.

It was miked and amplified, with pickups riding the four fat coil springs at the corners and contact mikes taped at random to rusting machine fragments. Somewhere the Lo Teks had an amp and a synthesizer, and now I made out the shapes of speakers overhead, above the cruel white floods.

A drumbeat began, electronic, like an amplified heart, steady as a metronome.

She'd removed her leather jacket and boots; her T-shirt was sleeveless, faint telltales of Chiba City circuitry traced along her thin arms. Her leather jeans gleamed under the floods. She began to dance.

She flexed her knees, white feet tensed on a flattened gas tank, and the Killing Floor began to heave in response. The sound it made was like a world ending, like the wires that hold heaven snapping and coiling across the sky.

He rode with it, for a few heartbeats, and then he moved, judging the movement of the Floor perfectly, like a man stepping from one flat stone to another in an ornamental garden.

He pulled the tip from his thumb with the grace of a man at ease with social gesture and flung it at her. Under the floods, the filament was a refracting thread of rainbow. She threw herself flat and rolled, jacknifing up as the molecule whipped past, steel claws snapping into the light in what must have been an automatic rictus of defense.

The drum pulse quickened, and she bounced with it, her dark hair wild around the blank silver lenses, her mouth thin, lips taut with concentration. The Killing Floor boomed and roared, and the Lo Teks were screaming their excitement.

He retracted the filament to a whirling meter-wide circle of ghostly polychrome and spun it in front of him, thumbless hand held level with his sternum. A shield.

And Molly seemed to let something go, something inside, and that was the real start of her mad-dog dance. She jumped, twisting, lunging sideways, landing with both feet on an alloy engine block wired directly to one of the coil springs. I cupped my hands over my ears and knelt in a vertigo of sound, thinking Floor and benches were on their way down, down to Nighttown, and I saw us tearing through the shanties, the wet wash, exploding on the tiles like rotten fruit. But the cables held, and the Killing Floor rose and fell like a crazy metal sea. And Molly danced on it.

And at the end, just before he made his final cast with the filament, I saw something in his face, an expression that didn't seem to belong there. It wasn't fear and it wasn't anger. I think it was disbelief, stunned incomprehension mingled with pure aesthetic revulsion at what he was seeing, hearing – at what was happening to him. He retracted the whirling filament, the ghost disk shrinking to the size of a dinner plate as he whipped his arm above his head and brought it down, the thumbtip curving out for Molly like a live thing.

The Floor carried her down, the molecule passing just above her head; the Floor whiplashed, lifting him into the path of the taut molecule. It should have passed harmlessly over his head and been withdrawn into its diamond-hard socket. It took his hand off just behind the wrist. There was a gap in the Floor in front of him, and he went through it like a diver, with a strange deliberate grace, a defeated kamikaze on his way down to Nighttown. Partly, I think, he took the dive to buy himself a few seconds of the dignity of silence. She'd killed him with culture shock.

The Lo Teks roared, but someone shut the amplifier off, and Molly rode the Killing Floor into silence, hanging on now, her face white and blank, until the pitching slowed and there was only a faint pinging of tortured metal and the grating of rust on rust.

We searched the Floor for the severed hand, but we never found it. All we found was a graceful curve in one piece of rusted steel, where the molecule went through. Its edge was bright as new chrome.

We never learned whether the Yakuza had accepted our terms, or even whether they got our message. As far as I know, their program is still waiting for Eddie Bax on a shelf in the back room of a gift shop on the third level of Sydney Central-5. Probably they sold the original back to Ono-Sendai months ago. But maybe they did get the pirate's broadcast, because nobody's come looking for me yet, and it's been nearly a year. If they do come, they'll have a long climb up through the dark, past Dog's sentries, and I don't look much like Eddie Bax these days. I let Molly take care of that, with a local anesthetic. And my new teeth have almost grown in.

I decided to stay up here. When I looked out across the Killing Floor, before he came, I saw how hollow I was. And I knew I was sick of being a bucket. So now I climb down and visit Jones, almost every night.

We're partners now, Jones and I, and Molly Millions, too. Molly handles our business in the Drome. Jones is still in Funland, but he has a bigger tank, with fresh seawater trucked in once a week. And he has his junk, when he needs it. He still talks to the kids with his frame of lights, but he talks to me on a new display unit in a shed that I rent there, a better unit than the one he used in the navy.

And we're all making good money, better money than I made before, because Jones's Squid can read the traces of anything that anyone ever stored in me, and he gives it to me on the display unit in languages I can understand. So we're learning a lot about all my former clients. And one day I'll have a surgeon dig all the silicon out of my amygdalae, and I'll live with my own memories and nobody else's, the way other people do. But not for a while.

In the meantime it's really okay up here, way up in the dark, smoking a Chinese filtertip and listening to the condensation that drips from the geodesics. Real quiet up here – unless a pair of Lo Teks decide to dance on the Killing Floor.

It's educational, too. With Jones to help me figure things out, I'm getting to be the most technical boy in town.

8

The Erotic Ontology of Cyberspace

Michael Heim

Michael Heim is the author of *Electric Language: A Philosophy of Word Processing* (Yale, 1999) and *The Metaphysics of Virtual Reality* (Oxford, 1993). Drawing on the thinking of eighteenth-century philosopher Gottfried Leibniz, this often-quoted essay suggests that cyberspace enables a poetic consciousness that supersedes material philosophy.

Cyberspace is more than a breakthrough in electronic media or in computer interface design. With its virtual environments and simulated worlds, cyberspace is a metaphysical laboratory, a tool for examining our very sense of reality.

When designing virtual worlds, we face a series of reality questions. How, for instance, should users appear to themselves in a virtual world? Should they appear to themselves in cyberspace as one set of objects among others, as third-person bodies that users can inspect with detachment? Or should users feel themselves to be headless fields of awareness, similar to our phenomenological experience? Should causality underpin the cyberworld so that an injury inflicted on the user's cyberbody likewise somehow damages the user's physical body? And who should make the ongoing design decisions? If the people who make simulations inevitably incorporate their own perceptions and beliefs, loading cyberspace with their prejudices as well as their insights, who should build the cyberworld? Should multiple users at any point be free to shape the qualities and dimensions of cyber entities? Should artistic users roam freely, programming and directing their own unique cyber cinemas that provide escape from the mundane world? Or does fantasy cease where the economics of the virtual workplace begins? But why be satisfied with a single virtual world? Why not several? Must we pledge allegiance to a single reality? Perhaps worlds should be layered like onion skins, realities within realities, or be loosely linked like neighborhoods, permitting free aesthetic pleasure to coexist with the task-oriented business world. Does the meaning of "reality" – and the keen existential edge of experience – weaken as it stretches over many virtual worlds?

Important as these questions are, they do not address the ontology of cyberspace itself, the question of what it means to *be* in a virtual world, whether one's own or another's world. They do not probe the reality status of our metaphysical tools or tell us why we invent virtual worlds. They are silent about the essence or soul of cyberspace. How does the metaphysical laboratory fit into human inquiry as a whole? What status do electronic worlds have within the entire range of human experience? What perils haunt the metaphysical origins of cyberspace?

In what follows, I explore the philosophical significance of cyberspace. I want to show the ontological origin from which cyber entities arise and then indicate the trajectory they seem to be on. The ontological question, as I see it, requires a two-pronged answer. We need to give an account of (1) the way entities exist within cyberspace and (2) the ontological status of cyberspace – the construct, the phenomenon – itself. The way in which we understand the ontological structure of cyberspace will determine how realities can exist within it. But the structure of cyberspace becomes clear only once we appreciate the distinctive way in which things appear within it. So we must begin with the entities we experience within the computerized environment.

My approach to cyberspace passes first through the ancient idealism of Plato and moves onward through the modern metaphysics of Leibniz. By connecting with intellectual precedents and prototypes, we can enrich our self-understanding and make cyberspace function as a more useful metaphysical laboratory.

Our Marriage to Technology

The phenomenal reality of cyber entities exists within a more general fascination with technology, and the fascination with technology is akin to aesthetic fascination. We love the simple, clear-cut linear surfaces that computers generate. We love the way that computers reduce complexity and ambiguity, capturing things in a digital network, clothing them in beaming colors, and girding them with precise geometrical structures. We are enamored of the possibility of controlling all human knowledge. The appeal of seeing society's data structures in cyberspace – if we begin with William Gibson's vision – is like the appeal of seeing the Los Angeles metropolis in the dark at five thousand feet: a great warmth of powerful, incandescent blue and green embers with red stripes that beckons the traveler to come down from the cool darkness. We are the moths attracted to flames, and frightened by them too, for there may be no home behind the lights, no secure abode behind the vast glowing structures. There are only the fiery objects of dream and longing.

Our love affair with computers, computer graphics, and computer networks runs deeper than aesthetic fascination and deeper than the play of the senses. We are searching for a home for the mind and heart. Our fascination with computers is more erotic than sensuous, more spiritual than utilitarian. Eros, as the ancient Greeks understood, springs from a feeling of insufficiency or inadequacy. Whereas the aesthete feels drawn to casual play and dalliance, the erotic lover reaches out to a fulfillment far beyond aesthetic detachment.

The computer's allure is more than utilitarian or aesthetic; it is erotic. Instead of a refreshing play with surfaces, as with toys or amusements, our affair with information machines announces a symbiotic relationship and ultimately a mental marriage to technology. Rightly perceived, the atmosphere of cyberspace carries the scent that once surrounded Wisdom. The world rendered as pure information not only fascinates our eyes and minds, but also captures our hearts. We feel augmented and empowered. Our hearts beat in the machines. This is Eros.

Cyberspace entities belong to a broad cultural phenomenon of the last third of the twentieth century: the phenomenon of computerization. Something becomes a phenomenon when it arrests and holds the attention of a civilization. Only then does our shared language articulate the presence of the thing so that it can appear in its steady identity as the moving stream of history.

Because we are immersed in everyday phenomena, however, we usually miss their overall momentum and cannot see where they are going or even what they truly are. A writer like William Gibson helps us grasp what is phenomenal in current culture because he captures the forward movement of our attention and shows us the future as it projects its claim back into our present. Of all writers, Gibson most clearly reveals the intrinsic allure of computerized entities, and his books – *Neuromancer*, *Count Zero*, and *Mona Lisa Overdrive* – point to the near-future, phenomenal reality of cyberspace. Indeed, Gibson coined the word *cyberspace*.

The Romance of *Neuromancer*

For Gibson, cyber entities appear under the sign of Eros. The fictional characters of *Neuromancer* experience the computer matrix – cyberspace – as a place of rapture and erotic intensity, of powerful desire and even self-submission. In the matrix, things attain a supervivid hyper-reality. Ordinary experience seems dull and unreal by comparison. Case, the data wizard of *Neuromancer*, awakens to an obsessive Eros that drives him back again and again to the information network:

> A year [in Japan] and he still dreamed of cyberspace, hope fading nightly.... [S]till he'd see the matrix in his sleep, bright lattices of logic unfolding across that colorless void.... [H]e was no [longer] console man, no cyberspace cowboy.... But the dreams came on in the Japanese night like livewire voodoo, and he'd cry for it, cry in his sleep, and wake alone in the dark, curled in his capsule in some coffin hotel, his hands clawed into the bedslab,... trying to reach the console that wasn't there.[1]

The sixteenth-century Spanish mystics John of the Cross and Teresa of Avila used a similar point of reference. Seeking words to connote the taste of spiritual divinity, they reached for the language of sexual ecstasy. They wrote of the breathless union of meditation in terms of the ecstatic blackout of consciousness, the *llama de amor viva* piercing the interior center of the soul like a white-hot arrow, the *cauterio suave* searing through the dreams of the dark night of the soul. Similarly, the intensity of Gibson's cyberspace inevitably conjures up the reference to orgasm, and vice versa:

Now she straddled him again, took his hand, and closed it over her, his thumb along the cleft of her buttocks, his fingers spread across the labia. As she began to lower herself, the images came pulsing back, the faces, fragments of neon arriving and receding. She slid down around him and his back arched convulsively. She rode him that way, impaling herself, slipping down on him again and again, until they both had come, his orgasm flaring blue in a timeless space, a vastness like the matrix, where the faces were shredded and blown away down hurricane corridors, and her inner thighs were strong and wet against his hips.[2]

But the orgasmic connection does not mean that Eros's going toward cyberspace entities terminates in a merely physiological or psychological reflex. Eros goes beyond private, subjective fantasies. Cyber Eros stems ultimately from the onto-logical drive highlighted long ago by Plato. Platonic metaphysics helps clarify the link between Eros and computerized entities.

In her speech in Plato's *Symposium*, Diotima, the priestess of love, teaches a doctrine of the escalating spirituality of the erotic drive. She tracks the intensity of Eros continuously from bodily attraction all the way to the mental attention of mathematics and beyond. The outer reaches of the biological sex drive, she explains to Socrates, extend to the mental realm where we continually seek to expand our knowledge.

On the primal level, Eros is a drive to extend our finite being, to prolong something of our physical selves beyond our mortal existence. But Eros does not stop with the drive for physical extension. We seek to extend ourselves and to heighten the intensity of our lives in general through Eros. The psyche longs to perpetuate itself and to conceive offspring, and this it can do, in a transposed sense, by conceiving ideas and nurturing awareness in the minds of others as well as our own. The psyche develops consciousness by formalizing perceptions and stabiliz-ing experiences through clearly defined entities. But Eros motivates humans to see more and to know more deeply. So, according to Plato, the fully explicit formal-ized identities of which we are conscious help us maintain life in a "solid state," thereby keeping perishability and impermanence at bay.

Only a short philosophical step separates this Platonic notion of knowledge from the matrix of cyberspace entities. (The word *matrix*, of course, stems from the Latin for "mother," the generative–erotic origin.) A short step in fundamental assumptions, however, can take centuries, especially if the step needs hardware support. The hardware for implementing Platonically formalized knowledge took centuries. Underneath, though, runs an ontological continuity, connecting the Platonic knowledge of ideal forms to the information systems of the matrix. Both approaches to cognition first extend and then renounce the physical embodiment of knowledge. In both, Eros inspires humans to outrun the drag of the "meat" – the flesh – by attaching human attention to what formally attracts the mind. As Platonists and Gnostics down through the ages have insisted, Eros guides us to Logos.

The erotic drive, however, as Plato saw it, needs education to attain its fulfill-ment. Left on its own, Eros naturally goes astray on any number of tangents, most of which come from sensory stimuli. In the *Republic*, Plato tells the well-known story of the Cave in which people caught in the prison of everyday life learn to love the fleeting, shadowy illusions projected on the walls of the dungeon of the flesh. With their attention forcibly fixed on the shadowy moving images cast by a flickering physical fire, the prisoners passively take sensory objects to be the highest and most interesting realities. Only later, when the prisoners manage to get free of their corporeal shackles, do they ascend to the realm of active thought, where they enjoy the shockingly clear vision of real things, things present not to the physical eyes but to the mind's eye. Only by actively processing things through mental logic, according to Plato, do we move into the upper air of reliable truth, which is also a lofty realm of intellectual beauty stripped of the imprecise impressions of the senses. Thus the liberation from the Cave requires a reeducation of human desires and interests. It entails a realization that what attracts us in the sensory world is no more than an outer projection of ideas we can find within us. Education must redirect desire toward the formally defined, logical aspects of things. Properly trained, love guides the mind to the well-formed, mental aspects of things.

Cyberspace is Platonism as a working product. The cybernaut seated before us, strapped into sensory-input devices, appears to be, and is indeed, lost to this world. Suspended in computer space, the cybernaut leaves the prison of the body and emerges in a world of digital sensation.

This Platonism is thoroughly modern, however. Instead of emerging in a sensationless world of pure concepts, the cybernaut moves among entities that are well formed in a special sense. The spatial objects of cyberspace proceed from the constructs of Platonic imagination not in the same sense that perfect solids or ideal numbers are Platonic constructs, but in the sense that inFORMation in cyberspace inherits the beauty of Platonic FORMS. The computer recycles ancient Platonism by injecting the ideal content of cognition with empirical specifics. Computerized representation of knowledge, then, is not the direct mental insight fostered by Platonism. The computer clothes the details of empirical experience so that they seem to share the ideality of the stable knowledge of the Forms. The mathematical machine uses a digital mold to reconstitute the mass of empirical material so that human consciousness can enjoy an integrity in the empirical data that would never have been possible before computers. The notion of ideal Forms in early Platonism has the allure of a perfect dream. But the ancient dream remained airy, a landscape of genera and generalities, until the hardware of information retrieval came to support the mind's quest for knowledge. Now, with the support of the electronic matrix, the dream can incorporate the smallest details of here-and-now existence. With an electronic infrastructure, the dream of perfect FORMS becomes the dream of inFORMation.

Filtered through the computer matrix, all reality becomes patterns of informa-tion. When reality becomes indistinguishable from information, then even Eros fits the schemes of binary communication. Bodily sex appears to be no more than an exchange of signal blips on the genetic corporeal network. Further, the erotic–generative source of formal idealism becomes subject to the laws of information management. Just as the later Taoists of ancient China created a yin–yang cosmo-logy that encompassed sex, cooking, weather, painting, architecture, martial arts, and the like, so too the computer culture interprets all knowable reality as transmissible information. The conclusion of *Neuromancer* shows us the transformation of sex and personality into the language of information.

> There was a strength that ran in her, . . . [s]omething he'd found and lost so many times. It belonged, he knew – he remembered – as she pulled him down, to the meat, the flesh the cowboys mocked. It was a vast thing, beyond knowing, a sea of information coded in spiral and pheromone, infinite intricacy that only the body, in its strong blind way, could ever read.
>
> . . . [H]e broke [the zipper], some tiny metal part shooting off against the wall as salt-rotten cloth gave, and then he was in her, effecting the transmission of the old message. Here, even here, in a place he knew for what it was, a coded model of some stranger's memory, the drive held.
>
> She shuddered against him as the stick caught fire, a leaping flare that threw their locked shadows across the bunker wall.[3]

The dumb meat once kept sex private, an inner sanctum, an opaque, silent, unknowable mystery. The sexual body held its genetic information with the strength of a blind, unwavering impulse. What is translucent you can manipulate, you can see. What stays opaque you cannot scrutinize and manipulate. It is an alien presence. The meat we either dismiss or come up against; we cannot ignore it. It remains something to encounter. Yet here, in *Neuromancer*, the protagonist, Case, makes love to a sexual body named Linda. Who is this Linda?

Gibson raises the deepest ontological question of cyberspace by suggesting that the Neuromancer master-computer *simulates* the body and personality of Case's beloved. A simulated, embodied personality provokes the sexual encounter. Why? Perhaps because the cyberspace system, which depends on the physical space of bodies for its initial impetus, now seeks to undermine the separate existence of human bodies that make it dependent and secondary. The ultimate revenge of the information system comes when the system absorbs the very identity of the human personality, absorbing the opacity of the body, grinding the meat into information, and deriding erotic life by reducing it to a transparent play of puppets. In an ontological turnabout, the computer counterfeits the silent and private body from which mental life originated. The machinate mind disdainfully mocks the meat. Information digests even the secret recesses of the caress. In its computerized version, Platonic Eros becomes a master of artificial intelligence, CYBEROS, the controller, the Neuromancer.

The Inner Structure of Cyberspace

Aware of the phenomenal reality of cyber entities, we can now appreciate the backdrop that is cyberspace itself. We can sense a distant source radiating an all-embracing power. For the creation of computerized entities taps into the most powerful of our psychobiological urges. Yet so far, this account of the distant source as Eros tells only half the story. For although Platonism provides the psychic makeup for cyberspace entities, only modern philosophy shows us the structure of cyberspace itself.

In its early phases – from roughly 400 B.C. to A.D. 1600 – Platonism exclusively addressed the speculative intellect, advancing a verbal–mental intellectuality over physical actuality. Later, Renaissance and modern Platonists gradually injected new features into the model of intelligence. The modern Platonists opened up the gates of verbal–spiritual understanding to concrete experiments set in empirical space and time. The new model of intelligence included the evidence of repeatable experience and the gritty details of experiment. For the first time, Platonism would have to absorb real space and real time into the objects of its contemplation.

The early Platonic model of intelligence considered space to be a mere receptacle for the purely intelligible entities subsisting as ideal forms. Time and space were refractive errors that rippled and distorted the mental scene of perfect unchanging realities. The bouncing rubber ball was in reality a round object, which was in reality a sphere, which was in reality a set of concentric circles, which could be analyzed with the precision of Euclidian geometry. Such a view of intelligence passed to modern Platonists, and they had to revise the classical assumptions. Thinkers and mathematicians would no longer stare at the sky of unchanging ideals. By applying mathematics to empirical experiment, science would absorb physical movement in space/time through the calculus. Mathematics transformed the intelligent observer from a contemplator to a calculator. But as long as the calculator depended on feeble human memory and scattered printed materials, a gap would still stretch between the longing and the satisfaction of knowledge. To close the gap, a computational engine was needed.

Before engineering an appropriate machine, the cyberspace project needed a new logic and a new metaphysics. The new logic and metaphysics of modernity came largely from the work of Gottfried Leibniz. In many ways, the later philosophies of Kant, Schopenhauer, Nietzsche, and Heidegger took their bearings from Leibniz.

As Leibniz worked out the modern Idealist epistemology, he was also experimenting with protocomputers. Pascal's calculator had been no more than an adding machine; Leibniz went further and produced a mechanical calculator that could also, by using stepped wheels, multiply and divide. The basic Leibnizian design became the blueprint for all commercial calculators until the electronics revolution of the 1970s. Leibniz, therefore, is one of the essential philosophical guides to the inner structure of cyberspace. His logic, metaphysics, and notion of representational symbols show us the hidden underpinnings of cyberspace. At the same time, his monadological metaphysics alerts us to the paradoxes that are likely to engulf cyberspace's future inhabitants.

Leibniz's Electric Language

Leibniz was the first to conceive of an "electric language," a set of symbols engineered for manipulation at the speed of thought. His *De arte combinatoria* (1666) outlines a language that became the historical foundation of contemporary symbolic logic. Leibniz's general outlook on language also became the ideological basis for computer-mediated telecommunications. A modern Platonist, Leibniz dreamed of the matrix.

The language that Leibniz outlined is an ideographic system of signs that can be manipulated to produce logical deductions without recourse to natural language. The signs represent primitive ideas gleaned from prior analysis. Once broken down into primitives and represented by stipulated signs, the component ideas can be paired and recombined to fashion novel configurations. In this way, Leibniz sought to mechanize the production of new ideas. As he described it, the encyclopedic collection and definition of primitive ideas would require the coordinated efforts of learned scholars from all parts of the civilized world. The royal academies that Leibniz promoted were the group nodes for an international republic of letters, a universal network for problem solving.

Leibniz believed all problems to be, in principle, soluble. The first step was to create a universal medium in which conflicting ideas could coexist and interrelate. A universal language would make it possible to translate all human notions and disagreements into the same set of symbols. His universal character set, *character-istica universalis*, rests on a binary logic, one quite unlike natural discourse in that it is neither restricted by material content nor embodied in vocalized sound. Contentless and silent, the binary language can transform every significant statement into the terms of a logical calculus, a system for proving argumentative patterns valid or invalid, or at least for connecting them in a homogeneous matrix. Through the common binary language, discordant ways of thinking can exist under a single roof. Disagreements in attitude or belief, once translated into matching symbols, can later yield to operations for ensuring logical consistency. To the partisans of dispute, Leibniz would say, "Let us upload this into our common system, then let us sit down and calculate." A single system would encompass all the combinations and permutations of human thought. Leibniz longed for his symbols to foster unified scientific research throughout the civilized world. The universal calculus would compile all human culture, bringing every natural language into a single shared database.

Leibniz's binary logic, disembodied and devoid of material content, depends on an artificial language remote from the words, letters, and utterances of everyday discourse. This logic treats reasoning as nothing more than a combining of signs, as a calculus. Like mathematics, the Leibnizian symbols erase the distance between the signifiers and the signified, between the thought seeking to express and the expression. No gap remains between symbol and meaning. Given the right motor, the Leibnizian symbolic logic – as developed later by George Boole, Bertrand Russell, and Alfred North Whitehead and then applied to electronic switching circuitry by Shannon – can function at the speed of thought. At such high speed, the felt semantic space closes between thought, language, and the thing expressed. Centuries later, John von Neumann applied a version of Leibniz's binary logic when building the first computers at Princeton.

In his search for a universal language of the matrix, Leibniz to some extent continued a premodern, medieval tradition. For behind his ideal language stands a premodern model of human intelligence. The medieval Scholastics held that human thinking, in its pure or ideal form, is more or less identical with logical reasoning. Reasoning functions along the lines of a superhuman model who remains unaffected by the vagaries of feelings and spatiotemporal experience. Human knowledge imitates a Being who knows things perfectly and knows them in their deductive connections. The omniscient Being transcends finite beings. Finite beings go slowly, one step at a time, seeing only moment by moment what is happening. On the path of life, a finite being cannot see clearly the things that remain behind on the path or the things that are going to happen after the next step. A divine mind, on the contrary, oversees the whole path. God sees all the trails below, inspecting at a single glance every step traveled, what has happened, and even what will happen on all possible paths below. God views things from the perspective of the mountaintop of eternity.

Human knowledge, thought Leibniz, should emulate this *visio dei*, this omniscient intuitive cognition of the deity. Human knowledge strives to know the way that a divine or an infinite Being knows things. No temporal unfolding, no linear steps, no delays limit God's knowledge of things. The temporal simultaneity, the all-at-once-ness of God's knowledge serves as a model for human knowledge in the modern world as projected by the work of Leibniz. What better way, then, to emulate God's knowledge than to generate a virtual world constituted by bits of information? To such a cyber world human beings could enjoy a God-like instant access. But if knowledge is power, who would handle the controls that govern every single particle of existence?

The power of Leibniz's modern logic made traditional logic seem puny and inefficient by comparison. For centuries, Aristotle's logic had been taught in the schools. Logic traditionally evaluated the steps of finite human thought, valid or invalid, as they occur in arguments in natural language. Traditional logic stayed close to spoken natural language. When modern logic absorbed the steps of Aristotle's logic into its system of symbols, modern logic became a network of symbols that could apply equally to electronic switching circuits as to arguments in natural language. Just as non-Euclidian geometry can set up axioms that defy the domain of real circles (physical figures), so too modern logic freed itself of any naturally given syntax. The universal logical calculus could govern computer circuits.

Leibniz's "electric language" operates by emulating the divine intelligence. God's knowledge has the simultaneity of all-at-once-ness, and so in order to achieve a divine access to things, the global matrix functions like a net to trap all language in an external present. Because access need not be linear, cyberspace does not, in principle, require a jump from one location to another. Science fiction writers have often imagined what it would be like to experience traveling at the speed of light, and one writer, Isaac Asimov, described such travel as a "jump through hyperspace." When his fictional space ship hits the speed of light, Asimov says that the ship makes a special kind of leap. At that speed, it is impossible to trace the discrete points of the distance traversed. In the novel *The Naked Sun*, Asimov depicts movement in hyperspace:

> There was a queer momentary sensation of being turned inside out. It lasted an instant and Baley knew it was a Jump, that oddly incomprehensible, almost mystical, momentary transition through hyperspace that transferred a ship and all it contained

from one point in space to another, light years away. Another lapse of time and another Jump, still another lapse, still another Jump.[4]

Like the fictional hyperspace, cyberspace unsettles the felt logical tracking of the human mind. Cyberspace is the perfect computer environment for accessing hypertext if we include all human perceptions as the "letters" of the "text." In both hyperspace and hypertext, linear perception loses track of the series of discernible movements. With hypertext, we connect things at the speed of a flash of intuition. The interaction with hypertext resembles movement beyond the speed of light. Hypertext reading and writing supports the intuitive leap over the traditional step-by-step logical chain. The jump, not the step, is the characteristic movement in hypertext.

As the environment for sensory hypertext, cyberspace feels like transportation through a frictionless, timeless medium. There is no jump because everything exists, implicitly if not actually, all at once. To understand this lightning speed and its perils for finite beings, we must look again at the metaphysics of Leibniz.

Monads Do Have Terminals

Leibniz called his metaphysics a *monadology*, a theory of reality describing a system of "monads." From our perspective, the monadology conceptually describes the nature of beings who are capable of supporting a computer matrix. The monadology can suggest how cyberspace fits into the larger world of networked, computerized beings.

The term *monadology* comes from the Greek *monas*, as in "monastic," "monk," and "monopoly." It refers to a certain kind of aloneness, a solitude in which each being pursues its appetites in isolation from all other beings, which also are solitary. The monad exists as an independent point of vital willpower, a surging drive to achieve its own goals according to its own internal dictates. Because they are a sheer, vital thrust, the monads do not have inert spatial dimensions but produce space as a by-product of their activity. Monads are monophysical, psychical substances whose forceful life is an immanent activity. For monads, there is no outer world to access, no larger, broader vision. What the monads see are the projections of their own appetites and their own ideas. In Leibniz's succinct phrase: "Monads have no windows."

Monads may have no windows, but they do have terminals. The mental life of the monad – and the monad has no other life – is a procession of internal representations. Leibniz's German calls these representations *Vorstellungen*, from *vor* (in front of) and *stellen* (to place). Realities are representations continually placed in front of the viewing apparatus of the monad, but placed in such a way that the system interprets or represents what is being pictured. The monad sees the pictures of things and knows only what can be pictured. The monad knows through the interface. The interface represents things, simulates them, and preserves them in a format that the monad can manipulate in any number of ways. The monad keeps the presence of things on tap, as it were, making them instantly available and disposable, so that the presence of things is represented or "canned." From the vantage point of physical phenomenal beings, the monad undergoes a surrogate experience. Yet the monad does more than think about or imagine things at the interface. The monad senses things, sees them and hears them as perceptions. But the perceptions of phenomenal entities do not occur in real physical space because no substances other than monads really exist. Whereas the interface with things vastly expands the monad's perceptual and cognitive powers, the things at the interface are simulations and representations.

Yet Leibniz's monadology speaks of monads in the plural. For a network to exist, more than one being must exist; otherwise, nothing is there to be networked. But how can monads coordinate or agree on anything at all, given their isolated nature? Do they even care if other monads exist? Leibniz tells us that each monad represents within itself the entire universe. Like Indra's Net, each monad mirrors the whole world. Each monad represents the universe in concentrated form, making within itself a *mundus concentratus*. Each microcosm contains the macrocosm. As such, the monad reflects the universe in a living mirror, making it a *miroir actif indivisible*, whose appetites drive it to represent everything to itself – everything, that is, mediated by its mental activity. Since each unit represents everything, each unit contains all the other units, containing them as represented. No direct physical contact passes between the willful mental units. Monads never meet face-to-face.

Although the monads represent the same universe, each one sees it differently. The differences in perception come from differences in perspective. These different perspectives arise not from different physical positions in space – the monads are not physical, and physical space is a by-product of mental perception – but from the varying degrees of clarity and intensity in each monad's mental landscape. The appetitive impulses in each monad highlight different things in the sequence of representational experience. Their different impulses constantly shift the scenes they see. Monads run different software.

Still, there exists, according to the monadology, one actual universe. Despite their ultimately solitary character, the monads belong to a single world. The harmony of all the entities in the world comes from the one underlying operating system. Although no unit directly contacts other units, each unit exists in synchronous time in the same reality. All their representations are coordinated through the supervisory role of the Central Infinite Monad, traditionally known as God. The Central Infinite Monad, we could say, is the Central System Operator (sysop), who harmonizes all the finite monadic units. The Central System Monad is the only being that exists with absolute necessity. Without a sysop, no one could get on line to reality. Thanks to the Central System Monad, each individual monad lives out its separate life according to the dictates of its own willful nature while still harmonizing with all the other monads on line.

Paradoxes in the Cultural Terrain of Cyberspace

Leibniz's monadological metaphysics brings out certain aspects of the erotic ontology of cyberspace. Although the monadology does not actually describe computerized space, of course, it does suggest some of the inner tendencies of computerized space. These tendencies are inherent in the structure of cyberspace and therefore affect the broader realities in which the matrix exists. Some paradoxes crop up. The monadological metaphysics shows us a cultural topography riddled with deep inconsistencies.

Cyberspace supplants physical space. We see this happening already in the familiar cyberspace of on-line communication – telephone, e-mail, newsgroups, and so forth. When on line, we break free, like the monads, from bodily existence. Telecommunication offers an unrestricted freedom of expression and personal contact, with far less hierarchy and formality than are found in the primary social world. Isolation persists as a major problem of contemporary urban society, and I mean spiritual isolation, the kind that plagues individuals even on crowded city streets. With the telephone and television, the computer network can function as a countermeasure. The computer network appears as a godsend in providing forums for people to gather in surprisingly personal proximity – especially considering today's limited band-widths – without the physical limitations of geography, time zones, or conspicuous social status. For many, networks and bulletin boards act as computer antidotes to the atomism of society. They assemble the monads. They function as social nodes for fostering those fluid and multiple elective affinities that everyday urban life seldom, in fact, supports.

Unfortunately, what technology gives with one hand, it often takes away with the other. Technology increasingly eliminates direct human interdependence. While our devices give us greater personal autonomy, at the same time they disrupt the familiar networks of direct association. Because our machines automate much of our labor, we have less to do with one another. Association becomes a conscious act of will. Voluntary associations operate with less spontaneity than do those having sprouted serendipitously. Because machines provide us with the power to flit about the universe, our communities grow more fragile, airy, and ephemeral even as our connections multiply.

Being a *body* constitutes the principle behind our separateness from one another and behind our personal presence. Our bodily existence stands at the forefront of our personal identity and individuality. Both law and morality recognize the physical body as something of a fence, an absolute boundary, establishing and protecting our privacy. Now the computer network simply brackets the physical presence of the participants, by either omitting or simulating corporeal immediacy. In one sense, this frees us from the restrictions imposed by our physical identity. We are more equal on the net because we can either ignore or create the body that appears in cyberspace. But in another sense, the quality of the human encounter narrows. The secondary or stand-in body reveals only as much of ourselves as we mentally wish to reveal. Bodily contact becomes optional; you need never stand face-to-face with other members of the virtual community. You can live your own separate existence without ever physically meeting another person. Computers may at first liberate societies through increased communication and may even forment revolutions (I am thinking of the computer print-outs in Tiananmen Square during the 1989 prodemocracy uprisings in China). They have, however, another side, a dark side.

The darker side hides a sinister melding of human and machine. The cyborg, or cybernetic organism, implies that the conscious mind steers – the meaning of the Greek *kybernetes* – our organic life. Organic life energy ceases to initiate our mental gestures. Can we ever be fully present when we live through a surrogate body standing in for us? The stand-in self lacks the vulnerability and fragility of our primary identity. The stand-in self can never fully represent us. The more we mistake the cyberbodies for ourselves, the more the machine twists ourselves into the prostheses we are wearing.

Gibson's fiction inspired the creation of role-playing games for young people. One of these games in the cybertech genre, *The View from the Edge: The Cyberpunk Handbook*, portrays the visage of humanity twisted to fit the shapes of the computer prosthesis. The body becomes literally "meat" for the implantation of information devices. The computer plugs directly into the bones of the wrist or skull and taps into major nerve trunks so that the chips can send and receive neural signals. As the game book wryly states:

> Some will put an interface plug at the temples (a "plug head"), just behind the ears (called a "frankenstein") or in the back of the head (a "puppethead"). Some cover them with inlaid silver or gold caps, others with wristwarmers. Once again, a matter of style. Each time you add a cybernetic enhancement, there's a corresponding loss of humanity. But it's not nice, simple and linear. Different people react differently to the cyborging process. Therefore, your humanity loss is based on the throw of random dice value for each enhancement. This is important, because it means that sheer luck could put you over the line before you know it. Walk carefully. Guard your mind.[5]

At the computer interface, the spirit migrates from the body to a world of total representation. Information and images float through the Platonic mind without a grounding in bodily experience. You can lose your humanity at the throw of the dice.

Gibson highlights this essentially Gnostic aspect of cybertech culture when he describes the computer addict who despairs at no longer being able to enter the computer matrix: "For Case, who'd lived for the bodiless exultation of cyberspace, it was the Fall. In the bars he'd frequented as a cowboy hotshot, the elite stance involved a certain relaxed contempt for the flesh. The body was meat. Case fell into the prison of his own flesh."[6] The surrogate life in cyberspace makes flesh feel like a prison, a fall from grace, a descent into a dark confusing reality. From the pit of life in the body, the virtual life looks like the virtuous life. Gibson evokes the Gnostic–Platonic–Manichean contempt for earthy, earthly existence.

Today's computer communication cuts the physical face out of the communication process. Computers stick the windows of the soul behind monitors, headsets, and datasuits. Even video conferencing adds only a simulation of face-to-face meeting, only a representation or an appearance of real meeting. The living, nonrepresentable face is the primal source of responsibility, the direct, warm link between private bodies. Without directly meeting others physically, our ethics languishes. Face-to-face communication, the fleshly bond between people, supports a long-term warmth and loyalty, a sense of obligation for which the computer-mediated communities have not yet been tested. Computer networks offer a certain sense of belonging, to be sure, but the sense of belonging circulates primarily among a special group of pioneers. How long and how deep are the personal relationships that develop outside embodied presence? The face is the primal interface, more basic than any machine mediation. The physical eyes are the windows that establish the neighborhood of trust. Without the direct experience of the human face, ethical awareness shrinks and rudeness enters. Examples abound. John Coates, spokesperson for the WELL in northern California says: "Some people just lose good manners on line. You can really feel insulated and protected from people if you're not looking at them – nobody can take a swing at you. On occasion, we've stepped in to request more diplomacy. One time we had to ask someone to go away."[7]

At the far end of distrust lies computer crime. The machine interface may amplify an amoral indifference to human relationships. Computers often eliminate the need to respond directly to what takes place between humans. People do not just observe one another, but become "lurkers." Without direct human presence, participation becomes optional. Electronic life converts primary bodily presence into telepresence, introducing a remove between represented presences. True, in bodily life we often play at altering our identity with different clothing, masks, and nicknames, but electronics installs the illusion that we are "having it both ways," keeping our distance while "putting ourselves on the line." On-line existence is intrinsically ambiguous, like the purchased passion of the customers in the House of Blue Lights in Gibson's *Burning Chrome*: "The customers are torn between needing someone and wanting to be alone at the same time, which has probably always been the name of that particular game, even before we had the neuroelectronics to enable them to have it both ways."[8] As the expanding global network permits the passage of bodily representations, "having it both ways" may reduce trust and spread cynical anomie.

A loss of innocence therefore accompanies an expanding network. As the on-line culture grows geographically, the sense of community diminishes. Shareware worked well in the early days of computers, and so did open bulletin boards. When the size of the user base increased, however, the spirit of community diminished, and the villains began appearing, some introducing viruses. Hackers invisibly reformatted hard disks, and shareware software writers moved to the commercial world. When we speak of a global village, we should keep in mind that every village makes villains, and when civilization reaches a certain degree of density, the barbaric tribes return, from within. Tribes shun their independent thinkers and punish individuality. A global international village, fed by accelerated competition and driven by information, may be host to an unprecedented barbarism. Gibson's vision of cyberspace works like a mental aphrodisiac, but it turns the living environment – electronic and real – into a harsh, nightmarish jungle. This jungle is more than a mere cyberpunk affectation, a matter of aestheticizing grit or conflict or rejection. It may also be an accurate vision of the intrinsic energies released in a cyberized society.

An artificial information jungle already spreads out over the world, duplicating with its virtual vastness the scattered geography of the actual world. The matrix already multiplies confusion, and future cyberspace may not simply reproduce a more efficient version of traditional information. The new information networks resemble the modern megalopolis, often described as a concrete jungle (New York) or a sprawl (Los Angeles). A maze of activities and hidden byways snakes around with no apparent center. Architecturally, the network sprawl suggests the absence of a philosophical or religious absolute. Traditional publishing resembles a medieval European city, with the center of all activity, the cathedral or church spire, guiding and gathering all the communal directions and pathways. The steeple visibly radiates like a hub, drawing the inhabitants into a unity and measuring the other buildings on a central model. Traditionally, the long-involved process of choosing which texts to print or which movies or television shows to produce serves a similar function. The book industry, for instance, provides readers with various cues for evaluating information. The publishers legitimize printed information by giving clues that affect the reader's willingness to engage in reading the book. Editorial attention, packaging, endorsements by professionals or colleagues, book design, and materials all add to the value of the publisher's imprint. Communication in contemporary cyberspace lacks the formal clues. In their place are private recommendations or just blind luck. The electronic world, unlike the traditional book industry, does not protect its readers or travelers by following rules that set up certain expectations. Already, in the electric element, the need for stable channels of content and reliable processes of choice grows urgent.

If cyberspace unfolds like existing large-scale media, we might expect a debasement of discriminating attention. If the economics of marketing forces the matrix to hold the attention of a critical mass of the population, we might expect a flashy liveliness and a flimsy currency to replace depth of content. Sustained attention will give way to fast-paced cuts. One British humanist spoke of the HISTORY forum on Bitnet in the following terms: "The HISTORY network has no view of what it exists for, and of late has become a sort of bar-room court-house for pseudo-historical discussion on a range of currently topical events. It really is, as Glasgow soccer players are often called, a waste of space." Cyberspace without carefully laid channels of choice may become a waste of space.

The Underlying Fault

Finally, on-line freedom seems paradoxical. If the drive to construct cyber entities comes from Eros in the Platonic sense, and if the structure of cyberspace follows the model of Leibniz's computer God, then cyberspace rests dangerously on an underlying fault of paradox. Remove the hidden recesses, the lure of the unknown, and you also destroy the erotic urge to uncover and reach further; you destroy the source of yearning. Set up a synthetic reality, place yourself in a computer-simulated environment, and you undermine the human craving to penetrate what radically eludes you, what is novel and unpredictable. The computer God's-eye view robs you of your freedom to be fully human. Knowing that the computer God already knows every nook and cranny deprives you of your freedom to search and discover.

Even though the computer God's-eye view remains closed to the human agents in cyberspace, they will know that such a view exists. Computerized reality synthesizes everything through calculation, and nothing exists in the synthetic world that is not literally numbered and counted. Here Gibson's protagonist gets a brief glimpse of this superhuman, or inhuman, omniscience:

> Case's consciousness divided like beads of mercury, arcing above an endless beach the color of the dark silver clouds. His vision was spherical, as though a single retina lined the inner surface of a globe that contained all things, if all things could be counted.
>
> And here things could be counted, each one. He knew the number of grains of sand in the construct of the beach (a number coded in a mathematical system that existed nowhere outside the mind that was Neuromancer). He knew the number of yellow food packets in the canisters in the bunker (four hundred and seven). He knew the number of brass teeth in the left half of the open zipper of the salt-crusted leather jacket that Linda Lee wore as she trudged along the sunset beach, swinging a stick of driftwood in her hand (two hundred and two).[9]

The erotic lover reels under the burden of omniscience: "*If* all things could be counted . . ." Can the beloved remain the beloved when she is fully known, when she is fully exposed to the analysis and synthesis of binary construction? Can we be touched or surprised – deeply astonished – by a synthetic reality, or will it always remain a magic trick, an illusory prestidigitation?

With the thrill of free access to unlimited corridors of information comes the complementary threat of total organization. Beneath the artificial harmony lies the possibility of surveillance by the all-knowing Central System Monad. The absolute sysop wields invisible power over all members of the network. The infinite CSM holds the key for monitoring, censoring, or rerouting any piece of information or any phenomenal presence on the network. The integrative nature of the computer shows up today in the ability of the CSM to read, delete, or alter private e-mail on any computer-mediated system. Those who hold the keys to the system, technically and economically, have access to anything on the system. The CSM will most likely place a top priority on maintaining and securing its power. While matrix users feel geographical and intellectual distances melt away, the price they pay is their ability to initiate uncontrolled and unsupervised activity.

According to Leibniz's monadology, the physical space perceived by the monads comes as an inessential by-product of experience. Spatiotemporal experience goes back to the limitations of the fuzzy finite monad minds, their inability to grasp the true roots of their existence. From the perspective of eternity, the monads exist by rational law and make no unprescribed movements. Whatever movement or change they make disappears in the lightning speed of God's absolute cognition. The flesh, Leibniz maintained, introduces a cognitive fuzziness. For the Platonic imagination, this fuzzy incarnate world dims the light of intelligence.

Yet the erotic ontology of cyberspace contradicts this preference for disembodied intelligibility. If I am right about the erotic basis of cyberspace, then the surrogate body undoes its genesis, contradicts its nature. The ideal of the simultaneous all-at-once-ness of computerized information access undermines any world that is worth knowing. The fleshly world is worth knowing for its distances and its hidden horizons. Thankfully, the Central System Monad never gets beyond the terminals into the physical richness of this world. Fortunately, here in the broader world, we still need eyes, fingers, mice, modems, and phone lines.

Gibson leaves us the image of a human group that instinctively keeps its distance from the computer matrix. These are the Zionites, the religiously tribal folk who prefer music to computers and intuitive loyalties to calculation. The Zionites constitute a human remnant in the environmental desolation of *Neuromancer*:

> Case didn't understand the Zionites.
> ...The Zionites always touched you when they were talking, hands on your shoulder. He [Case] didn't like that....
> "Try it," Case said [holding out the electrodes of the cyberspace deck].
> [The Zionite Aerol] took the band, put it on, and Case adjusted the trodes. He closed his eyes. Case hit the power stud. Aerol shuddered. Case jacked him back out.
> "What did you see, man?"
> "Babylon," Aerol said, sadly, handing him the trodes and kicking off down the corridor.[10]

As we suit up for the exciting future in cyberspace, we must not lose touch with the Zionites, the body people who remain rooted in the energies of the earth. They will nudge us out of our heady reverie in this new layer of reality. They will remind us of the living genesis of cyberspace, of the heartbeat behind the laboratory, of the love that still sprouts amid the broken slag and the rusty shells of oil refineries "under the poisoned silver sky."

Notes

1   William Gibson, *Neuromancer* (New York: Ace Books, 1984), pp. 4–5.
2   Ibid., p. 33.
3   Ibid., pp. 239–40.
4   Isaac Asimov, *The Naked Sun* (New York: Ballantine, 1957), p. 16.
5   Mike Pondsmith, *The View from the Edge: The Cyberpunk Handbook* (Berkeley, CA: R. Talsorian Games, 1988), pp. 20–2.
6   Gibson, *Neuromancer*, p. 6.
7   Quoted in Steve Rosenthal, "Turn On, Dial Up, Tune In," *Electric Word*, November–December 1989, p. 35.
8   William Gibson, *Burning Chrome* (New York: Ace Books, 1987), p. 191.
9   Gibson, *Neuromancer*, p. 258.
10 Ibid., p. 106.

9

Virtually Female: Body and Code

Margaret Morse

Margaret Morse, "Virtually Female: Body and Code," in Jennifer Terry and Melodie Calvert, eds., *Processed Lives: Gender and Technology in Everyday Life* (New York: Routledge, 1997), pp. 23–36.

Margaret Morse is an Associate Professor of Film and Video at the University of California, Santa Cruz. She has written on such wide-ranging topics as aerobics, rock video, and electronic art. Morse is the author of *Virtualities: Television, Media Art, and Cyberculture* (Indiana, 1998). In this essay she investigates the reason why many women "resist" technology.

Introduction: New Worlds and Tired Old Codes

Gender in, gender into, the gender of cyberspace – these are areas of some anxiety for women, considering the period in which we live. A major technologically driven, global reorganization of work and of the infrastructure is underway. What was once and largely still is a male-oriented domain of technology and the computer has generated a virtual realm, aka cyberspace, in which socio-economic activity and communications increasingly take place. Considering the actual distribution of practical and theoretical knowledge about science and technology by gender, it is no wonder that androcentric values dominate electronic culture. What will become of us as women and our limited successes in real space once the domains in which we have made our mark are dematerialized and put on the Net or in the Web? Is cyberspace genderless? When females are virtual, is feminism moot?

Information is the naked instrumentality of cyberspace, a commodity language stripped of its relation to a social and historical context and to the subjects who enunciate it. One might imagine a blank slate, unmarked and unconstrained by appearances on which to inscribe fresh aspirations. However, cyberspace is more like Freud's metaphor of the mystic writing pad: lift the sticky plastic page off the surface and all the delicate over-writing of the last quarter-century is whisked away. On the other hand, put the page back down on the sticky matrix and the lines of the "frontier" and "colonization" engraved deeply long ago map themselves unapologetically onto new cyberskin.[1] In a vacuum freed of mediating traditions and the ameliorating accretions of culture, old myths about technology and gender prevail: technology is posed against "the human body – comparatively unadaptable, vulnerable, mortal – that is felt to be the ultimate obstacle to the perfection of the machine environment."[2] Cynthia Cockburn notes in "The Circuit of Technology: Gender, Identity and Power," that the masculine identification of and with technology has survived the muscular period of the "heroic age of mechanization," and appropriated information technology, and one might add, fine motor movements for itself. Western femininity and its "constitution of identities organized around technological incompetence" have apparently survived fairly intact into the present as well.[3]

In contrast, in "Mysteries of the Bioapparatus," Nell Tenhaaf offers the provocative notion that cyberspace represents the femininization of the symbolic system.[4] If this is an invitation to join in a discursive struggle to define cyberspace, I gladly accept. My recent writing, "What Do Cyborgs Eat?" sought to debunk these disempowering assumptions, proposing the vision of a technology that is abject and mortal.[5] However, define cyberspace as I will, fashioning an inclusive and compassionate electronic culture out of the raw stuff of bits and bytes demands more than critique or what amounts to symbolically turning the table on masculine prerogatives. Even though we may have difficulty in setting the clock on our VCRs, the times demand that we re-engage information with our own values, in a practice that challenges emerging rules of ownership and exchange that exclude so many of us. However, when it comes to "hands-on" technology, why is volitional action or what amounts to willing myself into technological competence so much easier said than done?

Willing and Unwilling Bodies

The first challenge to shaping and taming this emerging world is the will itself and the human problem of unwill, especially in relation to femininity. I want to first discuss the somewhat embarrassing problem of technological ineptitude (not to be confused with technophobia) as it afflicts me and perhaps other klutzy women deeply involved in a critique of technological discourse to be accomplished by means of and even in the very medium we critique (yes, a double-bind).

Consider that my imperfect feminine identity, a construction of codes by trial and error, has been more virtual than unconscious or biologically determined all along. Beauty culture – the femininity you can buy – never provided enough coverage: I never felt feminine enough. Furthermore, since I've never been sure what it means to be a woman, I've had to rely on other people to tell me, "You can't do that." For example, after reading the literature distributed at a junior high career day in 1957, I decided to become a dentist. The reaction I received led me to the conclusion that femininity didn't include dentistry. The larger problem was that, in essence, none of the literature there was actually addressed to me.

At about that age, math phobia and technical ineptitude are culturally implanted in numerous American female adolescents. I think of the implant as a painful internal prosthesis, a glass ceiling within that subconsciously restricts the body from entering paths of desire that are tacitly forbidden. Of course, there are exceptions, women who are mechanics, experts in high mathematics and artists quite at home with machines of all kinds. Further, the "femininity" in question is culturally circumscribed: it is Western and probably heterosexual, as well as racially inflected with "whiteness" and by ethnic assumptions about whose job it is to mediate between the family and the world. My travels in Eastern Europe before the end of the Cold War revealed women as crane operators, mathematicians and engineers untransformed by beauty culture: these women questioned a lot of things, but never their femininity. In spite of recognizing and experiencing all this relativity, and try as I will, I remain divided, will against unwill, in awkward attempts toward technological competence in spite of something foreign in myself (that is, my specific kind of femininity implant) that deflects me from my resolute path.

Michel Foucault viewed power as the "infinitesimal mechanisms" that operate on the body of the individual, deploying subjectivity in this way and not that.[6] Then, will and unwill might be thought of as the internalized experiences of the minute and trivial that produce or don't produce *homo faber*. When it comes to my body in technological performances, unwill enters the page from the matrix below, like faulty instructions or an old program that has never been erased, causing slip-ups and occasional crashes. Unwill or the part of us that slips or forgets is also the part of us that is slothful, that loses motivation or a sense of purpose, *in nuce*, that resistance of the flesh to being harnessed or programmed by this or that ideology. Unwill is thus a hazy mixture of vegetative corporeality and an ineptitude that amounts to culturally inscribed hysteria. As a woman in a male-oriented techno-logical world that devalues the flesh, my struggle is thus against myself embodied as a woman – albeit a culturally constructed one. My unwill is then to some extent or other my femininity and my female flesh itself. Such unwill is not amenable to talking cures; even once instructions are recognized and lifted off the page, deep gouges in the matrix remain. How then do I get my disciplined and punished body to co-operate with my feminist (as opposed to feminine) ideals?

Recently I braved the throngs of screaming kids at the San Francisco Explor-atorium to try out an intermix of Web sites and installations. At a computer terminal linked to a virtual city, I got caught in an endless loop. Suddenly I noticed a little hand under mine, clicking the mouse. Someone was tucked onto my seat and giving me little pushes. Luckily for my self-esteem, the program wasn't working and the little guy now in charge of the computer was caught in a loop too. Yet, it was clear that something about our culture says to him, this is your place: claim it.

There have been few moments when I have felt this invitation to be addressed to me. One such epiphany, as ridiculous as it might seem, was viewing the opening screen of Christine Tamblyn's CD-ROM, *Mistaken Identities* (1995), namely, an image digitized from a woman's nightgown. The pink screen with tiny rosebuds on the monitor transformed the slick beige machine into something excessively feminine. I was surprised at my own reaction; I let out a deep breath and felt released and at ease.[7]

Gender in Cyberspace

What is cyberspace? My operating premise is that virtual communities and/or environments such as may be found on the Internet or in particular computer-supported worlds allow us to enter and move around inside in what amounts to our own symbolic system. In a three-dimensional pictorial and/or aural virtual world one is literally, albeit virtually, inside the visualization of a symbolic field; in language-generated worlds, this "insidedness" must be understood more figuratively. In either case, the point of view from inside can be revelatory.

Take, for instance, gender identity in a text-based virtual realm on-line such as an MUD or multi-user dungeon. Unlike situations determined by one's biological gender assignment and physical appearance, it is possible to become a member of any sex or species and to change oneself at will, creating personas and "rooms" which can express themselves to others. Such mutability would tend to underline the arbitrariness of gender and reveal its symbolic as opposed to its biological function. Oddly enough, however, judging from the experiences of my students in surfing the Net, virtual worlds do not necessarily or even commonly reveal interactions that transcend gender or cross culture. "Virtual females" told me how often they were hit upon (confronted in a sexually charged manner with demands or expectations to put out or perform sexually, albeit virtually). Why? Because the values encoded in the symbolic system prevail in the minds of the users. In physical reality, it's not so easy to become He-Man or Barbie, character dolls that are the crystallization of notions of masculinity and femininity; however, in a virtual world, stereotypical ideas about gender and sexuality can be simply brought to bear without the inevitable contingencies and imperfections that plague the act of physically embodying a gender identity. (Here the role of the body in moderating or impeding technology can be seen in a more positive light.) Even when male users are capable of successfully posing as women in virtual communities, a kind of gender polarization rather than a transcendence of gender takes place. Such interactions are caught with a vengeance in the very same dualisms that structure our language and relations to material reality, wasting the potential for insight that virtual play with symbolic forms could give us as a culture.

The Gender of Cyberspace

Some speculate that, like technology, cyberspace itself – what I think of as an externalization of symbolic code – is masculine.[8] Such a perspective seems to be from outside and to emphasize control of the virtual environment. Others, including cultural theorists who share a Kleinian psychoanalytic framework, think of it as feminine (especially, when considering the inside, an area enveloped like a fetus in a woman's body). Then, perhaps cyberspace is hermaphroditic, divided by gender inside and outside. The interiority of cyberspace, like the interior of a cave, is like being enclosed inside the womb. Furthermore, the interfaces of cybernetic space have been imagined as a seductive and dangerous garment. The fantasy of putting on such a second, virtual skin is said to express a longing "to become woman."[9] Perhaps this desire to put on the other (from a male point of view) explains the commonplace of men's fiction as female personas on the Net. Furthermore, its gender might depend on what it means to put on the other. My own experience of putting on the interface of virtual reality – the gloves and the head-mounted display – was like putting on a technological empowerment which, like the freedom of flight, allowed me to enter a masculine world otherwise foreclosed to me, even in my dreams. I was both psychically outside and in control and deliciously inside careening around in its illusory depths.[10]

However, this play with gender tends to be predictable, depending as it does on stereotypical notions of sexual identity. For instance, Sarah Kozol, a dancer who participated in Paul Sermon's *Telematic Dreaming* (1992 and 1994), a piece which electronically united two distant beds into one on screen, stressed how often the behavior of her bedpartners was part of well-worn scenarios connected with the bed as a symbolic space. Poetic innovation did take place, albeit rarely, and Kozol apparently revelled in the expansion and contraction of her body boundaries as she identified with the body in the screen image. The virtual body was composed of her own physical body partially hidden by a blue-screen sheet and electronically mixed with one or more physically distant participants into one monstrous combination that was none the less *her* body. Experiencing a vicious attack on her virtual body underlined the way in which virtual and material bodies were intertwined.[11] Thus, the assumption that the virtual is a separate realm of free play without actual consequences is misguided.

In my own experience, the virtual and the material are intertwined and superimposed on every aspect of cyberspace. In a recent talk, I described how I experienced an asthmatic panic much like I might under water while immersed in the multi-dimensional worlds of Char Davies, *Osmose* (1995). Unfortunately for me, the metaphor for the interface of the piece was one of diving under water; breathing in allowed one to ascend, breathing out to descend. One of the worlds consisted of machine code that scrolled upward relentlessly as I tried fruitlessly to escape it; other worlds were "under water." While I remained fully aware of the absurdity of the situation, I was having trouble breathing none the less. My unwill could be recognized but not negotiated; while this unwill has part of its roots in internalized, arbitrary, now even historical gender codes, it is also imbricated somatically with the body itself with needs other than ideological. Even the ability to breathe has psychic as well as avular components.

Access: Gender into Cyberspace

However willing or unwilling, the fundamental question before women is one of praxis: What is the contemporary situation for volitional action and intervention? I believe that the times are unusually propitious for speech-acts or performatives that constitute new realities, actual and virtual. On one hand, emerging notions and interpretations of reality are still quite soft, not yet hardened into their own rules of what kinds of statements can be made and who can make them. On the other, common sense has been undermined by implausible technological feats. This window of opportunity for volitional action is especially furthered by the spontaneous growth of a virtual public sphere on the Internet. However, access to this sphere is technologically circumscribed – you need to have knowledge and equipment to get in – and now that sphere itself is economically and legislatively threatened. In the meantime, social policy discourses have taken a hostile turn, side-tracked into making the beneficiaries of the safety net, from welfare mothers to school lunch programs, into the scapegoats for the deficiencies and failures of our society *per se*. Issues of civil rights and social justice for minorities and women in an information society have been deflected into a debate about affirmative action. Drifting amidst uncertainties, it seems that when we lost our enemy, "communism," internal others took on new importance, bearing the burden and the blame for vast socio-cultural changes and a restructuring of the nature of work.

Lack of access to the technology of information society threatens to screen out vast parts of the world population behind a curtain of silicon, producing socioeconomic disparities that are even more acute. After all, a network is defined as much by its holes or what it leaves out as by its links. To be left out is not merely privation – to some, freedom from constant technological innovation would be a welcome condition – but rather, to become part of a shadow world influenced by but having little influence on the flow of value and the exercise of power.

I recently spoke idealistically on the need to think of the holes in the net in relation to art:

> Art should not be ghettoized into the electronic and/or virtual environment versus the rest, but thought of as linked by metaphors across different degrees of materiality. That also means that an artist in Russia or Africa could participate beyond her or his material and technological means in what must be made a truly global dialogue with local positions. Then, for me, cyberspace is the manifestation of what some call the data sphere in perceptible – and that means largely metaphoric – forms. Relations to cyberspace as nightmare and/or utopia are understandably related to one's position in this economy and the mode of access to it, if any – the data entry worker is different from the programmer, the cultural entitlement of a little girl to cyberplay is not the same as a little boy's. The subsistence farmer's life, if not status, could not be more different than the fast food worker's, but they will be nonetheless ultimately related in a global system of integration and exclusion, like the strands and negative space of a net.[12]

So, when I was invited to compose a workshop panel for the International Symposium of Electronic Arts of ISEA 1995, convening in Helsinki, I tried to think of a productive way to follow my own prescription and produce a range of responses to a unifying metaphor, the cave. I was particularly keen to include a Hungarian-Romanian artist from Transylvania, Alexandru Antik, or as I later discovered, Sandor Antik, after seeing the cave-like *Imagination Held Prisoner/ Prisoner of the Imagination* at the first exhibition of electronic art in Bucharest in 1993.[13] His installation was a dark room, littered with the empty boxes in which film projectors that served now defunct provincial cinemas were once housed.

Flickering light, the projections of the slides of dead embryos and the video buzz of a trapped fly suggested a psychically devastated world in which the imagination had been nearly extinguished. Antik and the other participants in the exhibition had been given access and instruction in video for this occasion, though it was not clear how or if such access would continue beyond the show. For the Cave Panel, I matched Antik's presentation of a ritual that he had performed in a cellar in Cluj, with Jeffrey Shaw's EVE, an extremely high-tech apparatus for displaying virtual images.[14] Fran Dyson described the philosophy of the sound cave, while I introduced a wide range of recent pieces of electronic art on themes ranging from the prehistoric era and the cave of Hebron to virtual reality. Disparate themes and technologies resonated lyrically together in these evocative presentations. The limitations and infelicities of my plan only became clear to me later. Paradoxically, my strategy of inclusion had isolated the representative of the art and cave without technology, Antik, into a singular and exceptional position in a technologically rich gathering with which he had no language in common. Had I applied my own knowledge of what it feels like to be a woman in a male-oriented domain, I might have realized that the real problem in curation is not as I had framed it, in any one event, but in the creation of a domain.

That wasn't all: a woman in the audience for the panel asked, Why haven't you talked about the cave in relation to the female body? I suddenly realized I had left out a rich range of associations that included goddess worship and fertility figures in an unthinking act of self-censorship. I admitted in response that I was afraid, though I didn't realize at the time that it was a fear of being accused of falling into biological essentialism.[15] Accepting the idea that "woman" is a culturally con-structed category had evidently entailed corollaries in my mind that were far more questionable. They included an unresolved relation to the will – in line with the notion that "we are spoken" – and, sorriest of all, a difficulty or inner reserve about addressing and celebrating acts performed by women that change lives. In other words, I had confused the level of my post-structuralist convictions about the culturally constructedness of femininity with the actuality of women as subjects and agents, engendering worlds.

There are numerous organizations that promote female-oriented domains in cyberspace – WIM (Women in Multi-media), Women's Wire and WIT (Women in Technology) – and I have had contact with a few. However, there is a little known category of activist women in the arts about whom I have longed to write. I have come into contact with women curators in the last decade who do indeed generate domains that make the appearance of technologically-based art possible under the most unpromising of conditions. Their work often involves considerable personal sacrifice and seems to be sustained by a belief that the redeeming power of artistic expression should be made available to those who are excluded from the main-stream of information society. Their labors have a limited visibility, since they are collaborative and especially when there is no ongoing institutional relationship to support them. The common denominator of all of these women is that they did not occupy a niche or serve a pre-existing group, but crossed cultural boundaries and oppositions to create new domains that include technological have-nots. Their work has a feminine flavor – a cave building and garment fashioning that envelops or wraps a domain of technology and artistic creation. Among these practitioners I would include:

- Keiko Sei, who worked as a conduit to distribute camcorder work during the revolutions in Eastern Europe, by posing as a Japanese tourist. She was a co-convener of a symposium of artists and cultural workers on the Romanian Revolution held in Budapest in 1990 and assisted the artists in the media art show in Bucharest. She regularly works behind the scenes on media art projects in Eastern Europe and chooses to live in cities at the periphery of electronic culture that start with "B."
- Suzanne Meszoly, Director of the Soros Foundation for Contemporary Art in Budapest (and co-convener of the symposium on the Romanian Revolution), was active in establishing Soros Art Centers throughout the emerging countries of Eastern Europe. She has curated two major shows of media installations in Budapest, including "The Butterfly Effect" (1996).
- Kathy Rae Huffman is an American freelance media art curator and on-line networker and currently a member of HILUS intermediale project research group, Vienna. She frequently collaborates with Ars Electronica, Linz, the Internationale Stadt Berlin, and the Soros Centers for Contemporary Art Network. With Eva Wohlgemuth, Huffman created SIBERIAN DEAL, a real/virtual on-line journey in Siberia, in the fall of 1995 (http://www.t0.or.at/~Siberian). Huffman's prior history in media art was institutional (producer/curator of The CAT Fund, an artists' production project for WGBH TV, Boston, curator of media and performing arts at The ICA Boston and at Long Beach Museum) in a way that seems less supportable in the current climate of American culture. Her existence freelancing on the leading edge of technological art is a rewarding if precarious solution to domain creation.
- Ann Bray is Director of Los Angeles Freewaves, an annual event organized around what Bray and her twenty or so collaborators and curators think is what Los Angeles needs most at this time – from the period of the LA Rebellion to the present situation where survival of the arts is the problem among devastated art venues and supports. In many instances, LA Freewaves events are the first time a community has seen itself represented at all in any public forum. In the current even more reduced circumstances for the arts, the festival uses libraries and other existing venues as a means of organizing access to and exhibiting media art.

I would also include women who have links to the corporate world, considering that the very condition of possibility of some technological art forms may depend on not being free of commercial contexts.

- Machiko Kusahara was a pioneer in the production and criticism of computer imaging and animation in Japan (she has published a ten video-disk history of computer animation.) She has curated major shows supported by corporations in Japan beginning with the 1985 SIGGRAPH traveling art show shown at Sendai in 1986, in co-operation with an advertising company. (In Japan, most of the big exhibitions, except those organized by museums and special exhibitions like ARTEC, are organized and managed by advertising companies, Dentsu in particular.) She has worked on many exhibitions since, including a collaborative effort, Digital Image in 1990. Kusahara explained that one method she has used when seriously negotiating with a sponsor was to reveal her background in science. If that didn't work, she would add that she had studied mathematics (like, "by the way..."). "I learned from experience that many men have an inferiority complex about their ability in mathematics. Maybe they won't fall in love with a woman who studied math (I don't care!) but at least they feel some respect or fear."

• Lisa Goldman established the Interactive Media Festival of commercial, artistic and hybrid work with corporate underwriting. The second event in 1995 included a number of pieces on artificial life that caused me to rethink my first resistances to the very idea (or, as George Lakoff explains, metaphor.)[16] This cross-cultural venue (of art, commerce and technology) allowed me to appreciate the very idea of "interactivity" as a domain.

My admiration of women in adventures of art and technology is less for their adventures than for their practice and what I and others can learn from it. Just so, my own stories of awkwardness and of self-inflicted limits in praxis are also stories of self-discovery. However discouraging the snafus or exhilarating the successes, it is in setting precepts and ideals into praxis that I am able to shed those tired old codes, creating whatever it will mean, in my case at least, to be a woman.

Notes

1   For a critique of the "frontier" metaphor see Laura Miller's "Women and Children First: Gender and the Settling of the Electronic Frontier," in James Brook and Iain A. Boal (eds) *Resisting the Virtual Life: The Culture and Politics of Information* (San Francisco: City Lights, 1995), pp. 49–57.

2   As a result, "the human subject can only feel a sense of belittlement, incompleteness, lack" or "Promethean shame." Christopher Philips has unearthed Günther Anders' ["Other," born Stern] speculation that the desire to escape mortality and the flesh is behind the phenomenon of celebrity; in the reduction to a serially reproducible image, the celebrity becomes a relatively immortal machine. "Desiring Machines: Notes on Commodity, Celebrity, and Death in the Early Work of Andy Warhol," in *Public Information: Desire, Disaster, Document* (New York: Distributed Art Publishers and San Francisco Museum of Modern Art, 1994), pp. 39–47, citing and commenting on Günther Ander, *Die Antiquiertheit des Menschen: über die Schicksal der Seele in den zweiten industriellen Zeitalter* (Munich: H. Beck, 1956). Similar speculation abounds that the posthuman fantasy of having one's brain patterns downloaded and digitally preserved is "cyborg envy" (Allucquère Roseanne Stone) that may also be seen as a far from postgender "womb envy," that is, the power to give birth, in this case, to oneself as machine.

3   In Roger Silverstone and Eric Hirsch (eds) *Consuming Technologies: Media and Information in Domestic Spaces* (London and New York: Routledge, 1992), p. 41.

4   In Mary Anne Moser and Douglas MacLeod (eds) *Immersed in Technology: Art and Virtual Environments* (Cambridge, MA: MIT, 1996), pp. 51–71. What might be problematic in Tenhaaf's proposal is an assumption that immersion presumes a psychic state without much in the way of distance provided by disavowal or a fiction effect. She may be proposing a state much like the over- and under-identification associated with women in feminist approaches to film and television by Mary Anne Doane and Tania Modleski, for example. However, I have questioned the idea of immersion in cyberspace as a more total surrender to the fiction effect in a talk given at the Tate Gallery London in May 1995, to be published in a CD-ROM of the Symposium on Virtual Reality as a Fine Arts Medium; I also stressed that virtuality is not the same as fictionality.

5   "What Do Cyborgs Eat? Oral Logic in an Information Society," in Gretchen Bender and Timothy Druckrey (eds) *Culture on the Brink: Ideologies of Technology* (Seattle: Bay Press, 1994), pp. 157–89, 198–204, describes various imaginary ways of becoming machine-like or cyborg via interjection of smart drugs, electronic second skins or abandoning the flesh entirely by downloading human brain patterns into a computer. I, in turn, valorize the messy strategies of turning machine into flesh and question the omniscience and immortality not to mention intelligence that is projected onto machines. This line of thought found further expression as "Artificial Stupidity," a talk delivered at the International Symposium of Electronic Art in Montreal 1995, in which I question human–machine relations as the contact of the mortal and the divine.

6   See Cockburn's application of Foucault, in "The Circuit of Technology: Gender, Identity and Power" in Roger Silverstone and Eric Hirsch (eds) *Consuming Technologies,* op. cit., p. 44.

7   Looking to the next generation, Marsha Kinder, the author of *Playing with Power in Movies, Television and Video Games: From Muppet Babies to Teenage Mutant Ninja Turtles* (Berkeley: University of California Press, 1991), a book which explains how little boys are acculturated by video games, is producing an electronic game designed to attract little girls, as well as to play with concepts of gender.

8   Andreas Huyssen explained why mass culture, technology itself and machines are gendered female in his *After the Great Divide: Modernism, Mass Culture, Postmodernism* (Bloomington: Indiana University Press, 1986). For a male cyberspace, see Rob Milthorp's "Fascination, Masculinity and Cyberspace" in *Immersed in Technology,* pp. 129–50. Gillian Skirrow's "Hellivision" draws explicitly on Klein to describe a male and a female relation to the game world as inside the mother's body.

9   Allucquère Roseanne Stone, "Will the Real Body Please Stand Up?: Boundary Stories About Virtual Cultures" in Michael Benedikt (ed.) *Cyberspace: First Steps* (Cambridge, MA: MIT Press, 1991), cited and commented on in Alberto Moreiras, "Hacking a Private Site in Cyberspace" in Verena Andermatt Conley and the Miami Theory Collective (eds) *Rethinking Technologies* (Minneapolis: University of Minnesota Press, 1993), pp. 108 ff.

10 Further described in "Enthralling Spaces: The Aesthetics of Virtual Environments," in the catalogue of ISEA 1994, pp. 83–9.

11 Susan Kozol, "Spacemaking: Experiences of a Virtual Body," *Dance Theater Journal,* Summer 1994, pp. 12–13, 31, 46–7. For another description of a violation of the virtual body that is tantamount to rape, see Julian Dibbell, "A Rape in Cyberspace," *Village Voice,* 21 December 1993, pp. 36–42. On the other hand, Miller takes issue with the idea of virtual rape, pp. 53–7, by suggesting that it plays to stereotyped notions of women as victims. Perhaps then violation would be a more appropriate term.

12   From my talk at the Symposium on Art and Virtual Environments at the Banff Centre in 1994. A revised version was printed as: "Nature Morte: Landscape and Narrative in Virtual Environments" in the aforecited *Immersed in Technology*, pp. 195–232.

13   The piece is further described in my "Romanian Art and the Virtual Environment," in Calin Dan (ed.) *Ex Oriente Lux* (Bucharest: Soros Center for Contemporary Arts, 1994), pp. 67–8.

14   Shaw's EVE was a response to the CAVE, another image-surround developed in Chicago; rather than putting miniature televisions like goggles over one's eyes, as in virtual reality, the interior surface of a cube is covered with images. Whoever wears polarized glasses with a tracking device governs the point of view inside the virtual space. One the other hand, EVE is a very large spherical projection surface. Rather than projecting an entire image-surround, images appear only there, where the gaze of the person with the tracking device is directed. This piece makes the fantasy of producing the world through one's gaze explicit. I might add that so far, images for it have been borrowed rather than produced to fit its unique surface.

15   Several participants in "Questions of Feminism: 25 Responses," *October 71*, pp. 5–47, address the issue of essentialism from a contemporary standpoint. Mary Anne Staniszewski notes that "The problem with essentialist feminism was that its essentialism was patriarchal. Not unrelatedly, so are oppositions that restrict the way we would think and live and work", p. 43. Thanks to Christine Tamblyn for bringing the article to my attention. Nell Tenhaaf's aforementioned article also notes a need to rethink the notion of essentialism.

16   "Body, Brain and Communication," in *Resisting the Virtual Life*, pp. 124 ff.

10

Hypertext and Critical Theory

George Landow

George Landow, excerpt from "Hypertext and Critical Theory," from *Hypertext: The Convergence of Contemporary Critical Theory and Technology* (Baltimore and London: Johns Hopkins University Press, 1991), pp. 2–12. Copyright © 1991 George Landow.

George Landow is a professor of English and Art History at Brown University. This essay from his landmark book *Hypertext: The Convergence of Contemporary Critical Theory and Technology* (Johns Hopkins University Press, 1991) traces the development of computer-based systems for organizing text, linking the decentered architecture of the hypertext network to the philosophies of poststructuralist philosophers like Jacques Derrida.

> The problem of causality. It is not always easy to determine what has caused a specific change in a science. What made such a discovery possible? Why did this new concept appear? Where did this or that theory come from? Questions like these are often highly embarrassing because there are no definite methodological principles on which to base such an analysis. The embarrassment is much greater in the case of those general changes that alter a science as a whole. It is greater still in the case of several corresponding changes. But it probably reaches its highest point in the case of the empirical sciences: for the role of instruments, techniques, institutions, events, ideologies, and interests is very much in evidence; but one does not know how an articulation so complex and so diverse in composition actually operates.
>
> Michel Foucault
> *The Order of Things*

Hypertextual Derrida, Poststructuralist Nelson?

When designers of computer software examine the pages of *Glas* or *Of Grammatology*, they encounter a digitalized, hypertextual Derrida; and when literary theorists examine *Literary Machines*, they encounter a deconstructionist or poststructuralist Nelson. These shocks of recognition can occur because over the past several decades literary theory and computer hypertext, apparently unconnected areas of inquiry, have increasingly converged. Statements by theorists concerned with literature, like those by theorists concerned with computing, show a remarkable convergence. Working often, but not always, in ignorance of each other, writers in these areas offer evidence that provides us a way into the contemporary *episteme* in the midst of major changes. A paradigm shift, I suggest, has begun to take place in the writings of Jacques Derrida and Theodor Nelson, of Roland Barthes and Andries van Dam. I expect that one name in each pair will be unknown to most of my readers. Those working in computing will know well the ideas of Nelson and van Dam; those working in literary and cultural theory will know equally well the ideas of Derrida and Barthes.[1] All four, like many others who write on hypertext or literary theory, argue that we must abandon conceptual systems founded upon ideas of center, margin, hierarchy, and linearity and replace them with ones of multilinearity, nodes, links, and networks. Almost all parties to this paradigm shift, which marks a revolution in human thought, see electronic writing as a direct response to the strengths and weaknesses of the printed book. This response has profound implications for literature, education, and politics.

The many parallels between computer hypertext and critical theory have many points of interest, the most important of which, perhaps, lies in the fact that critical theory promises to theorize hypertext and hypertext promises to embody and thereby test aspects of theory, particularly those concerning textuality, narrative, and the roles or functions of reader and writer. Using hypertext, critical theorists will have, or now already have, a new laboratory, in addition to the conventional library of printed texts, in which to test their ideas. Most important, perhaps, an experience of reading hypertext or reading with hypertext greatly clarifies many of the most significant ideas of critical theory. As J. David Bolter points out in the course of explaining that hypertextuality embodies poststructuralist conceptions of the open text, "what is unnatural in print becomes natural in the electronic medium and will soon no longer need saying at all, because it can be shown."[2]

The Definition of Hypertext and its History as a Concept

In *S/Z*, Roland Barthes describes an ideal textuality that precisely matches that which has come to be called computer hypertext – text composed of blocks of words (or images) linked electronically by multiple paths, chains, or trails in an open-ended, perpetually unfinished textuality described by the terms *link, node, network, web,* and *path*: "In this ideal text," says Barthes, "the networks [*réseaux*] are many and interact, without any one of them being able to surpass the rest; this text is a galaxy of signifiers, not a structure of signifieds; it has no beginning; it is reversible; we gain access to it by several entrances, none of which can be author-itatively declared to be the main one; the codes it mobilizes extend *as far as the eye can reach*, they are indeterminable . . . ; the systems of meaning can take over this absolutely plural text, but their number is never closed, based as it is on the infinity of language" (emphasis in original).[3]

Like Barthes, Michel Foucault conceives of text in terms of network and links. In *The Archeology of Knowledge*, he points out that the "frontiers of a book are never clear-cut," because "it is caught up in a system of references to other books, other

texts, other sentences: it is a node within a network . . . [a] network of references."[4]
Like almost all structuralists and poststructuralists, Barthes and Foucault describe
text, the world of letters, and the power and status relations they involve in terms
shared by the field of computer hypertext.

Hypertext, a term coined by Theodor H. Nelson in the 1960s, refers also to a
form of electronic text, a radically new information technology, and a mode of
publication. "By 'hypertext,' " Nelson explains, "I mean *nonsequential writing* –
text that branches and allows choices to the reader, best read at an interactive
screen. As popularly conceived, this is a series of text chunks connected by links
which offer the reader different pathways."[5] Hypertext, as the term will be used in
the following pages, denotes text composed of blocks of text – what Barthes terms
a *lexia* – and the electronic links that join them. *Hypermedia* simply extends the
notion of the text in hypertext by including visual information, sound, animation,
and other forms of data. Since hypertext, which links a passage of verbal discourse
to images, maps, diagrams, and sound as easily as to another verbal passage,
expands the notion of text beyond the solely verbal, I do not distinguish between
hypertext and hypermedia. *Hypertext* denotes an information medium that links
verbal and nonverbal information. In the following pages, I shall use the terms
hypermedia and *hypertext* interchangeably. Electronic links connect lexias "external" to a work – say, commentary on it by another author or parallel or
contrasting texts – as well as within it and thereby create text that is experienced
as nonlinear, or, more properly, as multilinear or multisequential. Although conventional reading habits apply within each lexia, once one leaves the shadowy
bounds of any text unit, new rules and new experience apply.

The standard scholarly article in the humanities or physical sciences perfectly
embodies the underlying notions of hypertext as multisequentially read text. For
example, in reading an article on, say, James Joyce's *Ulysses*, one reads through
what is conventionally known as the main text, encounters a number or symbol
that indicates the presence of a foot- or endnote, and leaves the main text to read
that note, which can contain a citation of passages in *Ulysses* that supposedly
support the argument in question or information about the scholarly author's
indebtedness to other authors, disagreement with them, and so on. The note can
also summon up information about sources, influences, and parallels in other
literary texts. In each case, the reader can follow the link to another text indicated
by the note and thus move entirely outside the scholarly article itself. Having
completed reading the note or having decided that it does not warrant a careful
reading at the moment, one returns to the main text and continues reading until
one encounters another note, at which point one again leaves the main text.

This kind of reading constitutes the basic experience and starting point of
hypertext. Suppose now that one could simply touch the page where the symbol
of a note, reference, or annotation appeared, and thus instantly bring into view the
material contained in a note or even the entire other text – here all of *Ulysses* – to
which that note refers. Scholarly articles situate themselves within a field of relations, most of which the print medium keeps out of sight and relatively difficult to
follow, because in print technology the referenced (or linked) materials lie spatially
distant from the references to them. Electronic hypertext, in contrast, makes

individual references easy to follow and the entire field of interconnections obvious and easy to navigate. Changing the ease with which one can orient oneself within such a context and pursue individual references radically changes both the experience of reading and ultimately the nature of that which is read. For example, if one possessed a hypertext system in which our putative Joyce article was linked to all the other materials it cited, it would exist as part of a much larger system, in which the totality might count more than the individual document; the article would now be woven more tightly into its context than would a printed counterpart.

As this scenario suggests, hypertext blurs the boundaries between reader and writer and therefore instantiates another quality of Barthes's ideal text. From the vantage point of the current changes in information technology, Barthes's distinction between readerly and writerly texts appears to be essentially a distinction between text based on print technology and electronic hypertext, for hypertext fulfills

> the goal of literary work (of literature as work) [which] is to make the reader no longer a consumer, but a producer of the text. Our literature is characterized by the pitiless divorce which the literary institution maintains between the producer of the text and its user, between its owner and its customer, between its author and its reader. This reader is thereby plunged into a kind of idleness – he is intransitive; he is, in short, *serious*: instead of functioning himself, instead of gaining access to the magic of the signifier, to the pleasure of writing, he is left with no more than the poor freedom either to accept or reject the text: reading is nothing more than a *referendum*. Opposite the writerly text, then, is its countervalue, its negative, reactive value: what can be read, but not written: the *readerly*. We call any readerly text a classic text. (*S/Z*, 4)

Compare the way the designers of Intermedia, one of the most advanced hypertext systems thus far developed, describe the active reader that hypertext requires and creates:

> Both an author's tool and a reader's medium, a hypertext document system allows authors or groups of authors to *link* information together, create *paths* through a corpus of related material, *annotate* existing texts, and create notes that point readers to either bibliographic data or the body of the referenced text. . . . Readers can browse through linked, cross-referenced, annotated texts in an orderly but nonsequential manner.[6]

To get an idea of how hypertext produces Barthes's readerly text, let us examine how you, the reader of this book, would read it in a hypertext version. In the first place, instead of encountering it in a paper copy, you would begin to read it on a computer screen. Contemporary screens, which have neither the portability nor the tactility of printed books, make the act of reading somewhat more difficult. For people like me who do a large portion of their reading reclining on a bed or couch, screens also appear less convenient. At the same time, reading on Intermedia, the hypertext system with which I work, offers certain important compensations. Reading an Intermedia version of this book, for example, you could change the size and even style of font to make reading easier. Although you could not make such changes permanently in the text as seen by others, you could make them whenever you wished.

More important, since you would read this hypertext book on a large two-page graphics monitor, you would have the opportunity to place several texts next to one another. Thus, upon reaching the first note in the main text, which follows the passage just quoted from *S/Z*, you would activate the hypertext equivalent of a reference mark (button, link marker), and this action would bring the endnote into view. A hypertext version of a note differs from that in a printed book in several ways. First, it links directly to the reference symbol and does not reside in some sequentially numbered list at the rear of the main text. Second, once opened and either superimposed upon the main text or placed along side it, it appears as an independent, if connected, document in its own right and not as some sort of subsidiary, supporting, possibly parasitic text.

The note in question contains the following information: "Roland Barthes, *S/Z*, trans. Richard Miller (New York: Hill and Wang, 1974), 5–6." A hypertext lexia equivalent to this note could include this same information, or, more likely, take the form of the quoted passage, a longer section or chapter, or the entire text of Barthes's work. Furthermore, that passage could in turn link to other statements by Barthes of similar import, comments by students of Barthes, and passages by Derrida and Foucault that also concern this notion of the networked text. As a reader, you would have to decide whether to return to my argument, pursue some of the connections I have suggested by links, or, using other capacities of the system, search for connections I had not suggested. The multiplicity of hypertext, which appears in multiple links to individual blocks of text, calls for an active reader.

In addition, a full hypertext system, unlike a book and unlike some of the first approximations of hypertext currently available (HyperCard, Guide), offers the reader and writer the same environment. Therefore, by opening the text-processing program, or editor, as it is known, you can take notes, or you can write against my interpretations, against my text. Although you cannot change my text, you can write a response and then link it to my document. You thus have read the readerly text in two ways not possible with a book: You have chosen your reading path – and since you, like all readers, will choose individualized paths, the hypertext version of this book might take a very different form in your reading, perhaps suggesting the values of alternate routes and probably devoting less room in the main text to quoted passages. You might also have begun to take notes or produce responses to the text as you read, some of which might take the form of texts that either support or contradict interpretations proposed in my texts.

Other Convergences: Intertextuality, Multivocality, and De-centeredness

Like Barthes, Foucault, and Mikhail Bakhtin, Jacques Derrida continually uses the terms *link* (*liaison*), *web* (*toile*), *network* (*réseau*), and *interwoven* (*s'y tissent*), which cry out for hypertextuality;[7] but in contrast to Barthes, who emphasizes the read-erly text and its nonlinearity, Derrida emphasizes textual openness, intertextuality, and the irrelevance of distinctions between inside and outside a particular text. These emphases appear with particular clarity when he claims that "like any text, the text of 'Plato' couldn't not be involved, at least in a virtual, dynamic, lateral manner, with all the worlds that composed the system of the Greek language" (129). Derrida in fact here describes extant hypertext systems in which the active reader in the process of exploring a text, probing it, can call into play dictionaries with morphological analyzers that connect individual words to cognates, deriva-tions, and opposites. Here again something that Derrida and other critical theor-ists describe as part of a seemingly extravagant claim about language turns out precisely to describe the new economy of reading and writing with electronic virtual, rather than physical, forms.

Derrida properly acknowledges (in advance, one might say) that a new, freer, richer form of text, one truer to our potential experience, perhaps to our actual if unrecognized experience, depends upon discrete reading units. As he explains, in what Gregory Ulmer terms "the fundamental generalization of his writing,"[8] there also exists "the possibility of disengagement and citational graft which belongs to the structure of every mark, spoken and written, and which constitutes every mark in writing before and outside of every horizon of semio-linguistic communication.... Every sign, linguistic or nonlinguistic, spoken or written... can be *cited*, put between quotation marks." The implication of such citability and separability appears in the fact, crucial to hypertext, that, as Derrida adds, "in so doing it can break with every given context, engendering an infinity of new contexts in a manner which is absolutely illimitable."[9]

Like Barthes, Derrida conceives of text as constituted by discrete reading units. Derrida's conception of text relates to his "methodology of decomposition" that might transgress the limits of philosophy. "The organ of this new philosopheme," as Gregory Ulmer points out, "is the mouth, the mouth that bites, chews, tastes.... The first step of decomposition is the bite" (57). Derrida, who describes text in terms of something close to Barthes's lexias, explains in *Glas* that "the object of the present work, its style too, is the 'mourceau,'" which Ulmer translates as "bit, piece, morsel, fragment; musical composition; snack, mouthful." This *mourceau*, adds Derrida, "is always detached, as its name indicates and so you do not forget it, with the teeth," and these teeth, Ulmer explains, refer to "quotation marks, brackets, parentheses: when language is cited (put between quotation marks), the effect is that of releasing the grasp or hold of a controlling context" (58).

Derrida's groping for a way to foreground his recognition of the way text operates in a print medium – he is, after all, the fierce advocate of writing as against orality – shows the position, possibly the dilemma, of the thinker working with print who sees its shortcomings but for all his brilliance cannot think his way outside this *mentalité*. Derrida, the experience of hypertext shows, gropes toward a new kind of text: he describes it, he praises it, but he can present it only in terms of the devices – here those of punctuation – associated with a particular kind of writing. As the Marxists remind us, thought derives from the forces and modes of

production, though, as we shall see, few Marxists or Marxians ever directly confront the most important mode of literary production – that dependent upon the
techne of writing and print.

From this Derridean emphasis upon discontinuity comes the conception of
hypertext as a vast assemblage, what I have elsewhere termed the *metatext* and
what Nelson calls the "docuverse." Derrida in fact employs the word *assemblage*
for cinema, which he perceives as a rival, an alternative, to print. Ulmer points out
that "the gram or trace provides the 'linguistics' for collage/montage" (267), and
he quotes Derrida's use of *assemblage* in *Speech and Phenomena*: "The word
'assemblage' seems more apt for suggesting that the kind of bringing-together
proposed here has the structure of an interlacing, a weaving, or a web, which
would allow the different threads and different lines of sense or force to separate
again, as well as being ready to bind others together."[10] To carry Derrida's
instinctive theorizing of hypertext further, one may also point to his recognition
that such a montagelike textuality marks or foregrounds the writing process and
therefore rejects a deceptive transparency.

Hypertext and intertextuality

Hypertext, which is a fundamentally intertextual system, has the capacity to
emphasize intertextuality in a way that page-bound text in books cannot. As we
have already observed, scholarly articles and books offer an obvious example of
explicit hypertextuality in nonelectronic form. Conversely, any work of literature –
which for the sake of argument and economy I shall here confine in a most
arbitrary way to mean "high" literature of the sort we read and teach in universities – offers an instance of *implicit* hypertext in nonelectronic form. Again, take
Joyce's *Ulysses* as an example. If one looks, say, at the Nausicaa section, in which
Bloom watches Gerty McDowell on the beach, one notes that Joyce's text here
"alludes" or "refers" (the terms we usually employ) to many other texts or
phenomena that one can treat as texts, including the Nausicaa section of the
Odyssey, the advertisements and articles in the women's magazines that suffuse
and inform Gerty's thoughts, facts about contemporary Dublin and the Catholic
Church, and material that relates to other passages within the novel. Again, a
hypertext presentation of the novel links this section not only to the kinds of
materials mentioned but also to other works in Joyce's career, critical commentary,
and textual variants. Hypertext here permits one to make explicit, though not
necessarily intrusive, the linked materials that an educated reader perceives surrounding it.

Thaïs Morgan suggests that intertextuality, "as a structural analysis of texts in
relation to the larger system of signifying practices or uses of signs in culture,"
shifts attention from the triad constituted by author/work/tradition to another
constituted by text/discourse/culture. In so doing, "intertextuality replaces the
evolutionary model of literary history with a structural or synchronic model of
literature as a sign system. The most salient effect of this strategic change is to free
the literary text from psychological, sociological, and historical determinisms,
opening it up to an apparently infinite play of relationship."[11] Morgan well

describes a major implication of hypertext (and hypermedia) intertextuality: such opening up, such freeing one to create and perceive interconnections, obviously occurs. Nonetheless, although hypertext intertextuality would seem to devalue any historic or other reductionism, it in no way prevents those interested in reading in terms of author and tradition from doing so. Experiments thus far with Intermedia, HyperCard, and other hypertext systems suggest that hypertext does not necessarily turn one's attention away from such approaches. What is perhaps most interesting about hypertext, though, is not that it may fulfill certain claims of structuralist and poststructuralist criticism but that it provides a rich means of testing them.

Hypertext and multivocality

In attempting to imagine the experience of reading and writing with (or within) this new form of text, one would do well to pay heed to what Mikhail Bakhtin has written about the dialogic, polyphonic, multivocal novel, which he claims "is constructed not as the whole of a single consciousness, absorbing other consciousness as objects into itself, but as a whole formed by the interaction of several consciousnesses, none of which entirely becomes an object for the other."[12] Bakhtin's description of the polyphonic literary form presents the Dostoevskian novel as a hypertextual fiction in which the individual voices take the form of lexias.

If Derrida illuminates hypertextuality from the vantage point of the "bite" or "bit," Bakhtin illuminates it from the vantage point of its own life and force – its incarnation or instantiation of a voice, a point of view, a Rortyian conversation.[13] Thus, according to Bakhtin, "in the novel itself, nonparticipating 'third persons' are not represented in any way. There is no place for them, compositionally or in the larger meaning of the work" (*Problems*, 18). In terms of hypertextuality this points to an important quality of this information medium: hypertext does not permit a tyrannical, univocal voice. Rather the voice is always that distilled from the combined experience of the momentary focus, the lexia one presently reads, and the continually forming narrative of one's reading path.

Hypertext and de-centering

As readers move through a web or network of texts, they continually shift the center – and hence the focus or organizing principle – of their investigation and experience. Hypertext, in other words, provides an infinitely re-centerable system whose provisional point of focus depends upon the reader, who becomes a truly active reader in yet another sense. One of the fundamental characteristics of hypertext is that it is composed of bodies of linked texts that have no primary axis of organization. In other words, the metatext or document set – the entity that describes what in print technology is the book, work, or single text – has no center. Although this absence of a center can create problems for the reader and the writer, it also means that anyone who uses hypertext makes his or her own interests the de facto organizing principle (or center) for the investigation at the moment. One experiences hypertext as an infinitely de-centerable and re-centerable system, in part because hypertext transforms any document that has more than one link into a transient center, a directory document that one can employ to orient oneself and to decide where to go next.

Western culture imagined such quasi-magical entrances to a networked reality long before the development of computing technology. Biblical typology, which played such a major role in English culture during the seventeenth and nineteenth centuries, conceived sacred history in terms of types and shadows of Christ and his dispensation.[14] Thus, Moses, who existed in his own right, also existed as Christ, who fulfilled and completed the prophet's meaning. As countless seventeenth-century and Victorian sermons, tracts, and commentaries demonstrate, any particular person, event, or phenomenon acted as a magical window into the complex semiotic of the divine scheme for human salvation. Like the biblical type, which allows significant events and phenomena to participate simultaneously in many realities or levels of reality, the individual lexia inevitably provides a way into the network of connections. Given that evangelical Protestantism in America preserves and extends these traditions of biblical exegesis, one is not surprised to discover that some of the first applications of hypertext involved the Bible and its exegetical tradition.[15]

Not only do lexia work much in the manner of types, they also become Borgesian Alephs, points in space that contain all other points, because from the vantage point each provides one can see everything else – if not exactly simultaneously, then a short way distant, one or two jumps away, particularly in systems that have full text searching. Unlike Jorge Luis Borges's Aleph, one does not have to view it from a single site, neither does one have to sprawl in a cellar resting one's head on a canvas sack.[16] The hypertext document becomes a traveling Aleph.

Such capacity has an obvious relation to the ideas of Derrida, who emphasizes the need to shift vantage points by de-centering discussion. As Derrida points out in "Structure, Sign, and Play in the Discourse of the Human Sciences," the process or procedure he calls de-centering has played an essential role in intellectual change. He says, for example, that "ethnology could have been born as a science only at the moment when a de-centering had come about: at the moment when European culture – and, in consequence, the history of metaphysics and of its concepts – had been *dislocated*, driven from its locus, and forced to stop considering itself as the culture of reference."[17] Derrida makes no claim that an intellectual or ideological center is in any way bad, for, as he explains in response to a query from Serge Doubrovsky, "I didn't say that there was no center, that we could get along without the center. I believe that the center is a function, not a being – a reality, but a function. And this function is absolutely indispensable" (271).

All hypertext systems permit the individual reader to choose his or her own center of investigation and experience. What this principle means in practice is that the reader is not locked into any kind of particular organization or hierarchy. Experiences with Intermedia reveal that for those who choose to organize a session on the system in terms of authors – moving, say, from Keats to Tennyson – the system represents an old-fashioned, traditional, and in many ways still useful author-centered approach. On the other hand, nothing constrains the reader to work in this manner, and readers who wish to investigate the validity of period generalizations can organize their sessions in terms of such periods by using the Victorian and Romantic overviews as starting or midpoints while yet others can begin with ideological or critical notions, such as feminism or the Victorian novel. In practice most readers employ the materials developed at Brown University as a text-centered system, since they tend to focus upon individual works, with the result that even if they begin sessions by entering the system to look for information about an individual author, they tend to spend most time with lexias devoted to specific texts, moving between poem and poem (Swinburne's "Laus Veneris" and Keats's "La Belle Dame Sans Merci" or works centering on Ulysses by Joyce, Tennyson, and Soyinka) and between poem and informational texts ("Laus Veneris" and files on chivalry, medieval revival, courtly love, Wagner, and so on).

Notes

1 Here, right at the beginning, let me assure my readers that although I urge that Barthes and Derrida relate in interesting and important ways to computer hypertext, I do not take them – or semiotics and poststructuralism, or, for that matter, structuralism – to be essentially the same.

2 J. David Bolter, *Writing Space* (Hillsdale, NJ: Lawrence Erlbaum, 1990), p. 143.

3 Roland Barthes, *S/Z* (Paris: Éditions du Seuil, 1970), pp. 11–12; *S/Z*, trans. Richard Miller (New York: Hill and Wang, 1974), pp. 5–6. Subsequent references are to the English translation.

4 Michel Foucault, *The Archeology of Knowledge*, trans. A. M. Sheridan Smith (New York: Harper Colophon, 1976), p. 23.

5 Theodor H. Nelson, *Literary Machines* (Swarthmore, PA: self-published, 1981), p. 0/2. (Pagination begins with each section or chapter, thus 0/2 = prefatory matter, page 2).

6 Nicole Yankelovich, Norman Meyrowitz, and Andries van Dam, "Reading and Writing the Electronic Book," *IEEE Computer* 18 (October 1985), p. 18.

7 See, for example, Jacques Derrida, *La Dissémination* (Paris: Éditions de Seuil, 1972), pp. 71, 108, 172, 111; *Dissemination*, trans. Barbara Johnson (Chicago: University of Chicago Press, 1981), 96, 63, 98, 149. Subsequent references are to the English translation.

8 Gregory L. Ulmer, *Applied Grammatology: Post(e)-Pedagogy from Jacques Derrida to Joseph Beuys* (Baltimore: John Hopkins University Press, 1985), p. 58.

9 Jacques Derrida, "Signatiure Event Context," *Glyph I: Johns Hopkins Textual Studies* (Baltimore: Johns Hopkins University Press, 1977), p. 185. Quoted by Ulmer, *Applied Grammatology*, pp. 58–9.

10 Jacques Derrida, *Speech and Phenomena*, trans. David B. Allison (Evanston IL: Northwestern University Press, 1973), p. 131.

11 Thaïs E. Morgan, "Is There an Intertext in This Text?: Literary and Interdisciplinary Approaches to Intertextuality," *American Journal of Semiotics* 3 (1985), pp. 1–2.

12 Mikhail Bakhtin, *Problems of Dostoevsky's Poetics*, ed. and trans. Caryl Emerson (Minneapolis: University of Minnesota Press, 1984), p. 18.

13 I am thinking of Richard Rorty's description of edifying philosophy as a conversation: "To see keeping a conversation going as a sufficient aim of philosophy, to see wisdom

as consisting in the ability to sustain a conversation, is to see human beings as generators of new descriptions rather than beings one hopes to be able to describe accurately. To see the aim of philosophy as truth – namely, the truth about the terms which provide ultimate commensuration for all human inquiries and activities – is to see human beings as objects rather than subjects, as existing *en-soi* rather than as both *pour-soi* and *en-soi*, as both described objects and describing subjects" (*Philosophy and the Mirror of Nature* (Princeton: Princeton University Press, 1979), p. 378). To a large extent, Rorty can be thought of as the philosopher of hypertextuality.

14 George P. Landow, *Victorian Types, Victorian Shadows: Biblical Typology and Victorian Literature, Art, and Thought* (Boston: Routledge & Kegan Paul, 1980).

15 Examples include *GodSpeed Instant Bible Search Program*, from Kingdom Age Software in San Diego, California, and the Dallas Seminary CD-Word Project, which builds upon Guide, a hypertext system developed by OWL (Office Workstations Limited) International. See Steven J. DeRose, "Biblical Studies and Hypertext," in Paul Delany and George P. Landow, eds., *Hypermedia and Literary Studies* (Cambridge: MIT Press, 1991), pp. 185–204.

16 Jorge Luis Borges, "The Aleph," in *The Aleph and Other Stories, 1933–1969*, trans. Norman Thomas di Giovanni (New York: Bantam, 1971), p. 13: "In that single gigantic instant I saw millions of acts both delightful and awful; not one of them amazed me more than the fact that all of them occupied the same point in space, without overlapping or transparency. What my eyes beheld was simultaneous, but what I shall now write down will be successive, because language is successive.... The Aleph's diameter was probably little more than an inch, but all space was there, actual and undiminished. Each thing (a mirror's face, let us say) was infinite things, since I saw it from every angle of the universe."

17 Jacques Derrida, "Structure, Sign, and Play in the Discourse of the Human Sciences," in *The Structuralist Controversy: The Language of Criticism and the Sciences of Man* (Baltimore: Johns Hopkins University Press, 1972), p. 251.

11

Computers as Theatre

Brenda Laurel

Brenda Laurel is an author and researcher, known for her work on computer games and gender. Her publications include *The Art of Human–Computer Interface Design* (Addison-Wesley, 1990) and *Computers as Theatre* (Addison-Wesley, 1991) from which this section is drawn. The essay explores the human/computer interface (graphical forms, computer desktops, etc.) as constructed or "staged" experience.

[. . .]

The World's a Stage

For purposes of comparison, let's take a look at the theatre. We have observed that the theatre bears some similarities to interface design in that both deal with the representation of action. Drama, unlike novels or other forms of literature, incorporates the notion of *performance*; that is, plays are meant to be acted out. A parallel can be seen in interface design. In his book *The Elements of Friendly Software Design* [1982], Paul Heckel remarked, "When I design a product, I think of my program as giving a performance for its user." In the theatre, enactment typically occurs in a performance area called a stage. The stage is populated by one or more actors who portray characters. They perform actions in the physical context provided by the scene and light designers. The performance is typically viewed by a group of observers called an audience.

 Part of the technical "magic" that supports the performance is embodied in the scenery and objects on the stage (windows that open and close; teacups that break); the rest happens in the backstage and "wing" areas (where scenery is supported, curtains are opened and closed, and sound effects are produced), the "loft" area above the stage, which accommodates lighting instruments and backdrops or set pieces that can be raised and lowered, and the lighting booth, which is usually above the audience at the back of the auditorium. The magic is created by both people and machines, but who, what, and where they are *do not matter* to the audience.

It's not just that the technical underpinnings of theatrical performance are unimportant to audience members; when a play is "working," audience members are simply not aware of the technical aspects at all. For the audience member who is engaged by and involved in the play, the action on the stage is *all there is*. In this sense, plays are like movies: When you are engrossed in one, you forget about the projector, and you may even lose awareness of your own body. For the actor on stage, the experience is similar in that everything extraneous to the ongoing action is tuned out, with the exception of the audience's audible and visible responses, which are often used by the actors to tweak their performance in real time (this, by the way, reminds us that theatrical audiences are not strictly "passive" and may be said to influence the action). For actor and audience alike, the ultimate "reality" is what is happening in the imaginary world on the stage – the representation.

As researchers grapple with the notion of interaction in the world of computing, they sometimes compare computer users to theatrical audiences. "Users," the argument goes, are like audience members who are able to have a greater influence on the unfolding action than simply the fine-tuning provided by conventional audience response. In fact, I used this analogy in my dissertation in an attempt to create a model for interactive fantasy. The users of such a system, I argued, are like audience members who can march up onto the stage and become various characters, altering the action by what they say and do in their roles.

Let's reconsider for a minute. What would it be really like if the audience marched up on the stage? They wouldn't know the script, for starters, and there would be a lot of awkward fumbling for context. Their clothes and skin would look funny under the lights. A state of panic would seize the actors as they attempted to improvise action that could incorporate the interlopers and still yield something that had any dramatic integrity. Or perhaps it would degenerate into a free-for-all, as performances of avant-garde interactive plays in the 1960s often did.

The problem with the audience-as-active-participant idea is that it adds to the clutter, both psychological and physical. The transformation needs to be subtractive rather than additive. People who are participating in the representation aren't audience members anymore. It's not that the audience joins the actors on the stage; it's that they *become* actors – and the notion of "passive" observers disappears.

In a theatrical view of human-computer activity, the stage is a virtual world. It is populated by agents, both human and computer-generated, and other elements of the representational context (windows, teacups, desktops, or what-have-you). The technical magic that supports the representation, as in the theatre, is behind the scenes. Whether the magic is created by hardware, software, or wetware is of no consequence; its only value is in what it produces on the "stage." In other words, *the representation is all there is*. Think of it as existential WYSIWYG.[1]

[...]

An Artistic Perspective

In his seminal book, *The Elements of Friendly Software Design* [1982], Paul Heckel characterizes software design as primarily concerned with communication. He observes that "among all the art forms that can teach us about communication, the most appropriate is filmmaking." Heckel chooses filmmaking as an example over older forms (such as theatre) because it "illustrates the transition from an engineering discipline to an art form." He goes on to observe that movies did not achieve wide popular success until artists replaced engineers as the primary creators. Heckel's book is filled with references to illusion, performance, and other theatrical and filmic metaphors with software examples to illustrate each observation. He gives the use of metaphor in interface design a different twist by employing filmmaking, writing, acting, and other "communication crafts" as metaphors for the process of software design.

In 1967, Ted Nelson examined the evolution of film in order to understand how the new medium he envisioned – hypertext – should develop. In considering the ways in which the stage had influenced film, he noted that "stage content, when adapted, was appropriate and useful, while stage techniques (such as the notion of a proscenium and an insistence on continuous action within scenes) were not" [Nelson, 1967]. From the vantage point of 1990, we can see a migration of both techniques and content from film into the computer medium. If one takes the theatre and the film medium as subsets of a larger category, as representations of action in virtual worlds, then another key similarity between these media and computers is their fundamental elements of form and structure and their purpose.

Both Heckel and Nelson draw our attention to the centrality of "make-believe" in the conception and design of software. An engineer's view of software design is rooted in logic, realizing an orderly set of functions in an internally elegant program. In Heckel's view, the better approach is rooted in vision, which realizes an environment for action through evocative, consistent illusions. According to Nelson, it is the creation of "virtualities" – representations for things that may never have existed in the real world before [Nelson, 1990]. The role of imagination in creating interactive representations is clear and cannot be overrated. In an important sense, a piece of computer software is a collaborative exercise of the imaginations of the creator(s) of a program and people who use it.

Imagination supports a constellation of distinctively human phenomena that includes both symbolic thinking and representation-making. There is a story about a monkey and some bananas that every undergraduate psychology student has heard. A researcher places a monkey in a room with a bunch of bananas hanging from the ceiling and a box on the floor. The monkey tries various ways of getting the bananas – reaching, jumping, and so on – and eventually climbs up onto the box. A person in a similar situation would rehearse most of the possible strategies in her head and actively pursue only those that seemed promising, maybe only the successful one. For the monkey, the focus of attention is the real bananas; for the human, it's what's going on inside her head. Imagination is a shortcut through the process of trial and error.

But imagination is good for much more than real-world problem solving. The impulse to create interactive representations, as exemplified by human-computer activities, is only the most recent manifestation of the age-old desire to make what we imagine palpable – our insatiable need to exercise our intellect, judgment, and spirit in contexts, situations, and even personae that are different from those of our everyday lives. When a person considers how to climb a tree, imagination serves as a laboratory for virtual experiments in physics, biomechanics, and physiology. In matters of justice, art, or philosophy, imagination is the laboratory of the spirit.

What we do in our heads can be merely expedient or far-reaching, private or intended for sharing and communication. The novels of Ayn Rand, for instance or the plays of George Bernard Shaw create worlds where people address issues and problems, both concrete and abstract, and enact their discoveries, responses, and solutions. These representations are wholly contained in the realm of the imagination, yet they transport us to alternate possible perspectives and may influence us in ways that are more resonant and meaningful than experiences actually lived.

Art is the external *representation* of things that happen in the head of the artist. Art forms differ in terms of the materials they employ, the way the representations are created, what they purport to represent, and how they are manifest in the world. Different forms have different powers – the powers to engage, to provide pleasure and information, to evoke response. But all have as their end the *representation* of some internal vista that the artist wishes to create beyond the bounds of his or her own skull, making it available in some form to other people.

What are such representations good for? Aristotle defined *catharsis* as the end cause of a play and saw it as the pleasurable release of emotion, specifically those emotions evoked by the action represented in the play.[2] In his view, catharsis occurred during the actual "run-time" of the play, but some contemporary theorists disagree. The early twentieth-century German dramatist Bertolt Brecht extended the notion of catharsis beyond the temporal boundary of the performance [Brecht, 1964]. He posited that catharsis is not complete until the audience members take what they have assimilated from the representation and put it to work in their lives. In Brecht's hypothesis, the representation lives between imagination and reality, serving as a conductor, amplifier, clarifier, and motivator.

It seems to me that computer-based representations work in fundamentally the same way: a person participates in a representation that is not the same as real life but which has real-world effects or consequences. Representation and reality stand in a particular and necessary relation to one another. In much contemporary thinking about interfaces, however, the understanding of that relationship is muddy. On the one hand, we speak of "tools" for "users" to employ in the accomplishment of various tasks with computers. We plumb psychology for information about how people go about using tools and what is the best way to design them. We arrive at notions like "cut" and "paste" and even "write" that seem to suggest that people working with computers are operating in the arena of the concrete. We often fail to see that these are *representations* of tools and activities and to notice how that makes them different from (and often better than) the real thing.

On the other hand, we employ graphic artists to create icons and windows, pictures of little hands and file folders and lassos and spilling paint cans, to stand in for us in the computer's world. Here the idea of representation is used, but only in a superficial sense. Messy notions like "interface metaphor" are employed to gloss over the differences between representation and reality, attempting to draw little cognitive lines from the things we see on the screen to the "real" activities that psychologists tell us we are performing. Interface metaphors rumble along like Rube Goldberg machines, patched and wired together every time they break, until they are so encrusted with the artifacts of repair that we can no longer interpret them or recognize their referents.

This confusion over the nature of human-computer activity can be alleviated by thinking about it in terms of theatre, where the special relationship between representation and reality is already comfortably established, not only in theoretical terms but also in the way that people design and experience theatrical works. Both domains employ representations as contexts for thought. Both attempt to amplify and orchestrate experience. Both have the capacity to represent actions and situations that do not and cannot exist in the real world, in ways that invite us to extend our minds, feelings, and senses to envelop them.

In the view of semioticist Julian Hilton [1991], theatre is "essentially the art of showing, the art of the index . . . It involves the synthesis of symbolic and iconic systems (words and moving pictures) in a single indivisible performed event." Hilton employs the myth of Pygmalion and Galathea (familiar to many as the basis of George Bernard Shaw's *Pygmalion* and its musical adaptation, *My Fair Lady*) to express the relationship of the theatre to the domain of artificial intelligence. He describes the value of the theatre's ability to represent things that have no real-world referents in semiotic terms:

> Galathea in a literal sense imitates nothing, and as such defines a class of icon (the statue after all is a picture of itself) that can simultaneously be an index. It is this category of non-imitative index which enables the index to liberate its true power, whereby it has all the infinite valency of the symbol while retaining the immediate recognisability of the icon. [Hilton, 1991]

Computers are representation machines that can emulate any known medium, as Alan Kay observes:

> The protean nature of the computer is such that it can act like a machine or like a language to be shaped and exploited. It is a medium that can dynamically simulate the details of any other medium, including media that cannot exist physically. It is not a tool, although it can act like many tools. It is the first metamedium, and as such it has degrees of freedom for representation and expression never before encountered and as yet barely investigated. [Kay, 1984]

Thinking about interfaces is thinking too small. Designing human-computer experience isn't about building a better desktop. It's about creating imaginary worlds that have a special relationship to reality – worlds in which we can extent, amplify, and enrich our own capacities to think, feel, and act. Hopefully, this chapter has persuaded you that knowledge from the theatrical domain can help us in that task.

Notes

1 WYSIWYG stands for "what you see is what you get," coined by Warren Teitelman at Xerox PARC. It has been held up as a paradigm for direct-manipulation interfaces, but some theorists have contested its value (see, for instance, Ted Nelson's 1990 article, "The Right Way to Think About Software Design" in *The Art of Human-Computer Interface Design*).

2 That's not to say that plays must arouse only pleasant emotions; the pleasure of release makes even nasty emotions enjoyable in a theatrical context. Catharsis is discussed more fully in Chapter 4 [of *Computers as Theatre*].

References

Brecht, Bertolt, *Brecht on Theatre*. Translated by John Willett. New York, 1964.

Heckel, Paul, *The Elements of Friendly Software Design* (New York: Warner Books, 1982).

Hilton, Julian, "Some Semiotic Reflections on the Future of Artificial Intelligence," in R. Trappl, ed., *Artificial Intelligence: Future, Impacts, Challenges* (New York: Hemisphere, 1991).

Kay, Alan. "Computer Software." *Scientific American*, vol. 251, no. 3 (September 1984), pp. 52–9.

Nelson, Theodor Holm, "Getting It Out of Our System," in George Schecter, ed., *Information Retrieval: A Critical View* (Philadelphia, Penn: Frankford Arsenal, 1967).

Nelson, Theodor Holm, "The Right Way to Think about Software Design," in Brenda Laurel, ed., *The Art of Human-Computer Interface Design* (Reading, MA: Addison-Wesley, 1990).

12

The Information War

Hakim Bey

Hakim Bey, "The Information War," in Timothy Druckrey, ed., *Electronic Culture: Technology and Visual Representation* (New York: Aperture, 1996), pp. 369–75.

Hakim Bey is a widely published author and political activist, whose writing has appeared in such books as *Poetic Terrorism* (Autonomedia, 1995), *Immediatism* (AK Press, 1995), and *Millennium* (Automedia, 1996), as well as periodicals like *In These Times* and *Mother Jones*. In this selection, Bey considers the utopia/dystopia divide in attitudes toward the "information revolution," with reference to the First World origins of these ideas.

Humanity has always invested heavily in any scheme that offers escape from the body. And why not? Material reality is such a mess. Some of the earliest "religious" artifacts, such as Neanderthal ochre burials, already suggest a belief in immortality. All modern (i.e., postpaleolithic) religions contain the "Gnostic trace" of distrust or even outright hostility to the body and the "created" world. Contemporary "primitive" tribes and even peasant-pagans have a concept of immortality and of going-outside-the-body (ecstasy) without necessarily exhibiting any excessive body hatred. The Gnostic trace accumulates very gradually (like mercury poisoning) until eventually it turns pathological. Gnostic dualism exemplifies the extreme position of this disgust by shifting all value from body to "spirit." This idea characterizes what we call "civilization." A similar trajectory can be traced through the phenomenon of "war." Hunter-gatherers practiced (and still practice, as amongst the Yanomamo) a kind of ritualized brawl (think of the Plains Indian custom of "counting coup"). "Real" war is a continuation of religion and economics (i.e., politics) by other means, and thus only begins historically with the priestly invention of "scarcity" in the Neolithic and the emergence of a "warrior caste." (I categorically reject the theory that war is a prolongation of "hunting.") World War II seems to have been the last "real" war. Hyperreal war began in Vietnam with the involvement of television, and recently reached full obscene revelation in the Gulf War of 1991. Hyperreal war is no longer "economic," no longer "the health of the state." The Ritual brawl is voluntary and nonhierarchic (war chiefs are always temporary); real war is compulsory and hierarchic; hyperreal war is imagistic and psychologically interiorized ("pure war"). In the first, the body is risked; in the second, the body is sacrificed; in the third, the body has disappeared. (See P. Clastres on war, in *Archaeology of Violence*.) Modern science also incorporates an antimaterialist bias, the dialectical outcome of its war against Religion – it has in some sense become Religion. Science as knowledge of material reality paradoxically decomposes the materiality of the real. Science has always been a species of priestcraft, a branch of cosmology, and an ideology, a justification of "the way things are." The deconstruction of the real in postclassical physics mirrors the vacuum of unreality which constitutes "the state." Once the image of Heaven on Earth, the state now consists of no more than the management of images. It is no longer a force but a disembodied patterning of information. But just as Babylonian cosmology justified Babylonian power, so too does the "finality" of modern science serve the ends of the Terminal State, the postnuclear state, the "information state." Or so the New Paradigm would have it. And "everyone" accepts the axiomatic premises of the New Paradigm. The New Paradigm is very spiritual.

Even the New Age with its gnostic tendencies embraces the New Science and its increasing etherealization as a source of proof-texts for its spiritualist world view. Meditation and cybernetics go hand in hand. Of course the information state somehow requires the support of a police force and prison system that would have stunned Nebuchadnezzar and reduced all the priests of Moloch to paroxysms of awe. And modern science still can't weasel out of its complicity in the very-nearly-successful conquest of Nature. Civilization's greatest triumph over the body.

But who cares? It's all relative isn't it? I guess we'll just have to "evolve" beyond the body. Maybe we can do it in a "quantum leap." Meanwhile the excessive mediation of the Social, which is carried out through the machinery of the Media, increases the intensity of our alienation from the body by fixating the flow of attention on information rather than direct experience. In this sense the Media serves a religious or priestly role, appearing to offer us a way out of the body by redefining spirit as information. The essence of information is the Image, the sacral and iconic data complex which usurps the primacy of the "material bodily prin-ciple" as the vehicle of incarnation, replacing it with a fleshless ecstasis beyond corruption. Consciousness becomes something which can be down loaded, excised from the matrix of animality and immortalized as information. No longer "ghost-in-the machine," but machine-as-ghost, machine as Holy Ghost, ultimate mediator, which will translate us from our mayfly-corpses to a pleroma of Light. Virtual reality as CyberGnosis. Jack in, leave Mother Earth behind forever. All science proposes a paradigmatic universalism – as in science, so in the social. Classical physics played midwife to capitalism, communism, fascism, and other modern ideologies.

Postclassical science also proposes a set of ideas meant to be applied to the social: relativity, quantum "unreality," cybernetics, information theory, etc. With some exceptions, the postclassical tendency is towards ever greater etherealization. Some proponents of Black Hole theory, for example, talk like pure Pauline theologians, while some of the information theorists are beginning to sound like virtual

Manichaeans.[1] On the level of the social these paradigms give rise to a rhetoric of bodylessness quite worthy of a third-century desert monk or a seventeenth-century New England Puritan – but expressed in a language of postindustrial, postmodern feel-good consumer frenzy. Our every conversation is infected with certain paradigmatic assumptions which are really no more than bald assertions, but which we take for the very fabric or *Urgrund* of reality itself. For instance, since we now assume that computers represent a real step toward artificial intelligence, we also assume that buying a computer makes us more intelligent. In my own field I've met dozens of writers who sincerely believe that owning a PC has made them better (not "more efficient," but better) writers. This is amusing – but the same feeling about computers when applied to a trillion dollar military budget churns out Star Wars, killer robots, etc. (See Manuel de Landa's *War in the Age of Intelligent Machines* on AI in modern weaponry.) An important part of this rhetoric involves the concept of an "information economy." The post-Industrial world is now thought to be giving birth to this new economy. One of the clearest examples of the concept can be found in a recent book by Bishop Hoeller, a man who is a libertarian, the bishop of a Gnostic Dualist Church in California and a learned and respected writer for *Gnosis* magazine:

> The industry of the past phase of civilization (sometimes called "low technology") was big industry, and bigness always implies oppressiveness. The new high technology, however, is not big in the same way. While the old technology produced and distributed material resources, the new technology produces and disseminates information. The resources marketed in high technology are less about matter and more about mind. Under the impact of high technology, the world is moving increasingly from a physical economy into what might be called a "metaphysical economy." We are in the process of recognizing that consciousness rather than raw materials or physical resources constitutes wealth.[2]

Modern neo-Gnosticism usually plays down the old Manichaean attack on the body for a gentler greener rhetoric. Bishop Hoeller for instance stresses the importance of ecology and environment (because we don't want to "foul our nest," the Earth) – but in his chapter on Native American spirituality he implies that a cult of the Earth is clearly inferior to the pure Gnostic spirit of bodylessness:

> But we must not forget that the nest is not the same as the bird. The exoteric and esoteric traditions declare that earth is not the only home for human beings, that we did not grow like weeds from the soil. While our bodies indeed may have originated on this earth, our inner essence did not. To think otherwise puts us outside of all of the known spiritual traditions and separates us from the wisdom of the seers and sages of every age. Though wise in their own ways. Native Americans have small connection with this rich spiritual heritage.[3]

In such terms (the body = the "savage"), the Bishop's hatred and disdain for the flesh illuminate every page of his book. In his enthusiasm for a truly religious economy, he forgets that one cannot eat "information." "Real wealth" can never become immaterial until humanity achieves the final etherealization of downloaded consciousness. Information in the form of culture can be called wealth metaphorically because it is useful and desirable – but it can never be wealth in precisely the same basic way that oysters and cream, or wheat and water, are wealth in themselves. Information is always only information about some thing. Like money, information is not the thing itself. Over time we can come to think of money as wealth (as in a delightful Taoist ritual which refers to "Water and Money" as the two most vital principles in the universe), but in truth this is sloppy abstract thinking. It has allowed its focus of attention to wander from the bun to the penny which symbolizes the bun.[4] In effect we've had an information economy ever since we invented money. But we still haven't learned to digest copper. The Aesopian crudity of these truisms embarrasses me, but I must perforce play the stupid lazy yokel plowing a crooked furrow when all the straight thinkers around me appear to be hallucinating.

Americans and other "First World" types seem particularly susceptible to the rhetoric of a "metaphysical economy" because we can no longer see (or feel or smell) around us very much evidence of a physical world. Our architecture has become symbolic, we have enclosed ourselves in the manifestations of abstract thought (cars, apartments, offices, schools), we work at "service" or information-related jobs, helping in our little way to move disembodied symbols of wealth around an abstract grid of Capital, and we spend our leisure largely engrossed in Media rather than in direct experience of material reality. The material world for us has come to symbolize catastrophe, as in our amazingly hysterical reaction to storms and hurricanes (proof that we've failed to "conquer Nature" entirely), or our neo-Puritan fear of sexual otherness, or our taste for bland and denatured (almost abstract) food. And yet, this "First World" economy is not self-sufficient. It depends for its position (top of the pyramid) on a vast substructure of old-fashioned material production. Mexican farmworkers grow and package all that Natural food for us so we can devote our time to stocks, insurance, law, computers, video games. Peons in Taiwan make silicon chips for our PCs. "Towel-heads" in the Middle East suffer and die for our sins. Life? Oh, our servants do that for us. We have no life, only "lifestyle" – an abstraction of life, based on the sacred symbolism of the Commodity, mediated by the priesthood of the stars, those larger-than-life abstractions who rule our values and people our dreams – the media-archetypes; or perhaps "mediarchs" would be a better term. Of course this Baudrillardian dystopia doesn't really exist – yet.[5] It's surprising, however, to note how many social radicals consider it a desirable goal, at least as long as it's called the "information revolution" or something equally inspiring. Leftists talk about seizing the means of information-production from the data monopolists.[6] In truth, information is everywhere – even atom bombs can be constructed on plans available in public libraries. As Noam Chomsky points out, one can always access information – provided one has a private income and a fanaticism bordering on insanity. Universities and "think tanks" make pathetic attempts to monopolize information – they, too, are dazzled by the notion of an information economy – but their conspiracies are laughable. Information may not always be "free," but there's a great deal more of it available than any one person could never possibly use. Books on every conceivable subject can actually still be found through interlibrary loan.[7] Meanwhile someone still has to grow pears and cobble shoes. Or, even if these "industries" can be completely mechanized, someone still has to eat pears and wear shoes. The body is still the basis of wealth. The idea of Images as wealth is a "spectacular delusion." Even a radical critique of information can still give rise to an overvaluation of abstraction and data. In a *prositu* zine from England called *No*, the following message was scrawled messily across the back cover of a recent issue:

> As you read these words, the Information Age explodes ... inside and around you – with the Misinformation Missiles and Propaganda bombs of outright Information Warfare.
>
> Traditionally, war has been fought for territory/economic gain. Information Wars are fought for the acquisition of territory indigenous to the Information Age, i.e., the human mind itself. . . . In particular, it is the faculty of the imagination that is under the direct threat of extinction from the onslaughts of multi-media overload . . . DANGER – YOUR IMAGINATION MAY NOT BE YOUR OWN . . . As a culture sophisticates, it deepens its reliance on its images, icons and symbols as a way of defining itself and communicating with other cultures. As the accumulating mix of a culture's images floats around in its collective psyche, certain isomorphic icons coalesce to produce and to project an "illusion" of reality. Fads, fashions, artistic trends. U KNOW THE SCORE. "I can take their images for reality because I believe in the reality of their images (their image of reality)." WHOEVER CONTROLS THE METAPHOR GOVERNS THE MIND. The conditions of total saturation are slowly being realized – a creeping paralysis – from the trivialization of special/technical knowledge to the specialization of trivia. The INFORMATION WAR is a war we cannot afford to lose. The result is unimaginable.[8]

I find myself very much in sympathy with the author's critique of media here, yet I also feel that a demonization of "information" has been proposed which consists of nothing more than the mirror image of information-as-salvation. Again Baudrillard's vision of the Commtech Universe is evoked, but this time as Hell rather than as the Gnostic Hereafter. Bishop Hoeller wants everybody jacked-in and downloaded and the anonymous post-situationist ranter wants you to smash your telly, but both of them believe in the mystic power of information. One proposes the pax technologica, the other declares war. Both exude a kind of Manichaean view of Good and Evil, but can't agree on which is which. The critical theorist swims in a sea of facts. We like to imagine it also as our Maquis, with ourselves as the "guerilla ontologists" of its datascape. Since the nineteenth century the evermutating "social sciences" have unearthed a vast hoard of information on everything from shamanism to semiotics. Each "discovery" feeds back into social science and changes it. We drift. We wish for poetic facts, data which will intensify and mutate our experience of the real. We invent new hybrid "sciences" as tools for this process: ethnopharmacology, ethnohistory, cognitive studies, history of ideas, subjective anthropology (anthropological poetics or ethno-poetics), dada epistemology, etc. We look on all this knowledge not as "good" in itself, but valuable only inasmuch as it helps us to seize or to construct our own happiness. In this sense we do know of "information as wealth"; nevertheless, we continue to desire wealth itself and not merely its abstract representation as information. At the same time we also know of "information as war";[9] nevertheless, we have not decided to embrace ignorance just because "facts" can be used like a poison gas. Ignorance is not even an adequate defense, much less a useful weapon in this war. We attempt neither to fetishize nor to demonize information. Instead we try to establish a set of values by which information can be measured and assessed. Our standard in this process can only be the body. According to certain mystics, spirit and body are "one." Certainly spirit has lost its ontological solidity (since Nietzsche, anyway) while body's claim to "reality" has been undermined by modern science to the point of vanishing in a cloud of "pure energy." So why not assume that spirit and body are one, after all, and that they are twin (or dyadic) aspects of the same underlying and inexpressible real? No body without spirit, no spirit without body. The Gnostic Dualists are wrong, as are the vulgar dialectical materialists. Body and spirit together make life. If either pole is missing, the result is death. This constitutes a fairly simple set of values, assuming we prefer life to death. Obviously I'm avoiding any strict definitions of either body or spirit. I'm speaking of "empirical" everyday experiences. We experience "spirit" when we dream or create; we experience "body" when we eat or shit (or maybe vice versa); we experience both at once when we make love. I'm not proposing metaphysical categories here. We're still drifting and these are ad hoc points of reference, nothing more. We needn't be mystics to propose this version of "one reality." We need only point out that no other reality has yet appeared within the context of our knowable experience. For all practical purposes, the "world" is "one."[10] Historically however, the body half of this unity has always received the insults, bad press, scriptural condemnation, and economic persecution of the spirit half. The self-appointed representatives of the spirit have called almost all the tunes in known history, leaving the body only a prehistory of primitive disappearance, and a few spasms of failed insurrectionary futility.

Spirit has ruled – hence we scarcely even know how to speak the language of the body. When we use the word information we reify it because we have always reified abstractions – ever since God appeared as a burning bush. (Information as the catastrophic decorporealization of "brute" matter.) We would now like to propose the identification of self with body. We're not denying that the body is also spirit, but we wish to restore some balance to the historical equation. We calculate all body hatred and world slander as our evil. We insist on the revival (and mutation) of "pagan" values concerning the relation of body and spirit. We fail to feel any great enthusiasm for the information economy because we see it as yet another mask for body hatred. We can't quite believe in the information war, since it also hypostatizes information but labels it "evil." In this sense, "information" would appear to be neutral. But we also distrust this third position as a lukewarm cop-out and a failure of theoretical vision. Every "fact" takes different meanings as we run it through our dialectical prism[11] and study its gleam and shadows. The fact is never inert or neutral, but it can be both good and evil (or beyond them) in countless variations and combinations. We, finally, are the artists of this immeasurable discourse. We create values. We do this because we are alive. Information is as big a mess as the material world it reflects and transforms. We embrace the mass, all of it. It's all life. But within the vast chaos of the alive, certain information and certain material things begin to coalesce into a poetics or a way-of-knowing or a way-of-acting. We can draw certain pro tem conclusions, as long as we don't plaster them over and set them up on altars. Neither information nor indeed any one "fact" constitutes a thing-in-itself. The very word *information* implies an ideology, or rather a paradigm, rooted in unconscious fear of the silence of matter and of the universe. Information is a substitute for certainty, a left over fetish of dogmatics, a *super-stitio*, a spook. "Poetic facts" are not assimilable into the doctrine of information. "Knowledge is freedom" is true only when freedom is understood as a psycho-kinetic skill. Information is a chaos; knowledge is the spontaneous ordering of that chaos; freedom is the surfing of the wave of that spontaneity. These tentative conclusions constitute the shifting and marshy ground of our "theory." The TAZ wants all information and all bodily pleasure in a great complex confusion of sweet data and sweet dates – facts and feasts – wisdom and wealth. This is our economy – and our war.

Notes

1 The new "life" sciences offer some dialectical opposition here, or could do so if they worked through certain paradigms. Chaos theory seems to deal with the material world in positive ways, as does Gaia theory, morphogenetic theory, and various other "soft" and "neohermetic" disciplines. Elsewhere I've attempted to incorporate these philosophical implications into a "festal" synthesis. The point is not to abandon all thought about the material world, but to realize that all science has philosophical and political implications, and that science is a way of thinking, not a dogmatic structure of incontrovertible Truth. Of course quantum, relativity, and information theory are all "true" in some way and can be given a positive interpretation. I've already done that in several essays. Now I want to explore the negative aspects.

2 Stephen A. Hoeller, *Freedom: Alchemy for a Voluntary Society* (Wheaton, IL: Quest, 1992), pp. 229–30.

3 Hoeller, *Freedom: Alchemy for a Voluntary Society*, p. 164.

4 Like Pavlov's dogs salivating at the dinner bell rather than the dinner – a perfect illustration of what I mean by "abstraction."

5 Although some might say that it already "virtually" exists. I just use heard from a friend in California of a new scheme for "universal prisons" – offenders will be allowed to live at home and go to work but will be electronically monitored at all times, like Winston Smith in *1984*. The universal panoption now potentially coincides one to one with the whole of reality; life and work will take the place of outdated physical incarceration – the Prison Society will merge with "electronic democracy" to form a Surveillance State or information totality, with all time and space compacted beneath the unsleeping gaze of RoboCop. On the level of pure tech, at least, it would seem that we have at last arrived at "the future." "Honest citizens" of course will have nothing to fear; hence terror will reign unchallenged and Order will triumph like the Universal Ice. Our only hope may lie in the "chaotic perturbation" of massively linked computers, and in the venal stupidity or boredom of those who program and monitor the system.

6 I will always remember with pleasure being addressed, by a Bulgarian delegate to a conference I once attended as a "fellow worker in philosophy." Perhaps the capitalist

version would be "entrepreneur in philosophy" as if one bought ideas like apples at roadside stands.

7   Of course information may sometimes be "occult" as in conspiracy theory. Information may be "disinformation." Spies and propagandists make up a kind of shadow information economy, to be sure. Hackers who believe in freedom of information have my sympathy especially since they've been picked as the latest enemies of the Spectacular State, and subjected to its spasms of control-by-terror. But hackers have yet to "liberate" a single bit of information useful in our struggle. Their impotence, and their fascination with Imagery, make them ideal victims of the Information State, which itself is based on pure stimulation. One needn't steal data from the post-military-industrial complex to know in general, what it's up to. We understand enough to form our critique. More information by itself will never take the place of the actions we have failed to carry out: data by itself will never reach critical mass. Despite my loving debt to thinkers like Robert Anton Wilson and T. Leary I cannot agree with their optimistic analysis of the cognitive function of information technology. It is not the neural system alone which will achieve autonomy, but the entire body.

8   "Nothing Is True," *NO* 6, Box 175, Liverpool L69 8DX, UK.

9   Indeed, the whole "poetic terrorism" project has been proposed only as a strategy in this very war.

10 "The 'world' is 'one' " can be and has been used to justify a totality, a metaphysical ordering of "reality" with a "center" or "apex": one god, one king, etc., etc. This is the monism of orthodoxy, which naturally opposes Dualism and its other source of power (evil) – orthodoxy also presupposes that the one occupies a higher ontological position than the many, that transcendence takes precedence over immanence. What I call radical (or heretical) monism demands unity of one and many on the level of immanence: hence it is seen by orthodoxy as a turning-upside-down, or saturnalia, which proposes that every one is equally divine. Radical monism is "on the side of" the many – which explains why it seems to lie at the heart of pagan polytheism and shamanism, as well as extreme forms of monotheism such as Ismailism or Ranterism, based on "inner light" teachings. "All is one", therefore, can be spoken by any kind of monist of anti-dualist and can mean many different things.

11 A proposal: the new theory of Taoist dialectics. Think of the yin/yang disk, with a spot of black in the white lozenge, and vice versa – separated not by a straight line but an s-curve. Amiri Baraka says that dialectics is just "separating out the good from the bad" – but the Taoist is "beyond good and evil." The dialectic is supple, but the Taoist dialectic is downright sinuous. For example, making use of the Taoist dialectic, we can reevaluate Gnosis once again. True, it presents a negative view of the body and of becoming. But also true that it has played the role of the eternal rebel against all orthodoxy, and this makes it interesting. In its libertine and revolutionary manifestations, the Gnosis possesses many secrets, some of which are actually worth knowing. The organizational forms of Gnosis – the crackpot cult, the secret society – seem pregnant with possibilities for the TAZ/Immediatist project. Of course, as I've pointed out elsewhere, not all Gnosis is dualistic. There also exists a monist Gnostic tradition, which sometimes borrows-heavily from Dualism and its often confused with it. Monist Gnosis is anti-eschatological, using religious language to describe this world, not Heaven or the Gnosis Pleroma. Shamanism, certain "crazy" forms of Taoism and Tantra and Zen, heterodox sutism and Ismailism. Christian antimonians such as the Ranters, etc. – share a conviction of the holiness of the "inner spirit", and of the actually real, the world. These are our spiritual ancestors.

Part III

Living in the Immaterial World

Digital culture promotes a utopia made possible by technology. Pick up any newspaper, magazine, or turn on a television, and you will see endless advertisements and news items suggesting that the latest digital phone, palm computer, minidisk player, or chip-implanted credit card will increase productivity, enliven leisure time, and enhance communication. Unlike prior utopias, this vision of the future is not the product of human idealism or insight. With the purchase of the appropriate products and services, a utopian existence will come from a multinational corporation. This vision isn't so new, really. Throughout history, business interests have cloaked their agendas in a rhetoric of social betterment and scientific innovation. General Electric's familiar "better living through technology" mantra of the 1950s was really just another way of focusing consumer attention on the added convenience of electric frying pans, blenders, dishwashers, and away from such technological by-products as environmental pollution and the mechanization of everyday life.

So, what is new about the digital Erewhon, if anything? Many would argue that it differs from prior utopias in the way it extends individual subjectivity, social relations, and institutional power into increasingly ephemeral and elusive dimensions. As people spend more and more time with their telephones, televisions, and computers, the physicality of experience diminishes. This has specific consequences for the world of commerce, where the production and sale of goods and services increasingly moves from the material to the immaterial. Computers and digital networks have created enormous new markets for Internet providers, software developers, Web designers, and e-commerce entrepreneurs – to name but a few. In this environment, new currencies emerge relating to speed, access, and privacy. How fast or how long a connection can one afford? How much software or computer is needed to make this possible? Where, when, and at what price can one access information? At how many points are ones' choices monitored, recorded, and sold?

Proponents of cybercommerce argue that the powerful wave of digital technology that has created so many millionaires in Silicon Valley will revolutionize life as we know it. Witness the seemingly endless production of essays and books by corporate CEOs masquerading as social visionaries. Driven by the mania of blazing Internet connections and spiraling stock prices, a seemingly unstoppable popular movement is gaining momentum. Appropriating a 1960s language of "freedom" and "equality," cyberenthusiasts rhapsodize over the pending global saturation of that Internet, as personal choice and expression become identified more with consumption than with voting. During the last decade the number of hosts (computers with direct access to the Internet) rose to 36 million, as the number of Internet users worldwide grew to 200 million. As dramatic as this sounds, it is important to recognize that Internet users represent less than four percent of the world's 6 billion people. Even as the digerati celebrate the growth of cyberspace, the fact remains that it is a far from ubiquitous medium. On many levels the vast expansion of information technology has created what the US Commerce Department has termed a "digital divide." Reports indicate that households with incomes under $25,000 were 20 times less likely to have Internet access than those with higher incomes, and people with little education were 25 percent less likely to be netizens than college graduates.

While occasionally acknowledging that the Internet replicates existing relations of commerce and identity, popular spokespeople for the electronic frontier generally overlook the self-serving character of cyberspace, as well as the way non-virtual space in the "real" world continues to define who people are and what they can do. Consolidation of commercial and residential capital into such technology-rich centers as Boston, Silicon Valley, and Seattle continues, while simultaneously producing growing transient or ghettoized populations in less fortunate regions or in the nations of the developing world that produce the majority of the world's silicon chips.

Awareness of these issues has prompted a growing body of critical literature, key examples of which are reproduced in this section. Essays by Stanley Aronowitz, Arthur Kroker, Michael A. Weinstein, and Shoshana Zuboff address the often-problematic ways that digital culture is reshaping labor, capital, and social class. The international dimensions of this transformation are discussed in contributions by Manuel Castells, the Critical Art Ensemble, and Herbert Schiller. Taken together, these selections offer a sobering note of caution in a digital culture overrun with entrepreneurial ebullience. In the prescient words of Andy Warhol, "Buying is more fun than thinking."

13

Dilemmas of Transformation in the Age of the Smart Machine

Shoshana Zuboff

Shoshana Zuboff, excerpt from "Dilemmas of Transformation in the Age of the Smart Machine," from *In The Age of the Smart Machine: The Future of Work and Power* (New York: Basic Books, 1988), pp. 3–12. Copyright © 1988 by Basic Books, Inc. Reprinted by permission of Basic Books, a member of Perseus Books, L.L.C.

Shoshana Zuboff is a professor in the Harvard Business School, whose 1988 landmark *In the Age of the Smart Machine: The Future of Work and Power* remains one of the most complete and important books on how computer technology fundamentally alters relations of labor and capital. This selection is drawn from the opening section of that classic book.

> The history of technology is that of human history in all its diversity. That is why specialist historians of technology hardly ever manage to grasp it entirely in their hands.
>
> – Fernand Braudel
> *The Structures of Everyday Life*

> We don't know what will be happening to us in the future. Modern technology is taking over. What will be our place?
>
> – A Piney Wood worker

Piney Wood, one of the nation's largest pulp mills, was in the throes of a massive modernization effort that would place every aspect of the production process under computer control. Six workers were crowded around a table in the snack area outside what they called the Star Trek Suite, one of the first control rooms to have been completely converted to microprocessor-based instrumentation. It looked enough like a NASA control room to have earned its name.

It was almost midnight, but despite the late hour and the approach of the shift change, each of the six workers was at once animated and thoughtful. "Knowledge and technology are changing so fast," they said, "what will happen to us?" Their visions of the future foresaw wrenching change. They feared that today's working assumptions could not be relied upon to carry them through, that the future would not resemble the past or the present. More frightening still was the sense of a future moving out of reach so rapidly that there was little opportunity to plan or make choices. The speed of dissolution and renovation seemed to leave no time for assurances that we were not heading toward calamity – and it would be all the more regrettable for having been something of an accident.

The discussion around the table betrayed a grudging admiration for the new technology – its power, its intelligence, and the aura of progress surrounding it. That admiration, however, bore a sense of grief. Each expression of gee-whiz-Buck-Rogers breathless wonder brought with it an aching dread conveyed in images of a future that rendered their authors obsolete. In what ways would computer technology transform their work lives? Did it promise the Big Rock Candy Mountain or a silent graveyard?

> In fifteen years there will be nothing for the workers to do. The technology will be so good it will operate itself. You will just sit there behind a desk running two or three areas of the mill yourself and get bored.

The group concluded that the worker of the future would need "an extremely flexible personality" so that he or she would not be "mentally affected" by the velocity of change. They anticipated that workers would need a great deal of education and training in order to "breed flexibility." "We find it all to be a great stress," they said, "but it won't be that way for the new flexible people." Nor did they perceive any real choice, for most agreed that without an investment in the new technology, the company could not remain competitive. They also knew that without their additional flexibility, the technology would not fly right. "We are in a bind," one man groaned, "and there is no way out." The most they could do, it was agreed, was to avoid thinking too hard about the loss of overtime pay, the diminished probability of jobs for their sons and daughters, the fears of seeming incompetent in a strange new milieu, or the possibility that the company might welsh on its promise not to lay off workers.

During the conversation, a woman in stained overalls had remained silent with her head bowed, apparently lost in thought. Suddenly, she raised her face to us. It was lined with decades of hard work, her brow drawn together. Her hands lay quietly on the table. They were calloused and swollen, but her deep brown eyes were luminous, youthful, and kind. She seemed frozen, chilled by her own insight, as she solemnly delivered her conclusion:

> I think the country has a problem. The managers want everything to be run by computers. But if no one has a job, no one will know how to do anything anymore. Who will pay the taxes? What kind of society will it be when people have lost their knowledge and depend on computers for everything?

Her voice trailed off as the men stared at her in dazzled silence. They slowly turned their heads to look at one another and nodded in agreement. The forecast seemed true enough. Yes, there was a problem. They looked as though they had just run a hard race, only to stop short at the edge of a cliff. As their heels skidded in the dirt, they could see nothing ahead but a steep drop downward.

Must it be so? Should the advent of the smart machine be taken as an invitation to relax the demands upon human comprehension and critical judgment? Does the massive diffusion of computer technology throughout our workplaces necessarily entail an equally dramatic loss of meaningful employment opportunities? Must the new electronic milieu engender a world in which individuals have lost control over their daily work lives? Do these visions of the future represent the price of economic success or might they signal an industrial legacy that must be overcome if intelligent technology is to yield its full value? Will the new information techno-logy represent an opportunity for the rejuvenation of competitiveness, productive vitality, and organizational ingenuity? Which aspects of the future of working life can we predict, and which will depend upon the choices we make today?

The workers outside the Star Trek Suite knew that the so-called technological choices we face are really much more than that. Their consternation puts us on alert. There is a world to be lost and a world to be gained. Choices that appear to be merely technical will redefine our lives together at work. This means more than simply contemplating the implications or consequences of a new technology. It means that a powerful new technology, such as that represented by the computer, fundamentally reorganizes the infrastructure of our material world. It eliminates former alternatives. It creates new possibilities. It necessitates fresh choices.

The choices that we face concern the conception and distribution of knowledge in the workplace. Imagine the following scenario: Intelligence is lodged in the smart machine at the expense of the human capacity for critical judgment. Organ-izational members become ever more dependent, docile, and secretly cynical. As more tasks must be accomplished through the medium of information technology (I call this "computer-mediated work"), the sentient body loses its salience as a source of knowledge, resulting in profound disorientation and loss of meaning. People intensify their search for avenues of escape through drugs, apathy, or adversarial conflict, as the majority of jobs in our offices and factories become increasingly isolated, remote, routine, and perfunctory. Alternatively, imagine this scenario: Organizational leaders recognize the new forms of skill and knowledge needed to truly exploit the potential of an intelligent technology. They direct their resources toward creating a work force that can exercise critical judgment as it manages the surrounding machine systems. Work becomes more abstract as it depends upon understanding and manipulating information. This marks the beginning of new forms of mastery and provides an opportunity to imbue jobs with more comprehensive meaning. A new array of work tasks offer unprecedented opportunities for a wide range of employees to add value to products and services.

The choices that we make will shape relations of authority in the workplace. Once more, imagine: Managers struggle to retain their traditional sources of authority, which have depended in an important way upon their exclusive control of the organization's knowledge base. They use the new technology to structure organizational experience in ways that help reproduce the legitimacy of their traditional roles. Managers insist on the prerogatives of command and seek methods that protect the hierarchical distance that distinguishes them from their subordinates. Employees barred from the new forms of mastery relinquish their sense of responsibility for the organization's work and use obedience to authority as a means of expressing their resentment. Imagine an alternative: This technological transformation engenders a new approach to organizational behavior, one in which relationships are more intricate, collaborative, and bound by the mutual responsibilities of colleagues. As the new technology integrates information across time and space, managers and workers each overcome their narrow functional perspectives and create new roles that are better suited to enhancing value-adding activities in a data-rich environment. As the quality of skills at each organizational level becomes similar, hierarchical distinctions begin to blur. Authority comes to depend more upon an appropriate fit between knowledge and responsibility than upon the ranking rules of the traditional organizational pyramid.

The choices that we make will determine the techniques of administration that color the psychological ambience and shape communicative behavior in the emerging workplace. Imagine this scenario: The new technology becomes the source of surveillance techniques that are used to ensnare organizational members or to subtly bully them into conformity. Managers employ the technology to circumvent the demanding work of face-to-face engagement, substituting instead techniques of remote management and automated administration. The new technological infrastructure becomes a battlefield of techniques, with managers inventing novel ways to enhance certainty and control while employees discover new methods of self-protection and even sabotage. Imagine the alternative: The new technological milieu becomes a resource from which are fashioned innovative methods of information sharing and social exchange. These methods in turn produce a deepened sense of collective responsibility and joint ownership, as access to ever-broader domains of information lend new objectivity to data and preempt the dictates of hierarchical authority.

This book is about these alternative futures. Computer-based technologies are not neutral; they embody essential characteristics that are bound to alter the nature of work within our factories and offices, and among workers, professionals, and managers. New choices are laid open by these technologies, and these choices are being confronted in the daily lives of men and women across the landscape of modern organizations. This book is an effort to understand the deep structure of these choices – the historical, psychological, and organizational forces that imbue our conduct and sensibility. It is also a vision of a fruitful future, a call for action that can lead us beyond the stale reproduction of the past into an era that offers a historic opportunity to more fully develop the economic and human potential of our work organizations.

The Two Faces of Intelligent Technology

The past twenty years have seen their share of soothsayers ready to predict with conviction one extreme or another of the alternative futures I have presented. From the unmanned factory to the automated cockpit, visions of the future hail information technology as the final answer to "the labor question," the ultimate opportunity to rid ourselves of the thorny problems associated with training and managing a competent and committed work force. These very same technologies have been applauded as the hallmark of a second industrial revolution, in which the classic conflicts of knowledge and power associated with an earlier age will be synthesized in an array of organizational innovations and new procedures for the production of goods and services, all characterized by an unprecedented degree of labor harmony and widespread participation in management process.[1] Why the paradox? How can the very same technologies be interpreted in these different ways? Is this evidence that the technology is indeed neutral, a blank screen upon which managers project their biases and encounter only their own limitations? Alternatively, might it tell us something else about the interior structure of information technology?

Throughout history, humans have designed mechanisms to reproduce and extend the capacity of the human body as an instrument of work. The industrial age has carried this principle to a dramatic new level of sophistication with machines that can substitute for and amplify the abilities of the human body. Because machines are mute, and because they are precise and repetitive, they can be controlled according to a set of rational principles in a way that human bodies cannot.

There is no doubt that information technology can provide substitutes for the human body that reach an even greater degree of certainty and precision. When a task is automated by a computer, it must first be broken down to its smallest components. Whether the activity involves spraying paint on an automobile or performing a clerical transaction, it is the information contained in this analysis that translates human agency into a computer program. The resulting software can be used to automatically guide equipment, as in the case of a robot, or to execute an information transaction, as in the case of an automated teller machine.

A computer program makes it possible to rationalize activities more comprehensively than if they had been undertaken by a human being. Programmability means, for example, that a robot will respond with unwavering precision because the instructions that guide it are themselves unvarying, or that office transactions will be uniform because the instructions that guide them have been standardized. Events and processes can be rationalized to the extent that human agency can be analyzed and translated into a computer program.

What is it, then, that distinguishes information technology from earlier generations of machine technology? As information technology is used to reproduce, extend, and improve upon the process of substituting machines for human agency, it simultaneously accomplishes something quite different. The devices that automate by translating information into action also register data about those automated activities, thus generating new streams of information. For example, computer-based, numerically controlled machine tools or microprocessor-based sensing devices not only apply programmed instructions to equipment but also convert the current state of equipment, product, or process into data. Scanner devices in supermarkets automate the checkout process and simultaneously generate data that can be used for inventory control, warehousing, scheduling of deliveries, and market analysis. The same systems that make it possible to automate office transactions also create a vast overview of an organization's operations, with many levels of data coordinated and accessible for a variety of analytical efforts.

Thus, information technology, even when it is applied to automatically reproduce a finite activity, is not mute. It not only imposes information (in the form of programmed instructions) but also produces information. It both accomplishes tasks and translates them into information. The action of a machine is entirely invested in its object, the product. Information technology, on the other hand, introduces an additional dimension of reflexivity: it makes its contribution to the product, but it also reflects back on its activities and on the system of activities to which it is related. Information technology not only produces action but also produces a voice that symbolically renders events, objects, and processes so that they become visible, knowable, and shareable in a new way.

Viewed from this interior perspective, information technology is characterized by a fundamental duality that has not yet been fully appreciated. On the one hand, the technology can be applied to automating operations according to a logic that hardly differs from that of the nineteenth-century machine system – replace the human body with a technology that enables the same processes to be performed with more continuity and control. On the other, the same technology simultaneously generates information about the underlying productive and administrative processes through which an organization accomplishes its work. It provides a deeper level of transparency to activities that had been either partially or completely opaque. In this way information technology supersedes the traditional logic of automation. The word that I have coined to describe this unique capacity is *informate*. Activities, events, and objects are translated into and made visible by information when a technology *informates* as well as *automates*.

The informating power of intelligent technology can be seen in the manufacturing environment when microprocessor-based devices such as robots, programmable logic controllers, or sensors are used to translate the three-dimensional production process into digitized data. These data are then made available within a two-dimensional space, typically on the screen of a video display terminal or on a computer printout, in the form of electronic symbols, numbers, letters, and graphics. These data constitute a quality of information that did not exist before. The programmable controller not only tells the machine what to do – imposing information that guides operating equipment – but also tells what the machine has done – translating the production process and making it visible.

In the office environment, the combination of on-line transaction systems, information systems, and communications systems creates a vast information presence that now includes data formerly stored in people's heads, in face-to-face conversations, in metal file drawers, and on widely dispersed pieces of paper. The same technology that processes documents more rapidly, and with less intervention, than a mechanical typewriter or pen and ink can be used to display those documents in a communications network. As more of the underlying transactional and communicative processes of an organization become automated, they too become available as items in a growing organizational data base.

In its capacity as an automating technology, information technology has a vast potential to displace the human presence. Its implications as an informating technology, on the other hand, are not well understood. The distinction between *automate* and *informate* provides one way to understand how this technology represents both continuities and discontinuities with the traditions of industrial history. As long as the technology is treated narrowly in its automating function, it perpetuates the logic of the industrial machine that, over the course of this century, has made it possible to rationalize work while decreasing the dependence on human skills. However, when the technology also informates the processes to which it is applied, it increases the explicit information content of tasks and sets into motion a series of dynamics that will ultimately reconfigure the nature of work and the social relationships that organize productive activity.

Because this duality of intelligent technology has not been clearly recognized, the consequences of the technology's informating capacity are often regarded as unintended. Its effects are not planned, and the potential that it lays open remains relatively unexploited. Because the informating process is poorly defined, it often evades the conventional categories of description that are used to gauge the effects of industrial technology.

These dual capacities of information technology are not opposites; they are hierarchically integrated. Informating derives from and builds upon automation. Automation is a necessary but not sufficient condition for informating. It is quite possible to proceed with automation without reference to how it will contribute to the technology's informating potential. When this occurs, informating is experienced as an unintended consequence of automation. This is one point at which choices are laid open. Managers can choose to exploit the emergent informating capacity and explore the organizational innovations required to sustain and develop it. Alternatively, they can choose to ignore or suppress the informating process. In contrast, it is possible to consider informating objectives at the start of an automation process. When this occurs, the choices that are made with respect to how and what to automate are guided by criteria that reflect developmental goals associated with using the technology's unique informating power.

Information technology is frequently hailed as "revolutionary." What are the implications of this term? *Revolution* means a pervasive, marked, radical change, but *revolution* also refers to a movement around a fixed course that returns to the starting point. Each sense of the word has relevance for the central problem of this book. The informating capacity of the new computer-based technologies brings about radical change as it alters the intrinsic character of work – the way millions of people experience daily life on the job. It also poses fundamentally new choices for our organizational futures, and the ways in which labor and management respond to these new choices will finally determine whether our era becomes a time for radical change or a return to the familiar patterns and pitfalls of the traditional workplace. An emphasis on the informating capacity of intelligent technology can provide a point of origin for new conceptions of work and power. A more restricted emphasis on its automating capacity can provide the occasion for that second kind of revolution – a return to the familiar grounds of industrial society with divergent interests battling for control, augmented by an array of new material resources with which to attack and defend.

The questions that we face today are finally about leadership. Will there be leaders who are able to recognize the historical moment and the choices it presents? Will they find ways to create the organizational conditions in which new visions, new concepts, and a new language of workplace relations can emerge? Will they be able to create organizational innovations that can exploit the unique capacities of the new technology and thus mobilize their organization's productive potential to meet the heightened rigors of global competition? Will there be leaders who understand the crucial role that human beings from each organizational stratum can play in adding value to the production of goods and services? If not, we will be stranded in a new world with old solutions. We will suffer through the unintended consequences of change, because we have failed to understand this technology and how it differs from what came before. By neglecting the unique informating capacity of advanced computer-based technology and ignoring the need for a new vision of work and organization, we will have forfeited the dramatic business benefits it can provide. Instead, we will find ways to absorb the dysfunctions, putting out brush fires and patching wounds in a slow-burning bewilderment.

Note

1   See, for example, Michael Piore and Charles F. Sabel, *The Second Industrial Divide: Possibilities for Prosperity* (New York: Basic Books, 1984).

14

Technology and the Future of Work

Stanley Aronowitz

Stanley Aronowitz, "Technology and the Future of Work," in Gretchen Bender and Timothy Druckrey, eds., *Culture on the Brink: Ideologies of Technology* (Seattle: Bay Press, 1994), pp. 15–29.

Stanley Aronowitz is a professor of Sociology at the Graduate Center of the City University of New York. He is the author of *Science as Power: Discourse and Ideology in Modern Society* (Minnesota, 1980) and *The Jobless Future: Sci-Tech and the Dogma of Work* (Minnesota, 1995). This essay critiques the belief that technology solves all modern problems, when in fact it exacerbates longstanding inequalities and exploitative labor practices.

No doubt the main ideology of modern technologies is that *virtually* all of our problems – ethical, economic, political – are subject to technical solutions. For example, cybernetics is presented as the genie that, once liberated from the bottle, will possess the powers of an old-time elixir: it can cure virtually any disease (except death) or even change the genetic makeup of the human species, eliminating those characteristics "we" agree are unwanted, and it can solve most economic ills by spurring growth. (Indeed, an American, Robert Solow, won a Nobel Prize in economics for this amazing insight.) If any employer's profits are squeezed by skyrocketing costs, install a computer: watch heads roll and the bottom line soar. A new science, teledildonics, is being born, which may offer virtual sex (at a distance, of course) to the weary hacker – an innovation that, together with cybernetically charged virtual toys, promises to cool us out.

We live in a postcritical period; not only practical but also intellectual luddism seems irreversibly weakened. The merger of the intellect with technology signals the demise of the ancient naysayer. This negative dialectic yields to the power of positive thinking: while philosophers and social critics ask what implications this wraparound technology has for such old metaphysical questions as the integrity of the "self," the celebrants of (take your pick) cyberspace, cyberpunk, virtual reality, hyperreality, and its literary form, hypertexts, refuse the question as a modernist hangover. When not following the poststructuralist Nietzschean mantra about the "death" of the subject of which, in classical Anglo-American philosophy, the self is an outgrowth, the new technophiles gleefully announce that we are totally wired and it is entirely futile to cling to the old formulations of, say, the Frankfurt School, which speak of technological domination of the once autonomous subject.

Apocalyptic ruminations by philosophers and social theorists of the thorough commodification and technicization of social life are refuted but also mirrored by the strategic amnesia of the technophiles. Perhaps we need to comprehend what has occurred in Donna Haraway's openly ironic terms: humans have migrated to cyborg, "a hybrid of machine and organism, a creature of social reality as well as a creature of fiction."[1] Haraway calls our attention to borderlands, not only between reality and fiction and between machine and organism but perhaps more saliently between the biological and the social self which is congealed in our most ubiquitous production: the machine. Far from a happy conjunction, "the relation between organism and machine has been a border war. The stakes in the border war have been the territories of production, reproduction, and imagination."[2]

Whether employed as a powerful instrument in the corporate panopticon or as a way to facilitate the emergence of a democratic workplace in which *techné* signifies the unity of humans and nature rather than a technologically driven split, the machine is indeterminate from the perspective of the internal constitution of the technology. I suggest that many of the widely cited instances in which the introduction of the computer into the professional work formerly performed either by hand (as with engineering) or by conventional oral and printed texts (as with teaching) manage to elide the panopticon of power only by "forgetting" the context within which computer-mediated work is done.

The critique of science and technology that reemerged in the 1950s and 1960s hinged, in the final accounting, on the judgment, most forcefully articulated by the Frankfurt School, that reason under late capitalist conditions had become identical with instrumental rationality, whose basis is the capacity of scientifically based technology to facilitate a new social deal. The key element of the deal was that technology could "deliver the goods" to the underlying population in the West (and possibly elsewhere as well), in return for which culture surrendered its autonomy to the technological imperative. For Max Horkheimer, the new technology that came into existence and provided the material conditions for institutions of massified, electronically mediated culture signified nothing less than the eclipse of reason as a transcendent principle and, accordingly, the end of history. The consequence of technological domination was nothing less than the disappearance of historical agency, if by that term we mean both the will and the capacity of exploited and otherwise excluded social categories to participate in the polity as well as share control of society.

These powerful suggestions partly animated the massive student revolts of the 1960s and the "Third World" revolutions of the postwar era. Although they have outlived their moment of ideological power, they nevertheless retain much more than a marginal existence among important sectors of Western intellectuals to this day. However, in the past twenty years the technoculture that was once received as merely a brilliant and dystopian anticipation in social theory of what Daniel Bell and Alain Touraine would dub "postindustrial" society – a society in which social contradictions give way to conflicts that are subject to technologically based solutions – has become an ineluctable feature of everyday existence (conjoined, undoubtedly, with the ebbing of the most politicized manifestations of the resistance).

Technoculture has its prophets as well as its critics; like all other cultural spheres – education, sexuality, sports, art – technoculture realigns the discursive combat. One may no longer *derive* a position on the new computer-driven culture from familiar ideological premises. For example, within the new discursive boundaries, it is difficult to discern the differences on the basis of the traditional divisions between Marxists and liberals, since both argue (from different premises, to be sure) that the task of public policy is to free the new scientifically based technologies from the thrall of arcane social arrangements. In turn, critics of the scientific and technological revolution of our time have emerged from both conservative and radical camps, and their elegiac invocations of past civilization are remarkably similar.

Martin Heidegger's subtle questioning of the instrumental view – according to which technology is merely purposive activity subsumed under the characterization "means" – may be taken as a starting point for investigating the various claims concerning the new technologies. Recall that Heidegger brought us back to the Greek origin of the meaning of the term *techné* in order to free technology from its subsumption under instrumental reason. Where modern culture views technology as a regime of powerful tools by which human purposes may be served, particularly the domination of nature, *techné* signifies an uncovering, a way to the truth. Heidegger's point is that *techné* signified human activity itself rather than a "tool" of production and organization. In this reprise nature is not held at a distance as "other" but, as in ancient times, humans are *part of nature*. Thus, contrary to the practices of the past five centuries, nature is not perceived as an inert object. Its immanence includes us.

In contrast to *techné*, by which the object, nature, discloses itself, modern technology is an "ordering revealing," and technology becomes a process by which reality is teleologically enframed. This enframing blocks the truth of the world from "shining forth." In this regime, the world stands "in reserve" of human purpose, and it loses its own essence, at least provisionally. Of course, Heidegger's project is to restore to nature an autonomous existence from which *techné* then receives its rationale. The instrumental view, according to which technology is a means, does not, thereby, lose its power even if we restore *techné*; the history of the last twenty-five hundred years is irreversible. Rather, instrumental action becomes a local activity subordinate to its meaning as a way of revealing the being-of-the-world.

We can discern in Heidegger's discourse a not-too-veiled attack on the position of the Frankfurt School and other critics of modern technology. Against those for whom technology has *become* culture in late industrial societies, to the detriment of the autonomy of thought and being, Heidegger – despite his acknowledgement of the force of this critical view – wants to reconcile modern technology with culture by reviving the former's status as an end that extends beyond the category of domination. Echoing the early Marxist lament – that as machinery rendered human labor increasingly productive, labor is less able to control not only its product but also the process of labor – the Frankfurt School attempted to show that this dialectic strengthened domination. Specifically, to the extent that technological development signified the enlargement of human mastery over nature, it also created new mechanisms for human domination. However, by the mid-sixties, Herbert Marcuse had become ambivalent about this judgment. He returned to Marx's last meditation on technology, which saw technology's most subversive effect in its tendency to "liberate" labor from the production process. Automation would free labor for creative activity, some of which would be devoted to further reducing necessary labor.

Technoculture is a discourse of the identity of technology and culture. As we have seen, in its most sweeping expression, the cyborg, the distinction between humans and nature is called into question. While the organism and the machine may be historically, even analytically separate, Haraway's invocation of the metaphor of the border is only one version of a much larger movement in philosophy and culture theory. Thirty years ago, Louis Althusser's interrogation of the doctrine of humanism demonstrated the historicity of the pristine concept of "man." Invoking the figure of Spinoza, Gilles Deleuze's work seeks to free philosophy and culture theory from its idealist remnants, which, like Althusser, he finds in the Hegelian legacy. Deleuze has restored Spinoza's doctrine, which sunders the separation of spirit from "dead" matter in favor of immanence: all there is the material world.

From this doctrine follows the materialist refusal of the Frankenstein/golem imagery invoked by technology's humanist critics. No longer critical, it accepts, even celebrates, computer-mediated technology as liberating. For example, in this postcritical technology we are informed of the wonders of cyberspace, where overworked professionals can play therapy against stress with innovations such as virtual reality. In cyberspace the old-fashioned "pressing of the flesh" yields to what Howard Rheingold calls teledildonics:

> The first fully functional teledildonics system will be a communication device, not a sex machine. You probably will not use erotic telepresence technology in order to have sexual experiences with machines. Thirty years from now, when portable tele-diddlers become ubiquitous, most people will use them to have sexual experiences with other people, at a distance, in combinations and configurations undreamed of by pre-cybernetic voluptuaries. Through a marriage of virtual reality technology and telecommunication networks, you will be able to reach out and touch someone – or an entire population – in ways humans have never before experienced. Or so the scenario goes.[3]

Rheingold tells us that "You can reach out your virtual hand, pick up a virtual block, and by running your fingers over the object, feel the virtual surfaces and edges, by means of the effectors that exert counterforces against your skin."[4]

But, of course, the use of cybernetics for play or for producing nonlinear texts (hypertexts) are only a few of the uses of this technology. Equally, if not more to the point, cybernetics has revolutionized the workplace, biological science, and so on; it presents a whole new set of medical problems as well as possibilities.

Ironically, economic discourse has almost entirely disappeared from technophilic rhetorics. For those who herald cyberspace as the fulfillment of *homo ludens*, as the new sphere of the playful intellect, the disappearance of *homo faber* is considered an accomplished fact; postwork is taken as a given of the contemporary world. In the bargain, celebrates of the new technological revolution engage in massive historical amnesia or, worse, have chosen to refrain from commentary on the major practical consequence of cybernetics: the destruction of labor. It might be said here that those who would refuse to speak of this massively central function of the scientific-technological revolution should also keep silent about its playful aspects.

Put simply, cybernetics is the means by which labor is more and more removed from the industrial, commercial, and professional workplace. Its major function in our culture is to institutionalize unwork. Its effect is to raise the question "Why work?" in ways that were once part of the utopian discourse of technophiles.

Computer-Aided Design and Drafting (CADD), for example, has *virtually* eliminated the drafter in, and radically changed the character of, engineering. The articulation, by means of a computer, of design with execution (manufacturing) has increased productivity exponentially, wiped out whole occupations, and transformed the work from its tactile, craft character into a surveillance function.

Throughout the modern epoch, proponents of the scientific enlightenment have taken the position that the "idyllic" relations of precapitalist societies were impossibly repressive to the human spirit, and that capitalism, the evils of exploitation notwithstanding, had its one redeeming feature in the will to change the world – led by scientific and technological transformations. However, it is not excessive to argue that the computer, even more than its anterior concomitants (for example, steam power and electricity), provides an even more persuasive case for the claim, espoused by the newest technophiles, that finally, after nearly three centuries of rationalization, we can now envision the reintegration not only of work but also of humans with nature and with their own species. For some, these are not merely hyperbolic pronouncements, but practical opportunities for ending the estrangement of humans from their worlds. For, in its most visionary form, computer-driven technoculture claims to fulfill the dream of the "whole" person in the first place by healing the rupture between intellectual and manual labor. Technological utopians no longer see science and technology primarily within a discourse of social justice – namely, the freeing of labor from routine and back-breaking labor in order to free subjective time.

In the old design era, most of the architect's and engineer's time was taken up by making and remaking drawings and performing mathematical calculations. The three-dimensional graphics program and the math menu inscribed in CADD have drastically reduced the proportion of time spent on routines of drawing and calculating compared to actual design work in the activities of the engineer and architect. The consequences are already apparent. In the last five years, roughly the period of widespread introduction to CADD, hiring in civil, mechanical, and electrical engineering is confined to replacing some employees, but by no means on a one-to-one basis. Moreover, in civil engineering, owing to the broad perception that roads and bridges are seriously dilapidated, there has been a dramatic increase in public spending in construction and repair of these and other facilities.

But there has been no net increase of design jobs because these employees are now more productive. Similarly, those who herald technoculture as the fulfillment of the next and perhaps final frontier of human striving call on us not to mourn the passing of the old culture – if indeed a culture not intimately linked to technology ever existed – or to celebrate a new cornucopia of leisure; they call on us, rather, to take a new ground of social existence. At last, according to some, the full development of the individual is possible, because we have finally objectified both our physical and mental capacities in a machine.

Technoculture plays with the distinction, made first by the Greeks, between work and labor. Some have argued that, in contrast to the era of mechnical reproduction, computer-mediated work eliminates most of the repetitive tasks associated with Taylorism and Fordism, that this "smart machine" can interact with human intelligence as a playmate – hence the use of chess as a test of the possibilities of artificial intelligence. Chess is the ultimate criterion in that, even if a computer cannot exceed the boundaries established by its maker, it can nevertheless provide a mirror for our intelligence. Thus, the distinction between work and play that had characterized our collective preoccupation with scarcity throughout history is sundered: for the first time, work and play are identical for occupations beyond those of artists and scientists. To borrow a term from Alfred Whitehead, technology not only "ingresses" into events, but also has become an event that leaves virtually nothing untouched. It is not a worldview in the traditional sense; instead, it is the ingredient without which contemporary culture – work, art, science, and education, indeed the entire range of interactions – is unthinkable. So it is futile and even deeply conservative to rail against the technological revolution. The only remaining questions are associated with how to free technology from the thrall of the organization of labor, education, and play according to the canons of industrial society. In what follows, I will make some preliminary efforts to answer these questions.

Thirty-five years ago, business and labor leaders proclaimed the "automation" revolution, an event signaled by the introduction of the transfer machine into auto-assembly plants. In 1955, during a much publicized appearance at the General Motors Cleveland engine plant where the machine had recently been installed, GM CEO Charles E. Wilson, envisioning the fully automatic plant, is said to have asked United Auto Workers president Walter Reuther, "Who's going to pay union dues?" – to which Reuther shot back, "Who's going to buy your cars?" Now, the transfer machine was merely an electronically controlled assembly line: where thousands of workers formerly installed parts by hand (or by hand held electric tools), these operations were now performed by the machine itself. Early transfer machines simply applied to production the feedback mechanism of the thermostat, which by the mid fifties was already used in oil-, chemical-, and food-processing industries. And the machine weirdly bore a physical resemblance to human arms and hands – the prototype for which was already exhibited in that famous scene in *Modern Times*, in which Charlie is hooked up to an automatic feeding device that keeps his hands free to work while he eats lunch. The transfer machine's arms and hands are skeletonlike, bereft of flesh, but electric power multiplies the motive power once provided by muscle. In this regime of production, human labor is made ancillary to the machine and is absolutely needed only to repair it during its infrequent breakdowns.

Although the techniques of early automation were relatively elementary, at least in comparison to contemporary cybernetic practices, the fundamental purpose for its introduction into the workplace was crystal clear; later discourses about computerization, on the other hand, obscured the economic implications of computers. At the dawn of the latest technological revolution, most of those who were either its perpetrators or its objects understood what was at stake: to liberate labor from repetitive tasks and to enlarge profit margins by reducing the most expensive cost in production – manual labor. Recall the extent of unionization in the basic production industries at the end of the war: it was a historic development that established high wage and benefits levels.

On the eve of the Vietnam War, the recovering economies of Japan and Europe were already challenging, with higher technologies, U.S. industry to either modernize or close shop. However, the decade during which war industry-generated profits rolled in postponed the inevitable: when the United States turned its attention to civilian production in the 1970s, whether too late or not, U.S. corporations seemed to lack the will to take decisive steps to save the steel, rubber, electrical machinery, and a dozen other industries; the federal government was already in the thrall of an anti-interventionist ideology that paralyzed it even as dozens of key industrial plants closed down.

Yet, dire predictions of the decline and fall of U.S. world economic hegemony proved premature. Global capitalism, still largely based in the United States, where national boundaries are no longer – or never were – sacrosanct, produced a parallel industrial regime in the global assembly line. An "American-made" automobile is likely to contain a Japanese fuel pump, a Mexican exhaust system, and Malaysian windshield wipers, or to have been assembled in Japan or Korea. The only thing "American" about many Chryslers, for example, is the name. This describes a change, the abstract name for which is the "new international division of labor."

In the 1970s U.S.-based corporations went global, sacrificing in the process huge chunks of the domestic heavy- and light-production industries. Except for truck and aircraft manufacturers, the mass-transportation equipment industry virtually disappeared as U.S. competitiveness in shipbuilding and rail cars flagged. Japanese, German, and Italian steel was routinely imported into the United States, because the domestic steel corporations resolutely refused to modernize after the 1950s, specifically rejecting computer-driven basic ingot production processes. As late as 1980, most remaining U.S. auto-parts plants were ensconced in 1920s technology, even as overseas competitors had already introduced the major computer-mediated technologies of numerical controls, robotics, and lasers – all of which were developed in U.S. laboratories but were applied only in limited ways to U.S. production industries, notably the manufacture of aircraft engines.

Curiously, in this culture that has privileged practical applications over fundamental research, the United States still retains its lead in fundamental computer-hardware components, particularly in the very crucial memory chips, partially due to massive government funding of defense-related research and development activities in the 1950s and 1960s. And U.S. entrepreneurs still dominate the computer software field, although Japan and certain European countries, particularly Italy, are beginning to catch up.

Technoculture emerges from the ruins of the old mechanical-industrial culture. From the perspective of the industrial worker, whether in the factory or in the office, the second phase of automatic production – computerization – is merely a wrinkle of disempowerment. There are no exciting new skills needed to operate the console that controls a robot; only a small fraction of people get to program the numerical controls box perched atop the lathe, and to operate lasers, for example, requires no special technical training. Similarly, much clerical labor has been transformed by the computer. The typewriter is still employed in some smaller firms, but the personal computer has all but driven it from large offices. The computer is more versatile as a word processor than its ancestor, and its computational capacities exceed those of even the most advanced mechanical accounting devices. But while the typist gives way to the word-processing operator, and the skills menu required by the new machine varies and is, perhaps, marginally richer than the older one, the operators of the most complex electronically driven and computer-controlled technologies follow routine instructions. Moreover, after two decades of the computerized office, we have already discovered its dark side: for those who perform word processing, work can be dangerous to their health. Compounding widespread diseases of muscle and bone such as tendonitis and the more egregious Carpal Tunnel Syndrome and Repetitive Movement Disorder, which cripples arms and hands, some investigators have found that the incidence of birth defects among pregnant word-processing operators has multiplied beyond the statistical average for the general population.

There is no "culture" here, just a faster line. For office workers, the computerized workplace has tended to eliminate the amenities of socialized labor. Back-office workers in large commercial banks interact with their video display terminals (VDTs) more than with other human beings. VDT operators sit in individual carrels typing nothing but disembodied numbers all day. Naturally, this numbingly boring work causes enormous turnover among VDT operators.

In the large steel, machine, and metalworking plants that have been broadly computerized, there are fewer workers on the floor – a sometimes eerie experience for anyone of the older generation who remembers the camaraderie of the age of mechanical reproduction. The Marxist take on this – that the old factory was a prison, that the job dulled the mind and wore out the body – is true, but it wasn't lonely; and whether you had a diploma or not, you felt your power, because production literally depended on what Marx called "cooperative" labor. One need not invoke a sense of nostalgia for the preautomated assembly line to recognize some of its ambiguous virtues.

However, the worker is no longer the subject of production in the new technoculture because this technology is not rooted in the grand narratives of skilled and unskilled manual work, even as its function in the workplace (including in clerical work) is absolutely central. Even if these narratives were purposively sundered by the division of labor, they depended upon the great metaphor of man's conquest of nature through the coordination of head and hand. In the regime of industrial capitalism, the "whole" producer was divided (presumably in the interest of efficiency) and reunited by the function of management, now legitimated as a property of capital. The socialist project consisted largely of the promise to restore to the producer not so much the full product of his or her labor as self-management. Now, though, the function of direction would be shared by the direct producers, who might assign the coordinating tasks formerly ascribed to management as to any other task in the labor process, holding neither special privilege nor powers. At the same time, they would no longer be in the thrall of a division of labor in which what was called "intellectual" was sharply demarcated from what was called "manual." So even if "craft," the concept of which is identical with the unity of design and execution, no longer described the heart of the labor process, the formation of the detail laborer under capitalism – which also signified relations of power and powerlessness – would, under the new socialism, no longer be a signifier of social power; rather, it would become merely a technical description of certain functions within the labor process.

In the past twenty-five years, computer-mediated work has been employed, typically but not exclusively, in a manner that reproduces the hierarchies of managerial authority. The division between intellectual and manual labor, and the degradation of manual labor that characterized the industrializing era have been maintained, despite the integrative possibilities of the technology itself. But those who advocate it as the embodiment of the restoration of true profession or craft argue that its uses must be separated from its intrinsic character, and that it is in the interest neither of society nor of corporations to mechanically transpose the organization of work, perhaps appropriate in the industrializing era, to the new computerized workplace. On the contrary: some insist that computer-mediated work could provide unprecedented opportunities for the full development of the worker's knowledge and authority over the labor process.

On the other hand, the computer provides the basis for greatly extending the system of discipline and control inherited from nineteenth-century capitalism. Many corporations have used it to extend their panoptic worldview, which is to say, they have deployed the computer as a means of employee surveillance that far exceeds the most imperious dreams of the panopticon's inventor Jeremy Bentham, or those of any other nineteenth- or early twentieth-century capitalist.

Shoshana Zuboff, among others, insists that the computer invests communication with a new dimension by creating a richer social text, enabling people to communicate for all kinds of purposes – especially those of knowledge-sharing – to a degree that is impossible with either face-to-face interaction or print.[5] Conferencing, a technique made possible by computers, permits people in widely separate places to talk to each other by creating texts. The newspaper, the magazine, and the book occupy different temporal orders from those of the ordinary workplace, in which minutes and hours rather than days, weeks, and months are the primary unit.

However, Zuboff's most important claim for the computer – that it can facilitate more communications, and particularly make for shared decision making between the higher managerial echelons and subordinates – remains a hypothesis. Her studies of the industrial uses of the computer demonstrate the reverse, that Bentham's panopticon still marks the worldview of the managers. The opportunities for improved communications among peers are indeed greatly enhanced by the computer, because, logically enough, peers do not take the electronic text as a command; yet she reports that one manager was mortified by the rapidity with which a suggestion communicated via computer to subordinates was received as an order. This response is, of course, conditioned by the hierarchical regime of power in the corporate workplace.

It may be concluded that the computer is janus-faced, and that it mirrors its masters, the plural indicating merely a fissure among those who developed it. Although the idea of automatic production was already part of the lore of high industrial capitalism, the self-activating loom was seen as a more practical, business-oriented application of automation than was the calculator. Latter-day Babbages, though employed by corporations that have subsumed this invention under capital's requirements, retain the utopian – anarchist, even – impulse that infuses every effort to integrate design with execution, to finally abolish the socially constructed gulf between intellectual and manual labor.

With the introduction of cybernetics into a myriad of workplaces, the outlines of a new era of paid work have already come to the surface. A recent report by the International Labour Office, a United Nations agency, estimates world unemployment at more than 800 million. Of course, joblessness may not be attributed, exclusively, to the results of technological innovation. These numbers reflect vast underemployment of most of the world, which is still locked in agriculture; the worldwide glut of goods that resulted in mass permanent layoffs in every industrialized country in the early 1990s; and the tremendous growth of the labor force, especially women, owing to rapid urbanization but also to the equally cascading living standards, especially in the United States and Latin America.

Even as we are witnessing the rapid computerization of work, the national state is undergoing vast changes. The vaunted safety-net of welfare-state capitalism is increasingly full of holes, not only in the U.S., where it was never really strong, but also in Western Europe, where once the grand compromise between labor and capital insured cradle-to-grave security in many countries. In the wake of the state's weakness, even as a series of repressive apparatuses, millions are falling through the holes, including a significant segment of the middle class which, no less than manual workers, is experiencing the deleterious effects of computerization.

This leads to the conclusion that the current celebration of the coming of the cyborg, the possibilities of transforming labor into play, the hype about the wonderful world of the electronic superhighway and the vast horizon of the deployment of computers for music, film, and other visual arts must be tempered by the recognition that the *main* use of computers and other cybernetic technologies is to *destroy paid work*. We can rejoice at the possibility that humankind is being liberated from the oppressions of tradition, even of the newly eclipsed mechanical era. These include drudgery, boredom, repetitive mind-numbing operations, and many of the dangers of the old industrial factory. But computerization also entails the passing of a certain type of skill, that associated with the close coordination of feeling and reason, of intuition and calculation. Now the old organic self is subsumed under the cyborg self: we we are wired, simulacra.

It's all very exciting, but is Philip K. Dick's dark vision more plausible than that of the new utopians? Since the great nineteenth-century industrializing era never resolved the daunting problems posed by urbanism, international migration, and the carnage left by out-of-control production, are we heirs to the return of the repressed?

Notes

1   Donna J. Haraway, "A Cyborg Manifesto: Science, Technology, and Socialist-Feminism in the Late Twentieth Century," in *Simians, Cyborgs, and Women: The Reinvention of Nature* (New York: Routledge, 1991), p. 149.
2   Ibid., p. 150.
3   Howard Rheingold, *Virtual Reality: The Revolutionary Technology of Computer-Generated Artificial Worlds – and How It Promises to Transform Society* (New York: Simon & Schuster, 1991), p. 345.
4   Ibid., p. 346.
5   Shoshana Zuboff, *In the Age of the Smart Machine: The Future of Work and Power* (New York: Basic Books, 1988).

15

The Theory of the Virtual Class

Arthur Kroker and Michael A. Weinstein

Arthur Kroker and Michael A. Weinstein collaborated to write *Data Trash: The Theory of Virtual Class* (St. Martin's Press, 1994), from which this selection is excerpted. The book presents a critique of technological utopianism and its creation of a digital elite class. Kroker is a professor of Political Science at Concordia University and the editor of the online journal *C-THEORY*. Weinstein is a professor of Political Philosophy at Purdue University and a photography critic.

Wired Shut

Wired intends to profit from the Internet. And so do a lot of others. "People are going to have to realize that the Net is another medium, and it has to be sponsored commercially and it has to play by the rules of the marketplace," says John Battelle, *Wired*'s 28-year old managing editor. "You're still going to have sponsorship, advertising, the rules of the game, because it's just necessary to make commerce work." "I think that a lot of what some of the original Net god-utopians were thinking," continued Battelle, "is that there was just going to be this sort of huge anarchist, utopian, bliss medium, where there are no rules and everything is just sort of open. That's a great thought, but it's not going to work. And when the Time Warners get on the Net in a hard fashion it's going to be the people who first create the commerce and the environment, like *Wired*, that will be the market leaders."

Andrew Leonard, "Hot-Wired"
The Bay Guardian

The twentieth-century ends with the growth of cyber-authoritarianism, a stridently pro-technotopia movement, particularly in the mass media, typified by an obsession to the point of hysteria with emergent technologies, and with a consistent and very deliberate attempt to shut down, silence, and exclude any perspectives critical of technotopia. Not a wired culture, but a virtual culture that is wired shut: compulsively fixated on digital technology as a source of salvation from the reality of a lonely culture and radical social disconnection from everyday life, and determined to exclude from public debate any perspective that is not a cheerleader for the coming-to-be of the fully realized technological society. The virtual class is populated by would-be astronauts who never got the chance to go to the moon, and they do not easily accept criticism of this new Apollo project for the body telematic.

This is unfortunate since it is less a matter of being pro- or anti-technology, but of developing a critical perspective on the ethics of virtuality. When technology mutates into virtuality, the direction of political debate becomes clarified. If we cannot escape the hard-wiring of (our) bodies into wireless culture, then how can we inscribe primary ethical concerns onto the will to virtuality? How can we turn the virtual horizon in the direction of substantive human values: aesthetic creativity, social solidarity, democratic discourse, and economic justice? To link the relentless drive to cyberspace with ethical concerns is, of course, to give the lie to technological liberalism. To insist, that is, that the coming-to-be of the will to virtuality, and with it the emergence of our doubled fate as either body dumps or hyper-texted bodies, virtualizers or data trash, does not relax the traditional human injunction to give primacy to the ethical ends of the technological purposes we choose (or the will to virtuality that chooses us).

Privileging the question of ethics via virtuality lays bare the impulse to nihilism that is central to the virtual class. For it, the drive to planetary mastery represented by the will to virtuality relegates the ethical suasion to the electronic trashbin. Claiming with monumental hubris to be already beyond good and evil, it assumes perfect equivalency between the will to virtuality and the will to the (virtual) good. If the good is equivalent to the disintegration of experience into cybernetic interactivity or to the disappearance of memory and solitary reflection into massive Sunstations of archived information, then the virtual class is the leading exponent of the era of telematic ethics. Far from having abandoned ethical concerns, the virtual class has patched a coherent, dynamic, and comprehensive system of ethics onto the hard-line processors of the will to virtuality. Against economic justice, the virtual class practices a mixture of predatory capitalism and gung-ho technocratic rationalizations for laying waste to social concerns for employment, with insistent demands for "restructuring economies," "public policies of labor adjustment," and "deficit cutting," all aimed at maximal profitability. Against democratic discourse, the virtual class institutes anew the authoritarian mind, projecting its class interests onto cyberspace from which vantage-point it crushes any and all dissent to the prevailing orthodoxies of technotopia. For the virtual class, politics is about absolute control over intellectual property by means of war-like strategies of communication, control, and command. Against social solidarity, the virtual class promotes a grisly form of raw social materialism, whereby social experience is reduced to its prosthetic after-effects: the body becomes a passive archive to be processed, entertained, and stockpiled by the seduction-apertures of the virtual reality complex. And finally, against aesthetic creativity, the virtual class promotes the value of pattern-maintenance (of its own choosing), whereby human intelligence is reduced to a circulating medium of cybernetic exchange floating in the interfaces of the cultural animation machines. Key to the success of the virtual class is its promotion of a radically diminished vision of human experience and of a disintegrated conception of the human good: for virtualizers, the good is ultimately that which disappears human subjectivity, substituting the war-machine of cyberspace for the data trash of experience. Beyond this, the virtual class can achieve dominance today because its reduced vision of human experience consists of a digital superhighway, a fatal scene of circulation and gridlock, which corresponds to how the late twentieth-century mind likes to see itself. *Reverse nihilism*: not the nihilistic will as projected outwards onto an external object, but the nihilistic will turned inwards, decomposing subjectivity, reducing the self to an object of conscience and body vivisectioning. What does it mean when the body is virtualized without a sustaining ethical vision? Can anyone be strong enough for this? What results is rage against the body: a hatred of existence that can only be satisfied by an abandonment of flesh and subjectivity and, with it, a flight into virtuality. Virtuality without ethics is a primal scene of social suicide: a site of mass cryogenics where bodies are quick-frozen for future resequencing by the archived data networks. The virtual class can be this dynamic because it is already the aftershock of the living dead: body vivisectionists and early (mind) abandoners surfing the Net on a road trip to the virtual Inferno.

"Adapt or You're Toast"

The virtual class has driven to global power along the digital superhighway. Representing perfectly the expansionary interests of the recombinant commodity-form, the virtual class has seized the imagination of contemporary culture by conceiving a techno-utopian high-speed cybernetic grid for travelling across the electronic frontier. In this mythology of the new technological frontier, contemporary society is either equipped for fast travel down the main arterial lanes of the information highway, or it simply ceases to exist as a functioning member of technotopia. As the CEOs and the specialist consultants of the virtual class triumphantly proclaim: "Adapt or you're toast."

We now live in the age of dead information, dead (electronic) space, and dead (cybernetic) rhetoric. *Dead information*? That's our cooptation as servomechanisms of the cybernetic grid (the digital superhighway) that swallows bodies, and even whole societies, into the dynamic momentum of its telematic logic. Always working on the basis of the illusion of enhanced interactivity, the digital superhighway is really about the full immersion of the flesh into its virtual double. As *dead (electronic) space*, the digital superhighway is a big real estate venture in cybernetic form, where competing claims to intellectual property rights in an array of multi-media technologies of communication are at stake. No longer capitalism under the doubled sign of consumer and production models, the digital superhighway represents the disappearance of capitalism into colonized virtual space. And *dead (cybernetic) rhetoric*? That's the Internet's subordination to the predatory business interests of a virtual class, which might pay virtual lip service to the growth of electronic communities on a global basis, but which is devoted in actuality to shutting down the anarchy of the Net in favor of virtualized (commercial) exchange. Like a mirror image, the digital superhighway always means its opposite: not an open telematic autoroute for fast circulation across the electronic galaxy, but an immensely seductive harvesting machine for delivering bodies, culture, and labor to virtualization. The information highway is paved with (our) flesh. So consequently, *the theory of the virtual class*: cultural accomodation to technotopia is its goal, political consolidation (around the aims of the virtual class) its method, multi-media nervous systems its relay, and (our) disappearance into pure virtualities its ecstatic destiny.

That there is an inherent political contradiction between the attempt by the virtual class to liquidate the sprawling web of the Internet in favor of the smooth telematic vision of the digital superhighway is apparent. The information highway is the antithesis of the Net, in much the same way as the virtual class must destroy the *public dimension* of the Internet for its own survival. The informational technology of the Internet as a new *force* of virtual production provides the social conditions necessary for instituting fundamentally new *relations* of electronic creation. Spontaneously and certainly against the long-range interests of the virtual class, the Internet has been swamped by demands for meaning. Newly screen-radiated scholars dream up visions of a Virtual University, the population of Amsterdam goes on-line as Digital City, environmentalists become web weavers as they form a global Green cybernetic informational grid, and a new generation of fiction writers develops forms of telematic writing that mirror the crystalline structures and multi-phasal connections of hypertext.

But, of course, for the virtual class, content slows the speed of virtualized exchange, and meaning becomes the antagonistic contradiction of data. Accordingly, demands for meaning must be immediately denied as just another road-kill along the virtual highway. As such, the virtual class exercises its intense obsessive-compulsive drive to subordinate society to the telematic mythology of the digital superhighway. The democratic possibilities of the Internet, with its immanent appeal to new forms of global communication, might have been the seduction-strategy appropriate for the construction of the digital superhighway, but now that the cybernetic grid is firmly in control, the virtual class must move to liquidate the Internet. It is an old scenario, repeated this time in virtual form. Marx understood this first: every technology releases opposing possibilities towards emancipation and domination. Like its early bourgeois predecessors at the birth of capitalism, the virtual class christens the birth of technotopia by suppressing the potentially emancipatory relations of production released by the Internet in favor of the traditionally predatory force of production signified by the digital superhighway. Data is the anti-virus of meaning – telematic information refuses to be slowed down by the drag-weight of content. And the virtual class seeks to exterminate the *social* possibilities of the Internet. These are the first lessons of the theory of the virtual class.

Information Highway/Media-Net: Virtual Pastoral Power

The "information highway" has become the key route into virtuality. The "information highway" is another term for what we call the "media-net." It's a question
of whether we're cruising on a highway or being caught up in a Net, always already
available for (further) processing. The "highway" is definitely an answer to "Star
Wars": the communications complex takes over from the "military-industrial
complex." Unlike "Star Wars," however, the "highway" has already (de-)mater-
ialized in the world behind the monitors: cyberspace. For crash theory there is an
irony: the highway is a trompe l'oeil of possessive individualism covering the
individual possessed by the Net, sucked into the imploded, impossible world
behind the screen – related to the dubious world of ordinary perception through
cyber-space.

Information Highway vs. Media-Net

The prophet-hypesters of the information highway, from President Bill Clinton,
U.S.A., to President Bill Gates, Microsoft, proclaim a revolution to a higher level
of bourgeois consciousness. The highway is the utopia of the possessive individual:
the possessive individual now resides in technotopia.

This is how the higher level of bourgeois consciousness comes to be in grades
of perfection. Firstly, we enter an information highway which promises the
"individual" access to "information" from the universal archive instantly and
about anything. The capacity of the Net to hold information is virtually infinite
and, with the inevitable advances in microprocessors, its capacities to gather,
combine, and relay information will be equal to any demand for access. Are
you curious about anything? The answer is right at your fingertips. More seriously,
do you need to know something? A touch of a button will get you what you
need and eventually your brain waves alone (telekinesis fantasy) will do it. Here
is the world as information completely at the beck and call of the possessive
individual (the individual, that is, who is *possessed* by information). Here, everyone is a god who, if they are not omniscient all at once, can at least entertain
whatever information that they wish to have at any time they wish to have it.
Information is not the kind of thing that has to be shared. If everyone all at once
wanted to know who won the Stanley Cup in 1968 they could have the information simultaneously: cyberspace as the site of Unamuno's panarchy, where each
one is king.

At the next grade of perfection, the highway not only provides access to that
which is already given, but allows the "individual" to "interact" with other
"individuals," to create a society in cyberspace. The freedom to access information will be matched by the freedom to access individuals anywhere and at any
time, since eventually everyone will be wired. The hybridization of television,
telephone, and computer will produce every possible refinement of mediated
presence, allowing interactors an unprecedented range of options for finely

adjusting the distance of their relations. Through the use of profiles, data banks, and bulletin boards people will be able to connect with exactly those who will give them the most satisfaction, with whom they share interests, opinions, projects, and sexual preferences, and for whom they have need. Just as "individuals" will be able to access the realm of "information" (anything from their financial and insurance records to any movie ever made), they will also be able to access the domain of "human" communicators to find the ones who are best suited to them. As Bill Gates of Microsoft puts it: "The opportunity for people to reach out and share is amazing."[1]

The information highway as technotopia is the place where "individuals" command information for whatever purposes they entertain and find others with whom to combine to pursue those purposes. As Gates puts it, it is "empowering stuff." Technotopia is the seduction by which the flesh is drawn into the Net. What seduces is the fantasy of "empowerment," the center of the contemporary possessive individualist complex. By having whatever information one wants instantly and without effort, and by being linked to appropriate associates one saves an immense amount of time and energy, and is more likely to make better decisions for oneself. Who can complain about having more information, especially if it can be accessed easily and appropriately by a system of selectors that gives you what you ask for and nothing else, or even better, that knows you so well that it gives you what you really want (need?) (is good for you?), but did not even realize that you wanted?

The information highway means the death of the (human) agent and the triumph of the expert program, the wisdom that the greatest specialist would give you. Expert programs to diagnose you. Medical tests performed at home while you are hooked up to a computer that are interpreted by an expert program. In order to serve you, the "highway" will demand information from you. The selector systems will have to get to know you, scan you, monitor you, give you periodic tests. The expert program will be the new center for pastoral power. This is, of course, still enacted under capitalism. You will have to pay for information with money and there will be plenty of restrictions on its accessibility. Leave that as a contradiction of the virtual class between the capitalist organization of the highway and its technotopian vision: a contradiction within possessive individualism. More importantly, you will pay for information with information; indeed, you will be information.

The highway becomes the Net. What appears as "empowerment" is a trompe l'oeil, a seduction, an entrapment in a Baudrillardian loop in which the Net elicits information from the "user" and gives it back in what the selectors say is an appropriate form for that user. The great agent of possibility becomes the master tool of normalization now a micro-normalization with high specificity... perhaps uniqueness! Each "individual" has a unique disciplinary solution to hold them fast to the Net, where they are dumped for image processing and image reception. The information highway is the way by which bodies are drawn into cyberspace through the seduction of empowerment.

Bourgeois masculinity has always been pre-pubescent: the thoughts of little boys thinking about what they would do if they controlled the world, but now the world is cyberspace. The dream of being the god of cyberspace – public ideology as the fantasy of pre-pubescent males: a regression from sex to an autistic power drive.

[. . .]

The Virtual Class and Capitalism

The computer industry is in an intensive phase of "creative destruction," the term coined by Schumpeter and used by the neo-Darwinian macho apologists for capitalism to refer to the economic killing fields produced by rapid technological change. The Net is being brought into actuality through the offices of ruthless capitalist competition, in which vast empires fall and rise within a single decade (Big Blue/Microsoft). Under the disciplinary liberal night watchman's protection of "private" property-rights, capitalist freebooters destroy one another as they race to be the ones who actualize the Net, just like the railroads of the nineteenth-century racing across the continent. This means that the virtual class retains a strict capitalist determination and that its representative social type must be a capitalist, someone who is installing the highway to win a financial competition, if nothing else. If one is not so minded in today's computer industry they will be eaten alive. You will only be able to get personal kicks and pursue your (ressentiment-laden) idealistic views of computer democracy in this industry if you sell. So you hype your ideas and your ideals become hype – that is the twisted psychology of the virtual class: not hyped ideology, but something of, by, and for the Net: ideological hype.

There are pure capitalists in the cyber industry and there are capitalists who are also visionary computer specialists. The latter, in a spirit of vicious naivete, generate the ideological hype, a messianic element, that the former take up cynically. It's the old story of the good cop and the bad cop. How come the good cop tolerates the bad cop? So much for the computer democracy of cyber possessive-individualists. The economic base of the virtual class is the entire communications industry – everywhere it reaches. As a whole, this industry processes ideological hype for capitalist ends. It is most significantly constituted by cynicism, not viciously naive vision. Yet, though a small group in numerical proportion to the whole virtual class, the visionaries are essential to cyber-capitalism because they provide the ideological mediation to seduce the flesh into the Net. In this sense the cynical capitalists and the well-provided techies are merely drones, clearing the way for the Pied Piper's parade.

A frontier mentality rules the drive into cyberspace. It is one of the supreme ironies that a primitive form of capitalism, a retro-capitalism, is actualizing virtuality. The visionary cyber-capitalist is a hybrid monster of social Darwinism and techno-populist individualism. It is just such an imminently reversible figure that can provide the switching mechanism back and forth between cyberspace and the collapsing space of (crashed) perception.

The most complete representative of the virtual class is the visionary capitalist who is constituted by all of its contradictions and who, therefore, secretes its ideological hype. The rest of the class tends to split the contradictions: the vision-less-cynical-business capitalists and the perhaps visionary, perhaps skill-oriented, perhaps indifferent techno-intelligentsia of cognitive scientists, engineers, computer scientists, video-game developers, and all the other communication specialists, ranged in hierarchies, but all dependent for their economic support on the drive to virtualization. Whatever contradictions there are within the virtual class – that is, the contradictions stemming from the confrontation of bourgeois and proletarian – the class as a whole supports the drive into cyber-space through the wired world. This is the way it works in post late-capitalism, where the communication complex is repeating the pattern of class collaborationism that marked the old military-industrial complex. The drive into the Net is one of those great capitalist techno-projects that depends upon a concert of interests to sustain it, as it sucks social energy into itself. The phenomenon of a collaborationist complex harboring a retro-Darwinian competition is something new, but is stabilized, in the final analysis, by a broad consensus among the capitalist components of the virtual class that the liberal-fascist state structure is deserving of support. Indeed, in the U.S.A. in the 1990s the state is the greatest producer of the ideological hype of the "information highway." The virtual class has its administration in the White House. The concerted drive into cyberspace proceeds, all in the name of economic development and a utopian imaginary of possessive individualists.

The Hyper-Texted Body or Nietzsche Gets a Modem

But why be nostalgic? The old body type was always OK, but the wired body with its micro-flesh, multi-media channeled ports, cybernetic fingers, and bubbling neuro-brain finely interfaced to the "standard operating-system" of the Internet is infinitely better. Not really the wired body of sci-fi with its mutant designer look, or body flesh with its ghostly reminders of nineteenth-century philosophy, but the hyper-texted body as both: a wired nervous system embedded in living (dedicated) flesh.

The hyper-texted body with its dedicated flesh? That is our telematic future, and it's not necessarily so bleak. Technology has always been our sheltering environment: not second-order nature, but primal nature for the twenty-first-century body. In the end, the virtual class is very old-fashioned. It clings to an antiquated historical form – capitalism – and, on its behalf, wants to shut down the creative possibilities of the Internet. Dedicated flesh rebels against the virtual class. It does not want to be interfaced to the Net through modems and external software black boxes, but *actually wants to be an Internet*. The virtual class wants to appropriate emergent technologies for purposes of authoritarian political control over cyberspace. It wants to drag technotopia back to the age of the primitive politics of predatory capitalism. But dedicated (geek) flesh wants something very different. Unlike the (typically European) rejection of technotopia in favor of a newly emergent nostalgia movement under the sign of "Back to Vinyl" in digital sound or "Back to Pencils" in literature, dedicated flesh wants to deeply instantiate the age of technotopia. Operating by means of the aesthetic strategy of over-identification with the feared and desired object, the hyper-texted body insists that ours is already the era of post-capitalism, and even post-technology. Taking the will to virtuality seriously, it demands its telematic rights to be a functioning interfaced body: to be a multi-media thinker, to patch BUS ports on its cyber-flesh as it navigates the gravity well of the Internet, to create aesthetic visions equal to the pure virtualities found everywhere on the now superceded digital superhighway, and to become data to such a point of violent implosion that the body finally breaks free of the confining myth of "wired culture" and goes wireless.

The wireless body? That is the floating body, drifting around in the debris of technotopia: encrypted flesh in a sea of data. The perfect evolutionary successor to twentieth-century flesh, the wireless body fuses the speed of virtualized exchange into its cellular structure. DNA-coated data is inserted directly through spinal taps into dedicated flesh for better navigation through the treacherous shoals of the electronic galaxy. Not a body without memory or feelings, but the opposite. The wireless body is the battleground of the major political and ethical conflicts of late-twentieth- and early-twenty-first-century experience.

Perhaps the wireless body will be just a blank data dump, a floating petri dish where all the brilliant residues of technotopia are mixed together in newly recombinant forms. In this case, the wireless body would be an indefinitely reprogrammable chip: micro-soft flesh where the "standard operating-system" of the new electronic age comes off the top of the TV set, flips inside the body organic, and is soft-wired to a waiting vat of remaindered flesh.

But the wireless body could be, and already is, something very different. Not the body as an organic grid for passively sampling all the drifting bytes of recombinant culture, but the wireless body as a highly-charged theoretical and political site: a moving field of aesthetic contestation for remapping the galactic empire of technotopia. Data flesh can speak so confidently of the possibility of multi-media democracy, of sex without secretions, and of integrated (cyber-) relationships because it has already burst through to the other side of technotopia: to that point of brilliant dissolution where the Net comes alive, and begins to speak the language of wireless bodies in a wireless world.

There are already many wireless bodies on the Internet: Many data travelers on the virtual road have managed under the weight of the predatory capitalism of the virtual class and the even weightier humanist prejudices against geek flesh, to make of the Internet a charmed site for fusing the particle waves of all the passing data into a new body type: hyper-texted bodies circulating as "web weavers" in electronic space.

Refusing to be remaindered as flesh dumped by the virtual class, the hyper-texted body bends virtuality to its own purposes. Here, the will to virtuality ceases to be one-dimensional, becoming a doubled process, grisly yet creative, spatial yet memoried, in full violent play as the hyper-texted body. Always schizoid yet fully integrated, the hyper-texted body swallows its modem, cuts its wired connections to the information highway, and becomes its own system-operating software, combining and remutating the surrounding data storm into new virtualities. And why not? Human flesh no longer exists, except as an incept of the wireless world. Refuse, then, nostalgia for the surpassed past of remaindered flesh, and hyper-text your way to the (World Wide) Webbed body: the body that actually dances on its own data organs, sees with multi-media graphical interface screens, makes new best tele-friends on the MOO, writes electronic poetry on the disappearing edges of video, sound, and text integrators, and insists on going beyond the tedious world of binary divisions to the new cyber-mathematics of FITS. The hyper-texted body, then, is the precursor of a new world of multi-media politics, fractualized economics, incept personalities, and (cybernetically) interfaced relationships. After all, why should the virtual class monopolize digital reality? It only wants to suppress the creative possibilities of virtualization, privileging instead the tendencies of technotopia towards new and more vicious forms of cyber-authoritarianism. The virtual class only wants to subordinate digital reality to the will of capitalism. The hyper-texted body responds to the challenge of virtualization by making itself a monstrous double: pure virtuality/pure flesh. Consequently, our telematic future: the wireless body on the Net as a sequenced chip microprogrammed by the virtual class for purposes of (its) maximal profitability, or the wireless body as the leading-edge of critical subjectivity in the twenty-first century. If the virtual class is the post-historical successor to the early bourgeoisie of primitive capitalism, then the hyper-texted body is the Internet equivalent of the Paris Commune: anarchistic, utopian, and in full revolt against the suppression of the general (tele-)human possibilities of the Net in favor of the specific (monetary) interests of the virtual class. Always already the past to the future of the hyper-texted body, the virtual class is the particular interest that must be overcome by the hyper-texted body of data trash if the Net is to be gatewayed by soft ethics.

Soft ethics? Nietzsche's got a modem, and he is already rewriting the last pages of *The Will to Power* as *The Will to Virtuality.* As the patron saint of the hyper-texted body, Nietzsche is data trash to the smooth, unbroken surface of the virtual class.

Note

1 John Seabrook, "E-mail from Bill," *The New Yorker*, LXIX, 45 (January 10, 1994), p. 54.

16

The Informational Economy

Manuel Castells

Manuel Castells is Professor of Planning at the University of California, Berkeley, and Professor of Sociology and Director of the Institute of Sociology at the University of Madrid. He has published over 20 books, including his series on global social and political movements, entitled "The Information Age: Economy, Society, and Culture." In this essay, Castells outlines five fundamental features of the new global information economy.

We live in a new economy, gradually formed over the past half century and characterized by five fundamental features which are systematically interrelated. The first such feature is that sources of productivity – and therefore of economic growth in real terms – are increasingly dependent upon the application of science and technology, as well as upon the quality of information and management, in the processes of production, consumption, distribution, and trade. The pathbreaking work of Robert Solow in 1957,[1] followed by the aggregate-production-function studies on the sources of economic productivity by Denison, Malinvaud, Jorgenson, and Kendrick, among others,[2] has shown that advanced economies increased their productivity not so much as a result of the amount of capital or labor added to the production process, as was the case in the early stages of industrialization, but as the outcome of a more efficient combination of the factors of production. Although econometric equations are obscure in identifying the precise sources of the new productivity pattern, the "statistical residual" found to be critical in the new production function has often been assimilated to the new inputs represented by the deeper penetration of science, technology, labor skills, and managerial know-how in the production process.[3]

A similar finding was reported on the evolution of the Soviet economy by Abel Aganbegyan, Gorbachev's first economic adviser. According to Aganbegyan's calculations, the Soviet economy grew at a robust rate until 1971, or as long as the state could rely on purely quantitative expansion by injecting more capital and labor and by pumping more and more natural resources into a rather primitive industrial structure. Once the Soviet economy became more complex, as a result of industrialization, it needed to introduce more sophisticated know-how into the production process in order to sustain growth. Because of the difficulty of developing and applying science and technology within a command economy, growth rates plummeted from 1971 onward, until reaching zero growth in the mid-1980s,[4] thus prompting the need for *perestroika* and precipitating the demise of Soviet communism.

Thus, it seems that the increasingly important role of applied knowledge and information is a characteristic of advanced economic systems, transcending the historical characteristics of their modes of production. It would also seem that the salient role of knowledge and technology is not exclusive to the late twentieth-century economy, nor has this economy resulted simply from a sudden change of production techniques. We are observing in fact a secular trend. Knowledge has always been important in organizing and fostering economic growth.[5] But the greater the complexity and productivity of an economy, the greater its informational component and the greater the role played by new knowledge and new applications of knowledge (as compared with the mere addition of such production factors as capital or labor) in the growth of productivity.[6]

The second feature of the new world economy – and another secular trend that has accelerated in recent years – is the shift, in advanced capitalist societies, from material production to information-processing activities, both in terms of proportion of GNP and in the proportion of the population employed in such activities.[7] This seems to be a more fundamental change than the one proposed by the notion of the transition from industry to services, for today's "service sector" is so diverse that it becomes a residual category, mixing fundamentally different activities (from computer-software writing to cleaning floors) to the point that any analysis of economic structure must now start with a typological differentiation of the so-called service activities.[8] Furthermore, as Cohen and Zysman have forcefully argued,[9] there is a systemic linkage between manufacturing and the service sector, so that many such activities are in fact an integral part of the industrial production process.

Thus, the real transformation of the economic structure of advanced societies is the emergence of what Marc Porat in his seminal 1977 study labelled "the information economy," wherein an ever-growing role is played by the manipulation of symbols in the organization of production and in the enhancement of productivity.[10] In 1990, 47.4 percent of the employed population in the United States, 45.8 percent in the United Kingdom, 45.1 percent in France, and 40.0 percent in West Germany were engaged in information-processing activities, whether in the production of goods or in the provision of services,[11] and the proportion continues to rise over time.[12] Moreover, the quality of the information and one's efficiency in acquiring and processing it now constitute the strategic factor in both competitiveness and productivity for firms, regions, and countries.[13]

Along with the fundamental changes taking place in the production process itself is a third feature of the new economy: a profound transformation in the *organization* of production and of economic activity in general. This change can be described as a shift from standardized mass production to flexible customized production and from vertically integrated, large-scale organizations to vertical disintegration and horizontal networks between economic units.[14] This trend has sometimes been assimilated to the dynamic role played by small and medium-size businesses (expressions of the new flexibility) in opposition to bureaucratized large corporations, as in the formulation of Piore and Sabel,[15] and has been discussed in the context of the so-called Third Italy Model of industrial development.[16] The organizational transformation of the economy, however, goes beyond the size of the firm and does not contradict the fundamental trend toward the concentration of economic power in a few major conglomerates. While it is true that small businesses have shown great resilience, becoming dynamic units in an advanced economy, the organizational pattern of decentralization and flexibility is also characteristic of large corporations, both in their internal structure and in their relationship to a network of ancillary firms, as is illustrated by the "just in time" supply technique introduced by the large Japanese automobile firms. Thus, the matter at hand is not so much the decline of the large corporation (still the dominant agent of the world economy) as it is the organizational transformation of all economic activity, emphasizing flexibility and adaptability in response to a changing, diversified market.

Fourth, the new economy is a global economy, in which capital, production, management, markets, labor, information, and technology are organized across national boundaries. Although nation-states are still fundamental realities to be reckoned with in thinking about economic structures and processes, what is significant is that the unit of economic accounting, as well as the frame of reference for economic strategies, can no longer be the national economy. Competition is played out globally,[17] not only by the multinational corporations, but also by small and medium-size enterprises that connect directly or indirectly to the world market through their linkages in the networks that relate them to the large firms.[18] What is new, then, is not that international trade is an important component of the economy (in this sense, we can speak of a world economy since the seventeenth century), but that the national economy now works as a unit at the world level in real time. In this sense, we are not only seeing a process of internationalization of the economy, but a process of globalization – that is, the interpenetration of economic activities and national economies at the global level. The coming integration into the world economy of Eastern Europe, the former Soviet Union, and China – probably over the course of the next decade – will complete this process of globalization which, while not ignoring national boundaries, simply includes national characteristics as important features within a unified, global system.

Finally, these economic and organizational transformations in the world economy take place (and not by accident) in the midst of one of the most significant technological revolutions of human history.[19] The core of that revolution is in information technologies (microelectronics, informatics, and telecommunications) around which a constellation of major scientific discoveries and applications (in biotechnology, new materials, lasers, renewable energy, etc.) is transforming the material basis of our world in fewer than twenty years. This technological revolution has been stimulated in its applications by a demand generated by the economic and organizational transformations discussed above. In turn, the new technologies constitute the indispensable material base for such transformations.[20] Thus, the enhancement of telecommunications has created the material infrastructure needed for the formation of a global economy,[21] in a movement similar to that which lay behind the construction of the railways and the formation of national markets during the nineteenth century. The fact that new information technologies are available at the very moment when the organization of economic activity relies increasingly on the processing of a vast amount of information, moreover, contributes to removing the fundamental obstacle to labor-productivity growth as economies evolve from material production to information processing as the source of employment for most workers. In the United States, the differential of productivity growth between information jobs and noninformation jobs increased until 1980; thereafter, however, the trend was projected to turn around as new information technologies diffused throughout the economy.[22] Furthermore, these information technologies are also the critical factor allowing for flexibility and decentralization in production and management: production and trade units can function autonomously yet be reintegrated functionally through information networks, constituting in fact a new type of economic space, which I have called "the space of flows."[23]

Thus, with the revolution in information technology as the material basis of the emerging system, the various features of structural economic transformation that we have identified relate closely to each other. In fact, they join together to form a new type of economy that I, along with a growing number of economists and sociologists,[24] propose to call the "informational economy"[25] because, at its core, the fundamental source of wealth generation lies in an ability to create new knowledge and apply it to every realm of human activity by means of enhanced technological and organizational procedures of information processing.[26] The informational economy tends to be, in its essence, a global economy; and its structure and logic define, within the emerging world order, a new international division of labor.

Notes

1   Robert Solow, "Technical Change and the Aggregate Production Function," *Review of Economics and Statistics* 39 (1957), pp. 312–20.
2   For a thorough discussion of the literature on the question of productivity sources, see Richard R. Nelson, "Research of Productivity Growth and Productivity Differences: Dead Ends and New Departures," *Journal of Economic Literature* 19 (September 1981), pp. 1029–64.
3   See Christian Sautter, "L'Efficacité et la rentabilité de l'économie française de 1954 à 1974," *Economie et Statistique* 68 (1976); Edward Denison, *Trends in American Economic Growth 1929–1982* (Washington, DC: Brooking, 1985).
4   Abel Aganbegyan, *The Economic Challenge of Perestroika* (Bloomington: Indiana University Press, 1988), pp. 10–11.

5   See Nathan Rosenberg and L. E. Birdzell, *How the West Grew Rich: The Economic Transformation of the Industrial World* (New York: Basic Books, 1986).

6   Jerome A. Mark and William H. Waldorf, "Multifactor Productivity: A New BLS Measure," in *Monthly Labor Review* 106 (December 1983), pp. 3–15.

7   Tom Stonier, *The Wealth of Information: A Profile of the Postindustrial Economy* (London: Thames Methuen, 1983).

8   See Pascal Petit, *Slow Growth and the Service Economy* (London: Pinter, 1986).

9   Stephen S. Cohen and John Zysman, *Manufacturing Matters: The Myth of the Post-industrial Economy* (New York: Basic Books, 1987).

10 See Marc Porat, *The Information Economy: Definition and Measurement*, Special Publication 77–12(1) (Washington, DC: U.S. Department of Commerce, Office of Telecommunications, 1977).

11 Research in progress: data elaborated by Manuel Castells and Yuko Aoyama, University of California–Berkeley, 1992.

12 See Mark Hepworth, *Geography of the Information Economy* (London: Belhaven Press, 1989).

13 See Bruce R. Guile and Harvey Brooks (eds.), *Technology and Global Industry: Companies and Nations in the World Economy* (Washington, DC: National Academy Press, 1987).

14 See Robert Boyer, *Technical Change and the Theory of Regulation* (Paris: CEPREMAP, 1987).

15 Michael Piore and Charles Sabel, *The Second Industrial Divide* (New York: Basic Books, 1984).

16 See Vittorio Capecchi, "The Informal Economy and the Development of Flexible Specialization in Emilia-Romagna," in A. Portres, M. Castells, and L. Benton (eds.), *The Informal Economy: Studies in Advanced and Less Developed Countries* (Baltimore: Johns Hopkins University Press, 1989).

17 See A. Michael Spence and Heather A. Hazard (eds.), *International Competitiveness* (Cambridge, MA: Ballinger, 1988).

18 See Manuel Castells, Lee Goh, and R.W.Y. Kwok, *The Shek Kip Mei Syndrome: Economic Development and Public Policy in Hong Kong and Singapore* (London: Pion, 1990).

19 See Tom Forester, *High Tech Society* (Oxford: Basil Blackwell, 1987).

20 See Manuel Castells et al., *Nuevas tecnologías, economía y sociedad en España* (Madrid: Alianza Editorial, 1986).

21 See François Bar, "Configuring the Telecommunications Infrastructure for the Computer Age: The Economics of Network Control" (PhD dis., University of California–Berkeley, 1990).

22 See C. Jonscher, "Information Resources and Economic Productivity," *Information Economics and Policy* 2, no. 1 (1983), pp. 13–35.

23 See Manuel Castells, *The Informational City: Information Technology, Economic Restructuring, and the Urban-Regional Process* (Oxford: Basil Blackwell, 1989).

24 See J. Beniger, *The Control Revolution: Technological and Economic Origins of the Information Society* (Cambridge: Harvard University Press, 1986); and "Prospective sociologiche per la società postindustriale. Lo scenario internazionale," *Sociologia* (Rome), no. 1 (1989).

25 I prefer "informational economy" to Daniel Bell's "postindustrial society" because it gives substantive content to an otherwise purely descriptive notion.

26 See Ralph Landau and Nathan Rosenberg (eds.), *The Positive Sum Strategy: Harnessing Technology for Economic Growth* (Washington, DC: National Academy Press, 1986).

17

The Global Information Highway: Project for an Ungovernable World

Herbert I. Schiller

Herbert I. Schiller, excerpt from "The Global Information Highway: Project for an Ungovernable World," in James Brook and Iain A. Bola, eds., *Resisting the Virtual Life: The Culture and Politics of Information* (San Francisco: City Lights, 1995).

Herbert I. Schiller is a visiting professor at New York University and Professor of Communication Emeritus at the University of California, San Diego. His many books include *Living in the Number One Country: Reflections from a Critic of American Empire* (Seven Stories Press, 2000) and *Information Inequality: The Deepening Crisis* (Routledge, 1996). With particular emphasis on the information economy, this essay describes the global consolidation of power and wealth in the hands of a few.

While plans abound and steps are taken to construct the electronic information highway as rapidly as possible *inside* the continental boundaries, the design for a global system is hardly overlooked. In March 1994, Vice President Al Gore traveled to Buenos Aires, the site of an International Telecommunications Union Conference, at which representatives from 132 countries were present.

Before an international audience, Gore repeated the great promise he saw in electronic communication: "we now have at hand the technological breakthroughs and economic means to bring all the communities in the world together. We now can at last create a planetary information network that transmits messages and images with the speed of light from the largest city to the smallest village on every continent."

After offering this transcendental vision, Gore concluded more pragmatically. This information network, he stated, "will be a means by which families and friends will transcend the barriers of time and distance ... and it will make possible a global information marketplace, where consumers can buy and sell products."

Buying and selling information goods on the global network, no less than on the domestic one, Gore insisted, required that private industry be in charge. "We propose that private investment and competition be the foundations for development of the GII [Global Information Infrastructure]." (Gore 1994; see also Nathaniel C. Nash, "Gore Sees World Data Privatizing," *The New York Times*, March 22, 1994).

Months earlier, a somewhat different emphasis was given to the electronic communication project in a domestic venue. In September 1993, the White House described the information superhighway as a means "to enable U.S. firms to compete and win in the global economy" and to give the domestic economy a "competitive edge" internationally (NII 1993).

Not mentioned in Buenos Aires, but clearly in the forefront of White House thinking, is the global command and direction of the world economy, through information control, and the benefits that flow therefrom.

This is hardly a recent ambition, expressed for the first time by a new administration. For more than half a century, beginning while World War II was still being waged, U.S. leadership recognized the centrality of information control for gaining world advantage. Well before most of the world could do much about it, U.S. groups, private and governmental, were actively promoting information and cultural primacy on all continents. The policy had many elements in it, not all of them necessarily deliberate.

In the 1990s, for example, when a new generation of leadership is coming into authority around the world, it is common to discover that this or that individual, taking over the reins in this or that country, has been educated in the United States. Mexico provides a striking case in point: its departing president is a Harvard graduate, its newly designated one a Yale product. The education and training of foreign students in American schools and universities, expanded greatly after World War II, are now producing their harvest of graduates who assume high office at home. They have imbibed free market and other doctrines and values ladled out in America's premier schools.

But U.S. global cultural influence has not been limited to formal education. U.S. films and TV programs are the chief fare of national systems in most countries. News programs, especially CNN, offer U.S. perspectives, sometimes the only perspective provided, to world audiences. U.S. recorded music, theme parks, and advertising now comprise a major part of the world's cultural environment.

No less remarkable is the ad hoc adoption of English as the world's second language, facilitated by the waves of U.S. pop culture that have washed across all frontiers for forty years. And once the preeminence of English had been established, Anglo-American ideas, values, and cultural products generally have been received with familiarity and enthusiasm.

All this is well known and amply documented, though the domestic media and political establishments are shy about acknowledging their de facto cultural domination of what they like to refer to as "the global market." What is of special interest here, however, is the skillful combination of information instrumentation with philosophic principle – a mix that fuels the push toward concentrated cultural power. Not the laws of chance but strategic planning, rarely identified as such, underlies this development. It has succeeded well beyond the initial expectations of its formulators.

At the outset of what some hoped would be an American century (Schiller 1992), a vital doctrine was promoted: the free flow of information. Considered out of context, this principle seems unexceptional and indeed, entitled to respect. Yet when viewed alongside the reality of the early postwar years, it conferred unmatchable advantage on U.S. cultural industries. No rival foreign film industry, TV production center, publishing enterprise, or news establishment could possibly have competed on equal terms with the powerful U.S. media-entertainment companies at that time. And so it has gone to this day. The free flow of information, as implemented, has meant the ascendance of U.S. cultural product worldwide.

Under the "free-flow" principle, U.S. global strategy supported the rapid and fullest development of transport and information technologies, which under-pinned the capability for the cultural domination that was being constructed. For example, most of the civilian airliners in operation in most countries are U.S. made. These vehicles have enabled the massive growth of the world tourist industry, which has in turn leaned heavily on U.S. modes of entertaining and nurturing tourists – chain hotels, packaged tours, constructed spectacles, and so on.

Two key sectors received special attention and unstinting resources from the U.S. government in the never-ending pursuit of winning and holding the global market for U.S. products and services: satellite communications radically improved telecommunications and suppressed distance as a factor in global production, and computerization has become the basis of the information-using economy. Both have long been the recipients of heavy subsidies and favored treatment, Washing-ton's enthusiastic rhetoric for "free markets," notwithstanding.

Current plans to construct an information superhighway closely follow the historical model of the U.S. development and deployment of the communication satellite. The satellite project had a single unambiguous goal: capturing control of international communication circuits from British cable interests. The imperial rule of Great Britain in the nineteenth and early twentieth centuries had been facilitated greatly by control of the underwater message flow between the colonies and London. The American-built and -controlled satellite bypassed the cable and helped break the empire's monopoly on trade and investment and to reduce the British role in international communication (Schiller 1992).

Control of information instrumentation invariably goes hand in hand with control of the message flow and its content, surveillance capability, and all forms of information intelligence. To be sure, the revenues from such control are hardly afterthoughts in the minds of the builders and owners of the information super-highway.

Yet again, the "promise" of the communications instrumentation represented by the GII stresses the general social benefit. However, the conditions attached to the proposal – private creation and ownership – make it inevitable that the network will be of greatest value to those who have the financial ability to satisfy their need for instantaneous and voluminous global message flows.

These "information users" are none other than transnational corporations. They constitute the driving force for the creation of a global marketplace, for a deregulated world arena, and for global production sites selected for profitability and convenience – which are also the central considerations behind the National Information Infrastructure (NII) and the GII.

The launching of the global information superhighway project comes at a time when most of the preconditions for a corporate global "order" are in place. There is, first and foremost, the actual existence of a global economy, organized and directed by a relatively tiny number of transnational corporations. According to a survey of this global economic apparatus, 37,000 companies comprise the system. Given that there are millions of businesses in the United States, not counting those in Germany, Japan, and elsewhere, the extent of the concentration of economic influence in this global system cannot be overstated.

And though 37,000 companies occupy the command posts of the world economic order, the largest 100 transnational companies, in 1990, "had about $3.2 trillion in global assets of which $1.2 trillion was outside their own home countries" (*World Investment Report* 1993). These few megafirms are the true power-wielders of our time.

This world corporate order is a major force in reducing greatly the influence of nation states. As private economic decisions increasingly govern the global and national allocation of resources, the amount and character of investment, the value of currencies, and the sites and modes of production, important duties of government are silently appropriated by these giant private economic aggregates (Barnet and Cavenaugh 1994).

These corporations are the leading force in promoting deregulation and privatization of industry in all countries, notably but not exclusively in the telecommunications sector. In a 1994 report *Business Week* notes, for example: "From Italy to Taiwan, scores of governments, caught up in a free market frenzy and needing cash, are selling shares of state-run companies to the public. This sweeping global privatization movement, involving more than 50 nations and expected to raise some $300 billion over five years..." (*Business Week*, April 18, 1994).

One effect of the large-scale deregulation of industry and the massive privatizations is the increasing ineffectiveness of national authority. Unaccountability of the transnational corporation is now the prevailing condition in most countries. The world-active company makes fundamental decisions that affect huge numbers of people but reports to no one except its own executives and major shareholders.

At the same time, the strength of the transnational sector continues to grow, and the companies comprising it are themselves engaged in uninterrupted expansion and concentration. These developments are especially notable in the communication-media sphere, which, naturally, is also the site of the strongest sentiments in favor of the information superhighway. As U.S. media and cultural product flow more heavily into the global market, the interests of this sector become increasingly congruent with general transnational corporate objectives and policies.

While nonmedia companies – oil, heavy equipment, aerospace, agribusiness, and others – seek ever-improved means of communication to carry on and extend their international operations, the media-communication sector is only too happy to make these facilities available, at a price. For, of course, this sector strives to expand markets for its own specific outputs.

The recent rush to integration in the media-communication sector is itself a remarkable development. What can only be described as *total communication* capability – sometimes called "one-stop communication" – has become a short-term goal of the major firms in this sector. This translates into giant companies that possess the hardware and software to fully control messages and images from the conceptual stage to their ultimate delivery to users and audiences.

In brief, what is intended is the creation of private domains that will produce data and entertainment (films, interactive TV programs and video games, recordings, news), package them, and transmit them through satellite, cable, and telephone lines into living rooms and offices. Which companies ultimately will dominate the world and domestic markets is still uncertain. Time Warner, Viacom, Hearst, Bell Atlantic, Sega, US West, Microsoft, AT&T, IBM, Comcast, Telecommunications, Inc., are a few of the big players that are experimenting with different systems of "full-service" communication and vying with each other for advantageous market position (Ken Auletta, "The Magic Box," *The New Yorker*, April 11, 1994).

"The long-term economic opportunities" of these activities, Ken Auletta points out, "excite the business imagination for the rewards can be stupendous." The sums involved warrant this excitement:

> The cable and telephone businesses today [1994] generate close to two hundred billion dollars a year in revenues. Shopping by catalogue and other forms of shopping at home now constitute an eighty-billion-annual business. Entertainment – video stores, movie theatres, theme parks, music, books, video games, theatre, gambling – is a three-hundred-and-forty-billion-dollar business, and is growing twice as fast as over-all consumer spending.

And this is only the *domestic* market, which continues its expansion! The dimensions of the global market are yet to be discovered. In any event, corporate communication-entertainment titans are readying their capabilities to fill the cultural space of hundreds of millions of users and viewers, at home and abroad. More disturbing still, these global enterprises hope to enjoy and extend their relative immunity to oversight, locally and internationally.

The information superhighway is being promoted as a powerful means to even out the disparities and inequalities that afflict people inside the United States and throughout the world economy. In their many statements about the information superhighway, Vice President Gore and President Clinton insist that the project will reduce the gulf that separates the haves from the have-nots in education, health, and income. But the very basis, the nonnegotiable foundation of the project contradicts that promise.

A privately constructed and owned electronic information system will, of necessity, embody the essential features of a private enterprise economy: inequality of income along with the production of goods and services for profit. As production and sales are inseparably connected to income, the overall economy is directed, by the logic of market forces, to producing for and seeking out customers with the most income – because this strategy offers the greatest possibility of profit. It follows that a privately owned and managed information superhighway will be turned toward the interests and needs and income of the most advantaged sectors of the society. Significant modification of this systemic tendency requires the pressure of a strong political movement.

The most developed countries all exhibit wide income inequalities, and the United States is no exception. In the U.S., the top income levels, representing a tiny fraction of the population, receive more than the amount paid to half of the wage earners.

In less-industrialized countries, most of them still in some sort of economic dependency, the differentials are wider still. In India, for example, 120 million people now enjoy middle-class incomes, but 70 percent of the country's population remain mired in poverty ("As Prosperity Rises, Past Shackles India," *The New York Times*, February 18, 1994).

A recent report (James Brooke, "Colombia Booms Despite Its Violence," *The New York Times*, February 10, 1994) noted that in Colombia

> The number of people living below the poverty line has increased by about one million since 1990, to include about half of Colombia's population of 33 million people. In 15 years, the gap between average rural and urban incomes doubled.

This widening gap occurred in a period of "growth."

In a 1994 Human Development report of the United Nation's Development Program, wide income gaps between sections of a nation's population are seen as widespread around the world and threatening chaos in the afflicted areas. Egypt, South Africa, Nigeria, and Brazil, among others, "are countries now in danger of joining the world's list of failed states" (Paul Lewis, "U.N. Lists 4 Lands at Risk Over Income Gaps," *The New York Times*, June 2, 1994).

Similar growth with immiseration is found in the United States. "Today," writes an economic reporter for the *New York Times*, "the economy can keep on growing with the wealthiest 40 percent of the nation's families getting 68 percent of the income, even though 60 percent of the population is unhappily on the sidelines" (Louis Uchitelle, "Is Growth Moral?" *The New York Times Book Review*, March 27, 1994).

Will the creation of privately financed and privately owned, high-speed, multi-capability circuits carrying broad streams of messages and images reduce the gaps in living conditions across the globe? Time Warner, AT&T, Microsoft, and their rivals cannot be preoccupied with social inequality. Their focus is on revenue. Profits can come only from those who already have the income to purchase the services that are being prepared for sale.

Failing major political interventions – hardly to be expected in a time of world-wide deregulation and political conservatism – income gaps will widen, not diminish, at home and abroad. The inevitable corollary in communication is the employment of the electronic circuitry for transnational marketing, internal corporate operations, and the ideological objectives of businesses. Corporate data flows, Hollywood films and TV programs, business statistics, home gambling, video games, virtual reality shows, and shopping channels are the likely fare on the new electronic circuitry.

Yet there is at least one cloud on the market-forces horizon: *the question of how this corporately organized world will be governed*. If national authority continues to decline and corporate resource-allocation and general decision making continue to grow, and the welfare of approximately two-thirds of the world's population goes unattended and even deteriorates, what will prevent these conditions from provoking large-scale political convulsions in one place after another? And how can the globally privileged, wherever they may be, insulate themselves from these inevitable upheavals? What authority can check these powerful centrifugal currents?

These matters do not come up regularly on the nation's talk shows, concerned as they are with Madonna's underwear or the suicides of pathetic rock stars. Yet some attention is paid to these issues in more rarefied locales – the cozy diplomatic and foreign policy establishments, private and governmental, that generate the initiatives that eventually become national foreign policy.

In this era of eroding national authority, it is not surprising that some policy formulators have rediscovered the United Nations. In existence for half a century, and bypassed by its most powerful member for most of that time, the UN has, as a result of the changed international scene, drifted back into at least a blurry focus for some national influence-wielders. Yet since its inception, the UN has been a problem for U.S. diplomats. It is an *inclusive* body made up of representatives of all but a very few of the nations in the world, a circumstance that makes it difficult for a few still imperially minded societies to keep 185 national voices from having their say in governing the world.

The original design of the UN aimed to overcome this "obstacle" by putting major decision authority in the Security Council, which is dominated by a small club of the most powerful states. Still, this too proved an unacceptable limitation on U.S. postwar aims, especially given the presence on the council of a rival nonmarket society armed with atomic weapons.

In the early days of the UN there was almost constant deadlock. The creation of NATO (North Atlantic Treaty Organization) and other regional alliances served by design to deprive the one truly international organization of its global role and importance.

The former Soviet Union's frequent blockage of U.S. goals received heavy U.S. media attention, which generally obscured the source of disagreement – U.S. unwillingness to allow the loss of any part of the world market economy. Instead, the fraught messages and scary headlines helped convince Americans of Russian unreasonableness and the need for a gigantic arms program.

The UN was deemed an unworkable organization by U.S. leaders for other reasons as well. The most important objection, rarely made explicit, was to the presence of a large bloc of nations, the former colonial territories. These states, at least in their early postindependence years, constituted a vocal opposition to U.S. and Western efforts to retain or reimpose economic and cultural arrangements that perpetuated these nations' dependency.

The clash of interests between the few highly industrialized and powerful states, with the United States acting as militant whip, and the overwhelming majority of have-nots was epitomized in the struggle, first, for a New International Economic

Order (NIEO) and, soon after, a New International Information Order (NIIO). The West refused to allow changes in the prevailing world economic and cultural patterns that favored and perpetuated their interests.

The lesson Washington took away from these engagements in the 1960s and 1970s was to regard the United Nations as an oppositional force. The American media presented the UN as a body inimical to the American way of life. Within a short time, polls would demonstrate convincingly that the American public wanted nothing to do with the UN, and this "public opinion" became the justification for Washington's further anti-UN behavior. It was also a good example, so dear to the hearts of TV executives, of "giving the people what they want" – *after* they have been repeatedly "informed" by the information managers.

The collapse and disappearance of Soviet power made changes inevitable in this long-cultivated popular outlook. A United Nations with a supplicant Russia, instead of a veto-exercising superpower, is more attractive to Washington strategists. Yet the will to dominate without an international mediating body remains strong in some sections of the governing elite.

Elite opinion is split between the strategy of using the United Nations as an instrument for advancing U.S. national interests and the pursuit of an uncompromising unilateralist position. Both perspectives assume that state power will remain in place and continue to prevail, an assumption that gives an air of unreality to both tendencies. Promoters of increased U.S. interest in a Soviet-free UN see that as the best way of organizing and stabilizing the world in accord with the market system. In this view, the post-Cold War UN is a useful extension of U.S. policy. The opposing view believes that state power remains decisive in international affairs – and thus the U.S. should not yield its unilateral control to an international body.

The president and his secretary of state, the top command of the foreign-policy establishment, are deeply attached to the "leadership syndrome." From the beginning of his administration, President Clinton has emphasized, "we are, after all, the world's only superpower. We do have to lead the world" (*The New York Times*, April 24, 1993). And Secretary of State Warren Christopher has chimed in: "I think our need to lead is not constrained by our resources... I think that where we need to lead... we will find the resources to accomplish that" (Steven A. Holmes, "Christopher Reaffirms Leading U.S. Role in World," *The New York Times*, May 28, 1993).

One glaring weakness of the "leadership syndrome" is Christopher's confident assertion of the resource capability of the U.S. to "lead" the world. This claim is precisely what is called into question by a Rand Corporation analyst. To be a successful hegemonic power, he writes,

> is a wasting proposition. A hegemonic power forced to place such importance on military security must divert capital and creativity from the civilian sector, even as other states, freed from onerous spending for security, add resources to economically productive investments. As America's relative economic strength erodes, so does the comparative advantage over other powers upon which its hegemony is founded.... It is difficult to see, therefore, how capitalism can survive the decline of the Pax

Americana. (Benjamin C. Schwarts, "Is Capitalism Doomed?" *The New York Times*, May 23, 1994)

A still greater problem confronts those who look forward to a long era of U.S. world "leadership": the reduced capability of all political formations, state, local, regional, to manage, much less control, the vast private economic forces that now are embodied in the transnational corporate system. (We leave aside here the impact on national governance of the renewed strength and clamor of nationalistic and ethnic forces in many parts of the world. These feed on the economic chaos produced by the global market system.)

Early on in his administration, President Clinton outlined succinctly the features of the present world order and some of the dilemmas they produced (speech at the American University, February 26, 1993; text in *The New York Times*, February 27, 1993):

> Capital clearly has become global. Some three trillion dollars race around the world every day. And when a firm wants to build a new factory, it can turn to financial markets now open 24 hours a day from New York to Singapore. Products have clearly become more global. Now, if you buy an American car, it may be an American car built with some parts from Taiwan, designed by Germans, sold with British-made advertisements – or a combination of others in a different mix.

The president elaborated on this transnational corporate scenario:

> Services have become global. The accounting firm that keeps the books for a small business in Wichita may also be helping new entrepreneurs in Warsaw. And the same fast food restaurant that your family goes to – or at least I go to – also may be serving families from Manila to Moscow, and managing its business globally with information, technologies and satellites.

Clinton noted at least a trace of the effects of the operations of this private system:

> Could it be, that the world's most powerful nation has also given up a significant measure of its sovereignty in the quest to lift the fortunes of people throughout the world?

The answer is yes – but not for the reason Clinton offers. "Lifting the fortunes" of people around the world is hardly the motivation of the global corporate system that is reducing the authority of governments everywhere.

Still, from this partial understanding of the workings of the global economy, the Clinton White House has come to a fundamental conclusion concerning the role and importance of information in the routines and practices of the economic order. Here, too, the president's grasp of the new reality commands attention: "Most important of all, information has become global and has become king of the global economy." It follows that "In earlier history, wealth was measured in land, in gold, in oil, in machines. Today, the principal measure of our wealth is information: its quality, its quantity, and the speed with which we acquire it and adapt to it...."

It is this assessment that explains the genesis of the Clinton administration's preoccupation with and support for the new electronic information infrastructure. It is the vast information capabilities that the new infrastructure will provide that excites the government and that prompts the presidential assertion that mastery of this technology will enable the U.S. "to win in the 21st century" (NII 1993).

The reasoning is straightforward. If, in fact, information has become the vital element in the world and domestic economy, the expansion of information capability must confer increased, even uncontested authority on those who have it. This conclusion reinforces the unilateralist position. Why offer support to the United Nations or any other international body if the means of global authority – information control – are at hand? But is it so simple?

Those who believe state power will be enhanced by the new information technologies and expanded information flows may be overlooking one critical point. The main beneficiaries of the new instrumentation and its product are likely to be the transnational corporations. They will always be the first to install and use these advanced communication technologies.

The strength, flexibility, and range of global business will become more remarkable. The capability of the state, including the still very powerful United States, to enforce its will on the economy, domestic or international, will be further diminished. This may be partly obscured for a time because the national security state will have at its disposal an enhanced military and intelligence capability, derived from the new information technologies.

Interest rates, capital investment, employment, business-cycle policy, local working conditions, education, and entertainment increasingly elude national jurisdiction. Creation of a far-flung information superhighway will accelerate the process. This suggests that the government's information policy is a recipe for further diminution of national power, one that will encourage even greater concentration of private, unaccountable economic influence in geographically dispersed locales.

Some people see this corporate undermining of state power as a development to be encouraged. Given the long history of coercive state power, this view is certainly appealing. But politics must take account of prevailing power relationships: while the national state remains a potentially repressive force, today private, unaccountable economic power constitutes a greater threat to individual and community well-being.

The contours of the world-in-the-making, of progressively enfeebled governments, are shadowy, but one description, heavily influenced by the role of the new information technologies, is offered by Alvin Toffler. Toffler, one of the early boosters of the information-using economy and, accordingly, a darling of the speculative financial community, has long called the current historical epoch "the Third Wave" (Toffler 1980). In his typology, this denotes the shift first from agricultural to industrial society and now to an information-using society.

According to Toffler, global organization, production, distribution, work, living arrangements, and war itself have been profoundly affected. More cognizant than most of emerging realities, Toffler foresees the development of global "niche economies." Though he doesn't define them as such, niche economies can only be understood as enclaves of successful, transnational corporate activity. Some of the sites Toffler mentions include regions in southern China, parts of the former Soviet Union, the Baltic states, and southern Brazil – highlighting the fact that the sharp divisions between the well-off and the disadvantaged occur *within* as well as between countries.

Though inequality in the social order is nothing new, capitalist "development" accentuates and deepens this condition. And the new information technologies extend inequality by providing additional capabilities – mobility, flexibility, instantaneity – to the global corporation.

In *The Global City*, Saskia Sassen views the rise of what she calls global cities – Tokyo, London, New York, and lesser centers – as the direct outcome of the operations of the transnational corporations. These giant firms require a wide range of what Sassen calls "producer services" – advertising, design, accounting, financial, legal, management, security, and personnel – which can be concentrated in a few metropolitan centers. The life of these new centers may offer a glimpse of the future for some parts of the world population (Sassen 1991).

For Kenichi Ohmae, writing in the *Wall Street Journal*, the future is already here:

> No longer will managers organize international activities of their companies on the basis of national borders. Now the choice will be not whether to go into, say, China, but which region of China to enter.... The primary linkages of these natural economic zones are not to their "host" countries but to the global economy.

Ohmae finds that the best example of what he is describing

> is Dalian, a prosperous city of 5.2 million people in Liaoning Province in northern China. Dalian's prosperity has been driven not by clever management from Beijing but by an infusion of foreign capital and the presence of foreign corporations. Of the 3,500 corporations operating there, as many as 2,500 are affiliates of foreign companies from all over the world.... In Dalian you can virtually smell the global economy at work (Kenichi Ohmae, "New World Order: The Rise of the Region-State," *The Wall Street Journal*, August 16, 1994).

Toffler's "niche economies" also contribute to what he terms "the Revolt of the Rich." In the past, it was invariably the poor who revolted against the rich. But now well-off groups and locales want to preserve and extend their advantages. They do their best to distance themselves from, and to discard, their lagging and disadvantaged countrymen, regions, states.

Toffler's explanations may be deficient, but his descriptions are accurate enough. The poor, a good part of the minority population, and the inadequately educated are increasingly cordoned off in urban centers, jails, hospitals, and isolating areas and institutions.

Similarly, privileged countries today try to seal themselves off from masses of desperate people who wish to escape from destitute home areas. Western Europe tries to keep out the Africans and the East Europeans, Japan maintains tight control over immigration, Washington is wary of the human tide from the Southern Hemisphere that presses against the continental borders.

Can the rich enclaves, favored groups, and still relatively viable nation-states succeed in severing their ties with their poor neighbors, inside and outside their borders? While Toffler doesn't directly address this central question, he does speak about "niche war," making the connection clear. He regards the Persian Gulf War as an early model of what may be in store for those seeking to challenge the new world corporate order. Toffler puts it this way:

> [I]f we are now in the process of transforming the way we create wealth, from the industrial to the informational . . . there is a parallel change taking place with warfare, of which the Gulf War gives only the palest, palest little hint. The transition actually started back in the late 1970s, early 1980s, to a new form of warfare based on information superiority. It mirrors the way the economy has become information-dependent.

Toffler further predicts that

> In military terms there will be attempts to coordinate all the knowledge-intensive activities of the military from education and training to high-precision weaponry to espionage to everything that involves the mind – propaganda – into coherent strategies. ("Shock Wave Anti-Warrior," *Wired*, November 1993)

Along with the "niche war" strategy to overcome social eruptions, Toffler endorses the transmission of news and information to disaffected areas. CNN, for example, is regarded favorably as a suitable channel in such endeavors, as are the BBC and Japan's NHK. These networks are seen as unproblematic, reliable vehicles, dispensing "news" and information that will undermine the dissidents, whoever they may be.

Washington's plan for an information superhighway does not mention these applications, but the thinking underlying the project surely takes them into account. What else can it mean when the installation of the new information technologies are regarded as the vehicle to "win in the 21st century"?

But can precision warfare with a high information component and control of global news flows keep the world orderly while privately initiated economic forces are contributing to wildly disproportionate income distribution and gravely distorted resource utilization, locally and globally?

The deepening crisis that is provoked by advanced technology, used mainly for corporate advantage and implemented according to the rules of the market, may summon forth even less promising "solutions." Direct military interventions in nations "where governments have crumbled and the most basic conditions for civilized life have disappeared . . . is a trend that should be encouraged," writes one historian whose views have had respectful attention in the mainstream media.

According to this writer, the root cause of problems in many Third World countries, especially African nations, "is obvious but is never publicly admitted: some states are not yet fit to govern themselves" (Paul Johnson, "Colonialism's Back – and Not a Moment Too Soon," *The New York Times Sunday Magazine*,

April 18, 1992). But it is not a matter of being fit to govern oneself, a patronizing, if not racist charge. In the last years of the twentieth century, satisfactory governance is in crisis almost everywhere. The crisis derives from the weakening of state authority that has been brought about by a half a century of Cold War conflict, in tandem with the expansion of unaccountable private economic power. Information technologies at the disposal of this power further exacerbate already bad conditions. The response to this global crisis demands a totally different economic, political, and cultural direction from what now prevails.

References

Barnet, Richard, and Cavenaugh, John. 1994. *Global Dreams.* New York: Simon & Schuster.

Gore, Albert. 1994. Remarks delivered at the meeting of the International Telcommunications Union, Buenos Aires (March 21).

The National Information Infrastructure (NII). 1993. Agenda for Action, Executive Summary. Washington (September 15).

Sassen, Saskia. 1991. *The Global City.* Princeton: Princeton University Press.

Schiller, Herbert I. 1992. *Mass Communications and American Empire.* New ed. Boulder: Westview.

Toffler, Alvin. 1980. *The Third Wave.* New York: William Morrow.

World Investment Report. 1993. Transnational Corporation and Integrated International Production. United Nations Conference on Trade and Development, Programme on Transnational Corporations. New York: United Nations.

18

The Coming of Age of the Flesh Machine

Critical Art Ensemble

Critical Art Ensemble, "The Coming of Age of the Flesh Machine," in *Flesh Machine: Cyborgs, Designer Babies, and New Eugenic Consciousness* (Brooklyn: Autonomedia, 1998). Anti-copyrighted. Publishers state in the book that the contents may be freely used or "pirated," as long as they receive notice.

Critical Art Ensemble is an anonymous collective of five artists dedicated to exploring the intersections of art, technology, radical politics, and critical theory. "The Coming of Age of the Flesh Machine" is a cautionary piece about the danger posed as technology increasingly influences politics, science, and attitudes toward the body.

Over the past century, the two machines that comprise the general state apparatus have reached a level of sophistication which neither is likely to transcend. These complex mechanisms, the war machine and the sight machine, will go through many generations of refinement in the years to come; for the time being, however, the boundaries of their influence have stabilized.

The war machine is the apparatus of violence engineered to maintain the social, political, and economic relationships that support its continued existence in the world. The war machine consumes the assets of the world in classified rituals of uselessness (for example, missile systems that are designed never to be used, but rather to pull competing systems of violence into high-velocity cycles of war-tech production) and in spectacles of hopeless massacre (such as the Persian Gulf war). The history of the war machine has generally been perceived in the West as history itself (although some resistance to this belief began during the 19th century), and while the war machine has not followed a unilinear course of progress, due to disruptions by moments of inertia caused by natural disasters or cultural exhaustion, its engines have continued to creep toward realizing the historical construction of becoming the totality of social existence. Now it has reached an unsurpassable peak – a violence of such intensity that species annihilation is not only possible, but probable. Under these militarized conditions, the human condition becomes one of continuous alarm and preparation for the final moment of collective mortality.

The well-known counterpart of the war machine is the sight machine. It has two purposes: to mark the space of violent spectacle and sacrifice, and to control the symbolic order. The first task is accomplished through surveying and mapping all varieties of space, from the geographic to the social. Through the development of satellite-based imaging technologies, in combination with computer networks capable of sorting, storing, and retrieving vast amounts of visual information, a holistic representation has been constructed of the social, political, economic, and geographical landscape(s) that allows for near-perfect surveillance of all areas, from the micro to the macro. Through such visualization techniques, any situation or population deemed unsuitable for perpetuating the war machine can be targeted for sacrifice or for containment.

The second function of the sight machine, to control the symbolic order, means that the sight machine must generate representations that normalize the state of war in everyday life, and which socialize new generations of individuals into their machinic roles and identities. These representations are produced using all types of imaging technologies, from those as low-tech as a paint brush to ones as high-tech as supercomputers. The images are then distributed through the mass media in a ceaseless barrage of visual stimulation. To make sure that an individual cannot escape the imperatives of the sight machine for a single waking moment, ideological signatures are also deployed through the design and engineering of all artifacts and architectures. This latter strategy is ancient in its origins, but combined with the mass media's velocity and its absence of spatial restrictions, the sight machine now has the power to systematically encompass the globe in its spectacle. This is not to say that the world will be homogenized in any specific sense. The machinic sensibility understands that differentiation is both useful and necessary. However, the world will be homogenized in a general sense. Now that the machines are globally and specifically interlinked with the ideology and practices of pancapitalism, we can be certain that a hyper-rationalized cycle of production and consumption, under the authority of nomadic corporate-military control, will become the guiding dynamic of the day. How a given population or territory arrives at this principle is open to negotiation, and is measured by the extent to which profit (tribute paid to the war machine) increases within a given area or among a given population.

In spite of the great maturity of these machines, a necessary element still seems to be missing. While representation has been globally and rationally encoded with the imperatives of pancapitalism, the flesh upon which these codings are further inscribed has been left to reproduce and develop in a less than instrumental manner. To be sure, the flesh machine has intersected both the sight and war machines since ancient times, but comparatively speaking, the flesh machine is truly the slowest to develop. This is particularly true in the West, where practices in health and medicine, genetic engineering, or recombinant organisms have thoroughly intersected nonrational practices (particularly those of the spirit). Even when they were secularized after the Renaissance, these practices have consistently been less successful, when compared to their counterparts, in insuring the continuance of a given regime of state power. Unlike the war machine and the sight machine, which have accomplished their supreme tasks – the potential for species annihilation for the former, and global mapping and mass distribution of ideologically coded representation for the latter – the flesh machine has utterly failed to concretize its imagined world of global eugenics.

The simple explanation for the flesh machine's startling lack of development is cultural lag. As the West shifted from a feudal to a capitalist economy, demonstrating the benefits of rationalizing production in regard to war was a relatively simple task. National wealth and border expansion were clearly marked and blended well with the trace leftovers of feudal ideology. Manifest destiny, for example, did not stand in contradiction to Christian expansionism. War, economy, politics, and ideology (the slowest of social manifestations to change) were still working toward a common end (total domination). The rationalization of the flesh, however, could not find a point of connection with theologically informed ideology. Flesh ideology could only coexist as parallel rather than as intersecting tracks. For this reason it is no surprise that one of the fathers of flesh machine ideology was a man of God. The work of Thomas Malthus represents the ideological dilemma presented to the flesh machine on the cusp of the feudal/capitalist economic shift.

Malthus argued that the flesh did not have to be rationalized through secular engineering, since it was already rationalized by the divine order of the cosmos designed by God Himself. Although the nonrational motivation of original sin would guarantee replication of the work force, God had placed "natural checks" on the population, so only those who were needed would be produced. The uncivilized lower classes could be encouraged to have as many children as possible without fear that the population would overrun those in God's grace, because God would sort the good from the bad through famine, disease, and other natural catastrophes. For this reason, the flesh could be left to its own means, free of human intervention, and human progress could focus on fruition through economic progress. Spencerian philosophy, arriving half a century later, complemented this notion by suggesting that those fit for survival would be naturally selected in the social realm. The most skillful, intelligent, beautiful, athletic, etc., would be naturally selected by the structure of the society itself – that of "open" capitalist competition. Hence the flesh machine was still in no need of vigorous attention; however, Spencer did act as a hinge for the development of eugenic consciousness. Spencer constructed an ideological predisposition for conflating natural and social models of selection (the former arrived a decade or so after Spencer's primary theses were published). This made it possible for genetic engineering to become a naturalized social function, intimately tied to social progress without being a perversion of nature – in fact, it was now a part of nature. At this point eugenic consciousness could continue to develop uninterrupted by feudal religious dogma until its traces evaporated out of capitalist economy, or until it could be better reconfigured to suit the needs of capitalism. While the idea of a eugenic world continued to flourish in all capitalist countries, and culminated in the Nazi flesh experiment of the 30s and early 40s, the research never materialized that would be necessary to elevate the flesh machine to a developmental level on a par with the war machine.

Perhaps there is an even simpler explanation. Machinic development can only occur at the pace of one machine at a time, since scarce resources allow for only so much indirect military research. After the war machine came to full fruition with the implementation of fully matured total war during World War II, along with the attendant economic expansion, it became possible to allocate a generous helping of excess capital for the expansion of the next machine. In this case, it was the sight machine which had proved its value during the war effort with the development of radar and sonar, and thereby jumped to the front of the line for maximum investment. It was also clearly understood at this point that global warfare required new attention to logistic organization. The road between strategic and tactical weapons and logistical needs had leveled out, and this realization also pushed the sight machine to the front of the funding line. Conversely, the need of the Allied powers to separate themselves ideologically as far as possible from Nazi ideology pushed the desired development of the flesh machine back into the realm of nonhuman intervention. Consequently, the alliance between the war machine and the sight machine continued without interruption, delivering ever-increasingly sophisticated weapons of mass destruction. It also created an ever more enveloping visual/information apparatus – most notably satellite technology, television, video, computers, and the Net.

While the war machine reached relative completion in the 60s, the sight machine did not reach relative completion until the 80s (die-hard Web-users might want to argue for the 90s). Now a third machine can claim its share of excess capital, so the funds are flowing in increasing abundance to a long deferred dream. The flesh machine is here. It has been turned on, and like its siblings, the war machine and the sight machine, it cannot be turned off. As is to be expected, the flesh machine replicates elements of the sight and war machines in its construction. It is these moments of replication which are of interest in this essay.

A Brief Note on Scientific Imagination, Ethics, and the Flesh Machine

In the best of all possible worlds, ethical positions relevant to the flesh machine would be primary to any discussion about it. In fact, to read the literature on the flesh machine (which at this point is dominated by the medical and scientific establishments), one would think that ethics is of key concern to those in the midst of flesh machine development; however, nothing could be further from reality. The scientific establishment has long since demonstrated that when it comes to machinic development, ethics has no real place other than its ideological role as spectacle. Ethical discourse is not a point of blockage in regard to machinic development. Take the case of nuclear weapons development. The ethical argument that species annihilation is an unacceptable direction for scientific inquiry should certainly have been enough to block the production of such weaponry; however, the needs of the war machine rendered this discourse silent. In fact, the need of the war machine to overcome competing machinic systems moved nuclear weapons development along at top velocity. Handsome rewards and honors were paid to individuals and institutions participating in the nuclear initiative. In a word, ethical discourse was totally ignored. If big science can ignore nuclear holocaust and species annihilation, it seems very safe to assume that concerns about eugenics or any of the other possible flesh catastrophes are not going to be very meaningful in its deliberations about flesh machine policy and practice. Without question, it is in the interest of pancapitalism to rationalize the flesh, and consequently it is in the financial interest of big science to see that this desire manifests itself in the world.

Another problem with machinic development could be the institutionally-contained panglossian reification of the scientific imagination. Consider the following quote from Eli Friedman, president of the International Society for Artificial Organs, in regard to the development of artificial organs:

> Each of us attempting to advance medical science – whether an engineer, chemist, theoretician, or physician – depends on personal enthusiasm to sustain our work. Optimistic, self-driven investigators succeed beyond the point where the pessimist, convinced that the project cannot be done, has given up. Commitment to the design, construction, and implanting of artificial internal organs requires a positive, romantic, and unrestrained view of what may be attainable. Members of our society share a bond gained by the belief that fantasy can be transformed into reality.

and:

> ISAO convenes an extraordinary admixture of mavericks, "marchers to different drums," and very smart scientists capable of converting "what if" into "why not."

These lovely rhetorical flourishes primarily function to rally the troops in what will be a hard-fought battle for funding. It's time to move fast (the less reflection the better) if the AO model is to dominate the market; after all, there is serious competition from those who believe that harvesting organs from animals (transgenic animals if need be) is the better path along which to proceed. But it is the subtext of such thinking that is really of the greatest interest. From this perspective, science lives in a transcendental world beyond the social relationships of domination. If something is perceived as good in the lab, it will be good in the world, and the way a scientist imagines a concept/application to function in the world is the way it will in fact function. The most horrifying notion however, is the idea (bred from a maniacal sense of entitlement) that "if you can imagine it, you may as well do it," as if science is unconnected to any social structures or dynamics other than utopia and progress.

Perhaps the only hope is that the funding and the optimism becomes so excessive that it undermines machinic development. Star Wars is a perfect example of incidental resistance from the scientific establishment. During the Reagan-era big bonanza for war machine funding, the most ludicrous promises were made by big science in order to obtain research funds. The result was a series of contraptions that truly defines the comedy of science. Two of the finest examples are the rail gun that self-destructed upon launching its pellet projectile, and the deadly laser ray that had a range of only three feet. While the American taxpayers might see red over the excessive waste, a major section of the scientific establishment was apparently distracted enough by the blizzard of money that they failed to make any useful lethal devices.

If I Can See It, It's Already Dead

The war machine and the sight machine intersect at two key points – in the visual targeting of enemy forces (military sites, production sites, and population centers), and in visualizing logistical routes. Once sited and accurately placed within a detailed spatial grid, the enemy may be dispatched at the attacker's leisure, using the most efficient routes and means of attack. As long as the enemy can remain invisible, determining proper strategic action is difficult, if not impossible. Hence any successful offensive military action begins with visualization and representation. A strong defensive posture also requires proper visual intelligence. The better the vision, the more time available to configure a counterattack. The significant principle here – the one being replicated in the development of the flesh machine – is that vision equals control. Therefore the flesh machine, like its counterparts, is becoming increasingly photocentric.

Not surprisingly, much of the funding for the flesh machine is intended to develop maps of the body and to design imaging systems that will expedite this process. From the macro to the micro (the Human Genome Project being the best known), no stone can remain unturned. Every aspect of the body must be open to the vision of medical and scientific authority. Once the body is thoroughly mapped and its "mechanistic" splendor revealed, any body invader (organic or otherwise) can be eliminated, and the future of that body can be accurately predicted. While such developments sound like a boon to humanity, one need not be an expert in the field to be skeptical of such prospects.

While it is hard to doubt the success of the war machine in reducing military activity to the mechanized (that is, fully rationalized structures and dynamics), it is questionable whether the body can be reduced to a similar state regardless of how well it is represented. One major problem is that the body cannot be separated from its environment, since so many of its processes are set in motion by environmental conditions. For example, a toxic environment can produce undesirable effects in the body. Visual representation alerts medicine to an invasion, so action can be taken to contain or eliminate the invader. In this situation, medicine is reactive rather than preventive, and treats only the effect and not the cause. In fact, it diverts causality away from ecological pathologies, and reinvests it back in the body. In this manner, medicine becomes an alibi for whatever created the toxic situation that infected the body in the first place, by acting as if the infectant emerged internally. The problem raised here is the limited frame of representation in regard to the body map, in conjunction with an emphasis on tactical solutions to physical pathologies. This situation is, of course, understandable, since strategic action would have an undermining effect on the medical market. The one exception to this rule is when the toxic body emerges due to behavioral factors. In this case, the scientific/medical establishment can expand its authority over the body by suggesting and often enforcing behavioral restrictions on patients. In this situation, the science and medical establishment functions as a benevolent police force deployed against individuals to better mold them to the needs of the state.

To complicate matters further, flesh machine science and medicine have the unfortunate but necessary habit of putting the cart before the horse. The flesh machine, unlike its counterparts, does not have the luxury of developing its visual and weapons systems simultaneously, nor can weapons development precede advanced visual capabilities. The visual apparatus must come first. For example, antibiotics probably could not have been invented before the development of a microscope. Consequently, as in most research and development, a shotgun method is employed, whereby all varieties of vision machines are developed in the hopes that a few may be of some use. This leads to thrilling headlines like the following from Daniel Haney of the Associated Press: "Brain Imagery Exposes a Killer." What this headline refers to is a new medical map, acquired through the use of positron-emission tomography, which reveals the part of the brain affected by Alzheimer's disease, and the degree to which the brain has been eroded by the disease. This map can help physicians to diagnose Alzheimer's up to ten years before symptom onset. The comedy begins with the admission that there is no way to predict when symptoms will begin to appear, and that there is still no known treatment for the disease. All that medical science can do is tell the patient that s/he has the disease, and that s/he will be feeling its effect sometime in the future. The excitement over being able to visualize this disease comes from the belief that if the disease can be seen, then cure is near at hand. Or, in the words of the war machine, "If I can see it, it's already dead."

Since the process of visualization and representation in this case is at best only an indication of a far-off possibility for cure, and hence is of little use for the patient already diagnosed with the disease, it must be asked: Who could benefit from this information? Alzheimer's is in fact doubly problematic because it can be visualized before symptom onset, and because genetic mapping can also be used to indicate an individual's likelihood of developing it. The flesh machine's intersection with the surveying function of the sight machine becomes dramatically clear in this situation. Those who would benefit most from this information are insurance companies and the employer of the person likely to be afflicted with the ailment. Such information would be a tremendous cost-cutting device for both. However, ethical discussions about collecting bio-data lead one to believe that such information would remain confidential in the doctor-patient relationship. Perhaps privacy will be maintained. However, it seems more likely that if the information is perceived to lead to significantly higher profits, resources will be allocated by corporate sources to acquire it. The most common strategy to watch for is legislative initiatives pursued under the spectacle of benevolence. Mandatory drug testing for some private and public employment, under the authority of employee and public security, is an example of the means by which privacy can be eroded.

Finally there is the problem of representation itself. As the war machine demonstrates, the greater the visualization of a frontier territory, the greater the degree of contestation at the visualized sight. In other words, the more that is seen, the more power realizes what needs to be controlled and how to control it. The brain is certainly going to be the key, but happily, at this point, the research is too immature to warrant strategic intervention on behalf of state power. There are, however, good indicators of how the coming battle will take shape. One need only think of the visualization of the body and its connection to varieties of smoking bans from the legalistic to the normative, or in terms of populist countersurveillance, the relationship of toxins (DDT, for example) in the environment to body visualization, to understand the connection between vision, discipline, and contestation. The prizewinner, however, is the visualization of uterine space. Feminist critics have long shown how this point of ultra-violent contestation is but the beginning of the age of flesh machine violence. (This is also a point of great hope, as the discourse of the flesh machine has been appropriated from the experts. At the same time, this conflict has shown how fascist popular fronts are just as adept at appropriation.) In regard to uterine space, feminist critics have consistently pointed out that this variety of representation loads the ideological dice by presenting the space as separate from the wholistic bio-system of the woman, thus reinforcing the notion of "fetal space." This idea acts as a basis for "fetal rights," which are then argued as taking precedence over the rights of women.

A new era of bio-marginality has surely begun. Certainly this situation will only be reinforced by the visualization of either diseases or abnormalities (actual or potential) in subjects soon to be classified under the sign of the unfit. The unfit will be defined in accordance with their utility in relationship to the machine world of pancapitalism. The mapped body is the quantified body. Its use is measured down to the penny. Without such a development, how could any consumer trust in the markets of the flesh machine?

Selling Flesh

One of the oldest manifestations of the flesh machine is the idea of engineering the breeding of plants and livestock to produce what are perceived to be the most functional products within a given cultural situation. Increased knowledge about this task has certainly contributed to the great abundance in the food supply in the first world, thus shifting an individual's relationship to food from one of need to one of desire. In light of this achievement, industrial food producers have been faced with the task of developing foods that meet the logistical demands of broad-based distribution, while still maintaining a product that the manufacturer can market as desirable. The most productive solution thus far is the manufacture of processed foods; however, the market for food cannot be limited to processed food. The desire for perishable foods is too deeply etched into the culture, and no amount of spectacle can root out this desire. Fortunately for the producers of perishable foods, the product and the market can be rationalized to a great extent. This particular market is of interest because it provides at this moment the best illustration of the market imperatives that are being replicated in the industrial production and distribution of human flesh products. (This is not to say that flesh production will not one day be more akin to processed food, it is only to argue that at present the means of production are still too immature.)

To better illuminate this point, consider the case of apples. At the turn of the century, there were dozens of various types of apples available to the buying public.

Now when a consumer cruises through a supermarket in search of apples, the choice has been limited to three (red, green, and yellow). Choice has become increasingly limited partly because of logistical considerations. Like most perishable fruits and vegetables these days, apples are bred to have a long shelf life. In order to have apples all year round, they must be transported from locations that have the conditions to produce them when other locations cannot. Hence these apples must be able to survive an extended distribution process, and not all varieties of apples are capable of resisting rotting for long periods of time. However, logistics alone does not adequately explain choice limitations. Perhaps more important to the formula are market considerations.

Marketing agencies have understood for decades that desire is intensified most through visual appeal. How a product looks determines the probability of a consumer purchase more than any other variable. For apples, the consumer wants brightly colored surfaces, a rounded form, and white inner flesh. In other words, consumers want the perfect storybook apple that they have seen represented since they were children. Apples are bred to suit the cultural construction of "an apple," and only a few varieties of apples can simulate this appearance and meet this desire. This situation is yet another case of Baudrillard's universe of platonic madness, where consumers are caught in the tyranny of representation that passes as essence.

Along with the domination of vision, there comes the need of the producer to offer the consumer a reliable product, meaning that the apples one buys tomorrow will look and taste like the ones bought today. Consequently, there is an elimination of sense data other than the visual. If all that is needed to excite desire is a good visual, why bother to develop taste and smell? Especially when a good product can be guaranteed if it is completely tasteless (one can be sure that the apple purchased tomorrow will taste like the one purchased today)? In this situation, the tyranny of the image becomes glaringly apparent; one would think that smell and taste would be the dominating senses when buying foods, since they would best articulate the pleasure of consumption. Not so, it is vision, and unfortunately many of the most tasty apples do not look very good because they have none of the necessary storybook appeal. Consequently various types of apples have been eliminated, or limited to distribution in localized markets.

If the principles of product reliability and visual appeal are applied to the production/consumption components (as opposed to those concerned with control) of the flesh machine, the reasons for some recent developments become a little clearer. The first problem that flesh producers must face is how to get a reliable product. At present too little is known about genetic processes to fulfill this necessary market imperative. Consequently, they have had to rely on fooling the naive consumer. For example, one characteristic commonly sought after by those in the techno-baby market is intelligence. Unfortunately this characteristic cannot be guaranteed; in fact, flesh producers haven't the slightest idea how to replicate intelligence. However, they can promise breeding materials from intelligent donors. While using the sperm of a Nobel Prize winner in no way guarantees a smart child, and doesn't even increase the probability (nor does it decrease the probability of having a below average child), flesh dealers are able to use false analogies to sell their product. (If two tall parents have a child, the probability of the child being tall is increased, so wouldn't it be correct to say that if two people of above average intelligence have a child, that it would increase the probability that the child will have above average intelligence?) Many consumers believe this line of thought (the myth of hard genetic determinism has always been very seductive) and are therefore willing to pay higher prices for the sperm of an intelligent man than they are for the sperm of an average donor. Although this fraud will probably not continue indefinitely in the future, an important ideological seed is being sown. People are being taught to think eugenically. The perception is growing that in order to give a child every possible benefit in life, its conception should be engineered.

Another common strategy to better regulate flesh products is to take a genetic reading of the embryo while still in the petri dish. If a genetic characteristic is discovered that is deemed defective, the creature can be terminated before implantation. Again, parents-to-be can have their eugenic dreams come true within the limits of the genetic test. Even parents using the old-fashioned method of conception at least have the option of visualization (sonar) to make sure that the desired gender characteristic is realized. In each of these cases, better visualization and representation, along with an expanded range of genetic tests, will help to insure that desired characteristics are always a part of the flesh product, which leads to the conclusion that better vision machines are as important for profit as they are for control.

At the same time, remember that the marketing practices of postmodernity do not wholly apply to the flesh machine, and at present tend to function on an as-needed basis. Fertility clinics, for example, participate as much in the economy of scarcity (although it must be noted that these products and processes do not intersect the economy of need) as they do in the economy of desire. While they may use the practices described above, they also have the luxury of being the only option for those who have been denied the ability to produce flesh materials. Those clinics that can boast a product success rate of over 20% (most notably the Center for Reproductive Medicines and Infertility at New York Hospital-Cornell Medical Center, with a success rate of 34%) cannot meet the demand for their goods and services. Apparently, the market for flesh goods and services has been preconstructed in the bio-ideology of capitalism.

When Worlds Collide

Assuming that the flesh machine is guided by the pancapitalist imperatives of control and profit, what will occur if these two principles come into conflict with one another? This has been known to happen as social machines march toward maturity. The sight machine is currently facing this very contradiction in the development of the Net. Currently the Net has some space that is relatively open to the virtual public. In these free zones, one can get information on anything, from radical politics to the latest in commodity development. As to be expected, a lot of information floating about is resistant to the causes and imperatives of pancapitalism, and from the perspective of the state is badly in need of censorship. However, the enforcement of limited speech on the Net would require measures that would be devastating to on-line services and phone service providers, and could seriously damage the market potential of this new tool. (The Net has an unbelievably high concentration of wealthy literate consumers. It's a market pool that corporate authority does not want to annoy.) The dominant choice at present is to let the disorder of the Net continue until the market mechanisms are fully in place, and the virtual public is socialized to their use; then more repressive measures may be considered. Social conservatism taking a back seat to fiscal conservatism seems fairly representative of pancapitalist conflict resolution. The question is, will this policy replicate itself in the flesh machine?

A good example to speculate on in regard to this issue is the ever-elusive "gay gene," always on the verge of discovery, isolation, and visualization. Many actually anxiously await this discovery to prove once and for all that gayness is an essential quality and not just a "lifestyle" choice. However, once placed in the eugenic matrix this discovery might elicit some less positive associations. In the typical alarmist view, if the gene comes under the control of the flesh machine, then it will be eliminated from the gene pool, thus giving compulsory heterosexuality a whole new meaning. Under the imperative of control this possibility seems likely; however, when the imperative of marketability is considered, a different scenario emerges. There may well be a sizable market population for whom the selection of a gay gene would be desirable. Why would a good capitalist turn his back on a population that represents so much profit, not to mention that gay individuals as a submarket (CAE is assuming that some heterosexuals would select the gay gene too) must submit to the flesh machine to reproduce? Again, market and social imperatives come into conflict, but it is unknown which imperative will be selected for enforcement.

Such an issue at least demonstrates the complexity of the flesh machine, and how difficult the task of analyzing this third leviathan will be. What is certain is that the flesh machine is interdependent with and interrelated to the war machine and the sight machine of pancapitalism, and that it is certainly going to intensify the violence and the repression of its predecessors through the rationalization of the final component (i.e., the flesh) of the production/consumption process. Until maps are produced for the purpose of resistance and are crossed-referenced through the perspectives of numerous contestational voices, there will be no way, practical or strategic, to resist this new attack on liberationist visions, discourse, and practice.

Part IV

Performing Identity in Cyberspace

"There is no race. There is no gender. There is no age. There are no infirmities. There are only minds. Utopia? No, internet." This recent ad from MCI Worldcom typifies the boosterism that posits the Net as colorless, carefree, and democratic. In the face of enormous disparities in access and literacy, commercial promoters of digital technology assert its egalitarian character – even as they target their advertising to upscale market segments and specific geographic sites. It's no secret to residents of what have been termed Internet "dead zones" in states like Georgia, Mississippi, Maine, and Wyoming that low density regions are falling behind the rest of the nation in their access to high-speed telephone lines. In this light it is important to remember that little more than a decade ago admission to cyberspace required membership in an elite community: the university. Now one needs access to a computer, modem, phone line, and Internet provider – criteria that still exclude poor people and certain communities of color in disproportionate numbers.

Much of the idealized discourse of cyberspace discounts such materialist exigencies, but it does something else as well. Paul Virilio has explained how formulations of "cyberspace," the "Infobahn," and the like seem to encourage thinking that minimizes or smoothes over issues of difference. "The negative aspect of these information superhighways is precisely this loss of orientation regarding alterity, this disturbance in the relationship with the other."[1] Needed are conversations about technology that address these absences, erasures, or confusions. Indeed it is in writing that engages difference and identity that some of the most powerful analyses of technology are emerging. Certainly the writing of Anne Balsamo, Donna Haraway, Sandy Stone, and other feminist theorists addresses gendered technologies of power and control and thus begins to tackle the ways that science has been used in very real ways to sexualize and regulate the body. Whether one is discussing fad diets, prosthetic limbs, HIV research, or the general exclusion of women from network "communities," this focus on social technologies and physical regulation anchors futuristic speculation in the lived experience of human subjects.

Placed in a more global context, the very experience of networked communication, of digital aesthetics, reproduces a Western, specifically Cartesian, spatial model of representation, not unlike that of the cinema, creating a viewing subject occupying a privileged vantage point that is apart from the world viewed, and that permits that world to be constructed as something to be examined, manipulated, or owned. As Cameron Bailey explains in this volume, this creates a "self/other representational model that constructs a center/margin epistemology privileging the cybersubject as male, white, straight, able bodied, and dominant classed."

To get specific for a moment, one need only look to the cliquish language of the online world that excludes outsiders with a technical jargon of *MUDs*, *MOOs*, *avatars*, and *spam*. This constitutes an interpretive community predicated on a set of exclusionary rules and "netiquette" that is far from civil. In any visit to an online chat room one will observe voluminous anti-Semitic, racist, homophobic, and especially sexist speech, giving the lie to the myth of a disembodied or colorless cyberspace. Does the Internet encourage such behavior from otherwise polite individuals or does it attract bigots? Regardless, the experience of Internet use among women, people of color, lesbian women, gay men, is to foreground their identities while erasing them.

Significant in this regard is the extent to which a disembodied presence on the Internet permits an obfuscation of corporeal presence. By allowing people to mask their identities, the Net permits a kind of "identity performance" that has been used for purposes ranging from role-playing, masquerade, and subversion to deception, fraud, and assault. From the general analyses by Sandy Stone and Sherry Turkle to the more specific discussions by Julian Dibbell, Laura Miller, Lisa Nakamura, and Steve Silberman, the essays in this section address different aspects of such performitivity. What conclusions, if any, can one draw about identity in cyberspace? As discussed throughout this book, the age-old dream of a transcendent or idealized virtuality will remain flawed as long as its agents stay tethered to the non-virtual world. And they always will. The challenge facing digital culture is to examine the character of that tethering, and to struggle to understand the many reasons it is ignored, obscured, or denied.

Note

1 Paul Virilio, "The Third Interval: A Critical Transition," in Verena Andermatt Conley, ed., *Rethinking Technologies (Minneapolis: Minnesota, 1993), p. 3.*

19

Will the Real Body Please Stand Up?: Boundary Stories about Virtual Cultures

Allucquère Rosanne (Sandy) Stone

Sandy Stone, excerpt from "Will the Real Body Please Stand Up? Boundary Stories about Virtual Cultures," in Michael Benedikt, ed., *Cyberspace: First Steps* (Cambridge, MA: MIT Press, 1991). Reprinted by permission of The MIT Press.

Allucquère Rosanne (Sandy) Stone is a professor and Director of the Advanced Communications Technologies Laboratory (ACT Lab) at the University of Texas at Austin. Used extensively in courses, this essay provides a social history of virtual communities throughout human history and a comprehensive discussion of contemporary cyber-identity and community.

The Machines Are Restless Tonight

After Donna Haraway's "Promises of Monsters" and Bruno Latour's papers on actor networks and artifacts that speak, I find it hard to think of any artifact as being devoid of agency. Accordingly, when the dryer begins to beep complainingly from the laundry room while I am at dinner with friends, we raise eyebrows at each other and say simultaneously, "The machines are restless tonight…"

It's not the phrase, I don't think, that I find intriguing. Even after Haraway (1991) and Latour (1988), the phrase is hard to appreciate in an intuitive way. It's the ellipsis I notice. You can hear those three dots. What comes after them? The fact that the phrase – obviously a send-up of a vaguely anthropological chestnut – seems funny to us, already says a great deal about the way we think of our complex and frequently uneasy imbrications with the unliving. I, for one, spend more time interacting with Saint-John Perse, my affectionate name for my Macintosh computer, than I do with my friends. I appreciate its foibles, and it gripes to me about mine. That someone comes into the room and reminds me that Perse is merely a "passage point" for the work practices of a circle of my friends over in Silicon Valley changes my sense of facing a vague but palpable sentience squatting on my desk not one whit. The people I study are deeply imbricated in a complex social network mediated by little technologies to which they have delegated significant amounts of their time and agency, not to mention their humor. I say to myself: Who am I studying? A group of people? Their machines? A group of people and or in their machines? Or something else?

When I study these groups, I try to pay attention to all of their interactions. And as soon as I allow myself to see that most of the interactions of the people I am studying involve vague but palpable sentiences squatting on their desks, I have to start thinking about watching the machines just as attentively as I watch the people, because, for them, the machines are not merely passage points. Haraway and other workers who observe the traffic across the boundaries between "nature," "society," and "technology" tend to see nature as lively, unpredictable, and, in some sense, actively resisting interpretations. If nature and technology seem to be collapsing into each other, as Haraway and others claim, then the unhumans can be lively too.

One symptom of this is that the flux of information that passes back and forth across the vanishing divides between nature and technology has become extremely dense. Cyborgs with a vengeance, one of the groups I study, is already talking about colonizing a social space in which the divide between nature and technology has become thoroughly unrecognizable, while one of the individuals I study is busy trying to sort out how the many people who seem to inhabit the social space of her body are colonizing her. When I listen to the voices in these new social spaces I hear a multiplicity of voices, some recognizably human and some quite different, all clamoring at once, frequently saying things whose meanings are tantalizingly familiar but which have subtly changed.
[. . .]

Decoupling the Body and the Subject

The illusion will be so powerful you won't be able *to tell what's real and what's not.* Steve Williams

In her complex and provocative 1984 study *The Tremulous Private Body,* Frances Barker suggests that, because of the effects of the Restoration on the social and political imaginary in Britain (1660 and on), the human body gradually ceased to be perceived as public spectacle, as had previously been the case, and became privatized in new ways. In Barker's model of the post-Jacobean citizen, the social economy of the body became rearranged in such a way as to interpose several layers between the individual and public space. Concomitant with this removal of the body from a largely public social economy, Barker argues that the subject, the "I" or perceiving self that Descartes had recently pried loose from its former unity with the body, reorganized, or was reorganized, in a new economy of its own. In particular, the subject, as did the body, ceased to constitute itself as public spectacle and instead fled from the public sphere and constituted itself in *text* – such as Samuel Pepys' diary (1668).

Such changes in the social economy of both the body and the subject, Barker suggests, very smoothly serve the purposes of capital accumulation. The product of a privatized body and of a subject removed from the public sphere is a social monad more suited to manipulation by virtue of being more isolated. Barker also makes a case that the energies of the individual, which were previously absorbed in a complex public social economy and which regularly returned to nourish the sender, started backing up instead, and needing to find fresh outlets. The machineries of capitalism handily provided a new channel for productive energy. Without this damming of creative energies, Barker suggests, the industrial age, with its vast hunger for productive labor and the consequent creation of surplus value, would have been impossible.

In Barker's account, beginning in the 1600s in England, the body became progressively more hidden, first because of changing conventions of dress, later by conventions of spatial privacy. Concomitantly, the self, Barker's "subject," retreated even further inward, until much of its means of expression was through texts. Where social communication had been direct and personal, a warrant was developing for social communication to be indirect and delegated through communication technologies – first pen and paper, and later the technologies and market economics of print. The body (and the subject, although she doesn't lump them together in this way) became "the site of an operation of power, of an exercise of meaning . . . a transition, effected over a long period of time, from a socially visible object to one which can no longer be seen" (Barker 1984: 13).

While the subject in Barker's account became, in her words, "raging, solitary, productive," what it produced was text. On the other hand, it was the newly hidden Victorian body that became physically productive and that later provided the motor for the industrial revolution; it was most useful as a brute body, for which the creative spark was an impediment. In sum, the body became more physical, while the subject became more textual, which is to say nonphysical.

If the information age is an extension of the industrial age, with the passage of time the split between the body and the subject should grow more pronounced still. But in the fourth epoch the split is simultaneously growing and disappearing. The socioepistemic mechanism by which bodies mean is undergoing a deep restructuring in the latter part of the twentieth century, finally fulfilling the furthest extent of the isolation of those bodies through which its domination is authorized and secured.

I don't think it is accidental that one of the earliest, textual, virtual communities – the community of gentlemen assembled by Robert Boyle during his debates with Hobbes – came into existence at the moment about which Barker is writing. The debate between Boyle and Hobbes and the production of Pepys' diary are virtually contemporaneous. In the late twentieth century, Gibson's *Neuromancer* is simultaneously a perverse evocation of the Restoration subject and its annihilation in an implosion of meaning from which arises a new economy of signification.

Barker's work resonates in useful ways with two other accounts of the evolution of the body and the subject through the interventions of late twentieth-century technologies: Donna Haraway's "A Manifesto for Cyborgs" and "The Biopolitics of Postmodern Bodies" (1985, 1988). Both these accounts are about the collapse of categories and of the boundaries of the body. (Shortly after being introduced to Haraway's work I wrote a very short paper called "Sex And Death among the

Cyborgs." The thesis of "Sex And Death" was similar to Haraway's.) The bound-aries between the subject, if not the body, and the "rest of the world" are under-going a radical refiguration, brought about in part through the mediation of technology. Further, as Baudrillard and others have pointed out, the boundaries between technology and nature are themselves in the midst of a deep restructur-ing. This means that many of the usual analytical categories have become unreli-able for making the useful distinctions between the biological and the technological, the natural and artificial, the human and mechanical, to which we have become accustomed.

François Dagognet suggests that the recent debates about whether nature is becoming irremediably technologized are based on a false dichotomy: namely that there exists, here and now, a category "nature" which is "over here," and a category "technology" (or, for those following other debates, "culture") which is "over there." Dagognet argues on the contrary that the category "nature" has not existed for thousands of years...not since the first humans deliberately planted gardens or discovered slash-and-burn farming. I would argue further that "Nature," instead of representing some pristine category or originary state of being, has taken on an entirely different function in late twentieth-century economies of meaning. Not only has the character of nature as yet another coconstruct of culture become more patent, but it has become nothing more (or less) than an ordering factor – a construct by means of which we attempt to *keep technology visible* as something separate from our "natural" selves and our everyday lives. In other words, the category "nature," rather than referring to any object or category in the world, is a *strategy* for maintaining boundaries for political and economic ends, and thus a way of making meaning. (In this sense, the project of reifying a "natural" state over and against a technologized "fallen" one is not only one of the industries of postmodern nostalgia, but also part of a binary, opposi-tional cognitive style that some maintain is part of our society's pervasively male epistemology.)

These arguments imply as a corollary that "technology," as we customarily think of it, does not exist either; that we must begin to rethink the category of techno-logy as also one that exists only because of its imagined binary opposition to another category upon which it operates and in relation to which it is constituted. In a recent paper Paul Rabinow asks what kind of being might thrive in a world in which nature is becoming increasingly technologized. What about a being who has learned to live in a world in which, rather than nature becoming technologized, technology *is* nature – in which the boundaries between subject and environment have collapsed?

Phone sex workers and VR engineers

I have recently been conducting a study of two groups who seemed to instantiate productive aspects of this implosion of boundaries. One is phone sex workers. The other is computer scientists and engineers working on VR systems that involve making humans visible in the virtual space. I was interested in the ways in which these groups, which seem quite different, are similar. For the work of both is about representing the human body through limited communication channels, and both groups do this by coding cultural expectations as tokens of meaning.

Computer engineers seem fascinated by VR because you not only program a world, but in a real sense inhabit it. Because cyberspace worlds can be inhabited by communities, in the process of articulating a cyberspace system, engineers must model cognition and community; and because communities are inhabited by bodies, they must model bodies as well. While cheap and practical systems are years away, many workers are already hotly debating the form and character of the communities they believe will spring up in their quasi-imaginary cyberspaces. In doing so, they are articulating their own assumptions about bodies and sociality and projecting them onto the codes that define cyberspace systems. Since, for example, programmers create the codes by which VR is generated in interaction with workers in widely diverse fields, how these heterogeneous co-working groups understand cognition, community, and bodies will determine the nature of cognition, community, and bodies in VR.

Both the engineers and the sex workers are in the business of constructing tokens that are recognized as objects of desire. Phone sex is the process of provoking, satisfying, *constructing* desire through a single mode of communication, the telephone. In the process, participants draw on a repertoire of cultural codes to construct a scenario that compresses large amounts of information into a very small space. The worker verbally codes for gesture, appearance, and proclivity, and expresses these as tokens, sometimes in no more than a word. The client uncompresses the tokens and constructs a dense, complex interactional image. In these interactions desire appears as a product of the tension between embodied reality and the emptiness of the token, in the forces that maintain the preexisting codes by which the token is constituted. The client mobilizes expectations and preexisting codes for body in the modalities that are not expressed in the token; that is, tokens in phone sex are purely verbal, and the client uses cues in the verbal token to construct a multimodal object of desire with attributes of shape, tactility, odor, etc. This act is thoroughly individual and interpretive; out of a highly compressed token of desire the client constitutes meaning that is dense, locally situated, and socially particular.

Bodies in cyberspace are also constituted by descriptive codes that "embody" expectations of appearance. Many of the engineers currently debating the form and nature of cyberspace are the young turks of computer engineering, men in their late teens and twenties, and they are preoccupied with the things with which postpubescent men have always been preoccupied. This rather steamy group will generate the codes and descriptors by which bodies in cyberspace are represented. Because of practical limitations, a certain amount of their discussion is concerned with data compression and tokenization. As with phone sex, cyberspace is a relatively narrow-bandwidth representational medium, visual and aural instead of purely aural to be sure, but how bodies are represented will involve how *re*cognition works.

One of the most active sites for speculation about how *re*cognition might work in cyberspace is the work of computer game developers, in particular the area known as interactive fantasy (IF). Since Gibson's first book burst onto the hackers' scene, interactive fantasy programmers (in particular, Laurel and others) have been taking their most durable stock-in-trade and speculating about how it will be deployed in virtual reality scenarios. For example, how, if they do, will people make love in cyberspace? – a space in which everything, including bodies, exists as something close to a metaphor. Fortunately or unfortunately, however, everyone is still preorgasmic in virtual reality.

When I began the short history of virtual systems, I said that I wanted to use accounts of virtual communities as an entry point into a search for two things: an apparatus for the production of community and an apparatus for the production of body. Keeping in mind that this chapter is necessarily brief, let me look at the data so far:

- Members of electronic virtual communities act as if the community met in a physical public space. The number of times that on-line conferences refer to the conference as an architectural place and to the mode of interaction in that place as being social is overwhelmingly high in proportion to those who do not. They say things like "This is a nice place to get together" or "This is a convenient place to meet."
- The virtual space is most frequently visualized as Cartesian. On-line conferencees tend to visualize the conference system as a three-dimensional space that can be mapped in terms of Cartesian coordinates, so that some branches of the conference are "higher up" and others "lower down." (One of the commands on the Stuart II conference moved the user "sideways.") Gibson's own visualization of cyberspace was Cartesian. In consideration of the imagination I sometimes see being brought to bear on virtual spaces, this odd fact invites further investigation.
- Conferences act as if the virtual space were inhabited by bodies. Conferencees construct bodies on-line by describing them, either spontaneously or in response to questions, and articulate their discourses around this assumption.
- Bodies in virtual space have complex erotic components. Conferencees may flirt with each other. Some may engage in "netsex," constructing elaborate erotic mutual fantasies. Erotic possibilities for the virtual body are a significant part of the discussions of some of the groups designing cyberspace systems. The consequences of virtual bodies are considerable in the local frame, in that conferences mobilize significant erotic tension in relation to their virtual bodies. In contrast to the conferences, the bandwidth for physicalities in phone sex is quite limited. (One worker said ironically, "(o)n the phone, every female sex worker is white, five feet four, and has red hair.")
- The meaning of locality and privacy is not settled. The field is rife with debates about the legal status of communications within the networks. One such, for example, is about the meaning of inside and outside. Traditionally, when sending a letter one preserves privacy by enclosing it in an envelope. But in electronic mail, for example, the address is part of the message. The distinction between inside and outside has been erased, and along with it the possibility of privacy. Secure encryption systems are needed.[1]

- Names are local labels. "Conferencees" seem to have no difficulty addressing, befriending, and developing fairly complex relationships with the delegated puppets – agents – of other conferences. Such relationships remain stable as long as the provisional name ("handle") attached to the puppet does not change, but an unexpected observation was that relationships remain stable when the conference decides to change handles, as long as fair notice is given. Occasionally a conferencee will have several handles on the same conference, and a constructed identity for each. Other conferences may or may not be aware of this. Conferencees treat others' puppets as if they were embodied people meeting in a public space nonetheless.

Private Body, Public Body, and Cyborg Envy

Partly, my interest in VR engineers stems from observations that suggest that while they are surely engaged in saving the project of late-twentieth-century capitalism, they are also inverting and disrupting its consequences for the body as an object of power relationships. They manage both to preserve the privatized sphere of the individual – which Barker characterizes as "raging, solitary, productive" – as well as to escape to a position that is of the spectacle and incontrovertibly public. But this occurs under a new definition of public and private: one in which warrantability is irrelevant, spectacle is plastic and negotiated, and desire no longer grounds itself in physicality. Under these conditions, one might ask, will the future inhabitants of cyberspace "catch" the engineers' societal imperative to construct desire in gendered, binary terms – coded into the virtual body descriptors – or will they find more appealing the possibilities of difference unconstrained by relationships of dominance and submission? Partly this will depend upon how "cyberspaceians" engage with the virtual body.

Vivian Sobchack, in her 1988 discussion of cinematic space excludes the space of the video and computer screen from participation in the production of an "apparatus of engagement." Sobchack describes engagement with cinematic space as producing a thickening of the present . . . a "temporal simultaneity (that) also extends presence spatially – transforming the 'thin' abstracted space of the machine into a thickened and concrete world." Contrasted with video, which is to say with the electronic space of the CRT screen and with its small, low-resolution, and serial mode of display, the viewer of cinema engages with the apparatus of cinematic production in a way that produces "a space that is deep and textural, that can be materially inhabited . . . a specific and mobile engagement of embodied and enworlded subjects/objects whose visual/visible activity prospects and articulates a shifting field of vision from a world that always exceeds it." Sobchack speaks of electronic space as "a phenomenological structure of sensual and psychological experience that seems to belong to no-body." Sobchack sees the computer screen as "spatially decentered, weakly temporalized and quasi-disembodied."

This seems to be true, as long as the mode of engagement remains that of spectator. But it is the quality of direct physical and kinesthetic engagement, the enrolling of hapticity in the service of both the drama and the dramatic, which is not part of the cinematic mode. The cinematic mode of engagement, like that of conventional theater, is mediated by two modalities; the viewer experiences the presentation through sight and hearing. The electronic screen is "flat," so long as we consider it in the same bimodal way. But it is the potential for interaction that is one of the things that distinguishes the computer from the cinematic mode, and that transforms the small, low-resolution, and frequently monochromatic electronic screen from a novelty to a powerfully gripping force. Interaction is the physical concretization of a desire to escape the flatness and merge into the created system. It is the sense in which the "spectator" is more than a participant, but becomes both participant in and creator of the simulation. In brief, it is the sense of unlimited power which the dis/embodied simulation produces, and the different ways in which socialization has led those always-embodied participants confronted with the sign of unlimited power to respond.

In quite different terms from the cinematic, then, cyberspace "thickens" the present, producing a space that is deep and textural, and one that, in Sobchack's terms, can be materially inhabited. David Tomas, in his article "The Technophilic Body" (1989), describes cyberspace as "a purely spectacular, kinesthetically exciting, and often dizzying sense of bodily freedom." I read this in the additional sense of freedom *from* the body, and in particular perhaps, freedom from the sense of loss of control that accompanies adolescent male embodiment. Cyberspace is surely also a concretization of the psychoanalytically framed desire of the male to achieve the "kinesthetically exciting, dizzying sense" of freedom.

Some fiction has been written about multimodal, experiential cinema. But the fictional apparatus surrounding imaginary cybernetic spaces seems to have proliferated and pushed experiential cinema into the background. This is because cyberspace is part of, not simply the medium for, the action. Sobchack, on the other hand, argues that cinematic space possesses a power of engagement that the electronic space cannot match:

> Semiotically engaged as subjective and intentional, as presenting representation of the objective world ... The spectator(s) can share (and thereby to a degree interpretively alter) a film's presentation and representation of embodied experience. (1992)

Sobchack's argument for the viewer's intentional engagement of cinematic space, slightly modified, however, works equally well for the cybernetic space of the computer. That is, one might say that the console cowboy is also "... semiotically engaged as subjective and intentional, as presenting representation of a *subj*ective world ... the spectator can share (and thereby to a high degree interpretively alter) a simulation's presentation and representation of experience which may be, through cybernetic/semiotic operators not yet existent but present and active in fiction (the cyberspace deck), mapped back upon the physical body."

In psychoanalytic terms, for the young male, unlimited power first suggests the mother. The experience of unlimited power is both gendered, and, for the male, fraught with the need for control, producing an unresolvable need for reconciliation with an always absent structure of personality. An "absent structure of personality" is also another way of describing the peculiarly seductive character of the computer that Turkle characterizes as the "second self." Danger, the sense of threat as well as seductiveness that the computer can evoke, comes from both within and without. It derives from the complex interrelationships between human and computer, and thus partially within the human; and it exists quasi-autonomously within the simulation. It constitutes simultaneously the senses of erotic pleasure and of loss of control over the body. Both also constitute a constellation of responses to the simulation that deeply engage fear, desire, pleasure, and the need for domination, subjugation, and control.

It seems to be the engagement of the adolescent male within humans of both sexes that is responsible for the seductiveness of the cybernetic mode. There is also a protean quality about cybernetic interaction, a sense of physical as well as conceptual mutability that is implied in the sense of exciting, dizzying physical movement within purely conceptual space. I find that reality hackers experience a sense of longing for an embodied conceptual space like that which cyberspace suggests. This sense, which seems to accompany the desire to cross the human/machine boundary, to penetrate and merge, which is part of the evocation of cyberspace, and which shares certain conceptual and affective characteristics with numerous fictional evocations of the inarticulate longing of the male for the female, I characterize as *cyborg envy.*

Smoothness implies a seductive tactile quality that expresses one of the characteristics of cyborg envy: In the case of the computer, a desire literally to enter into such a discourse, to penetrate the smooth and relatively affectless surface of the electronic screen and enter the deep, complex, and tactile (individual) cybernetic space or (consensual) cyberspace within and beyond. Penetrating the screen involves a state change from the physical, biological space of the embodied viewer to the symbolic, metaphorical "consensual hallucination" of cyberspace; a space that is a locus of intense desire for refigured embodiment.

The act of programming a computer invokes a set of reading practices both in the literary and cultural sense. "Console cowboys" such as the cyberspace warriors of William Gibson's cyberpunk novels proliferate and capture the imagination of large groups of readers. Programming itself involves constant creation, interpretation, and reinterpretation of languages. To enter the discursive space of the program is to enter the space of a set of variables and operators to which the programmer assigns names. To enact naming is simultaneously to possess the power of, and to render harmless, the complex of desire and fear that charge the signifiers in such a discourse; to enact naming within the highly charged world of surfaces that is cyberspace is to appropriate the surfaces, to incorporate the surfaces into one's own. Penetration translates into envelopment. In other words, to enter cyberspace is to physically *put on* cyberspace. To become the cyborg, to put on the seductive and dangerous cybernetic space like a garment, is to put on the *female*. Thus cyberspace both *dis*embodies, in Sobchack's terms, but also *re*embodies in the polychrome, hypersurfaced cyborg character of the console cowboy. As the charged, multigendered, hallucinatory space collapses onto the personal physicality of the console cowboy, the intense tactility associated with such a reconceived and refigured body constitutes the seductive quality of what one might call the *cybernetic act*.

In all, the unitary, bounded, safely warranted body constituted within the frame of bourgeois modernity is undergoing a gradual process of translation to the refigured and reinscribed embodiments of the cyberspace community. Sex in the age of the coding metaphor – absent bodies, absent reproduction, perhaps related to desire, but desire itself refigured in terms of bandwidth and internal difference – may mean something quite unexpected. Dying in the age of the coding metaphor – in selectably inhabitable structures of signification, absent warrantability – gives new and disturbing meaning to the title of Steven Levine's book about the process, *Who Dies?*

Cyberspace, Sociotechnics, and Other Neologisms

Part of the problem of "going on in much the same way," as Harry Collins put it, is in knowing what the same way is. At the close of the twentieth century, I would argue that two of the problems are, first, as in Paul Virilio's analysis, *speed*, and second, tightly coupled to speed, what happens as human physical evolution falls further and further out of synchronization with human cultural evolution. The product of this growing tension between nature and culture is stress.

Stress management is a major concern of industrial corporations. Donna Haraway points out that

> (t)he threat of intolerable rates of change and of evolutionary and ideological obsol-
> escence are the framework that structure much of late twentieth-century medical,
> social and technological thought. Stress is part of a complex web of technological
> discourses in which the organism becomes a particular kind of communications
> system, strongly analogous to the cybernetic machines that emerged from the war
> to reorganize ideological discourse and significant sectors of state, industrial, and
> military practice.... Utilization of information at boundaries and transitions, bio-
> logical or mechanical, is a critical capacity of systems potentially subject to stress,
> because failure to correctly apprehend and negotiate rapid change could result in
> communication breakdown – a problem which engages the attention of a broad
> spectrum of military, governmental, industrial and institutional interests. (1990:
> 186–230 passim)

The development of cyberspace systems – which I will refer to as part of a new *technics* – may be one of a widely distributed constellation of responses to stress, and secondly a way of continuing the process of collapsing the categories of nature and culture that Paul Rabinow sees as the outcome of the new genetics. Cyber-space can be viewed as a toolkit for refiguring consciousness in order to permit things to go on in much the same way. Rabinow suggests that nature will be modeled on culture; it will be known and remade through technique. Nature will finally become artificial, just as culture becomes natural.

Haraway (1985) puts this in a slightly different way: "The certainty of what counts as nature," she says, "(that is, as) a source of insight, a subject for knowledge, and a promise of innocence – is undermined, perhaps fatally." The change in the permeability of the boundaries between nature and technics that these accounts suggest does not simply mean that nature and technics mix – but that, seen from the technical side, technics become natural, just as, from Rabinow's anthropological perspective on the culture side, culture becomes artificial. In technosociality, the social world of virtual culture, technics is nature. When exploration, rationalization, remaking, and control mean the same thing, then nature, technics, and the structure of meaning have become indistinguishable. The technosocial subject is able successfully to navigate through this treacherous new world. S/he is constituted as part of the evolution of communications technology and of the human organism, in a time in which technology and organism are collapsing, imploding, into each other.

Electronic virtual communities represent flexible, lively, and practical adaptations to the real circumstances that confront persons seeking community in what Haraway (1987) refers to as "the mythic time called the late twentieth century." They are part of a range of innovative solutions to the drive for sociality – a drive that can be frequently thwarted by the geographical and cultural realities of cities increasingly structured according to the needs of powerful economic interests rather than in ways that encourage and facilitate habitation and social interaction in the urban context. In this context, electronic virtual communities are complex and ingenious strategies for *survival*. Whether the seemingly inherent seductiveness of the medium distorts the aims of those strategies, as television has done for literacy and personal interaction, remains to be seen.

So Much for Community. What about the Body?

No matter how virtual the subject may become, there is always a body attached. It may be off somewhere else – and that "somewhere else" may be a privileged point of view – but consciousness remains firmly rooted in the physical. Historically, body, technology, and community constitute each other.

In her 1990 book *Gender Trouble*, Judith Butler introduces the useful concept of the "culturally intelligible body," or the criteria and the textual productions (including writing on or in the body itself) that each society uses to produce physical bodies that it recognizes as members. It is useful to argue that most cultural production of intelligibility is about reading or writing and takes place through the mediation of texts. If we can apply textual analysis to the narrow-bandwidth modes of computers and telephones, then we can examine the production of gendered bodies in cyberspace also as a set of tokens that code difference within a field of ideal types. I refer to this process as the production of the *legible* body.

The opposite production, of course, is of the *illegible* body, the "boundary-subject" that theorist Gloria Anzaldúa calls the *Mestiza*, one who lives in the borderlands and is only partially recognized by each abutting society. Anzaldúa describes the Mestiza by means of a multiplicity of frequently conflicting accounts. There is no position, she shows, outside of the abutting societies themselves from which an omniscient overview could capture the essence of the Mestiza's predicament, nor is there any single account from within a societal framework that constitutes an adequate description.

If the Mestiza is an illegible subject, existing quantumlike in multiple states, then participants in the electronic virtual communities of cyberspace live in the borderlands of both physical and virtual culture, like the Mestiza. Their social system includes other people, quasi people or delegated agencies that represent specific individuals, and quasi agents that represent "intelligent" machines, clusters of people, or both. Their ancestors, lower on the chain of evolution, are network conferencers, communities organized around texts such as Boyle's "community of gentlemen" and the religious traditions based in holy scripture, communities organized around broadcasts, and communities of music such as the Deadheads. What separates the cyberspace communities from their ancestors is that many of the cyberspace communities interact in real time. Agents meet face-to-face, though as I noted before, under a redefiniton of both "meet" and "face."

I might have been able to make my point regarding illegible subjects without invoking the Mestiza as an example. But I make an example of a specific kind of person as a way of keeping the discussion grounded in individual bodies: in Paul Churchland's words, in the "situated biological creatures" that we each are. The work of science is *about* bodies – not in an abstract sense, but in the complex and protean ways that we daily manifest ourselves as physical social beings, vulnerable to the powerful knowledges that surround us, and to the effects upon us of the transformative discourses of science and technology that we both enable and enact.

I am particularly conscious of this because much of the work of cyberspace researchers, reinforced and perhaps created by the soaring imagery of William Gibson's novels, assumes that the human body is "meat" – obsolete, as soon as consciousness itself can be uploaded into the network. The discourse of visionary virtual world builders is rife with images of imaginal bodies, freed from the constraints that flesh imposes. Cyberspace developers foresee a time when they will be able to forget about the body. But it is important to remember that virtual community originates in, and must return to, the physical. No refigured virtual body, no matter how beautiful, will slow the death of a cyberpunk with AIDS. Even in the age of the technosocial subject, life is lived through bodies.

Forgetting about the body is an old Cartesian trick, one that has unpleasant consequences for those bodies whose speech is silenced by the act of our forgetting; that is to say, those upon whose labor the act of forgetting the body is founded – usually women and minorities. On the other hand, as Haraway points out, forgetting can be a powerful strategy; through forgetting, that which is already built becomes that which can be discovered. But like any powerful and productive strategy, this one has its dangers. Remembering – discovering – that bodies and communities constitute each other surely suggests a set of questions and debates for the burgeoning virtual electronic community. I hope to observe the outcome.

Acknowledgments

Thanks to Mischa Adams, Gloria Anzaldúa, Laura Chernaik, Heinz von Foerster, Thyrza Goodeve, John Hartigan, Barbara Joans, Victor Kytasty, Roddey Reid, Chela Sandoval, Susan Leigh Star, and Sharon Traweek for their many suggestions; to Bandit (Seagate), Ron Cain (Borland), Carl Tollander (Autodesk), Ted Kaehler (Sun), Jane T. Lear (Intel), Marc Lentczner, Robert Orr (Amdahl), Jon Singer (soulmate), Brenda Laurel (Telepresence Research and all-around Wonderful Person); Joshua Susser, the Advanced Technology Group of Apple Computer, Inc., Tene Tachyon, Jon Shemitz, John James, and my many respondents in the virtual world of online BBSs. I am grateful to Michael Benedikt and friends and to the University of Texas School of Architecture for making part of the research possible, and to the participants in The First Conference on Cyberspace for their ideas as well as their collaboration in constituting yet another virtual community. In particular I thank Donna Haraway, whose work and encouragement have been invaluable.

Note

1 Although no one has actually given up on encryption systems, the probable reason that international standards for encryption have not proceeded much faster has been the United States Government's opposition to encryption key standards that are reasonably secure. Such standards would prevent such agencies as the CIA from gaining access to communications traffic. The United States' diminishing role as a superpower may change this. Computer industries in other nations have overtaken the United States' lead in electronics and are beginning to produce secure encryption equipment as well. A side effect of this will be to enable those engaged in electronic communication to reinstate the inside-outside dichotomy, and with it the notion of privacy in the virtual social space.

Bibliography

Anzaldúa, Gloria, *Borderlands/La Frontera: The New Mestiza* (San Francisco: Spinsters/ Aunt Lute, 1987).

Barker, Francis, *The Tremulous Private Body: Essays in Subjection* (London: Methuen, 1984).

Baudrillard, Jean, *The Ecstasy of Communication*, trans. Bernard and Caroline Schutze, Sylvere Lotringer (New York: Semiotext(e), 1987).

Butler, Judith, *Gender Trouble: Feminism and the Subversion of Identity* (New York: Routledge, 1990).

Gibson, William, *Neuromancer* (New York: Ace, 1984).

Habermas, J., *Communication and the Evolution of Society* (Boston: Beacon Press, 1979).

Haraway, Donna, "A Manifesto for Cyborgs: Science, technology and socialist feminism in the 1980s," *Socialist Review* 1985, 80, pp. 65–107.

Haraway, Donna, "Donna Haraway Reads National Geographic" (Paper Tiger, 1987) Video.

Haraway, Donna, "The Biopolitics of Postmodern Bodies: Determinations of Self and Other in Immune System Discourse," *Wenner Gren Foundation Conference on Medical Anthropology*, Lisbon, Portugal, 1988.

Haraway, Donna, "Washburn and the New Physical Anthropology," in *Primate Visions: Gender, Race, and Nature in the World of Modern Science* (New York: Routledge, 1990).

Haraway, Donna "The Promises of Monsters: A regenerative politics for inappropriate/d others," in P. Treichler and G. Nelson (eds.), *Cultural Studies Now and in the Future* (1991).

Latour, Bruno, *The Pasteurization of France*, trans. Alan Sheridan and John Law (Cambridge: Harvard University Press, 1988).

Laurel, Brenda, "Interface as Mimesis," in D. A. Norman and S. Draper (eds.), *User Centered System Design: New Perspectives on Human-Computer Interaction* (Hillsdale, NJ: Lawrence Erlbaum Associates, 1986).

Laurel, Brenda, "Reassessing Interactivity," *Journal of Computer Game Design*, 1987, 1, p. 3.

Laurel, Brenda, "Culture Hacking," *Journal of Computer Game Design*, 1988, 1, p. 8.

Laurel, Brenda, "Dramatic Action and Virtual Reality," in *Proceedings of the 1989 NCGA Interactive Arts Conference*, 1989a.

Laurel, Brenda, "New Interfaces for Entertainment," *Journal of Computer Game Design*, 1989b, 2, p. 5.

Laurel, Brenda, "A Taxonomy of Interactive Movies," *New Media News* (The Boston Computer Society), 1989c, 3, p. 1.

Lehman-Wilzig, Sam, "Frankenstein Unbound: Toward a legal definition of artificial intelligence," *Futures*, December 1981, p. 447.

Levine, Steven, *Who Dies? An Investigation of Conscious Living and Conscious Dying* (Bath: Gateway Press, 1988).

Sobchack, Vivian, "The Address of the Eye: A *Phenomenology of Film Experience* (Princeton: Princeton University Press, 1992).

Sobchack, Vivian, "The Scene Of The Screen: Toward a phenomenology of cinematic and electronic 'presence,'" in H. V. Gumbrecht and L. K. Pfeiffer, eds., *Materialitat des Kommunikation* (GDR: Suhrkamp-Verlag, 1988).

Tomas, David, "The Technophilic Body: On technicity in William Gibson's cyborg culture," *New Formations*, 8, Spring, 1989.

20

A Rape in Cyberspace; or How an Evil Clown, a Haitian Trickster Spirit, Two Wizards, and a Cast of Dozens Turned a Database into a Society

Julian Dibbell

Julian Dibbell, excerpt from "A Rape in Cyberspace," from *Village Voice* (December 21, 1993), pp. 36–42. Reprinted by permission of the author.

Julian Dibbell is a journalist whose writing on technology appears in *Details*, *Spin*, *Wired*, and the *New York Times*. He is the author of *My Tiny Life: Crime and Passion in a Virtual World* (Owl Books, 1999). Originally published in the *Village Voice*, Dibbell's account of an assault that occurred on the Internet is one of the most frequently cited essays about cloaked identity in cyberspace.

They say he raped them that night. They say he did it with a cunning little doll, fashioned in their image and imbued with the power to make them do whatever he desired. They say that by manipulating the doll he forced them to have sex with him, and with each other, and to do horrible, brutal things to their own bodies. And though I wasn't there that night, I think I can assure you that what they say is true, because it all happened right in the living room – right there amid the well-stocked bookcases and the sofas and the fireplace – of a house I've come to think of as my second home.

Call me Dr. Bombay. Some months ago – let's say about halfway between the first time you heard the words *information superhighway* and the first time you wished you never had – I found myself tripping with compulsive regularity down the well-traveled information lane that leads to LambdaMOO, a very large and very busy rustic chateau built entirely of words. Nightly, I typed the commands that called those words onto my computer screen, dropping me with what seemed a warm electric thud inside the mansion's darkened coat closet, where I checked my quotidian identity, stepped into the persona and appearance of a minor character from a long-gone television sitcom, and stepped out into the glaring chatter of the crowded living room. Sometimes, when the mood struck me, I emerged as a dolphin instead.

I won't say why I chose to masquerade as Samantha Stevens's outlandish cousin, or as the dolphin, or what exactly led to my mild but so-far incurable addiction to the semifictional digital otherworlds known around the Internet as multi-user dimensions, or MUDs. This isn't my story, after all. It's the story of a man named Mr. Bungle, and of the ghostly sexual violence he committed in the halls of LambdaMOO, and most importantly of the ways his violence and his victims challenged the 1000 and more residents of that surreal, magic-infested mansion to become, finally, the community so many of them already believed they were.

That I was myself one of those residents has little direct bearing on the story's events. I mention it only as a warning that my own perspective is perhaps too steeped in the surreality and magic of the place to serve as an entirely appropriate guide. For the Bungle Affair raises questions that – here on the brink of a future in which human life may find itself as tightly enveloped in digital environments as it is today in the architectural kind – demand a clear-eyed, sober, and unmystified consideration. It asks us to shut our ears momentarily to the techno-utopian ecstasies of West Coast cyberhippies and look without illusion upon the present possibilities for building, in the on-line spaces of this world, societies more decent and free than those mapped onto dirt and concrete and capital. It asks us to behold the new bodies awaiting us in virtual space undazzled by their phantom powers, and to get to the crucial work of sorting out the socially meaningful differences between those bodies and our physical ones. And most forthrightly it asks us to wrap our late-modern ontologies, epistemologies, sexual ethics, and common sense around the curious notion of rape by voodoo doll – and to try not to warp them beyond recognition in the process.

In short, the Bungle Affair dares me to explain it to you without resort to dime-store mysticisms, and I fear I may have shape-shifted by the digital moonlight one too many times to be quite up to the task. But I will do what I can, and can do no better I suppose than to lead with the facts. For if nothing else about Mr. Bungle's case is unambiguous, the facts at least are crystal clear.

The facts begin (as they often do) with a time and a place. The time was a Monday night in March, and the place, as I've said, was the living room – which, due to the inviting warmth of its decor, is so invariably packed with chitchatters as to be roughly synonymous among LambdaMOOers with a party. So strong, indeed, is the sense of convivial common ground invested in the living room that a cruel mind could hardly imagine a better place in which to stage a violation of LambdaMOO's communal spirit. And there was cruelty enough lurking in the appearance Mr. Bungle presented to the virtual world – he was at the time a fat, oleaginous, Bisquick-faced clown dressed in cum-stained harlequin garb and girdled with a mistletoe-and-hemlock belt whose buckle bore the quaint inscription "KISS ME UNDER THIS, BITCH!" But whether cruelty motivated his choice of crime scene is not among the established facts of the case. It is a fact only that he did choose the living room.

The remaining facts tell us a bit more about the inner world of Mr. Bungle, though only perhaps that it couldn't have been a very comfortable place. They tell us that he commenced his assault entirely unprovoked, at or about 10 P.M. Pacific Standard Time. That he began by using his voodoo doll to force one of the room's occupants to sexually service him in a variety of more or less conventional ways. That this victim was legba, a Haitian trickster spirit of indeterminate gender, brown-skinned and wearing an expensive pearl gray suit, top hat, and dark glasses. That legba heaped vicious imprecations on him all the while and that he was soon ejected bodily from the room. That he hid himself away then in his private chambers somewhere on the mansion grounds and continued the attacks without interruption, since the voodoo doll worked just as well at a distance as in proximity. That he turned his attentions now to Starsinger, a rather pointedly nondescript female character, tall, stout, and brown-haired, forcing her into unwanted liaisons with other individuals present in the room, among them legba, Bakunin (the well-known radical), and Juniper (the squirrel). That his actions grew progressively violent. That he made legba eat his/her own pubic hair. That he caused Starsinger to violate herself with a piece of kitchen cutlery. That his distant laughter echoed evilly in the living room with every successive outrage. That he could not be stopped until at last someone summoned Zippy, a wise and trusted old-timer who brought with him a gun of near wizardly powers, a gun that didn't kill but enveloped its targets in a cage impermeable even to a voodoo doll's powers. That Zippy fired his gun at Mr. Bungle, thwarting the doll at last and silencing the evil, distant laughter.

These particulars, as I said, are unambiguous. But they are far from simple, for the simple reason that every set of facts in virtual reality (or VR, as the locals abbreviate it) is shadowed by a second, complicating set: the "real-life" facts. And while a certain tension invariably buzzes in the gap between the hard, prosaic RL facts and their more fluid, dreamy VR counterparts, the dissonance in the Bungle case is striking. No hideous clowns or trickster spirits appear in the RL version of the incident, no voodoo dolls or wizard guns, indeed no rape at all as any RL court of law has yet defined it. The actors in the drama were university students for the most part, and they sat rather undramatically before computer screens the entire time, their only actions a spidery flitting of fingers across standard QWERTY keyboards. No bodies touched. Whatever physical interaction occurred consisted of a mingling of electronic signals sent from sites spread out between New York City and Sydney, Australia. Those signals met in Lambda-MOO, certainly, just as the hideous clown and the living room party did, but what was LambdaMOO after all? Not an enchanted mansion or anything of the sort – just a middlingly complex database, maintained for experimental purposes inside a Xerox Corporation research computer in Palo Alto and open to public access via the Internet.

To be more precise about it, LambdaMOO was a MUD. Or to be yet more precise, it was a subspecies of MUD known as a MOO, which is short for "MUD, Object-Oriented." All of which means that it was a kind of database especially designed to give users the vivid impression of moving through a physical space that in reality exists only as descriptive data filed away on a hard drive. When users dial into LambdaMOO, for instance, the program immediately presents them with a brief textual description of one of the rooms of the database's fictional mansion (the coat closet, say). If the user wants to leave this room, she can enter a command to move in a particular direction and the database will replace the original description with a new one corresponding to the room located in the direction she chose. When the new description scrolls across the user's screen it lists not only the fixed features of the room but all its contents at that moment – including things (tools, toys, weapons) and other users (each represented as a "character" over which he or she has sole control).

As far as the database program is concerned, all of these entities – rooms, things, characters – are just different subprograms that the program allows to interact according to rules very roughly mimicking the laws of the physical world. Characters may not leave a room in a given direction, for instance, unless the room subprogram contains an "exit" at that compass point. And if a character "says" or "does" something (as directed by its user-owner), then only the users whose characters are also located in that room will see the output describing the statement or action. Aside from such basic constraints, however, LambdaMOOers are allowed a broad freedom to create – they can describe their characters any way they like, they can make rooms of their own and decorate them to taste, and they can build new objects almost at will. The combination of all this busy user activity with the hard physics of the database can certainly induce a lucid illusion of presence – but when all is said and done the only thing you *really* see when you visit LambdaMOO is a kind of slow-crawling script, lines of dialogue and stage direction creeping steadily up your computer screen.

Which is all just to say that, to the extent that Mr. Bungle's assault happened in real life at all, it happened as a sort of Punch-and-Judy show, in which the puppets and the scenery were made of nothing more substantial than digital code and snippets of creative writing. The puppeteer behind Bungle, as it happened, was a young man logging in to the MOO from a New York University computer. He could have been Al Gore for all any of the others knew, however, and he could have written Bungle's script that night any way he chose. He could have sent a command to print the message "Mr. Bungle, smiling a saintly smile, floats angelic near the ceiling of the living room, showering joy and candy kisses down upon the heads of all below" – and everyone then receiving output from the database's subprogram #17 (a/k/a the "living room") would have seen that sentence on their screens.

Instead, he entered sadistic fantasies into the "voodoo doll," a subprogram that served the not exactly kosher purpose of attributing actions to other characters that their users did not actually write. And thus a woman in Haverford, Pennsylvania, whose account on the MOO attached her to a character she called Starsinger, was given the unasked-for opportunity to read the words "As if against her will, Starsinger jabs a steak knife up her ass, causing immense joy. You hear Mr. Bungle laughing evilly in the distance." And thus the woman in Seattle who had written herself the character called legba, with a view perhaps to tasting in imagination a deity's freedom from the burdens of the gendered flesh, got to read similarly constructed sentences in which legba, messenger of the gods, lord of crossroads and communications, suffered a brand of degradation all-too-customarily reserved for the embodied female.

"Mostly voodoo dolls are amusing," wrote legba on the evening after Bungle's rampage, posting a public statement to the widely read in-MOO mailing list called *social-issues*, a forum for debate on matters of import to the entire populace. "And mostly I tend to think that restrictive measures around here cause more trouble than they prevent. But I also think that Mr. Bungle was being a vicious, vile fuckhead, and I . . . want his sorry ass scattered from #17 to the Cinder Pile. I'm not calling for policies, trials, or better jails. I'm not sure what I'm calling for. Virtual castration, if I could manage it. Mostly, [this type of thing] doesn't happen here. Mostly, perhaps I thought it wouldn't happen to me. Mostly, I trust people to conduct themselves with some veneer of civility. Mostly, I want his ass."

Months later, the woman in Seattle would confide to me that as she wrote those words posttraumatic tears were streaming down her face – a real-life fact that should suffice to prove that the words' emotional content was no mere playacting. The precise tenor of that content, however, its mingling of murderous rage and eyeball-rolling annoyance, was a curious amalgam that neither the RL nor the VR facts alone can quite account for. Where virtual reality and its conventions would have us believe that legba and Starsinger were brutally raped in their own living room, here was the victim legba scolding Mr. Bungle for a breach of "civility." Where real life, on the other hand, insists the incident was only an episode in a free-form version of Dungeons and Dragons, confined to the realm of the symbolic and at no point threatening any player's life, limb, or material well-being, here now was the player legba issuing aggrieved and heartfelt calls for Mr. Bungle's dismemberment. Ludicrously excessive by RL's lights, woefully understated by VR's, the tone of legba's response made sense only in the buzzing, dissonant gap between them.

Which is to say it made the only kind of sense that *can* be made of MUDly phenomena. For while the *facts* attached to any event born of a MUD's strange, ethereal universe may march in straight, tandem lines separated neatly into the virtual and the real, its meaning lies always in that gap. You learn this axiom early in your life as a player, and it's of no small relevance to the Bungle case that you usually learn it between the sheets, so to speak. Netsex, tinysex, virtual sex – however you name it, in real-life reality it's nothing more than a 900-line encounter stripped of even the vestigial physicality of the voice. And yet as any but the most inhibited of newbies can tell you, it's possibly the headiest experience the very heady world of MUDs has to offer. Amid flurries of even the most cursorily described caresses, sighs, and penetrations, the glands do engage, and often as throbbingly as they would in a real-life assignation – sometimes even more so, given the combined power of anonymity and textual suggestiveness to unshackle deep-seated fantasies. And if the virtual setting and the interplayer vibe are right, who knows? The heart may engage as well, stirring up passions as strong as many that bind lovers who observe the formality of trysting in the flesh.

To participate, therefore, in this disembodied enactment of life's most body-centered activity is to risk the realization that when it comes to sex, perhaps the body in question is not the physical one at all, but its psychic double, the bodylike self-representation we carry around in our heads. I know, I know, you've read

Foucault and your mind is not quite blown by the notion that sex is never so much an exchange of fluids as it is an exchange of signs. But trust your friend Dr. Bombay, it's one thing to grasp the notion intellectually and quite another to feel it coursing through your veins amid the virtual steam of hot netnookie. And it's a whole other mind-blowing trip altogether to encounter it thus as a college frosh, new to the net and still in the grip of hormonal hurricanes and high-school sexual mythologies. The shock can easily reverberate throughout an entire young worldview. Small wonder, then, that a newbie's first taste of MUD sex is often also the first time she or he surrenders wholly to the slippery terms of MUDish ontology, recognizing in a full-bodied way that what happens inside a MUD-made world is neither exactly real nor exactly make-believe, but profoundly, compellingly, and emotionally meaningful.

And small wonder indeed that the sexual nature of Mr. Bungle's crime provoked such powerful feelings, and not just in legba (who, be it noted, was in real life a theory-savvy doctoral candidate and a longtime MOOer, but just as baffled and overwhelmed by the force of her own reaction, she later would attest, as any panting undergrad might have been). Even players who had never experienced MUD rape (the vast majority of male-presenting characters, but not as large a majority of the female-presenting as might be hoped) immediately appreciated its gravity and were moved to condemnation of the perp. legba's missive to *social issues* followed a strongly worded one from Zippy ("Well, well," it began, "no matter what else happens on Lambda, I can always be sure that some jerk is going to reinforce my low opinion of humanity") and was itself followed by others from Moriah, Raccoon, Crawfish, and evangeline. Starsinger also let her feelings ("pissed") be known. And even Jander, the Clueless Samaritan who had responded to Bungle's cries for help and uncaged him shortly after the incident, expressed his regret once apprised of Bungle's deeds, which he allowed to be "despicable."

A sense was brewing that something needed to be done – done soon and in something like an organized fashion – about Mr. Bungle, in particular, and about MUD rape, in general. Regarding the general problem, evangeline, who identified herself as a survivor of both virtual rape ("many times over") and real-life sexual assault, floated a cautious proposal for a MOO-wide powwow on the subject of virtual sex offenses and what mechanisms if any might be put in place to deal with their future occurrence. As for the specific problem, the answer no doubt seemed obvious to many. But it wasn't until the evening of the second day after the incident that legba, finally and rather solemnly, gave it voice: "I am requesting that Mr. Bungle be toaded for raping Starsinger and I. I have never done this before, and have thought about it for days. He hurt us both."

That was all. Three simple sentences posted to *social*. Reading them, an outsider might never guess that they were an application for a death warrant. Even an outsider familiar with other MUDs might not guess it, since in many of them "toading" still refers to a command that, true to the gameworlds' sword-and-sorcery origins, simply turns a player into a toad, wiping the player's description and attributes and replacing them with those of the slimy amphibian. Bad luck for sure, but not quite as bad as what happens when the same command is invoked in the MOOish strains of MUD: not only are the description and attributes of the toaded player erased, but the account itself goes too. The annihilation of the character, thus, is total.

And nothing less than total annihilation, it seemed, would do to settle LambdaMOO's accounts with Mr. Bungle. Within minutes of the posting of legba's appeal, SamIAm, the Australian Deleuzean, who had witnessed much of the attack from the back room of his suburban Sydney home, seconded the motion with a brief message crisply entitled "Toad the fukr." SamIAm's posting was seconded almost as quickly by that of Bakunin, covictim of Mr. Bungle and well-known radical, who in real life happened also to be married to the real-life legba. And over the course of the next 24 hours as many as 50 players made it known, on *social and in a variety of other forms and forums, that they would be pleased to see Mr. Bungle erased from the face of the MOO. And with dissent so far confined to a dozen or so antitoading hardliners, the numbers suggested that the citizenry was indeed moving towards a resolve to have Bungle's virtual head.

There was one small but stubborn obstacle in the way of this resolve, however, and that was a curious state of social affairs known in some quarters of the MOO as the New Direction. It was all very fine, you see, for the LambdaMOO rabble to get it in their heads to liquidate one of their peers, but when the time came to actually do the deed it would require the services of a nobler class of character. It would require a wizard. Master-programmers of the MOO, spelunkers of the database's deepest code-structures and custodians of its day-to-day administrative trivia, wizards are also the only players empowered to issue the toad command, a feature maintained on nearly all MUDs as a quick-and-dirty means of social control. But the wizards of LambdaMOO, after years of adjudicating all manner of interplayer disputes with little to show for it but their own weariness and the smoldering resentment of the general populace, had decided they'd had enough of the social sphere. And so, four months before the Bungle incident, the archwizard Haakon (known in RL as Pavel Curtis, Xerox researcher and LambdaMOO's principal architect) formalized this decision in a document called "LambdaMOO Takes a New Direction," which he placed in the living room for all to see. In it, Haakon announced that the wizards from that day forth were pure technicians. From then on, they would make no decision affecting the social life of the MOO, but only implement whatever decisions the community as a whole directed them to. From then on, it was decreed, LambdaMOO would just have to grow up and solve its problems on its own.

Faced with the task of inventing its own self-governance from scratch, the LambdaMOO population had so far done what any other loose, amorphous agglomeration of individuals would have done: they'd let it slide. But now the task took on new urgency. Since getting the wizards to toad Mr. Bungle (or to toad the likes of him in the future) required a convincing case that the cry for his head came from the community at large, then the community itself would have to be defined; and if the community was to be convincingly defined, then some form of social organization, no matter how rudimentary, would have to be settled on. And thus, as if against its will, the question of what to do about Mr. Bungle began to shape itself into a sort of referendum on the political future of the MOO.

Arguments broke out on *social and elsewhere that had only superficially to do with Bungle (since everyone agreed he was a cad) and everything to do with where the participants stood on LambdaMOO's crazy-quilty political map. Parliamentarian legalist types argued that unfortunately Bungle could not legitimately be toaded at all, since there were no explicit MOO rules against rape, or against just about anything else – and the sooner such rules were established, they added, and maybe even a full-blown judiciary system complete with elected officials and prisons to enforce those rules, the better. Others, with a royalist streak in them, seemed to feel that Bungle's as-yet-unpunished outrage only proved this New Direction silliness had gone on long enough, and that it was high time the wizardocracy returned to the position of swift and decisive leadership their player class was born to.

And then there were what I'll call the technolibertarians. For them, MUD rapists were of course assholes, but the presence of assholes on the system was a technical inevitability, like noise on a phone line, and best dealt with not through repressive social disciplinary mechanisms but through the timely deployment of defensive software tools. Some asshole blasting violent, graphic language at you? Don't whine to the authorities about it – hit the @gag command and the asshole's statements will be blocked from your screen (and only yours). It's simple, it's effective, and it censors no one.

But the Bungle case was rather hard on such arguments. For one thing, the extremely public nature of the living room meant that gagging would spare the victims only from witnessing their own violation, but not from having others witness it. You might want to argue that what those victims didn't directly experience couldn't hurt them, but consider how that wisdom would sound to a woman who'd been, say, fondled by strangers while passed out drunk and you have a rough idea how it might go over with a crowd of hard-core MOOers. Consider, for another thing, that many of the biologically female participants in the Bungle debate had been around long enough to grow lethally weary of the gag-and-get-over-it school of virtual-rape counseling, with its fine line between empowering victims and holding them responsible for their own suffering, and its shrugging indifference to the window of pain between the moment the rape-text starts flowing and the moment a gag shuts it off. From the outset it was clear that the technolibertarians were going to have to tiptoe through this issue with care, and for the most part they did.

Yet no position was trickier to maintain than that of the MOO's resident anarchists. Like the technolibbers, the anarchists didn't care much for punishments or policies or power elites. Like them, they hoped the MOO could be a place where people interacted fulfillingly without the need for such things. But their high hopes were complicated, in general, by a somewhat less thoroughgoing faith in technology ("Even if you can't tear down the master's house with the master's tools" – read a slogan written into one anarchist player's self-description – "it is a damned good place to start".) And at present they were additionally complicated by the fact that the most vocal anarchists in the discussion were none other than legba, Bakunin, and SamIAm, who wanted to see Mr. Bungle toaded as badly as anyone did.

Needless to say, a pro death penalty platform is not an especially comfortable one for an anarchist to sit on, so these particular anarchists were now at great pains to sever the conceptual ties between toading and capital punishment. Toading, they insisted (almost convincingly), was much more closely analogous to banishment; it was a kind of turning of the communal back on the offending party, a collective action which, if carried out properly, was entirely consistent with anarchist models of community. And carrying it out properly meant first and foremost building a consensus around it – a messy process for which there were no easy technocratic substitutes. It was going to take plenty of good old-fashioned, jawbone-intensive grassroots organizing.

So that when the time came, at 7 P.M. PST on the evening of the third day after the occurrence in the living room, to gather in evangeline's room for her proposed real-time open conclave, Bakunin and legba were among the first to arrive. But this was hardly to be an anarchist-dominated affair, for the room was crowding rapidly with representatives of all the MOO's political stripes, and even a few wizards. Hagbard showed up, and Autumn and Quastro, Puff, JoeFeedback, L-dopa and Bloaf, HerkieCosmo, Silver Rocket, Karl Porcupine, Matchstick – the names piled up and the discussion gathered momentum under their weight. Arguments multiplied and mingled, players talked past and through each other, the textual clutter of utterances and gestures filled up the screen like thick cigar smoke. Peaking in number at around 30, this was one of the largest crowds that ever gathered in a single LambdaMOO chamber, and while evangeline had given her place a description that made it "infinite in expanse and fluid in form," it now seemed anything but roomy. You could almost feel the claustrophobic air of the place, dank and overheated by virtual bodies, pressing against your skin.

I know you could because I too was there, making my lone and insignificant appearance in this story. Completely ignorant of any of the goings-on that had led to the meeting, I wandered in purely to see what the crowd was about, and though I observed the proceedings for a good while, I confess I found it hard to grasp what was going on. I was still the rankest of newbies, then, my MOO legs still too unsteady to make the leaps of faith, logic, and empathy required to meet the spectacle on its own terms. I was fascinated by the concept of virtual rape, but I couldn't quite take it seriously.

In this, though, I was in a small and mostly silent minority, for the discussion that raged around me was of an almost unrelieved earnestness, bent it seemed on examining every last aspect and implication of Mr. Bungle's crime. There were the central questions, of course: thumbs up or down on Bungle's virtual existence? And if down, how then to insure that his toading was not just some isolated lynching but a first step toward shaping LambdaMOO into a legitimate community? Surrounding these, however, a tangle of weighty side issues proliferated. What, some wondered, was the real-life legal status of the offense? Could Bungle's university administrators punish him for sexual harassment? Could he be prosecuted under California state laws against obscene phone calls? Little enthusiasm was shown for pursuing either of these lines of action, which testifies both to the uniqueness of the crime and to the nimbleness with which the discussants were negotiating its idiosyncracies. Many were the casual references to Bungle's deed as simply "rape," but these in no way implied that the players had lost sight of all distinctions between the virtual and physical versions, or that they believed Bungle should be dealt with in the same way a real-life criminal would. He had committed a MOO crime, and his punishment, if any, would be meted out via the MOO.

On the other hand, little patience was shown toward any attempts to downplay the seriousness of what Mr. Bungle had done. When the affable HerkieCosmo proposed, more in the way of an hypothesis than an assertion, that "perhaps it's better to release ... violent tendencies in a virtual environment rather than in real life," he was tut-tutted so swiftly and relentlessly that he withdrew the hypothesis altogether, apologizing humbly as he did so. Not that the assembly was averse to putting matters into a more philosophical perspective. "Where does the body end and the mind begin?" young Quastro asked, amid recurring attempts to fine-tune the differences between real and virtual violence. "Is not the mind a part of the body?" "In MOO, the body IS the mind," offered HerkieCosmo gamely, and not at all implausibly, demonstrating the ease with which very knotty metaphysical conundrums come undone in VR. The not-so-aptly named Obvious seemed to agree, arriving after deep consideration of the nature of Bungle's crime at the hardly novel yet now somehow newly resonant conjecture "All reality might consist of ideas, who knows."

On these and other matters the anarchists, the libertarians, the legalists, the wizardists – and the wizards – all had their thoughtful say. But as the evening wore on and the talk grew more heated and more heady, it seemed increasingly clear that the vigorous intelligence being brought to bear on this swarm of issues wasn't going to result in anything remotely like resolution. The perspectives were just too varied, the memescape just too slippery. Again and again, arguments that looked at first to be heading in a decisive direction ended up chasing their own tails; and slowly, depressingly, a dusty haze of irrelevance gathered over the proceedings.

It was almost a relief, therefore, when midway through the evening Mr. Bungle himself, the living, breathing cause of all this talk, teleported into the room. Not that it was much of a surprise. Oddly enough, in the three days since his release from Zippy's cage, Bungle had returned more than once to wander the public spaces of LambdaMOO, walking willingly into one of the fiercest storms of ill will and invective ever to rain down on a player. He'd been taking it all with a curious and mostly silent passivity, and when challenged face to virtual face by both legba and the genderless elder statescharacter PatGently to defend himself on *social, he'd demurred, mumbling something about Christ and expiation. He was equally quiet now, and his reception was still uniformly cool. legba fixed an arctic stare on him – "no hate, no anger, no interest at all. Just ... watching." Others were more actively unfriendly. "Asshole," spat Karl Porcupine, "creep." But the harshest of the MOO's hostility toward him had already been vented, and the attention he drew now was motivated more, it seemed, by the opportunity to probe the rapist's mind, to find out what made it tick and if possible how to get it to tick differently. In short, they wanted to know why he'd done it. So they asked him.

And Mr. Bungle thought about it. And as eddies of discussion and debate continued to swirl around him, he thought about it some more. And then he said this:

> I engaged in a bit of a psychological device that is called thought-polarization, the fact that this is not RL simply added to heighten the affect of the device. It was purely a sequence of events with no consequence on my RL existence.

They might have known. Stilted though its diction was, the gist of the answer was simple, and something many in the room had probably already surmised: Mr. Bungle was a psycho. Not, perhaps, in real life – but then in real life it's possible for reasonable people to assume, as Bungle clearly did, that what transpires between word-costumed characters within the boundaries of a make-believe world is, if not mere play, then at most some kind of emotional laboratory experiment. Inside the MOO, however, such thinking marked a person as one of two basically subcompetent types. The first was the newbie, in which case the confusion was understandable, since there were few MOOers who had not, upon their first visits as anonymous "guest" characters, mistaken the place for a vast playpen in which they might act out their wildest fantasies without fear of censure. Only with time and the acquisition of a fixed character do players tend to make the critical passage from anonymity to pseudonymity, developing the concern for their character's reputation that marks the attainment of virtual adulthood. But while Mr. Bungle hadn't been around as long as most MOOers, he'd been around long enough to leave his newbie status behind, and his delusional statement therefore placed him among the second type: the sociopath.

And as there is but small percentage in arguing with a head case, the room's attention gradually abandoned Mr. Bungle and returned to the discussions that had previously occupied it. But if the debate had been edging toward ineffectuality before, Bungle's anticlimactic appearance had evidently robbed it of any forward motion whatsoever. What's more, from his lonely corner of the room Mr. Bungle kept issuing periodic expressions of a prickly sort of remorse, interlaced with sarcasm and belligerence, and though it was hard to tell if he wasn't still just conducting his experiments, some people thought his regret genuine enough that maybe he didn't deserve to be toaded after all. Logically, of course, discussion of the principal issues at hand didn't require unanimous belief that Bungle was an irredeemable bastard, but now that cracks were showing in that unanimity, the last of the meeting's fervor seemed to be draining out through them.

People started drifting away. Mr. Bungle left first, then others followed – one by one, in twos and threes, hugging friends and waving goodnight. By 9:45 only a handful remained, and the great debate had wound down into casual conversation, the melancholy remains of another fruitless good idea. The arguments had been well-honed, certainly, and perhaps might prove useful in some as-yet-unclear long run. But at this point what seemed clear was that evangeline's meeting had died, at last, and without any practical results to mark its passing.

It was also at this point, most likely, that JoeFeedback reached his decision. JoeFeedback was a wizard, a taciturn sort of fellow who'd sat brooding on the sidelines all evening. He hadn't said a lot, but what he had said indicated that he took the crime committed against legba and Starsinger very seriously, and that he felt no particular compassion toward the character who had committed it. But on the other hand he had made it equally plain that he took the elimination of a fellow player just as seriously, and moreover that he had no desire to return to the days of wizardly fiat. It must have been difficult, therefore, to reconcile the conflicting impulses churning within him at that moment. In fact, it was probably impossible, for as much as he would have liked to make himself an instrument of LambdaMOO's collective will, he surely realized that under the present order of things he must in the final analysis either act alone or not act at all.

So JoeFeedback acted alone.

He told the lingering few players in the room that he had to go, and then he went. It was a minute or two before ten. He did it quietly and he did it privately, but all anyone had to do to know he'd done it was to type the @ who command, which was normally what you typed if you wanted to know a player's present location and the time he last logged in. But if you had run a @ who on Mr. Bungle not too long after JoeFeedback left evangeline's room, the database would have told you something different.

"Mr. Bungle," it would have said, "is not the name of any player."

The date, as it happened, was April Fool's Day, and it would still be April Fool's Day for another two hours. But this was no joke: Mr. Bungle was truly dead and truly gone.

They say that LambdaMOO has never been the same since Mr. Bungle's toading. They say as well that nothing's really changed. And though it skirts the fuzziest of dream-logics to say that both these statements are true, the MOO is just the sort of fuzzy, dreamlike place in which such contradictions thrive.

Certainly whatever civil society now informs LambdaMOO owes its existence to the Bungle Affair. The archwizard Haakon made sure of that. Away on business for the duration of the episode, Haakon returned to find its wreckage strewn across the tiny universe he'd set in motion. The death of a player, the trauma of several others, and the angst-ridden conscience of his colleague JoeFeedback presented themselves to his concerned and astonished attention, and he resolved to see if he couldn't learn some lesson from it all. For the better part of a day he brooded over the record of events and arguments left in *social*, then he sat pondering the chaotically evolving shape of his creation, and at the day's end he descended once again into the social arena of the MOO with another history-altering proclamation.

It was probably his last, for what he now decreed was the final, missing piece of the New Direction. In a few days, Haakon announced, he would build into the database a system of petitions and ballots whereby anyone could put to popular vote any social scheme requiring wizardly powers for its implementation, with the results of the vote to be binding on the wizards. At last and for good, the awkward gap between the will of the players and the efficacy of the technicians would be closed. And though some anarchists grumbled about the irony of Haakon's dictatorially imposing universal suffrage on an unconsulted populace, in general the citizens of LambdaMOO seemed to find it hard to fault a system more purely democratic than any that could ever exist in real life. Eight months and a dozen ballot measures later, widespread participation in the new regime has produced a small arsenal of mechanisms for dealing with the types of violence that called the system into being. MOO residents now have access to a @boot command, for instance, with which to summarily eject berserker "guest" characters. And players can bring suit against one another through an ad hoc arbitration system in which mutually agreed-upon judges have at their disposition the full range of wizardly punishments – up to and including the capital.

Yet the continued dependence on death as the ultimate keeper of the peace suggests that this new MOO order may not be built on the most solid of foundations. For if life on LambdaMOO began to acquire more coherence in the wake of the toading, death retained all the fuzziness of pre-Bungle days. This truth was rather dramatically borne out, not too many days after Bungle departed, by the arrival of a strange new character named Dr. Jest. There was a forceful eccentricity to the newcomer's manner, but the oddest thing about his style was its striking yet unnameable familiarity. And when he developed the annoying habit of stuffing fellow players into a jar containing a tiny simulacrum of a certain deceased rapist, the source of this familiarity became obvious:

Mr. Bungle had risen from the grave.

In itself, Bungle's reincarnation as Dr. Jest was a remarkable turn of events, but perhaps even more remarkable was the utter lack of amazement with which the LambdaMOO public took note of it. To be sure, many residents were appalled by the brazenness of Bungle's return. In fact, one of the first petitions circulated under the new voting system was a request for Dr. Jest's toading that almost immediately gathered 52 signatures (but has failed so far to reach ballot status). Yet few were unaware of the ease with which the toad proscription could be circumvented – all the toadee had to do (all the ur-Bungle at NYU presumably had done) was to go to the minor hassle of acquiring a new Internet account, and Lambda-MOO's character registration program would then simply treat the known felon as an entirely new and innocent person. Nor was this ease generally understood to represent a failure of toading's social disciplinary function. On the contrary, it only underlined the truism (repeated many times throughout the debate over Mr. Bungle's fate) that his punishment, ultimately, had been no more or less symbolic than his crime.

What *was* surprising, however, was that Mr. Bungle/Dr. Jest seemed to have taken the symbolism to heart. Dark themes still obsessed him – the objects he created gave off wafts of Nazi imagery and medical torture – but he no longer radiated the aggressively antisocial vibes he had before. He was a lot less unpleasant to look at (the outrageously seedy clown description had been replaced by that of a mildly creepy but actually rather natty young man, with "blue eyes . . . suggestive of conspiracy, untamed eroticism, and perhaps a sense of understanding of the future"), and aside from the occasional jar-stuffing incident, he was also a lot less dangerous to be around. It was obvious he'd undergone some sort of personal transformation in the days since I'd first glimpsed him back in evangeline's crowded room – nothing radical maybe, but powerful nonetheless, and resonant enough with my own experience, I felt, that it might be more than professionally interesting to talk with him, and perhaps compare notes.

For I too was undergoing a transformation in the aftermath of that night in evangeline's, and I'm still not entirely sure what to make of it. As I pursued my runaway fascination with the discussion I had heard there, as I pored over the *social debate and got to know legba and some of the other victims and witnesses, I could feel my newbie consciousness falling away from me. Where before I'd found it hard to take virtual rape seriously, I now was finding it difficult to remember how I could ever *not* have taken it seriously. I was proud to have arrived at this perspective – it felt like an exotic sort of achievement, and it definitely made my ongoing experience of the MOO a richer one.

But it was also having some unsettling effects on the way I looked at the rest of the world. Sometimes, for instance, it was hard for me to understand why RL society classifies RL rape alongside crimes against person or property. Since rape can occur without any physical pain or damage, I found myself reasoning, then it must be classed as a crime against the mind – more intimately and deeply hurtful, to be sure, than cross burnings, wolf whistles, and virtual rape, but undeniably located on the same conceptual continuum. I did not, however, conclude as a result that rapists were protected in any fashion by the First Amendment. Quite the opposite, in fact: the more seriously I took the notion of virtual rape, the less seriously I was able to take the notion of freedom of speech, with its tidy division of the world into the symbolic and the real.

Let me assure you, though, that I am not presenting these thoughts as arguments. I offer them, rather, as a picture of the sort of mind-set that deep immersion in a virtual world has inspired in me. I offer them also, therefore, as a kind of prophecy. For whatever else these thoughts tell me, I have come to believe that they announce the final stages of our decades-long passage into the Information Age, a paradigm shift that the classic liberal firewall between word and deed (itself a product of an earlier paradigm shift commonly known as the Enlightenment) is not likely to survive intact. After all, anyone the least bit familiar with the workings of the new era's definitive technology, the computer, knows that it operates on a principle impracticably difficult to distinguish from the pre-Enlightenment principle of the magic word: the commands you type into a computer are a kind of speech that doesn't so much communicate as *make things happen*, directly and ineluctably, the same way pulling a trigger does. They are incantations, in other words, and anyone at all attuned to the technosocial megatrends of the moment – from the growing dependence of economies on the global flow of intensely fetishized words and numbers to the burgeoning ability of bioengineers to speak the spells written in the four-letter text of DNA – knows that the logic of the incantation is rapidly permeating the fabric of our lives.

And it's precisely this logic that provides the real magic in a place like Lambda-MOO – not the fictive trappings of voodoo and shapeshifting and wizardry, but the conflation of speech and act that's inevitable in any computer-mediated world, be it Lambda or the increasingly wired world at large. This is dangerous magic, to be sure, a potential threat – if misconstrued or misapplied – to our always precarious freedoms of expression, and as someone who lives by his words I do not take the threat lightly. And yet, on the other hand, I can no longer convince myself that our wishful insulation of language from the realm of action has ever been anything but a valuable kludge, a philosophically damaged stopgap against oppression that would just have to do till something truer and more elegant came along.

Am I wrong to think this truer, more elegant thing can be found on Lambda-MOO? Perhaps, but I continue to seek it there, sensing its presence just beneath the surface of every interaction. I have even thought, as I said, that discussing with Dr. Jest our shared experience of the workings of the MOO might help me in my search. But when that notion first occurred to me, I still felt somewhat intimidated by his lingering criminal aura, and I hemmed and hawed a good long time before finally resolving to drop him MOO-mail requesting an interview. By then it was too late. For reasons known only to himself, Dr. Jest had stopped logging in. Maybe he'd grown bored with the MOO. Maybe the loneliness of ostracism had gotten to him. Maybe a psycho whim had carried him far away or maybe he'd quietly acquired a third character and started life over with a cleaner slate.

Wherever he'd gone, though, he left behind the room he'd created for himself – a treehouse "tastefully decorated" with rare-book shelves, an operating table, and a life-size William S. Burroughs doll – and he left it unlocked. So I took to checking in there occasionally, and I still do from time to time. I head out of my own cozy nook (inside a TV set inside the little red hotel inside the Monopoly board inside the dining room of LambdaMOO), and I teleport on over to the treehouse, where the room description always tells me Dr. Jest is present but asleep, in the conventional depiction for disconnected characters. The not-quite-emptiness of the abandoned room invariably instills in me an uncomfortable mix of melancholy and the creeps, and I stick around only on the off chance that Dr. Jest will wake up, say hello, and share his understanding of the future with me.

He won't, of course, but this is no great loss. Increasingly, the complex magic of the MOO interests me more as a way to live the present than to understand the future. And it's usually not long before I leave Dr. Jest's lonely treehouse and head back to the mansion, to see some friends.

21

Women and Children First:
Gender and the Settling of the
Electronic Frontier

Laura Miller

Laura Miller, "Women and Children First: Gender and the Settling of the Electronic Frontier," in James Brooks and Ian Boa, eds., *Resisting the Virtual Life* (San Francisco: City Light Books, 1995), pp. 49–58.

Laura Miller is a widely published journalist and critic, whose writing has appeared in such publications as the *San Francisco Examiner*, *SF Weekly*, and *Harpers Bazarre*. Miller is also a worker-owner of the Good Vibrations sex products store in San Francisco. This essay presents a succinct discussion of gender online, with attention to Julian Dibbel's "Rape in Cyberspace" piece, which appears as chapter 20 in this volume.

When *Newsweek* (May 16, 1994) ran an article entitled "Men, Women and Computers," all hell broke out on the Net, particularly on the on-line service I've participated in for six years, The Well (Whole Earth 'Lectronic Link). "Cyberspace, it turns out," declared *Newsweek*'s Nancy Kantrowitz, "isn't much of an Eden after all. It's marred by just as many sexist ruts and gender conflicts as the Real World. . . . Women often feel about as welcome as a system crash." "It was horrible. Awful, poorly researched, unsubstantiated drivel," one member wrote, a sentiment echoed throughout some 480 postings.

However egregious the errors in the article (some sources maintain that they were incorrectly quoted), it's only one of several mainstream media depictions of the Net as an environment hostile to women. Even women who had been complaining about on-line gender relations found themselves increasingly annoyed by what one Well member termed the "cyberbabe harassment" angle that seems to typify media coverage of the issue. Reified in the pages of *Newsweek* and other journals, what had once been the topic of discussion by insiders – on-line commentary is informal, conversational, and often spontaneous – became a journalistic "fact" about the Net known by complete strangers and novices. In a matter of months, the airy stuff of bitch sessions became widespread, hardened stereotypes.

At the same time, the Internet has come under increasing scrutiny as it mutates from an obscure, freewheeling web of computer networks used by a small elite of academics, scientists, and hobbyists to ... well, nobody seems to know exactly what. But the business press prints vague, fevered prophecies of fabulous wealth, and a bonanza mentality has blossomed. With it comes big business and the government, intent on regulating this amorphous medium into a manageable and profitable industry. The Net's history of informal self-regulation and its wide libertarian streak guarantee that battles like the one over the Clipper chip (a mandatory decoding device that would make all encrypted data readable by federal agents) will be only the first among many.

Yet the threat of regulation is built into the very mythos used to conceptualize the Net by its defenders – and gender plays a crucial role in that threat. However revolutionary the technologized interactions of on-line communities may seem, we understand them by deploying a set of very familiar metaphors from the rich figurative soup of American culture. Would different metaphors have allowed the Net a different, better historical trajectory? Perhaps not, but the way we choose to describe the Net now encourages us to see regulation as its inevitable fate. And, by examining how gender roles provide a foundation for the intensification of such social controls, we can illuminate the way those roles proscribe the freedoms of men as well as women.

For months I mistakenly referred to the EFF (an organization founded by John Perry Barlow and Lotus 1-2-3 designer Mitch Kapor to foster access to, and further the discursive freedom of, on-line communications) as "The Electronic Freedom Foundation," instead of by its actual name, "The Electronic Frontier Foundation." Once corrected, I was struck by how intimately related the ideas "frontier" and "freedom" are in the Western mythos. The *frontier*, as a realm of limitless possibilities and few social controls, hovers, grail-like, in the American psyche, the dream our national identity is based on, but a dream that's always, somehow, just vanishing away.

Once made, the choice to see the Net as a frontier feels unavoidable, but it's actually quite problematic. The word "frontier" has traditionally described a place, if not land then the limitless "final frontier" of space. The Net, on the other hand, occupies precisely no physical space (although the computers and phone lines that make it possible do). It is a completely bodiless, symbolic thing with no discernable boundaries or location. The land of the American frontier did not become a "frontier" until Europeans determined to conquer it, but the continent existed before the intention to settle it. Unlike land, the Net was created by its pioneers.

Most peculiar, then, is the choice of the word "frontier" to describe an artifact so humanly constructed that it only exists as ideas or information. For central to the idea of the frontier is that it contains no (or very few) other people – fewer than two per square mile according to the nineteenth-century historian Frederick Turner. The freedom the frontier promises is a liberation from the demands of society, while the Net (I'm thinking now of Usenet) has nothing but society to offer. Without other people, news groups, mailing lists, and files simply wouldn't exist and e-mail would be purposeless. Unlike real space, cyberspace must be shared.

Nevertheless, the choice of a spatial metaphor (credited to the science-fiction novelist William Gibson, who coined the term "cyberspace"), however awkward, isn't surprising. Psychologist Julian Jaynes has pointed out that geographical analogies have long predominated humanity's efforts to conceptualize – map out – consciousness. Unfortunately, these analogies bring with them a heavy load of baggage comparable to Pandora's box: open it and a complex series of problems have come to stay.

The frontier exists beyond the edge of settled or owned land. As the land that doesn't belong to anybody (or to people who "don't count," like Native Americans), it is on the verge of being acquired; currently unowned, but still ownable. Just as the ideal of chastity makes virginity sexually provocative, so does the unclaimed territory invite settlers, irresistibly so. Americans regard the lost geographical frontier with a melancholy, voluptuous fatalism – we had no choice but to advance upon it and it had no alternative but to submit. When an EFF member compares the Clipper chip to barbed wire encroaching on the prairie, doesn't he realize the surrender implied in his metaphor?

The psychosexual undercurrents (if anyone still thinks of them as "under") in the idea of civilization's phallic intrusion into nature's passive, feminine space have been observed, exhaustively, elsewhere. The classic Western narrative is actually far more concerned with social relationships than conflicts between man and nature. In these stories, the frontier is a lawless society of men, a milieu in which physical strength, courage, and personal charisma supplant institutional authority and violent conflict is the accepted means of settling disputes. The Western narrative connects pleasurably with the American romance of individualistic masculinity; small wonder that the predominantly male founders of the Net's culture found it so appealing.

When civilization arrives on the frontier, it comes dressed in skirts and short pants. In the archetypal 1939 movie *Dodge City*, Wade Hatton (Errol Flynn) refuses to accept the position of marshal because he prefers the footloose life of a trail driver. Abbie Irving (Olivia de Haviland), a recent arrival from the civilized East, scolds him for his unwillingness to accept and advance the cause of law; she can't function (in her job as crusading journalist) in a town governed by brute force. It takes the accidental killing of a child in a street brawl for Hatton to realize that he must pin on the badge and clean up Dodge City.

In the Western mythos, civilization is necessary because women and children are victimized in conditions of freedom. Introduce women and children into a frontier town and the law must follow because women and children must be protected. Women, in fact, are usually the most vocal proponents of the conversion from frontier justice to civil society.

The imperiled women and children of the Western narrative make their appearance today in newspaper and magazine articles that focus on the intimidation and sexual harassment of women on line and reports of pedophiles trolling for victims in computerized chat rooms. If on-line women successfully contest these attempts to depict them as the beleaguered prey of brutish men, expect the pedophile to assume a larger profile in arguments that the Net is out of control.

In the meantime, the media prefer to cast women as the victims, probably because many women actively participate in the call for greater regulation of on-line interactions, just as Abbie Irving urges Wade Hatton to bring the rule of law to Dodge City. These requests have a long cultural tradition, based on the idea that women, like children, constitute a peculiarly vulnerable class of people who require special protection from the elements of society men are expected to confront alone. In an insufficiently civilized society like the frontier, women, by virtue of this childlike vulnerability, are thought to live under the constant threat of kidnap, abuse, murder, and especially rape.

Women, who have every right to expect that crimes against their person will be rigorously prosecuted, should nevertheless regard the notion of special protections (chivalry, by another name) with suspicion. Based as it is on the idea that women are inherently weak and incapable of self-defense and that men are innately predatory, it actually reinforces the power imbalance between the sexes, with its roots in the concept of women as property, constantly under siege and requiring the vigilant protection of their male owners. If the romance of the frontier arises from the promise of vast stretches of unowned land, an escape from the restrictions of a society based on private property, the introduction of women spoils that dream by reintroducing the imperative of property in their own persons.

How does any of this relate to on-line interactions, which occur not on a desert landscape but in a complex, technological society where women are supposed to command equal status with men? It accompanies us as a set of unexamined assumptions about what it means to be male or female, assumptions that we believe are rooted in the imperatives of our bodies. These assumptions follow us into the bodiless realm of cyberspace, a forum where, as one scholar put it, "participants are washed clean of the stigmata of their real 'selves' and are free to invent new ones to their tastes." Perhaps some observers feel that the replication of gender roles in a context where the absence of bodies supposedly makes them superfluous proves exactly how innate those roles are. Instead, I see in the relent-less attempts to interpret on-line interactions as highly gendered, an intimation of just how artificial, how created, our gender system is. If it comes "naturally," why does it need to be perpetually defended and reasserted?

Complaints about the treatment of women on line fall into three categories: that women are subjected to excessive, unwanted sexual attention, that the prevailing style of on-line discussion turns women off, and that women are singled out by male participants for exceptionally dismissive or hostile treatment. In making these assertions, the *Newsweek* article and other stories on the issue do echo grievances that some on-line women have made for years. And, without a doubt, people have encountered sexual come-ons, aggressive debating tactics, and ad hominem attacks on the Net. However, individual users interpret such events in widely different ways, and to generalize from those interpretations to describe the experiences of women and men as a whole is a rash leap indeed.

I am one of many women who don't recognize their own experience of the Net in the misogynist gauntlet described above. In researching this essay, I joined America Online and spent an hour or two "hanging out" in the real-time chat rooms reputed to be rife with sexual harassment. I received several "instant messages" from men, initiating private conversation with innocuous questions about my hometown and tenure on the service. One man politely inquired if I was interested in "hot phone talk" and just as politely bowed out when I declined. At no point did I feel harassed or treated with disrespect. If I ever want to find a phone-sex partner, I now know where to look but until then I probably won't frequent certain chat rooms.

Other women may experience a request for phone sex or even those tame instant messages as both intrusive and insulting (while still others maintain that they have received much more explicit messages and inquiries completely out of the blue). My point isn't that my reactions are the more correct, but rather that both are the reactions of women, and no journalist has any reason to believe that mine are the exception rather than the rule.

For me, the menace in sexual harassment comes from the underlying threat of rape or physical violence. I see my body as the site of my heightened vulnerability as a woman. But on line – where I have no body and neither does anyone else – I consider rape to be impossible. Not everyone agrees. Julian Dibbell, in an article for *The Village Voice*, describes the repercussions of a "rape" in a multiuser dimension, or MUD, in which one user employed a subprogram called a "voodoo doll" to cause the personae of other users to perform sexual acts. Citing the "conflation of speech and act that's inevitable in any computer-mediated world," he moved toward the conclusion that "since rape can occur without any physical pain or damage, then it must be classified as a crime against the mind." Therefore, the offending user had committed something on the same "conceptual continuum" as rape. Tellingly, the incident led to the formation of the first governmental entity on the MUD.

No doubt the cyber-rapist (who went by the nom de guerre Mr. Bungle) appreciated the elevation of his mischief-making to the rank of virtual felony: all of the outlaw glamour and none of the prison time (he was exiled from the MUD). Mr. Bungle limited his victims to personae created by women users, a choice that, in its obedience to prevailing gender roles, shaped the debate that followed his crimes. For, in accordance with the real-world understanding that women's smaller, physically weaker bodies and lower social status make them subject to violation by men, there's a troubling notion in the real and virtual worlds that women's minds are also more vulnerable to invasion, degradation, and abuse.

This sense of fragility extends beyond interactions with sexual overtones. The *Newsweek* article reports that women participants can't tolerate the harsh, contentious quality of on-line discussions, that they prefer mutual support to heated debate, and are retreating wholesale to women-only conferences and newsgroups. As someone who values on-line forums precisely because they mandate equal time for each user who chooses to take it and forestall various "alpha male" rhetorical tactics like interrupting, loudness, or exploiting the psychosocial advantages of greater size or a deeper voice, I find this perplexing and disturbing. In these laments I hear the reluctance of women to enter into the kind of robust debate that characterizes healthy public life, a willingness to let men bully us even when they've been relieved of most of their traditional advantages. Withdrawing into an electronic purdah where one will never be challenged or provoked, allowing the ludicrous ritual chest-thumping of some users to intimate us into silence – surely women can come up with a more spirited response than this.

And of course they can, because besides being riddled with reductive stereotypes, media analyses like *Newsweek*'s simply aren't accurate. While the on-line population is predominantly male, a significant and vocal minority of women contribute regularly and more than manage to hold their own. Some of The Well's most bombastic participants are women, just as there are many tactful and conciliatory men. At least, I think there are, because, ultimately, it's impossible to be sure of anyone's biological gender on line. "Transpostites," people who pose as members of the opposite gender, are an established element of Net society, most famously a man who, pretending to be a disabled lesbian, built warm and intimate friendships with women on several CompuServe forums.

Perhaps what we should be examining is not the triumph of gender differences on the Net, but their potential blurring. In this light, *Newsweek*'s stout assertion that in cyberspace "the gender gap is real" begins to seem less objective than defensive, an insistence that on-line culture is "the same" as real life because the idea that it might be different, when it comes to gender, is too scary. If gender roles can be cast off so easily, they may be less deeply rooted, less "natural" than we believe. There may not actually be a "masculine" or "feminine" mind or outlook, but simply a conventional way of interpreting individuals that recognizes behavior seen as in accordance with their biological gender and ignores behavior that isn't.

For example, John Seabury wrote in the *New Yorker* (June 6, 1994) of his stricken reaction to his first "flame," a colorful slice of adolescent invective sent to him by an unnamed technology journalist. Reading it, he begins to "shiver" like a burn victim, an effect that worsens with repeated readings. He writes that "the technology greased the words . . . with a kind of immediacy that allowed them to slide easily into my brain." He tells his friends, his coworkers, his partner – even his mother – and, predictably, appeals to CompuServe's management for recourse – to no avail. Soon enough, he's talking about civilization and anarchy, how the liberating "lack of social barriers is also what is appalling about the net," and calling for regulation.

As a newcomer, Seabury was chided for brooding over a missive that most Net veterans would have dismissed and forgotten as the crude potshot of an envious jerk. (I can't help wondering if my fellow journalist never received hate mail in response to his other writings; this bit of e-mail seems comparable, par for the course when one assumes a public profile.) What nobody did was observe that Seabury's reaction – the shock, the feelings of violation, the appeals to his family and support network, the bootless complaints to the authorities – reads exactly like many horror stories about women's trials on the Net. Yet, because Seabury is a man, no one attributes the attack to his gender or suggests that the Net has proven an environment hostile to men. Furthermore, the idea that the Net must be more strictly governed to prevent the abuse of guys who write for the *New Yorker* seems laughable – though who's to say that Seabury's pain is less than any woman's? Who can doubt that, were he a woman, his tribulations would be seen as compelling evidence of Internet sexism?

The idea that women merit special protections in an environment as incorporeal as the Net is intimately bound up with the idea that women's minds are weak, fragile, and unsuited to the rough and tumble of public discourse. It's an argument that women should recognize with profound mistrust and resist, especially when we are used as rhetorical pawns in a battle to regulate a rare (if elite) space of gender ambiguity. When the mainstream media generalize about women's experiences on line in ways that just happen to uphold the most conventional and pernicious gender stereotypes, they can expect to be greeted with howls of disapproval from women who refuse to acquiesce in these roles and pass them on to other women.

And there are plenty of us, as The Well's response to the *Newsweek* article indicates. Women have always participated in on-line communications, women whose chosen careers in technology and the sciences have already marked them as gender-role resisters. As the schoolmarms arrive on the electronic frontier, their female predecessors find themselves cast in the role of saloon girls, their willingness to engage in "masculine" activities like verbal aggression, debate, or sexual experimentation marking them as insufficiently feminine, or "bad" women. "If that's what women on line are like, I must be a Martian," one Well woman wrote in response to the shrinking female technophobes depicted in the *Newsweek* article. Rather than relegating so many people to the status of gender aliens, we ought to reconsider how adequate those roles are to the task of describing real human beings.

22

We're Teen, We're Queer, and We've Got E-Mail

Steve Silberman

Steve Silberman is a journalist and senior correspondent for *Wired News*, an Internet subsidiary of *Wired* magazine. He is the co-author of the book *Skeleton Keys: A Dictionary for Deadheads* (Doubleday, 1994). In this article Silberman discusses the development of a gay online community.

There's a light on in the Nerd Nook: John Teen Ø is composing e-mail into the night. The Nerd Nook is what John's mother calls her 16-year-old's bedroom – it's more cramped than the bridge of the Enterprise, with a Roland CM-322 that makes "You've got mail" thunder like the voice of God.

John's favourite short story is "The Metamorphosis." Sure, Kafka's fable of waking up to discover you've morphed into something that makes everyone tweak speaks to every teenager. But John especially has had moments of feeling insectoid – like during one school choir trip, when, he says, the teacher booking rooms felt it necessary to inform the other students' parents of John's "orientation." When they balked at their kids sharing a room with him, John was doubled up with another teacher – a fate nearly as alienating as Gregor Samsa's.

The choir trip fiasco was but one chapter in the continuing online journal that has made John Teen Ø – or as his parents and classmates know him, John Erwin – one of the most articulate voices in America Online's Gay and Lesbian Community Forum.

From: John Teen Ø

My high school career has been a sudden and drastic spell of turbulence and change that has influenced every aspect of life. Once I was an automaton, obeying external, societal, and parental expectations like a dog, oblivious of who I was or what I wanted. I was the token child every parent wants – student body president, color guard, recipient of the general excellence award, and outstanding music student of the year. I conformed to society's paradigm, and I was rewarded. Yet I was miserable. Everything I did was a diversion from thinking about myself. Finally, last summer, my subconsciousness felt comfortable enough to be able to connect myself with who I really am, and I began to understand what it is to be gay.

John Teen Ø is a new kind of gay kid, a 16-year-old not only out, but already at home in the online convergence of activists that Tom Reilly, the co-founder of Digital Queers, calls the "Queer Global Village." Just 10 years ago, most queer teens hid behind a self-imposed don't-ask-don't-tell policy until they shipped out to Oberlin or San Francisco, but the Net has given even closeted kids a place to conspire. Though the Erwins' house is in an unincorporated area of Santa Clara County in California, with goats and llamas foraging in the backyard, John's access to AOL's gay and lesbian forum enables him to follow dispatches from queer activists worldwide, hone his writing, flirt, try on disposable identities, and battle bigots – all from his home screen.

John's ambitions to recast national policy before the principal of Menlo School even palms him a diploma (John's mother refers to him as her "little mini-activist") are not unrealistic. Like the un-narrative of every videogame, the saga of gay teens online is one of metamorphosis, of "little mini" nerds becoming warriors in a hidden Stronghold of Power. For young queers, the Magic Ring is the bond of community.

John's posts have the confidence and urgency of one who speaks for many who must keep silent:

> The struggle for equal rights has always taken place on the frontier of the legal wilderness where liberty meets power. Liberty has claimed much of that wilderness now, but the frontier always lies ahead of us.... The frontier of liberty may have expanded far beyond where it began, but for those without rights, it always seems on the horizon, just beyond their reach.

And the messages that stream back into John's box are mostly from kids his own age, many marooned far from urban centers for gay and lesbian youth. Such is Christopher Rempel, a witty, soft-spoken Ace of Base fan from (as he puts it) "redneck farmer hell." Christopher borrowed the principal's modem to jack into a beekeepers BBS and gopher his way to the Queer Resources Directory, a multimeg collection of text files, news items, and services listings.

> My name is Christopher and I am 15 years old. I came to terms that I was gay last summer and, aside from some depression, I'm OK. I am "not" in denial about being gay.
> I would like to write to someone that I can talk to about issues I can't talk about with my friends. I don't play sports very much, but I make it up in my knowledge of computers. I am interested in anybody with an open mind and big aspirations for the future.

A decade ago, the only queer info available to most teens was in a few dour psychology texts under the nose of the school librarian. Now libraries of files await them in the AOL forum and elsewhere – the Queer Resources Directory alone contains hundreds – and teens can join mailing lists like Queercampus and

GayNet, or tap resources like the Bridges Project, a referral service that tells teens not only how to get in touch with queer youth groups, but how to jump-start one themselves.

Kali is an 18-year-old lesbian at a university in Colorado. Her name means "fierce" in Swahili. Growing up in California, Kali was the leader of a young women's chapter of the Church of Jesus Christ of Latter-Day Saints. She was also the "Girl Saved by E-mail," whose story ran last spring on CNN. After mood swings plummeted her into a profound depression, Kali – like too many gay teens – considered suicide. Her access to GayNet at school gave her a place to air those feelings, and a phone call from someone she knew online saved her life.

Kali is now a regular contributor to Sappho, a women's board she most appreciates because there she is accepted as an equal. "They forgive me for being young," Kali laughs, "though women come out later than guys, so there aren't a lot of teen lesbians. But it's a high of connection. We joke that we're posting to 500 of our closest friends."

"The wonderful thing about online services is that they are an intrinsically decentralized resource," says Tom Reilly, who has solicited the hardware and imparted the skills to get dozens of queer organizations jacked in. "Kids can challenge what adults have to say and make the news. One of the best examples of teen organizing in the last year was teens working with the Massachusetts legislature to pass a law requiring gay and lesbian education in the high schools. If teen organizers are successful *somewhere* now, everyone's gonna hear about it. This is the most powerful tool queer youth have ever had."

Another power that teenagers are now wielding online is their anger. "Teens are starting to throw their weight around," says Quirk, the leader of the AOL forum. (Quirk maintains a gender-neutral identity online, to be an equal-opportunity sounding board for young lesbians and gay men.) "They're *complaining*. It used to be, 'Ick – I think I'm gay, I'll sneak around the forum and see what they're doing.' With this second wave of activism, it's like, 'There's gay stuff here, but it's not right for *me*.' These kids are computer literate, and they're using the anger of youth to create a space for themselves."

The powers that be at AOL, however, have not yet seen fit to allow that space to be named by its users – the creation of chat rooms called "gay teen" anything is banned. "AOL has found that the word 'gay' with the word 'youth' or 'teen' in a room name becomes a lightning rod for predators," says Quirk. "I've been in teen conferences where adult cruising so overwhelmed any kind of conversation about being in high school and 'What kind of music do you like?' that I was furious. Until I can figure out a way to provide a safe space for them, I'm not going to put them at risk."

Quirk and AOL are in a tight place. Pedophilia has become the trendy bludgeon with which to trash cyberspace in the dailies, and concerned parents invoke the P-word to justify limiting teens' access to gay forums. At the same time, however, postings in the teens-only folder of the Gay and Lesbian Community Forum flame not only the invasion of teen turf by adults trolling for sex, but also the adults claiming to "protect" them by limiting their access to one another.

One anonymous 17-year-old poster on AOL dissed the notion that queer teens are helpless victims of online "predators":

> There are procedures for dealing with perverts, which most teens (in contrast with most of the adults we've encountered) are familiar with. Flooding e-mail boxes of annoying perverts, "IGNORE"-ing them in chat rooms, and shutting off our Instant Messages are all very effective methods. We are not defenseless, nor innocent.

The issue is further complicated by the fact that the intermingling of old and young people online is good for teens. The online connection allows them to open dialogs with mentors like Deacon Maccubbin, co-owner of Lambda Rising bookstore in Washington, D.C. As "DeaconMac," Maccubbin has been talking with gay kids on CompuServe and AOL for eight years. One of the young people DeaconMac corresponded with online, years ago, was Tom Reilly. "Deacon was the first openly gay man I'd ever had a conversation with, and he had a very clear idea of what his role was. He was nurturing and mentoring; he sent me articles; and he didn't come on to me," says Reilly. "I'll never forget it as long as I live."

In the past, teens often had to wait until they were old enough to get into a bar to meet other gay people – or hang around outside until someone noticed them. Online interaction gives teens a chance to unmask themselves in a safe place, in a venue where individuals make themselves known by the acuity of their thought and expression, rather than by their physical appearance.

When JohnTeen Ø logged his first post in the gay AOL forum, he expressed outrage that the concerns of queer teens – who are at a disproportionately high risk for suicide – were being shunted aside by adult organizations. His post was spotted by Sarah Gregory, a 26-year-old anarchist law student who helped get the National Gay and Lesbian Task Force wired up. "I really wanted to hit this kid between the eyes with the fact that a national organization saw what he was saying and cared that gay youth were killing themselves," Gregory recalls. A correspondence and friendship began that would have been unlikely offline – for, as Gregory says, "I don't notice 16-year-old boys in the real world."

Gregory explains: "I remember one particularly graphic letter I sent John in response to his questions. I wrote a *huge* disclaimer before and after it. But then I remembered how desperately I wanted to be talked to as an adult, and a sexual being, when I was 14. Thinking back, that's the point where John stopped sounding so formal, so much like a well-bred teenager talking to an authority figure, and became my friend. It's also the last time he talked about suicide. It scared me how easily his vulnerability could have been exploited, but I'd do it again in a heartbeat."

"I didn't even listen to music," moans John recalling his nerdhood, when the only thing he logged in for was shareware. Now the background thrash for his late-night e-mail sessions is Pansy Division. "To keep myself in the closet, I surrounded myself with people I'd never find attractive. I had two different parts of my life: the normal part, where I worked hard in school and got good grades, and this other part, where I was interested in guys but didn't do anything about it." For many kids, writing to John or to other posters is where a more authentic life begins:

Dear John Teen:

I am so frustrated with life and all of its blind turns. Am I gay? What will happen if I tell friends and my mom? . . . (I still don't 100% know that I am gay only that I am not heterosexual SO WHAT AM I) I really want to fit somewhere and also to love someone (at this point I don't care who). . . . Please EMAIL back and enlighten me. You have been very inspirational to me. I have no idea how you gained the courage to come out. Thanks, James

But John Erwin must guard against JohnTeen Ø becoming a full-time gig: he not only has the frontiers of liberty to defend and his peers to "enlighten," but like any 16-year-old, he needs space to fuck up, be a normal teenage cockroach, and figure out who he is. And he'd like to find someone to love. Does he have anyone in mind? "Yes!" he grins, pulling out his yearbook and leafing to a photo of a handsome boy who says he's straight.

Is John's dream guy online?

"No, I wish," John says. "If he was online, I could tell him how I *feel*."

23

Race In/For Cyberspace: Identity Tourism and Racial Passing on the Internet

Lisa Nakamura

Lisa Nakamura, "Race In/For Cyberspace: Identity Tourism and Racial Passing on the Internet." A later version appears in Beth E. Kolko, Lisa Nakamura, Gilbert B. Rodman, eds., *Race in Cyberspace* (Routledge, 2000), pp. 15–27. Reproduced by permission of Taylor & Francis, Inc./Routledge, Inc., http://www. routledge-ny.com.

Lisa Nakamura is the co-editor of *Race in Cyberspace* (Routledge, 2000). From an Asian-American perspective, this essay discusses how spaces like Lambda-MOO enable participants to drop in and out of racially-specific identities, both reproducing and subverting stereotypes.

A cute cartoon dog sits in front of a computer, gazing at the monitor and typing away busily. The cartoon's caption jubilantly proclaims, "On the Internet, nobody knows you're a dog!" This image resonates with particular intensity for those members of a rapidly expanding subculture which congregates within the consensual hallucination defined as cyberspace. Users define their presence within this textual and graphical space through a variety of different activities – commercial interaction, academic research, netsurfing, real time interaction and chatting with interlocutors who are similarly "connected" – but all can see the humor in this image because it illustrates so graphically a common condition of being and self-definition within this space. Users of the Internet represent themselves within it solely through the medium of keystrokes and mouse-clicks, and through this medium they can describe themselves and their physical bodies any way they like; they perform their bodies as text. On the Internet, nobody knows that you're a dog; it is possible to "computer crossdress" (Stone, 1991) and represent yourself as a different gender, age, race, etc. The technology of the Internet offers its participants unprecedented possibilities for communicating with each other in real time, and for controlling the conditions of their own self-representations in ways impossible in face to face interaction. The cartoon seems to celebrate access to the Internet as a social leveler which permits even dogs to express freely themselves in discourse to their masters, who are deceived into thinking that they are their peers, rather than their property. The element of difference, in this cartoon the difference between species, is comically subverted in this image; in the medium of cyberspace, distinctions and imbalances in power between beings who perform themselves solely through writing seem to have been deferred, if not effaced.

This utopian vision of cyberspace as a promoter of a radically democratic form of discourse should not be underestimated. Yet the image can be read on several other levels as well. The freedom which the dog chooses to avail itself of is the freedom to "pass" as part of a privileged group, i.e. human computer users with access to the Internet. This is possible because of the discursive dynamic of the Internet, particularly in chat spaces like LambdaMOO where users are known to others by self-authored names which they give their "characters" rather than more telling email addresses with domain names. Defining gender is a central part of the discourse – players who choose to present themselves as "neuter," one of the several genders available to players on LambdaMOO, are often asked to "set gender," as if the choice to have a neuter gender is not a choice at all, or at least one that other players choose to recognize. Gender is an element of identity which must be defined by each player – though the creators of LambdaMOO try to contribute towards a reimagining of gender by offering four, two more than are acknowledged in "real life," still, one must be chosen (the choice is not optional). Each player must "enunciate" the gender that they choose, since this gender will be visible to other players who call up other players' physical descriptions on their screens. However, race is not an "option" which must be chosen – though players can elect to write it into their descriptions, it is not required that they do so. My study, which I would characterize as ethnographic, with certain important reservations, focuses on the ways in which race is "written," in the cyberspace locus called LambdaMOO, as well as the ways it is read by other players, the conditions under which it is enunciated, contested, and ultimately erased and suppressed, and the ideological implications of these performative acts of writing and reading otherness. What does the way race is written in LambdaMOO reveal about the enunciation of difference in new electronic media? Have the rules of the game changed, and if so, how?

Role-playing sites on the Internet such as LambdaMOO offer their participants programming features such as the ability to physically "set" one's gender, race, and physical appearance, through which they can, indeed are required to, project a version of the self which is inherently theatrical. Since the "real" identities of the interlocutors at Lambda are unverifiable (except by crackers and hackers, whose outlaw manipulations of code are unanimously construed by the Internet's citizens as a violation of both privacy and personal freedom) it can be said that everyone who participates is "passing," as it impossible to tell if a character's description matches a player's physical characteristics. Some of the uses to which this infixed theatricality are put are benign and even funny – descriptions of self as a human-size pickle or pot bellied pig are not uncommon, and generally are received in a positive, amused, tolerant way by other players. Players who elect to describe themselves in racial terms, as Asian, African American, Latino, or other members of oppressed and marginalized minorities, are often seen as engaging in a form of hostile performance, since they introduce what many consider a real life "divisive issue" into the phantasmatic world of cybernetic textual interaction. The borders and frontiers of cyberspace which had previously seemed so amorphous take on a keen sharpness when the enunciation of racial otherness is put into play as performance. While everyone is "passing," some forms of racial passing are condoned and practised since they do not threaten the integrity of a national sense of self which is defined as white.

The first act a participant in LambdaMOO performs is that of writing a self description – it is the primal scene of cybernetic identity, a postmodern performance of the mirror stage:

> Identity is the first thing you create in a MUD. You have to decide the name of your alternate identity – what MUDders call your character. And you have to describe who this character is, for the benefit of the other people who inhabit the same MUD. By creating your identity, you help create a world. Your character's role and the roles of the others who play with you are part of the architecture of belief that upholds for everybody in the MUD the illusion of being a wizard in a castle or a navigator aboard a starship: the roles give people new stages on which to exercise new identities, and their new identities affirm the reality of the scenario. (Rheingold, 1995)

In LambdaMOO it is required that one choose a gender; though two of the choices are variations on the theme of "neuter," the choice cannot be deferred because the programming code requires it. It is impossible to receive authorization to create a character without making this choice. Race is not only not a required choice, it is not even on the menu.[1] Players are given as many lines of text as they like to write any sort of textual description of themselves that they want. The "architecture of belief" which underpins social interaction in the MOO, that is, the belief that your interlocutors possess distinctive human identities which coalesce through and vivify the glowing letters scrolling down the computer screen, is itself built upon this form of fantastic autobiographical writing called the self-description. The majority of players in LambdaMOO do not mention race at all in their self description, though most do include eye and hair color, build, age, and the pronouns which indicate a male or a female gender.[2] In these cases when race is not mentioned as such, but hair and eye color is, race is still being evoked – a character with blue eyes and blond hair will be assumed to be white. Yet while the textual conditions of self-definition and self-performance would seem to permit players total freedom, within the boundaries of the written word, to describe themselves in any way they choose, this choice is actually an illusion. This is because the choice not to mention race does in fact constitute a choice – in the absence of racial description, all players are assumed to be white. This is partly due to the demographics of Internet users – most are white, male, highly educated, and middle class. It is also due to the utopian belief-system prevalent in the MOO. This system, which claims that the MOO should be a free space for play, strives towards policing and regulating racial discourse in the interest of social harmony. This system of regulation does permit racial role playing when it fits within familiar discourses of racial stereotyping, and thus perpetuates these discourses. I am going to focus on the deployment of Asian performance within the MOO because Asian personae are by far the most common non-white ones chosen by players and offer the most examples for study.

The vast majority of male Asian characters deployed in the MOO fit into familiar stereotypes from popular electronic media such as video games, television, and film, and popular literary genres such as science fiction and historical romance. Characters named Mr. Sulu, Chun Li, Hua Ling, Anjin San, Musashi, Bruce Lee, Little Dragon, Nunchaku, Hiroko, Miura Tetsuo, and Akira invoke their counterparts in the world of popular media; Mr. Sulu is the token "Oriental" in the television show "Star Trek," Hua Ling and Hiroko are characters in the science fiction novels *Eon* and *Red Mars*, Chun Li and Liu Kang are characters from the video games "Street Fighter" and "Mortal Kombat," the movie star Bruce Lee was nicknamed "Little Dragon," Miura Tetsuo and Anjin San are characters in James Clavell's popular novel and miniseries "Shogun," Musashi is a medieval Japanese folklore hero, and Akira is the title of a Japanese animated film of the genre called "anime." The name Nunchaku refers to a weapon, as do, in a more oblique way, all of the names listed above. These names all adapt the samurai warrior fantasy to cyberdiscursive role playing, and permit their users to perform a notion of the Oriental warrior adopted from popular media. This is an example of the crossing over effect of popular media into cyberspace, which is, as the latest comer to the array of electronic entertainment media, a bricolage of figurations and simulations. The Orientalized male persona, complete with sword, confirms the idea of the male oriental as potent, antique, exotic, and anachronistic.

This type of Orientalized theatricality is a form of identity tourism; players who choose to perform this type of racial play are almost always white, and their appropriation of stereotyped male Asiatic samurai figures allows them to indulge in a dream of crossing over racial boundaries temporarily and recreationally. Choosing these stereotypes tips their interlocutors off to the fact that they are not "really" Asian; they are instead "playing" in an already familiar type of performance. Thus, the Orient is brought into the discourse, but only as a token or "type." The idea of a non-stereotyped Asian male identity is so seldom enacted in LambdaMOO that its absence can only be read as a symptom of a suppression.

Tourism is a particularly apt metaphor to describe the activity of racial identity appropriation, or "passing" in cyberspace. The activity of "surfing" (an activity already associated with tourism in the mind of most Americans) the Internet not only reinforces the idea that cyberspace is not only a place where travel and mobility are featured attractions, but also figures it as a form of travel which is inherently recreational, exotic, and exciting, like surfing. The choice to enact oneself as a samurai warrior in LambdaMOO constitutes a form of identity tourism which allows a player to appropriate an Asian racial identity without any of the risks associated with being a racial minority in real life. While this might seem to offer a promising venue for non-Asian characters to see through the eyes of the Other by performing themselves as Asian through on-line textual interaction, the fact that the personae chosen are overwhelmingly Asian stereotypes blocks this possibility by reinforcing these stereotypes.

This theatrical fantasy of passing as a form of identity tourism has deep roots in colonial fiction, such as Kipling's *Kim* and T. E. Lawrence's *Seven Pillars of Wisdom*, and Sir Richard Burton's writings. The Irish orphan and spy Kim, who uses disguise to pass as Hindu, Muslim, and other varieties of Indian natives, experiences the pleasures and dangers of cross cultural performance. Said's (1987) insightful reading of the nature of Kim's adventures in cross cultural passing contrasts the possibilities for play and pleasure for white travelers in an imperialistic world controlled by the European empire with the relatively constrained plot resolutions offered that same boy back home. "For what one cannot do in one's own Western environment, where to try to live out the grand dream of a successful quest is only to keep coming up against one's own mediocrity and the world's corruption and degradation, one can do abroad. Isn't it possible in India to do everything, be anything, go anywhere with impunity?" (p. 42). To practitioners of identity tourism as I have described it above, LambdaMOO represents an phantasmatic imperial space, much like Kipling's Anglo-India, which supplies a stage upon which the "grand dream of a successful quest" can be enacted.

Since the incorporation of the computer into the white collar workplace the line which divides work from play has become increasingly fluid. It is difficult for employers and indeed, for employees, to always differentiate between doing "research" on the Internet and "playing": exchanging email, checking library catalogues, interacting with friends and colleagues through synchronous media like "talk" sessions, and videoconferencing offer enhanced opportunities for gossip, jokes, and other distractions under the guise of work.[3] Time spent on the Internet is a hiatus from "rl" (or real life, as it is called by most participants in virtual social spaces like LambdaMOO), and when that time is spent in a role playing space such as Lambda, devoted only to social interaction and the creation and maintenance of a convincingly "real" milieu modeled after an "international community," that hiatus becomes a full-fledged vacation. The fact that Lambda offers players the ability to write their own descriptions, as well as the fact that players often utilize this programming feature to write stereotyped Asian personae for themselves, reveal that attractions lie not only in being able to "go" to exotic spaces,[4] but to co-opt the exotic and attach it to oneself. The appropriation of racial identity becomes a form of recreation, a vacation from fixed identities and locales.

This vacation offers the satisfaction of a desire to fix the boundaries of cultural identity and exploit them for recreational purposes. As Said puts it, the tourist who passes as the marginalized Other during his travels partakes of a fantasy of social control, one which depends upon and fixes the familiar contours of racial power relations.

> It is the wish-fantasy of someone who would like to think that everything is possible, that one can go anywhere and be anything. T.E. Lawrence in *The Seven Pillars of Wisdom* expresses this fantasy over and over, as he reminds us how he – a blond and blue-eyed Englishman – moved among the desert Arabs as if he were one of them. I call this a fantasy because, as both Kipling and Lawrence endlessly remind us, no one – least of all actual whites and non-whites in the colonies – ever forgets that "going native" or playing the Great Game are facts based on rock-like foundations, those of European power. Was there ever a native fooled by the blue or green-eyed Kims and Lawrences who passed among the inferior races as agent adventures? I doubt it . . . (Said, 1987, p. 44)

As Donna Haraway (1991, p. 168) notes, high technologies "promise ultimate mobility and perfect exchange and incidentally enable tourism, that perfect practice of mobility and exchange, to emerge as one of the world's largest single industries." Identity tourism in cyberspaces like LambdaMOO functions as a fascinating example of the promise of high technology to enhance travel opportunities by redefining what constitutes travel – logging on to a phantasmatic space where one can appropriate exotic identities means that one need never cross a physical border or even leave one's armchair to go on vacation. This "promise" of "ultimate mobility and perfect exchange" is not, however, fulfilled for everyone in LambdaMOO. The suppression of racial discourse which does not conform to familiar stereotypes, and the enactment of notions of the Oriental which do conform to them, extends the promise of mobility and exchange only to those who wish to change their identities to fit accepted norms.

Performances of Asian female personae in LambdaMOO are doubly repressive because they enact a variety of identity tourism which cuts across the axes of gender and race, linking them in a powerful mix which brings together virtual sex, Orientalist stereotyping, and performance. A listing of some of the names and descriptions chosen by players who masquerade as "Asian" "females" at Lambda-MOO include: AsianDoll, Miss_Saigon, Bisexual_Asian_Guest, Michelle_Chang, Geisha_Guest, and Maiden Taiwan. They describe themselves as, for example, a "mystical Oriental beauty, drawn from the pages of a Nagel calendar," or, in the case of the Geisha_Guest, a character owned by a white American man living in Japan:

> a petite Japanese girl in her twenties. She has devoted her entire life to the perfecting the tea ceremony and mastering the art of lovemaking. She is multi-orgasmic. She is wearing a pastel kimono, 3 under-kimonos in pink and white. She is not wearing panties, and that would not be appropriate for a geisha. She has spent her entire life in the pursuit of erotic experiences.

Now, it is commonly known that the relative dearth of women in cyberspace results in a great deal of "computer cross dressing," or men masquerading as women. Men who do this are generally seeking sexual interaction, or "netsex" from other players of both genders. When the performance is doubly layered, and a user extends his identity tourism across both race and gender, it is possible to observe a double appropriation or objectification which uses the "Oriental" as part of a sexual lure, thus exploiting and reifying through performance notions of the Asian female as submissive, docile, a sexual plaything.

The fetishization of the Asian female extends beyond LambdaMOO into other parts of the Internet. There is a usenet newsgroup called "alt.sex.fetish.orientals" which is extremely active – it is also the only one of the infamous "alt.sex" newsgroups which overtly focuses upon race as an adjunct to sexuality.

Cyberspace is the newest incarnation of the idea of national boundaries. It is a phenomenon more abstract yet at the same time more "real" than outer space, since millions of participants deploy and immerse themselves within it daily, while space travel has been experienced by only a few people. The term "cyberspace" participates in a topographical trope which, as Stone points out, defines the activity of on-line interaction as taking place within a locus, a space, a "world" unto itself. This second "world," like carnival, possesses constantly fluctuating boundaries, frontiers, and dividing lines which separate it from both the realm of the "real" (that which takes place off line) and its corollary, the world of the physical body which gets projected, manipulated, and performed via on-line interaction. The title of the *Time* magazine cover story for July 25, 1994, "The Strange New World of Internet: Battles on the Frontiers of Cyberspace" is typical of the popular media's depictions of the Internet as a world unto itself with shifting frontiers and borders which are contested in the same way that national borders are. The "battle" over borders takes place on several levels which have been well documented elsewhere, such as the battle over encryption and the conflict between the rights of the private individual to transmit and receive information freely and the rights of government to monitor potentially dangerous, subversive, or obscene material which crosses state lines over telephone wires. These contests concern the distinction between public and private. It is, however, seldom acknowledged that the trope of the battle on the cyber frontier also connotes a conflict on the level of cultural self-definition. If, as Chris Chesher notes, "the frontier has been used since as a metaphor for freedom and progress, and . . . space exploration, especially, in the 1950s and 1960s was often called the 'new frontier,' " (1994, p. 18) the figuration of cyberspace as the most recent representation of the frontier sets the stage for border skirmishes in the realm of cultural representations of the Other. The discourse of space travel during this period solidified the American identity by limning out the contours of an cosmic, or "last" frontier.[5] The "race for space," or the race to stake out a border to be defended against both the non-human (aliens) and the non-American (the Soviets) translates into an obsession with race and a fear of racial contamination, always one of the distinctive features of the imperialist project. In films such as *Alien*, the integrity and solidarity of the American body is threatened on two fronts – both the anti-human (the alien) and the passing-as-human (the cyborg) seek to gain entry and colonize Ripley's human body. Narratives which locate the source of contaminating elements within a deceitful and uncanny technologically-enabled theatricality – the ability to pass as human – depict performance as an occupational hazard of the colonization of any space. New and futuristic technologies call into question the integrity of categories of the human since they enable the non-human to assume a human face and identity.

Recently, a character on Lambda named "Tapu" proposed a piece of legislation to the Lambda community in the form of a petition. This petition, entitled "Hate-Crime," was intended to impose penalties upon characters who harassed other characters on the basis of race. The players' publicly posted response to this petition, which failed by a narrow margin, reveals a great deal about the particular variety of utopianism common to real-time textual on-line social interaction. The petition's detractors argued that legislation or discourse designed to prevent or penalize racist "hate speech" were unnecessary since those offended in this way had the option to "hide" their race by removing it from their descriptions. A character named "Taffy" writes "Well, who knows my race unless I tell them? If race isn't important than why mention it? If you want to get in somebody's face with your race then perhaps you deserve a bit of flak. Either way I don't see why we need extra rules to deal with this." "Taffy," who signs himself "proud to be a sort of greyish pinky color with bloches" [sic] recommends a strategy of both blaming the victim and suppressing race, an issue which "isn't important" and shouldn't be mentioned because doing so gets in "somebody's face." The fear of the "flak" supposedly generated by players' decisions to include race in their descriptions of self is echoed in another post to the same group by "Nougat," who points out that "how is someone to know what race you are a part of? If [sic] this bill is meant to combat comments by towards people of different races, or just any comments whatsoever? Seems to me, if you include your race in your description, you are making yourself the sacrificial lamb. I don't include 'caucasian' in my description, simply because I think it is unnecessary. And thusly, I don't think I've ever been called 'honkey.'" Both of these posts emphasize that race is not, should not be, "necessary" to social interaction on LambdaMOO. The punishment for introducing this extraneous and divisive issue into the MOO, which represents a vacation space, a Fantasy Island of sorts, for its users, is to become a "sacrificial lamb." The attraction of Fantasy Island lay in its ability to provide scenarios for the fantasies of privileged individuals. And the maintenance of this fantasy, that of a race-free society, can only occur by suppressing forbidden identity choices.

While many of the members of social on-line communities like LambdaMOO are stubbornly utopian in their attitudes towards the power dynamics and flows of information within the technologically mediated social spaces they inhabit, most of the theorists are pessimistic. Andrew Ross and Constance Penley (1991) introduce the essays in their collection *Technoculture* by asserting that "the odds are firmly stacked against the efforts of those committed to creating technological counter-cultures" (p. xiii). Chesher concedes that "In spite of the claims that everyone is the same in virtual worlds, access to technology and necessary skills will effectively replicate class divisions of the rest of reality in the virtual spaces" (p. 28) and "will tend to reinforce existing inequalities, and propagate already dominant ideologies" (p. 29). Indeed, the cost of net access does contribute towards class divisions as well as racial ones; the vast majority of the Internet's users are white and middle-class. One of the dangers of identity tourism is that it takes this restriction across the axes of race/class in the "real world" to an even more subtle and complex degree by reducing non-white identity positions to part of a costume or masquerade to be used by curious vacationers in cyberspace. Asianness is co-opted as a "passing" fancy, an identity-prosthesis which signifies sex, the exotic, passivity when female, and anachronistic dreams of combat in its male manifestation. "Passing" as a samurai or geisha is diverting, reversible, and a privilege mainly used by white men. The paradigm of Asian passing masquerades on LambdaMOO itself works to suppress racial difference by setting the tone of the discourse in racist contours, which inevitably discourage "real life" Asian men and women from textual performance in that space, effectively driving race underground. As a result, a default "whiteness" covers the entire social space of LambdaMOO – race is "whited out" in the name of cybersocial hygiene.

The dream of a new technology has always contained within it the fear of total control, and the accompanying loss of individual autonomy. Perhaps the best way to subvert the hegemony of cybersocial hygiene is to use its own metaphors against itself. Racial and racist discourse in the MOO is the unique product of a machine and an ideology. Looking at discourse about race in cyberspace as a computer bug or ghost in the machine permits insight into the ways that it subverts that machine. A bug interrupts a program's regular commands and routines, causing it to behave unpredictably. "Bugs are mistakes, or unexpected occurrences, as opposed to things that are intentional" (Aker 1987–91, p. 12). Programmers routinely debug their work because they desire complete control over the way their program functions, just as Taffy and Nougat would like to debug LambdaMOO of its "sacrificial lambs," those who insist on introducing new expressions of race into their world. Discourse about race in cyberspace is conceptualized as a bug, something which an efficient computer user would eradicate since it contaminates their work/play. The "unexpected occurrence" of race has the potential, by its very unexpectedness, to sabotage the ideology-machine's routines. Therefore, its articulation is critical, as is the ongoing examination of the dynamics of this articulation. As Butler (1993, p. 118) puts it:

> Doubtlessly crucial is the ability to wield the signs of subordinated identity in a public domain that constitutes its own homophobic and racist hegemonies through the erasure or domestication of culturally and politically constituted identities. And insofar as it is imperative that we insist upon those specificities in order to expose the fictions of an imperialist humanism that works through unmarked privilege, there remains the risk that we will make the articulation of ever more specified identities into the aim of political activism. Thus every insistence on identity must at some point lead to a taking stock of the constitutive exclusions that reconsolidate hegemonic power differentials.

The erasure and domestication of Asianness on LambdaMOO perpetuates an Orientalist myth of social control and order. As Cornell West puts it, as Judith Butler puts it, "race matters," and "bodies matter." Programming language and Internet connectivity have made it possible for people to interact without putting into play any bodies but the ones they write for themselves. The temporary divorce which cyberdiscourse grants the mind from the body and the text from the body also separates race and the body. Player scripts which eschew repressive versions of the Oriental in favor of critical rearticulations and recombinations of race, gender, and class, and which also call the fixedness of these categories into question have the power to turn the theatricality characteristic of MOOspace into a truly innovative form of play, rather than a tired reiteration and reinstatement of old hierarchies. Role playing is a feature of the MOO, not a bug, and it would be absurd to ask that everyone who plays within it hew literally to the "rl" gender, race, or condition of life. A diversification of the roles which get played, which are permitted to be played, can enable a thought provoking detachment of race from the body, and an accompanying questioning of the essentialness of race as a category. Performing alternative versions of self and race jams the ideology-machine, and facilitates a desirable opening up of what Judith Butler (1993, p. 242) calls "the difficult future terrain of community" in cyberspace.

Notes

1 Some MUDS such as Diku and Phoenix require players to select races. These MUDs are patterned after the role playing game Dungeons and Dragons and unlike Lambda, which exists to provide a forum for social interaction and chatting, focus primarily on virtual combat and the accumulation of game points. The races available to players (orc, elf, dwarf, human, etc) are familiar to readers of the "sword and sorcery" genre of science fiction, and determine what sort of combat "attributes" a player can exploit. The combat metaphor which is a part of this genre of role playing reinforces the notion of racial difference.

2 Most players do not choose either spivak or neuter as their gender; perhaps because this type of choice is seen as a non choice. Spivaks and neuters are often asked to "set gender" by other players; they are seen as having deferred a choice rather than having made an unpopular one. Perhaps this is an example of the "informatics of domination" which Haraway describes.

3 Computer users who were using their machines to play games at work realized that it was possible for their employers and coworkers to spy on them while walking nearby and notice that they were slacking – hence, they developed screen savers which, at a keystroke, can instantly cover their "play" with a convincingly "work-like" image, such as a spreadsheet or business letter.

4 Microsoft's recent television and print media advertising campaign markets access to both personal computing and networking by promoting these activities as a form of travel; the ads ask the prospective consumer, "where do you want to go today?" Microsoft's promise to transport the user to new spaces where desire can be fulfilled is enticing in its very vagueness, offering an open ended invitation for travel and novel experiences.

5 The political action group devoted to defending the right to free speech in cyberspace against governmental control calls itself "The Electronic Frontier;" this is another example of the metaphorization of cyberspace as a colony to be defended against hostile takeovers.

References

Aker, Sharon et al., *Macintosh Bible*, 3rd edition (Berkeley: Goldstein and Blair, 1987–91).

Butler, Judith, *Bodies That Matter: On the Discursive Limits of "Sex"* (New York: Routledge, 1993).

Chesher, Chris, "Colonizing Virtual Reality: Construction of the Discourse of Virtual Reality, 1984–1992". *Cultronix*, vol. 1, issue 1, Summer 1994. *The English Server*. Online. 16 May 1995.

Elmer, Dewitt, Philip, "Battle for the Soul of the Internet." *Time*, 25 July 1994.

Haraway, Donna, *Simians, Cyborgs, and Women* (New York: Routledge, 1991).

Penley, Constance and Ross, Andrew, *Technoculture* (Minneapolis: University of Minnesota Press, 1991).

Rheingold, Howard, *The Virtual Community* (New York: HarperPerennial, 1993). *The Well*. Online. 16 May 1995.

Said, Edward, "Introduction," *Kim* by Rudyard Kipling (New York: Penguin, 1987), pp. 7–46.

Stone, Allucquère Rosanne, "Will the Real Body Please Stand Up?: Boundary Stories About Virtual Cultures," in Michael Benedikt (ed.), *Cyberspace: First Steps*. (Cambridge: MIT Press, 1991).

24

Who Am We?

Sherry Turkle

Sherry Turkle is a clinical psychologist and a professor of the Sociology of Science at the Massachusetts Institute of Technology. She has written extensively about the psychological and cultural implications of computer technology. Her books include *The Second Self: Computers and the Human Spirit* (Simon & Schuster, 1984) and *Life on the Screen: Identity in the Age of the Internet* (Simon & Schuster, 1995). This selection, which first appeared in *Wired* magazine, discusses identity in chatrooms and MUDs, with specific anecdotes about the experiences of children, teenagers, and adults.

> We are moving from modernist calculation toward postmodernist simulation, where the self is a multiple, distributed system.

There are many Sherry Turkles. There is the "French Sherry," who studied poststructuralism in Paris in the 1960s. There is Turkle the social scientist, trained in anthropology, personality psychology, and sociology. There is Dr. Turkle, the clinical psychologist. There is Sherry Turkle the writer of books – *Psychoanalytic Politics* (Basic Books, 1978) and *The Second Self: Computers and the Human Spirit* (Simon & Schuster, 1984). There is Sherry the professor, who has mentored MIT students for nearly 20 years. And there is the cyberspace explorer, the woman who might log on as a man, or as another woman, or as, simply, ST.

All of these Sherry Turkles have authored a new book, *Life on the Screen: Identity in the Age of the Internet*, published November 30 by Simon & Schuster. *Life on the Screen* tells how the computer profoundly shapes our ways of thinking and feeling, how ideas carried by technology are reshaped by people for their own purposes, how computers are not just changing our lives but changing our selves.

This story is borne of Turkle's past decade of research. In a series of pizza parties for MUDders in the Boston area, Turkle found conversations quickly turning to multiple personae, romance, and what can be counted on as "real" in virtual space. She soon turned to the world of Internet Relay Chat, newsgroups, bulletin boards, and commercial online services. She also examined the burgeoning cyberspace lives of children and teenagers.

What has she found? That the Internet links millions of people in new spaces that are changing the way we think and the way we form our communities. That we are moving from "a modernist culture of calculation toward a postmodernist culture of simulation." That life on the screen permits us to "project ourselves into our own dramas, dramas in which we are producer, director, and star. . . . Computer screens are the new location for our fantasies, both erotic and intellectual. We are using life on computer screens to become comfortable with new ways of thinking about evolution, relationships, sexuality, politics, and identity."

Turkle's own metaphor of windows serves well to introduce the following samplings from her new book. Those boxed-off areas on the screen, Turkle writes, allow us to cycle through cyberspace and real life, over and over. Windows allow us to be in several contexts at the same time – in a MUD, in a word-processing program, in a chat room, in e-mail.

"Windows have become a powerful metaphor for thinking about the self as a multiple, distributed system," Turkle writes. "The self is no longer simply playing different roles in different settings at different times. The life practice of windows is that of a decentered self that exists in many worlds, that plays many roles at the same time." Now real life itself may be, as one of Turkle's subjects says, "just one more window."

As recently as 10 to 15 years ago, it was almost unthinkable to speak of the computer's involvement with ideas about unstable meanings and unknowable truths. The computer had a clear intellectual identity as a calculating machine. In an introductory programming course at Harvard University in 1978, one professor introduced the computer to the class by calling it a giant calculator. Programming, he reassured the students, was a cut-and-dried technical activity whose rules were crystal clear.

Such reassurances captured the essence of what I call the modernist computational aesthetic. It's the computer as calculator: no matter how complicated a computer might seem, what happened inside it could be mechanically unpacked. Programming was a technical skill that could be done a right way or a wrong way. The right way was dictated by the computer's calculator essence. The right way was linear and logical. This linear, logical [model] guided thinking not only about technology and programming, but about economics, psychology, and social life. Computational ideas were one of the great modern metanarratives, stories of how the world worked that provided unifying pictures and analyzed complicated things by breaking them down into simpler parts. Computers, it was assumed, would become more powerful, both as tools and as metaphors, by becoming better and faster calculating machines, better and faster analytical engines.

From today's perspective, the fundamental lessons of computing are wrong. Programming is no longer cut and dried. Are you programming when you customize your word-processing software? When you design "organisms" to populate a simulation of Darwinian evolution in the computer game SimLife? Or when you build a room in a MUD so that opening a door to it will cause "Happy Un-Birthday" to ring out on all but one day of the year?

The lessons of computing today have to do not with calculation and rules, but with simulation, navigation, and interaction. The very image of the computer as a giant calculator has become quaint and dated. Fifteen years ago, most computer users were limited to typing commands. Today they use off-the-shelf products to manipulate simulated desktops, draw with simulated paints and brushes, and fly in simulated airplane cockpits.

Today's computational models of the mind often embrace a postmodern aesthetic of complexity and decentering. Mainstream computer researchers no longer aspire to program intelligence into computers but expect intelligence to emerge from the interactions of small subprograms.

In the games in the Sim series (SimCity, SimLife, SimAnt, SimHealth), you try to build a community, an ecosystem, or a public policy. The goal is to make a successful whole from complex, interrelated parts. Tim is 13, and among his friends, the Sim games are the subject of long conversations about what he calls Sim secrets. "Every kid knows," he confides, "that hitting Shift-F1 will get you a couple of thousand dollars in SimCity." But Tim knows that the Sim secrets have their limits. They are little tricks, but they are not what the game is about. The game is about making choices and getting feedback. Tim talks easily about the trade-offs in SimCity – between zoning restrictions and economic development, pollution controls and housing starts.

SimLife is Tim's favorite game, because "even though it's not a videogame, you can play it like one." By this he means that as in a videogame, events in the Sim world move things forward. ("My trilobytes went extinct. They must have run out of algae. I didn't give them algae. I forgot. I think I'll do that now.") He is able to act on a vague intuitive sense of what will work even when he doesn't have a verifiable model of the rules underneath the game's behavior. When he is populating his universe in a biology laboratory scenario, Tim puts in 50 each of his favorite creatures, such as trilobytes and sea urchins, but puts in only 20 sharks. ("I don't want 50 of these, I don't want to ruin this.") Tim can keep playing even when he has no idea what is driving events. For example, when his sea urchins become extinct, I ask him why.

TIM: I don't know, it's just something that happens.
ST: Do you know how to find out why it happened?
TIM: No.
ST: Do you mind that you can't tell why?
TIM: No. I don't let things like that bother me. It's not what's important.

"Your orgot is being eaten up," the game tells us. I ask Tim, "What's an orgot?" He doesn't know. "I just ignore that," he says. "You don't need to know that kind of stuff to play."

I am clearly having a hard time hiding my lifetime habit of looking up words that I don't understand, because Tim tries to appease me by coming up with a working definition of orgot. "I ignore the word, but I think it is sort of like an organism. I never read that, but just from playing, I would say that's what it is."

The orgot issue will not die: "Your fig orgot moved to another species," the game informs us. This time I say nothing, but Tim reads my mind: "Don't let it bother you if you don't understand. I just say to myself that I probably won't be able to understand the whole game any time soon. So I just play it."

I begin to look through dictionaries, in which orgot is not listed, and finally find a reference to it embedded in the game itself, in a file called READ ME. The file apologizes for the fact that orgot has been given several and in some ways contradictory meanings in this version of SimLife, but one of them is close to organism. Tim was right enough.

Children are comfortable with the idea that inanimate objects can both think and have a personality. But they no longer worry if the machine is alive. They know it is not. The issue of aliveness has moved into the background as though it is settled. But the notion of the machine has expanded to include its having a psychology. In talking about computers in a psychological way, children allow computational machines to retain an animistic trace, a mark of having passed through a stage in which the issue of the computer's aliveness was a focus of intense consideration.

Children also grant new capacities and privileges to the machine world on the basis of its animation if not its life. They endow artificial objects with properties, such as having intentions and ideas, previously reserved for living beings.

Granting a psychology to computers can mean that objects in the category "machine," like objects in the categories "people" and "pets," are fitting partners for dialog and relationship. Although children increasingly regard computers as mere machines, they are also increasingly likely to attribute qualities to them that undermine the machine/person distinction.

Children develop the two concepts in parallel and take what they understand to be the computer's psychological activity (interactivity as well as speaking, singing, and doing math) as a sign of consciousness. But they insist that breathing, having blood, being born, and, as one put it, "having real skin" are the true signs of life. Children today contemplate machines they believe to be intelligent and conscious yet not alive.

These children who so effortlessly split consciousness and life are forerunners of a larger cultural movement. Adults, less willing than children to grant that today's most advanced computer programs are even close to conscious, no longer flinch from the very idea of a self-conscious machine. Even a decade ago, the idea of machine intelligence provoked sharp debate. Today, the controversy about computers does not turn on their capacity for intelligence but on their capacity for life. We are willing to grant that the machine has a "psychology," but not that it can be alive.

People accept the idea that certain machines have a claim to intelligence and thus to their respectful attention. They are ready to engage with computers in a variety of domains. Yet when people consider what if anything might ultimately differentiate computers from humans, they dwell long and lovingly on those aspects of people that are tied to the sensuality and physical embodiment of life. It is as if they are seeking to underscore that although today's machines may be psychological in the cognitive sense, they are not psychological in a way that comprises our relationships with our bodies and with other people. Some computers might be considered intelligent and might even become conscious, but they are not born of mothers, raised in families, they do not know the pain of loss, or live with the certainty that they will die.

The 13-year-old Tim thinks that SimLife, unlike videogames and computer programming, is useful. "You get to mutate plants and animals into different species. You get to balance an ecosystem. You are part of something important." Tim thinks that the "animals that grow in the computer could be alive," although he adds, "This is kind of spooky."

Robbie, a 10-year-old who has been given a modem for her birthday, puts the emphasis not on communication but on mobility in considering whether the creatures she has evolved on SimLife are alive. "I think they are a little alive in the game, but you can turn it off and you cannot save your game, so that all the creatures you have evolved go away. But if they could figure out how to get rid of that part of the program so that you would have to save the game . . . if your modem were on, [the creatures] could get out of your computer and go to America Online."

Sean, 13, who has never used a modem, comes up with a variant on Robbie's ideas about travel. "The creatures could be more alive if they could get into DOS. If they were in DOS, they would be like a computer virus and they could get onto all of your disks, and if you loaned your disks to friends, it would be like they were traveling."

In the late 1970s and early 1980s, when I studied children's ideas about aliveness in dealing with stationary computer objects, the focus of children's thinking had shifted to an object's psychological properties. Today, in children's comments about the creatures that exist on simulation games, in talk about travel via circulating disks or over modems, in talk of viruses and networks, movement is resurfacing as a criterion for aliveness. Children widely assume that the creatures on Sim games have a desire to move out of the system into a wider digital world.

The creatures in simulation space challenge children to find a new language for talking about them and their status, as do mobile robots that wander about, making their "own decisions" about where to go. When MIT professor Rodney Brooks asked his 10-year-old daughter whether his mobots, or mobile robots, were alive, she said, "No, they just have control." For this child, and despite her father's work, life is biological. You can have consciousness and intentionality without being alive. At the end of the 1992 Artificial Life Conference, I sat next to 11-year-old Holly as we watched a group of robots with distinctly different "personalities" compete in a special robot Olympics. I told her I was studying robots and life, and Holly became thoughtful. Then she said unexpectedly, "It's like Pinocchio. First, Pinocchio was just a puppet. He was not alive at all. Then he was an alive puppet. Then he was an alive boy. A real boy. But he was alive even before he was a real boy. So I think the robots are like that. They are alive like Pinocchio [the puppet], but not like real boys."

In the early 1970s, the face-to-face role-playing game Dungeons and Dragons swept the game culture. The term "dungeon" persisted in the high-tech culture to connote a virtual place. So when virtual spaces were created that many computer users could share and collaborate within, they were deemed Multi-User Dungeons or MUDs, a new kind of social virtual reality. (Some games use software that make them technically MUSHes or MOOs, but the term MUD has come to refer to all of the multi-user environments.)

MUDs are a new kind of virtual parlor game and a new form of community. In addition, text-based MUDs are a new form of collaboratively written literature. MUD players are MUD authors, the creators as well as consumers of media content. In this, participating in a MUD has much in common with scriptwriting, performance art, street theater, improvisational theater, or even commedia dell'arte. But MUDs are something else as well.

As players participate, they become authors not only of text but of themselves, constructing new selves through social interaction. Since one participates in MUDs by sending text to a computer that houses the MUD's program and database, MUD selves are constituted in interaction with the machine. Take it away and the MUD selves cease to exist: "Part of me, a very important part of me, only exists inside PernMUD," says one player. Several players joke that they are like "the electrodes in the computer," trying to express the degree to which they feel part of its space.

All MUDs are organized around the metaphor of physical space. When you first enter a MUD, you may find yourself in a medieval church from which you can step out into the town square, or you may find yourself in the coat closet of a large, rambling house. For example, when you first log on to LambdaMOO, one of the most popular MUDs on the Internet, you see the following description:

> The Coat Closet. The Closet is a dark, cramped space. It appears to be very crowded in here; you keep bumping into what feels like coats, boots, and other people (apparently sleeping). One useful thing that you've discovered in your bumbling about is a metal doorknob set at waist level into what might be a door. There's a new edition of the newspaper. Type "news" to see it.

In the MUDs, virtual characters converse with each other, exchange gestures, express emotions, win and lose virtual money, and rise and fall in social status. A virtual character can also die. Some die of "natural" causes (a player decides to close them down), or they can have their virtual lives snuffed out. This is all achieved through writing, and this in a culture that had apparently fallen asleep in the audiovisual arms of television. Yet this new writing is a kind of hybrid: speech momentarily frozen into artifact, but curiously ephemeral artifact. In this new writing, unless it is printed out on paper, a screenful of flickers soon replaces the previous screen.

The anonymity of MUDs gives people the chance to express multiple and often unexplored aspects of the self, to play with their identity and to try out new ones. MUDs make possible the creation of an identity so fluid and multiple that it strains the limits of the notion. Identity, after all, refers to the sameness between two qualities, in this case between a person and his or her persona. But in MUDs, one can be many.

A 21-year-old college senior defends his violent characters as "something in me; but quite frankly I'd rather rape on MUDs where no harm is done." A 26-year-old clerical worker says, "I'm not one thing, I'm many things. Each part gets to be more fully expressed in MUDs than in the real world. So even though I play more than one self on MUDs, I feel more like 'myself' when I'm MUDding." In real life, this woman sees her world as too narrow to allow her to manifest certain aspects of the person she feels herself to be. Creating screen personae is thus an opportunity for self-expression, leading to her feeling more like her true self when decked out in an array of virtual masks.

MUDs imply difference, multiplicity, heterogeneity, and fragmentation. Such an experience of identity contradicts the Latin root of the word, idem, meaning "the same." But this contradiction increasingly defines the conditions of our lives beyond the virtual world. MUDs thus become objects-to-think-with for thinking about postmodern selves. Indeed, the unfolding of all MUD action takes place in a resolutely postmodern context. There are parallel narratives in the different rooms of a MUD. The cultures of Tolkien, Gibson, and Madonna coexist and interact. Since MUDs are authored by their players, thousands of people in all, often hundreds at a time, are all logged on from different places; the solitary author is displaced and distributed. Traditional ideas about identity have been tied to a notion of authenticity that such virtual experiences actively subvert. When each player can create many characters in many games, the self is not only decentered but multiplied without limit.

As a new social experience, MUDs pose many psychological questions: If a persona in a role-playing game drops defenses that the player in real life has been unable to abandon, what effect does this have? What if a persona enjoys success in some area (say, flirting) that the player has not been able to achieve? Slippages often occur in places where persona and self merge, where the multiple personae join to comprise what the individual thinks of as his or her authentic self.

Doug is a Midwestern college junior. He plays four characters distributed across three different MUDs. One is a seductive woman. One is a macho, cowboy type whose self-description stresses that he is a "Marlboros rolled in the T-shirt sleeve kind of guy." The third is a rabbit of unspecified gender who wanders its MUD introducing people to each other, a character he calls Carrot. Doug says, "Carrot is so low key that people let it be around while they are having private conversations. So I think of Carrot as my passive, voyeuristic character." Doug's fourth character is one that he plays only on a MUD in which all the characters are furry animals. "I'd rather not even talk about that character because my anonymity there is very important to me," Doug says. "Let's just say that on FurryMUDs I feel like a sexual tourist." Doug talks about playing his characters in windows and says that using windows has made it possible for him to "turn pieces of my mind on and off."

"I split my mind. . . . I can see myself as being two or three or more. And I just turn on one part of my mind and then another when I go from window to window. I'm in some kind of argument in one window and trying to come on to a girl in a MUD in another, and another window might be running a spreadsheet program or some other technical thing for school. . . . And then I'll get a real-time message that flashes on the screen as soon as it is sent from another system user, and I guess that's RL. RL is just one more window, and it's not usually my best one."

Play has always been an important aspect of our individual efforts to build identity. The psychoanalyst Erik Erikson called play a "toy situation" that allows us to "reveal and commit" ourselves "in its unreality." While MUDs are not the only "places" on the Internet in which to play with identity, they provide an unparalleled opportunity for such play. On a MUD one actually gets to build character and environment and then to live within the toy situation. A MUD can become a context for discovering who one is and wishes to be. In this way, the games are laboratories for the construction of identity.

Stewart, a 23-year-old physics graduate student, uses MUDs to have experiences he can't imagine for himself in RL. His intense online involvements engaged key issues in his life but ultimately failed to help him reach successful resolutions.

Stewart's real life revolves around laboratory work and his plans for a future in science. His only friend is his roommate, another physics student whom he describes as even more reclusive than himself. For Stewart, this circumscribed, almost monastic student life does not represent a radical departure from what has gone before. He has had heart trouble since he was a child; one small rebellion, a ski trip when he was a college freshman, put him in the hospital for a week. He has lived life within a small compass.

Stewart is logged on to one MUD or another for at least 40 hours a week. It seems misleading to call what he does there playing. He spends his time constructing a life that is more expansive than the one he lives in physical reality. Stewart, who has traveled very little and has never been to Europe, explains with delight that his favorite MUD, although played in English, is physically located on a computer in Germany and has many European players.

On the German MUD, Stewart shaped a character named Achilles, but he asks his MUD friends to call him Stewart as much as possible. He wants to feel that his real self exists somewhere between Stewart and Achilles. He wants to feel that his MUD life is part of his real life. Stewart insists that he does not role play, but that MUDs simply allow him to be a better version of himself.

On the MUD, Stewart creates a living environment suitable for his ideal self. His university dormitory is modest, but the room he has built for Achilles on the MUD is elegant and heavily influenced by Ralph Lauren advertising. He has named it "the home beneath the silver moon." There are books, a roaring fire, cognac, a cherry mantel "covered with pictures of Achilles's friends from around the world."

"You look up . . . and through the immense skylight you see a breathtaking view of the night sky. The moon is always full over Achilles's home, and its light fills the room with a warm glow."

Beyond expanding his social world, MUDs have brought Stewart the only romance and intimacy he has ever known. At a social event in virtual space, a "wedding" of two regular players on a German-based MUD I call Gargoyle, Achilles met Winterlight, a character played by one of the three female players on that MUD. Stewart, who has known little success in dating and romantic relationships, was able to charm this desirable player.

On their first virtual date, Achilles took Winterlight to an Italian restaurant close to Stewart's dorm. He had often fantasized being there with a woman. Stewart used a combination of MUD commands to simulate a romantic evening – picking Winterlight up at the airport in a limousine, driving her to a hotel room so that she could shower, and then taking her to the restaurant and ordering veal for her.

This dinner date led to others during which Achilles was tender and romantic, chivalrous and poetic. The intimacy Achilles experienced during his courtship of Winterlight is unknown to Stewart in other contexts. "She's a very, she's a good friend. I found out a lot of things, from things about physiology to the color of nail polish she wears." Finally, Achilles asked for Winterlight's hand. When she accepted, they had a formal engagement ceremony on the MUD.

At the engagement, Winterlight gave Achilles a rose she had worn in her hair; Achilles gave her 1,000 paper stars.

Although Stewart participated in this ceremony alone in his room with his computer and modem, a group of European players actually traveled to Germany, site of Gargoyle's host computer, and got together for food and champagne. Many of the 25 guests at the German celebration brought gifts and dressed specially for the occasion. Stewart felt as though he were throwing a party. This was the first time that he had ever entertained, and he was proud of his success. In real life, Stewart felt constrained by his health problems, his shyness and social isolation, and his narrow economic straits. In the Gargoyle MUD, he bypassed these obstacles, at least temporarily.

The psychological effects of life on the screen can be complicated: a safe place is not all that is needed for personal change. Stewart came to MUDding with serious problems, and for Stewart, playing on MUDs led to a net drop in self-esteem. MUDs did help Stewart talk about his troubles while they were still emotionally relevant; nevertheless, he is emphatic that MUDding has ultimately made him feel worse about himself. MUDding did not alter Stewart's sense of himself as with-drawn, unappealing, and flawed.

While Stewart has tried hard to make his MUD self, the "better" Achilles self, part of his real life, he says he has failed. He says, "I'm not social. I don't like parties. I can't talk to people about my problems." The integration of the social Achilles, who can talk about his troubles, and the asocial Stewart, who can only cope by putting them out of mind, has not occurred. From Stewart's point of view, MUDs have stripped away some of his defenses but have given him nothing in return. In fact, MUDs make Stewart feel vulnerable in a new way. Although he hoped that MUDs would cure him, it is MUDs that now make him feel sick. He feels addicted to MUDs: "When you feel you're stagnating and you feel there's nothing going on in your life and you're stuck in a rut, it's very easy to be on there for a very large amount of time."

Stewart cannot learn from his character Achilles's experience and social success because they are too different from the things of which he believes himself capable. Despite his efforts to turn Achilles into Stewart, Stewart has split off his strengths and sees them as possible only for Achilles in the MUD. It is only Achilles who can create the magic and win the girl. In making this split between himself and the achievements of his screen persona, Stewart does not give himself credit for the positive steps he has taken in real life. Like an unsuccessful psychotherapy, MUD-ding has not helped Stewart bring these good experiences inside himself or integrate them into his self-image.

Relationships during adolescence are usually bounded by a mutual understanding that they involve limited commitment. Virtual space is well suited to such relationships; its natural limitations keep things within bounds. As in Thomas Mann's The Magic Mountain, which takes place in the isolation of a sanatorium, relationships become intense very quickly because the participants feel isolated in a remote and unfamiliar world with its own rules. MUDs, like other electronic meeting places, can breed a kind of easy intimacy. In a first phase, MUD players feel the excitement of a rapidly deepening relationship and the sense that time itself is speeding up. "The MUD quickens things. It quickens things so much," says one player. "You know, you don't think about it when you're doing it, but you meet somebody on the MUD, and within a week you feel like you've been friends forever."

In a second phase, players commonly try to take things from the virtual to the real and are usually disappointed.

Gender-swapping on MUDs is not a small part of the game action. By some estimates, Habitat, a Japanese MUD, has 1.5 million users. Habitat is a MUD operated for profit. Among the registered members of Habitat, there is a ratio of four real-life men to each real-life woman. But inside the MUD the ratio is only three male characters to one female character. In other words, a significant number of players, many tens of thousands of them, are virtually cross-dressing.

What is virtual gender-swapping all about? Some of those who do it claim that it is not particularly significant. "When I play a woman I don't really take it too seriously," said 20-year-old Andrei. "I do it to improve the ratio of women to men. It's just a game." On one level, virtual gender-swapping is easier than doing it in real life. For a man to present himself as female in a chat room, on an IRC channel, or in a MUD, only requires writing a description. For a man to play a woman on the streets of an American city, he would have to shave various parts of his body; wear makeup, perhaps a wig, a dress, and high heels; perhaps change his voice, walk, and mannerisms. He would have some anxiety about passing, and there might be even more anxiety about not passing, which would pose a risk of violence and possibly arrest. So more men are willing to give virtual cross-dressing a try. But once they are online as female, they soon find that maintaining this fiction is difficult. To pass as a woman for any length of time requires understanding how gender inflects speech, manner, the interpretation of experience. Women attempting to pass as men face the same kind of challenge.

Virtual cross-dressing is not as simple as Andrei suggests. Not only can it be technically challenging, it can be psychologically complicated. Taking a virtual role may involve you in ongoing relationships. You may discover things about yourself that you never knew before.

Case, a 34-year-old industrial designer who is happily married to a co-worker, is currently MUDding as a female character. In response to my question, "Has MUDding ever caused you any emotional pain?" he says, "Yes, but also the kind of learning that comes from hard times."

"I'm having pain in my playing now. Mairead, the woman I'm playing in MedievalMUSH, is having an interesting relationship with a fellow. Mairead is a lawyer, and the high cost of law school has to be paid for by a corporation or a noble house. She fell in love with a nobleman who paid for her law school. [Case slips into referring to Mairead in the first person.] Now he wants to marry me although I'm a commoner, I finally said yes. I try to talk to him about the fact that I'm essentially his property. I'm a commoner...I've grown up with it, that's the way life is. He wants to deny the situation. He says, 'Oh no, no no...We'll pick you up, set you on your feet, the whole world is open to you.' But every time I behave like I'm now going to be a countess some day...as in, 'And I never liked this wallpaper anyway,' I get pushed down. The relationship is pull up, push down. It's an incredibly psychologically damaging thing to do to a person. And the very thing that he liked about her that she was independent, strong, said what was on her mind, it is all being bled out of her."

Case looks at me with a wry smile and sighs, "A woman's life." He continues: "I see her [Mairead] heading for a major psychological problem. What we have is a dysfunctional relationship. But even though it's very painful and stressful, it's very interesting to watch myself cope with this problem. How am I going to dig my persona's self out of this mess? Because I don't want to go on like this. I want to get out of it...You can see that playing this woman lets me see what I have in my psychological repertoire, what is hard and what is easy for me. And I can also see how some of the things that work when you're a man just backfire when you're a woman."

Case further illustrates the complexity of gender swapping as a vehicle for self-reflection. Case describes his RL persona as a nice guy, a "Jimmy Stewart type like my father." He says that in general he likes his father and he likes himself, but he feels he pays a price for his low-key ways. In particular, he feels at a loss when it comes to confrontation, both at home and in business dealings. Case likes MUD-ding as a female because it makes it easier for him to be aggressive and confrontational. Case plays several online "Katharine Hepburn types," strong, dynamic, "out there" women who remind him of his mother, "who says exactly what's on her mind and is a take-no-prisoners sort."

For Case, if you are assertive as a man, it is coded as "being a bastard." If you are assertive as a woman, it is coded as "modern and together."

Some women who play male characters desire invisibility or permission to be more outspoken or aggressive. "I was born in the South and taught that girls didn't speak up to disagree with men," says Zoe, a 34-year-old woman who plays male and female characters on four MUDs.

"We would sit at dinner and my father would talk and my mother would agree. I thought my father was a god. Once or twice I did disagree with him. I remember one time in particular when I was 10, and he looked at me and said, 'Well, well, well, if this little flower grows too many more thorns, she will never catch a man.'"

Zoe credits MUDs with enabling her to reach a state of mind where she is better able to speak up for herself in her marriage ("to say what's on my mind before things get all blown out of proportion") and to handle her job as the financial officer for a small biotechnology firm.

"I played a MUD man for two years. First I did it because I wanted the feeling of an equal playing field in terms of authority, and the only way I could think of to get it was to play a man. But after a while, I got very absorbed by MUDding. I became a wizard on a pretty simple MUD. I called myself Ulysses and got involved in the system and realized that as a man I could be firm and people would think I was a great wizard. As a woman, drawing the line and standing firm has always made me feel like a bitch and, actually, I feel that people saw me as one, too. As a man I was liberated from all that. I learned from my mistakes. I got better at being firm but not rigid. I practiced, safe from criticism."

Zoe's perceptions of her gender trouble are almost the opposite of Case's. While Case sees aggressiveness as acceptable only for women, Zoe sees it as acceptable only for men. These stories share a notion that a virtual gender swap gave people greater emotional range in the real. Zoe says: "I got really good at playing a man, so good that whoever was on the system would accept me as a man and talk to me as a man. So, other guys talked to Ulysses guy to guy. It was very validating. All those years I was paranoid about how men talked about women. Or I thought I was paranoid. Then I got a chance to be a guy and I saw that I wasn't paranoid at all."

Virtual sex, whether in MUDs or in a private room on a commercial online service, consists of two or more players typing descriptions of physical actions, verbal statements, and emotional reactions for their characters. In cyberspace, this activity is not only common but, for many people, it is the centerpiece of their online experience.

On MUDs, some people have sex as characters of their own gender. Others have sex as characters of the other gender. Some men play female personae to have netsex with men. And in the "fake-lesbian syndrome," men adopt online female personae in order to have netsex with women. Although it does not seem to be as widespread, I have met several women who say they present as male characters in order to have netsex with men. Some people have sex as nonhuman characters, for example, as animals on FurryMUDs. Some enjoy sex with one partner. Some use virtual reality as a place to experiment with group situations. In real life, such behavior (where possible) can create enormous practical and emotional confusion. Virtual adventures may be easier to undertake, but they can also result in significant complications.

Martin and Beth, both 41, have been married for 19 years and have four children. Early in their marriage, Martin regretted not having had more time for sexual experimentation and had an extramarital affair. The affair hurt Beth deeply, and Martin decided he never wanted to do it again. When Martin discovered MUDs he was thrilled. "I really am monogamous. I'm really not interested in something outside my marriage. But being able to have, you know, a Tiny romance is kind of cool." Martin decided to tell Beth about his MUD sex life and she decided to tell him that she does not mind. Beth has made a conscious decision to consider Martin's sexual relationships on MUDs as more like his reading an erotic novel than like his having a rendezvous in a motel room. For Martin, his online affairs are a way to fill the gaps of his youth, to broaden his sexual experience without endangering his marriage.

Other partners of virtual adulterers do not share Beth's accepting attitude. Janet, 24, a secretary at a New York law firm, is very upset by her husband Tim's sex life in cyberspace. After Tim's first online affair, he confessed his virtual infidelity. When Janet objected, Tim told her that he would stop "seeing" his online mistress. Janet says that she is not sure that he actually did stop. "The thing that bothers me most is that he wants to do it in the first place. In some ways, I'd have an easier time understanding why he would want to have an affair in real life. At least there, I could say to myself, 'Well, it is for someone with a better body, or just for the novelty.' It's like the first kiss is always the best kiss. But in MUDding, he is saying that he wants that feeling of intimacy with someone else, the 'just talk' part of an encounter with a woman, and to me that comes closer to what is most important about sex."

"First I told him he couldn't do it anymore. Then, I panicked and figured that he might do it anyway because, unlike in real life, I could never find out. All these thousands of people all over the world with their stupid fake names...no way I would ever find out. So, I pulled back and said that talking about it was strictly off limits. But now I don't know if that was the right decision. I feel paranoid whenever he is on the computer."

This distressed wife struggles to decide whether her husband is unfaithful when his persona collaborates on writing real-time erotica with another persona in cyberspace. And beyond this, should it make a difference if unbeknownst to the husband his cyberspace mistress turns out to be a 19-year-old male college freshman? What if "she" is an infirm 80-year-old man in a nursing home? And even more disturbing, what if she is a 12-year-old girl? Or a 12-year-old boy?

TinySex poses the question of what is at the heart of sex and fidelity. Is it the physical action? Is it emotional intimacy with someone other than one's primary partner? Is infidelity in the head or in the body? Is it in the desire or in the action? What constitutes the violation of trust?

And once we take virtuality seriously as a way of life, we need a new language for talking about the simplest things. Each individual must ask: What is the nature of my relationships? What are the limits of my responsibility? And even more basic: Who and what am I? What is the connection between my physical and virtual bodies? And is it different in different cyberspaces? These questions are equally central for thinking about community. What is the nature of our social ties? What kind of accountability do we have for our actions in real life and in cyberspace? What kind of society or societies are we creating, both on and off the screen?

When people adopt an online persona they cross a boundary into highly charged territory. Some feel an uncomfortable sense of fragmentation, some a sense of relief. Some sense the possibilities for self-discovery, even self-transformation. Serena, a 26-year-old graduate student in history, says, "When I log on to a new MUD and I create a character and know I have to start typing my description, I always feel a sense of panic. Like I could find out something I don't want to know." Arlie, a 20-year-old undergraduate, says, "I am always very self-conscious when I create a new character. Usually, I end up creating someone I wouldn't want my parents to know about . . . But that someone is part of me."

> Irony is about contradictions that do not resolve into larger wholes . . . about the tension of holding incompatible things together because both or all are necessary and true – Donna Haraway

As we stand on the boundary between the real and the virtual, our experience recalls what the anthropologist Victor Turner termed a liminal moment, a moment of passage when new cultural symbols and meanings can emerge. Liminal moments are times of tension, extreme reactions, and great opportunity. When Turner talked about liminality, he understood it as a transitional state, but living with flux may no longer be temporary. Technology is bringing postmodernism down to earth itself; the story of technology refuses modernist resolutions and requires an openness to multiple viewpoints.

Multiple viewpoints call forth a new moral discourse. The culture of simulation may help us achieve a vision of a multiple but integrated identity whose flexibility, resilience, and capacity for joy comes from having access to our many selves. But if we have lost reality in the process, we shall have struck a poor bargain. In Wim Wenders's film Until the End of the World, a scientist develops a device that translates the electrochemical activity of the brain into digital images. He gives this technology to his family and closest friends, who are now able to hold small battery driven monitors and watch their dreams. At first, they are charmed. They see their treasured fantasies, their secret selves. They see the images they otherwise would forget, the scenes they otherwise would repress. As with the personae one can play in a MUD, watching dreams on a screen opens up new aspects of the self.

However, the story soon turns dark. The images seduce. They are richer and more compelling than the real life around them. Wenders's characters fall in love with their dreams, become addicted to them. People wander about with blankets over their heads the better to see the monitors from which they cannot bear to be parted. They are imprisoned by the screens, imprisoned by the keys to their past that the screens seem to hold.

We, too, are vulnerable to using our screens in these ways. People can get lost in virtual worlds. Some are tempted to think of life in cyberspace as insignificant, as escape or meaningless diversion. It is not. Our experiences there are serious play. We belittle them at our risk. We must understand the dynamics of virtual experience both to foresee who might be in danger and to put these experiences to best use. Without a deep understanding of the many selves that we express in the virtual, we cannot use our experiences there to enrich the real. If we cultivate our awareness of what stands behind our screen personae, we are more likely to succeed in using virtual experience for personal transformation.

The imperative to self-knowledge has always been at the heart of philosophical inquiry. In the 20th century, it found expression in the psychoanalytic culture as well. One might say that it constitutes the ethic of psychoanalysis. From the perspective of this ethic, we work to know ourselves in order to improve not only our own lives, but those of our families and society. Psychoanalysis is a survivor discourse. Born of a modernist worldview, it has evolved into forms relevant to postmodern times. With mechanistic roots in the culture of calculation, psychoanalytic ideas become newly relevant in the culture of simulation. Some believe that we are at the end of the Freudian century. But the reality is more complex. Our need for a practical philosophy of self-knowledge has never been greater as we struggle to make meaning from our lives on the screen.

Part V

Searching for Community Online

In recent years it has become commonplace to discuss the Internet as a community – as a virtual place where people meet, chat, conduct business, and develop a sense of togetherness. Common definitions of communities describe "unified" bodies of individuals, or people living in a particular area, or groups with a common history or similar sociopolitical interests. Hence, it is important to stress that even in its most generic definitions, community is conceived as a relationship among people as much as a place. Long before the Internet existed as an idea, researchers looking at community recognized it as a type of "network" made possible by mail, telephones, automobiles, and such mass communications media as television and movies.

In this context, the idea of a community enabled by the Internet hardly seems like a great insight. Yet the online manifestation of the "virtual community" has generated great public enthusiasm. An unabashed advocate of the social potentials of virtual encounters, Howard Rheingold asserts that "people in virtual communities do just about everything people do in real life, but we leave our bodies behind." For obvious reasons, the notion of virtual community has become attractive in certain political circles. The allure of digital connectedness resonates powerfully at a time when people feel increasingly alienated from the ballot box and the old town square. This was the fundamental attraction of Ross Perot's vision of a national "electronic town meeting" for conducting instantaneous votes on public policy. This notion of a giant national conversation satisfies both the affective desire for an inclusive community and the "common sense" thinking that such a unified culture is possible and advisable.

Not surprisingly, democracy has emerged as a powerful theme in the romanticization of online community. Digital media and related forms of communication are regarded by many as means of leveling social inequalities and erasing problematic differences. Although not a political community in the conventional sense, the Internet has been used successfully to mobilize constituencies to write letters and communicate with legislators, as well as orchestrate online "demonstrations" resulting from mass e-mailings to single sites. Cyberspace is also used to mobilize community along less directly political lines. This is well recognized by the growing number of corporations who use the Internet as an advertising medium, not to mention investors who pay inflated rates for shares in Internet companies that make no profits. Like other mass media, the Net is becoming a major conduit for the reflection and manufacture of human desire.

What effects might these contradictory forms of Internet community have on democracy? Do they offer new forums for public discourse and civic participation, as is often suggested? Or do they simply refashion old forms of democracy with a new face? The essays in this section by Pierre Lévy, Mark Poster, and Howard Rheingold reach divergent conclusions on these issues, ranging from optimism to disappointment over the effect of the Internet on public life. Additional contributions by Guillermo Gómez-Peña and Avital Ronell provide views of the ways computer networks have served the interests of existing social groups.

The overarching question these essays seek to address is whether it is possible for a technology to create new political structures or understandings of political life, without changing the fundamental power structures and social organizations in which the technology operates. Some in this section argue that contemporary democracies are not failing because people lack the technical means to communicate or provide feedback. They are failing because people have lost faith in politicians, politics, and public institutions. Does the Internet have the capability of changing the way people conceive their relations to one another? If so, is it ever possible for such new understandings to escape the historical and cultural baggage from which they emerge? Or is it more likely, that the most new technologies offer is an improved way of addressing the world as it exists?

25

Collective Intelligence

Pierre Lévy

Pierre Lévy, "Collective Intelligence," excerpt from "Introduction" to Pierre Lévy, *Collective Intelligence* (Cambridge, MA: Perseus Books, 1997), pp. 1–10.

Pierre Lévy is a professor in the Department of Hypermedia at the University of Paris-VIII and scientific advisor to the TriVium Company. He is the author of *Becoming Virtual: Reality in the Digital Age* (Plenum, 1998) and *Collective Intelligence: Mankind's Emerging World in Cyberspace* (Perseus, 1997). In this essay, Lévy introduces his view of a unified human consciousness enabled by computer networks

The prosperity of a nation, geographical region, business, or individual depends on their ability to navigate the knowledge space. Power is now conferred through the optimal management of knowledge, whether it involves technology, science, communication, or our "ethical" relationship with the other. The more we are able to form intelligent communities, as open-minded, cognitive subjects capable of initiative, imagination, and rapid response, the more we will be able to ensure our success in a highly competitive environment. Our material relationship to the world is maintained through a formidable epistemological and logical infrastructure: educational and training institutions, communications networks, digitally supported intellectual technologies, the continuous improvement and distribution of skills. In the long term, everything is based on the flexibility and vitality of our networks of knowledge production, transaction, and exchange.

It would be a gross oversimplification to compare the transition to the age of knowledge with the shift to a service economy. Such a transition cannot be reduced to the displacement of industrial activities to the service sector, for the service sector itself is increasingly coming under siege by a variety of technological objects. It is becoming "industrialized," as characterized by the presence of ATMs, Web sites, educational software, expert systems, etc. To a greater and greater extent, industrial organizations see their activities as a form of service. To respond to the new conditions of economic life, businesses tend to organize themselves in such a way that they are receptive to *innovation networks*. This means, for example, that in a large corporation, departments can easily and quickly interact with one another, without the need for any kind of formal agreement, and with the continuous exchange of information and personnel. Interactive systems and contemporary innovation networks intersect one another, operating across the enterprise. The increasing growth of partnerships and alliances is a striking illustration of this process. New abilities must continuously be imported, produced, and introduced (in real time) in all sectors of the economy. Organizations must remain receptive to a constantly renewed stream of scientific, technical, social, and even aesthetic skills. Skill flow conditions cash flow. Once the process of renewal slows down, the company or organization is in danger of petrifaction and extinction. As Michel Serres has written, knowledge has become the new infrastructure.

Why did the so-called communist governments begin to decline sharply during the seventies, before finally collapsing at the beginning of the nineties? Without going into too many details on what is a complex issue, I can offer one hypothesis[1] that may be able to shed considerable light on our approach to the age of knowledge. The bureaucratically planned economy, which was still capable of functioning at the beginning of the sixties, was incapable of following the transformation of labor that resulted from the contemporary evolution of technological and organizational structure. Totalitarianism collapsed in the face of new forms of mobile and cooperative labor. *It was incapable of collective intelligence.*

The great shake-up of Western economies toward the tertiary sector was not the only factor involved in this, however. A more significant movement was under way, one that was anthropological. Beginning in the nineteen sixties, it became increasingly difficult for a laborer, employee, or engineer to inherit the traditions of a trade, to exercise and transmit this ability almost unchanged, to assume a lasting professional identity. Not only did technologies change with increasing velocity, but it became necessary to learn how to compare, regulate, communicate, and reorganize one's activity. It became necessary to exercise one's intellectual potential on a continuous basis. Moreover, new conditions of economic life gave a competitive edge to organizations in which each member was capable of taking the initiative for coordination, rather than submitting to some form of top-down planning. But this constant mobilization of social and cognitive abilities implicitly assumed a considerable degree of subjective involvement. No longer was it sufficient to passively identify oneself with a category, trade, or community. Now one's uniqueness, one's personal identity were implicated in professional life. It is precisely this form of subjective mobilization, highly individual as well as ethical and cooperative, that the bureaucratic and totalitarian universe was incapable of generating.

Quite obviously the interpenetration of leisure, culture, and work as a form of global social and subjective commitment remains the privilege of business leaders, the more highly qualified executives, certain professions, researchers, and artists. There are indications, however, that this model will expand, "trickle down" by a process of capillary motion, to all layers of society. The fact that the boundary between our professional life and personal development is beginning to blur signifies the death of a form of economic activity. Economic goals and technological efficiency can no longer operate within a closed circuit. As soon as genuine subjective commitment is required of individuals, economic needs must give way to politics in the broadest sense of the word, that is to ethics and civic respons-ibility. They must also reflect cultural significations. Pure economy and mere efficiency cease to become effective. Only by incorporating cultural and moral objectives, aesthetic experience, can business engage the subjectivity of its employ-ees, as well as its customers. The corporation no longer only consumes and produces goods and services, as in traditional economics. It is no longer satisfied with implementing, developing, and distributing skill and knowledge, as illustrated by the new cognitive approach to organizational structure. We must recognize the fact that the corporation, like other institutions, both encourages and promotes the development of subjectivity. Because it conditions all other activities, the continuous production of subjectivity will most likely be considered the major economic activity throughout the next century.

Under the wage system the individual sells his physical strength or labor time within a quantitative and easily measurable framework. Such a system could easily give way to a form of self-promotion, involving qualitatively differentiated abilities, by independent producers or small teams.[2] Individuals and microcorporations are more capable than large companies of continuous reorganization and optimal enhancement of the individual skills that are currently the requirements for suc-cess. Economic life will no longer be driven primarily by competition among large companies, which encourage quantitative and anonymous forms of labor. Rather, we are witnessing the development of complex forms of confrontational interde-pendence among skill zones that are fluid, delocalized, based on their singularities, and agitated by permanent molecular movements of association, exchange, and rivalry. The ability to rapidly form and reform intelligent communities will become the decisive weapon of regional skill centers competing within a globalized eco-nomic space. The emergence and constant redefinition of distributed identities will not only take place within the institutional framework of business, but through cooperative interactions in an international cyberspace.

Anthropology

Once knowledge becomes the prime mover, an unknown social landscape unfolds before our eyes in which the rules of social interaction and the identities of the players are redefined. A new anthropological space, the *knowledge space*, is being formed today, which could easily take precedence over the spaces of earth, territory, and commerce that preceded it. The second part of this book [Lévy's] is devoted to a detailed cartography of these spaces and their interrelation-ship.

What is an anthropological space? It is a system of proximity (space) unique to the world of humanity (anthropological), and thus dependent on human techno-logies, significations, language, culture, conventions, representations, and emo-tions. For example, in the anthropological space I refer to as "territorial," two individuals, living on either side of a border, are "farther" from one another than from people living in the same country, while this relationship might be reversed in the space of physical geography.

The *earth* was the first great space of signification formed by our species. It is based on the three primordial characteristics that distinguish *Homo sapiens*: language, technology, and complex forms of social organization ("religion" in the broadest sense of the word). Only humanity lives on *this* earth; animals inhabit ecological niches. Our relationship to the cosmos is the fundamental aspect of this first space, both from a point of view that we would today qualify as imaginary (animism, totemism), as well as from a very practical point of view, given the intimate contact between us and "nature." Myth and rite are the specific modes of knowledge of this first anthropological space. On earth, identity is inscribed within our bond to the cosmos as well as in our affiliation or alliance with other men. The first item on our resumé is generally our name, our symbolic inscription within an ancestral line.

A second, *territorial* space arose during the Neolithic period with the development of agriculture, the city, the state, and writing. This second space did not eliminate the great nomadic earth but partially covered it and attempted to turn it into something sedentary, domesticated. Hunting and gathering were no longer a source of wealth, but the possession and exploitation of fields. Within this second anthropological space the dominant modes of knowledge were based on writing: history and the development of systematic, theoretical, and hermeneutic knowledge. Here, the pivot of existence was no longer participation in the cosmos but the link to a territorial entity (affiliation, property, etc.) defined by its borders. Today, along with our name, we have an address, which serves to identify us within the territory of residents and taxpayers. The institutions in which we live are also territories, or juxtapositions of territories, with their hierarchies, bureaucracies, systems of rules, borders, logic, belonging, and exclusion.

A third anthropological space began to develop in the sixteenth century, which I will call the *commodity* space. It began to take shape with the initial development of a world market following the conquest of America by Europeans. The organizing principle of the new space is movement: the flow of energy, raw materials, merchandise, capital, labor, information. The great movement of *deterritorialization* that began to develop at the dawn of the modern era did not result in the suppression of territories but in their subversion, their subordination to economic flux. The commodity space did not eliminate the preceding spaces, but outpaced them. It became the new engine of evolution. Wealth was no longer based on controlling borders but on the control of movement. Industry now rules, in the general sense of processing materials and information. Modern experimental science is a typical mode of knowledge of the new space of continuous movement. But traditional science is itself undergoing a process of deterritorialization. Following the Second World War, it gave way to a "technoscience" driven by a permanent dynamic of research and economic innovation. The coupling of theory and experimental practice characteristic of classical science now had to compete with the growing power of simulation and digital modeling, which threatened conventional epistemological methods and provided a glimpse into the turmoil of a fourth space. To possess an identity, to exist in the space of commodity flow, means that we participate in economic production and exchange, occupy a position at the nodes of the various networks of production, transaction, and communication. To be unemployed within the commodity space is a sign of misfortune, for within it our social identity is defined by work, which means, for the majority of the population, a job and a salary. On our resumé, right after our name (position on earth) and address (position within the territory), we generally indicate our profession (position in the commodity space).

Is it possible to bring a new space into existence, in which we would possess a social identity even without a profession? Perhaps the current crisis of identity and social forms of identification signifies the dimly perceived and incomplete emergence of a new anthropological space, that of knowledge and collective intelligence, whose arrival is in no way guaranteed by any historical laws. Like the other anthropological spaces, the *knowledge space* will control preceding spaces rather than eliminate them. From this point forward, the existence of economic networks and territorial power will depend on mankind's capacity for the rapid acquisition of knowledge and the development of a collective imagination, as will the survival of the great nomadic earth.

Intelligence and human knowledge have always played a central role in social life. Our species is called *sapiens* for good reason. To each anthropological space there corresponds a specific mode of knowledge. But then, why refer to civilization's new horizon as the *knowledge space*? There are at least three aspects to this newness: the rate of evolution of knowledge, the number of people who will be asked to learn and produce new forms of knowledge, and finally, the appearance of new tools (cyberspatial tools) capable of bringing forth, within the cloud of information around us, unknown and distinct landscapes, singular identities characteristic of this space, new sociohistoric figures.

Speed. Never before has science and technology evolved so rapidly, with so many direct consequences on our daily life, work, modes of communication, our relation to our bodies, space, etc. Today it is within the universe of knowledge and skill that acceleration is greatest and the configurations most changeable. This is one of the reasons why knowledge (in the most general sense of the word) dominates the other dimensions of social life.

Mass. It has become impossible to restrict knowledge and its movement to castes of specialists. From now on, humanity as a whole must adapt, learn, and invent if it is to improve its lot in the complex and chaotic universe in which we now live.

Tools. The number of messages in circulation has never been as great as it is now, but we have few instruments to filter the pertinent data, make connections on the basis of significations and needs that are still subjective, or orient ourselves within the flux of information. It is at this point that the knowledge space ceases to be the object of established fact and becomes a project. Building the knowledge space will mean acquiring the institutional, technical, and conceptual instruments needed to make information navigable, so that each of us is able to orient ourselves and recognize others on the basis of mutual interests, abilities, projects, means, and identities within this new space. The deliberate creation of a system of expression for the knowledge space will enable us to correctly express, and perhaps even resolve, a number of crucial problems that we are currently unable to formulate adequately with the concepts and tools that have been used to express preceding spaces.

Our living knowledge, skills, and abilities are in the process of being recognized as the primary source of all other wealth. What then will our new communication tools be used for? The most socially useful goal will no doubt be to supply ourselves with the instruments for sharing our mental abilities in the construction of collective intellect or imagination. Internetworked data would then provide the technical infrastructure for the collective brain or *hypercortex*[3] of living communities. The role of information technology and digital communications is not to "replace mankind" but to promote the construction of intelligent communities in which our social and cognitive potential can be mutually developed and enhanced. Based on this approach, the major architectural project of the twenty-first century will be to imagine, build, and enhance an interactive and ever changing cyberspace. Perhaps it will then be possible to move beyond the society of the spectacle and enter a post-media era in which communications technologies will serve to filter and help us navigate knowledge, and enable us to think collectively rather than simply haul masses of information around with us. Unfortunately, although the promoters of the information highway may be aware of the problem, they remain mired in discussions about bandwidth. Fortunately, at present only a small minority considers the global system for delivering video on demand to be the *nec plus ultra* of imaginative thought concerning the art and architecture of cyberspace.

Notes

1   This hypothesis was inspired by the work of Bernard Perret. See *L'Economie contre la société. Affronter la crise de l'intégration culturelle et sociale*, by Bernard Perret and Guy Roustang (Paris: Editions du Seuil, 1993).

2   This long-range approach to the "end of employment" was suggested by Robert Reich, *The Work of Nations: Preparing Ourselves for 21st Century Capitalism* (New York: Random House, 1991).

3   The word was coined by Roy Ascott during the "Telenonia" conference held in Toulouse in 1992 as part of the FAUST project. See also, "Telenonia" in *Interactive Art, Intercommunication*, 7 (1994), pp. 114–23, and "Telenonia, On Line" in *Kunst im Netz* (Graz: Steirischen Kulturinitiative, 1993), pp. 135–46.

26

Cyberdemocracy: The Internet and the Public Sphere

Mark Poster

Mark Poster, "Cyberdemocracy: The Internet and the Public Sphere," in David Porter, ed., *Internet Culture* (New York and London: Routledge, 1997), pp. 201–18. The original version of this essay appeared in the journal *Lusitaria*.

Mark Poster is a professor of history at the University of California, Irvine, whose books include *The Mode of Information: Poststructuralism and Social Context* (Chicago, 1990) and *The Second Media Age* (Polity Press, 1995). This selection offers a comprehensive review of perspectives on the prospects of democratic enhancement via computers and networks, including background on the public sphere as discussed by Jürgen Habermas and Nancy Fraser.

I am an advertisement for a version of myself.

David Byrne

The Stakes of the Question

The discussion of the political impact of the Internet has focused on a number of issues: access, technological determinism, encryption, commodification, intellectual property, the public sphere, decentralization, anarchy, gender and ethnicity. While these issues may be addressed from a number of standpoints, only some of them are able to assess the full extent of what is at stake in the new communications technology at the cultural level of identity formation. If questions are framed in relation to prevailing political structures, forces and ideologies, for example, blinders are being imposed which exclude the question of the subject or identity construction from the domain of discussion. Instances of such apparently urgent but actually limiting questions are those of encryption and commodification. In the case of encryption, the United States government seeks to secure its borders from "terrorists" who might use the Internet and thereby threaten it. But the dangers to the population are and have always been far greater from this state apparatus itself than from so-called terrorists. If the prospects of democracy on the Internet are viewed in terms of encryption, then the security of the existing national government becomes the limit of the matter: what is secure for the nation-state is taken to mean true security for everyone, a highly dubious proposition.[1] The question of the potential for new forms of social space to empower individuals in new ways is foreclosed in favor of preserving existing relations of force as they are embodied in the state.

The issue of commodification also affords a narrow focus, often restricting the discussion of the politics of the Internet to the question of which corporation will be able to obtain what amount of income from which configuration of the Internet. Will the telephone companies, the cable companies or some amalgam of both be able to secure adequate markets and profits from providing the general public with railroad timetables, five hundred channels of television, the movie of one's choice on demand and so forth? From this vantage point the questions raised are as follows: Shall the Internet be used to deliver entertainment products, like some gigantic, virtual theme park? Or shall it be used to sell commodities, functioning as an electronic retail store or mall? These questions consume corporate managers around the country and their Marxist critics alike, though here again, as with the encryption issue, the Internet is being understood as an extension of or substitution for existing institutions.

While there is no doubt that the Internet folds into existing social functions and extends them in new ways, translating the act of shopping, for example, into an electronic form, what are far more cogent as possible long-term political effects of the Internet are the ways in which it institutes new social functions, ones that do not fit easily within those of characteristically modern organizations. The problem is that these new functions can only become intelligible if a framework is adopted that does not limit the discussion from the outset to modern patterns of interpretation. For example, if one understands politics as the restriction or expansion of the existing executive, legislative and judicial branches of government, one will not be able even to broach the question of new types of participation in government. To ask, then, about the relation of the Internet to democracy is to challenge or to risk challenging our existing theoretical approaches to these questions.

If one brackets political theories that address modern governmental institutions in order to assess the "postmodern" possibilities suggested by the Internet, two difficulties immediately emerge: 1. there is no adequate "postmodern" theory of politics and 2. the issue of democracy, the dominant political norm and ideal, is itself a "modern" category associated with the project of the Enlightenment. Let me address these issues in turn.

Recently theorists such as Philippe Lacoue-Labarthe and Jean-Luc Nancy have pointed to the limitations of a "left/right" spectrum of ideologies for addressing contemporary political issues.[2] Deriving from seating arrangements of legislators during the French Revolution of 1789, the modern ideological spectrum inscribes a grand narrative of liberation which contains several problematic aspects. The most important of these for our purposes is that this Enlightenment narrative establishes a process of liberation at the heart of history which requires at its base a pre-social, foundational, individual identity. The individual is posited as outside of and prior to history, only later becoming ensnared in externally imposed chains. Politics from this modern perspective is then the arduous extraction of an autonomous agent from the contingent obstacles imposed by the past. In its rush to ontologize freedom, the modern view of the subject hides the process of its historical construction. A postmodern orientation would have to allow for the constitution of identity within the social and within language, displacing the question of freedom from a presupposition of and a conclusion to theory to become instead a pre-theoretical or non-foundational discursive preference.

Postmodern theorists have discovered that modern theory's insistence on the freedom of the subject, its compulsive, repetitive inscription into discourse of the sign of the resisting agent, functions to restrict the shape of identity to its modern form, rather than contributing towards emancipation. Postmodern theory, then, must resist ontologizing any form of the subject, while simultaneously insisting on the constructedness of identity. In the effort to avoid the pitfalls of modern political theory, then, postmodern theory sharply restricts the scope of its ability to define a new political direction.

But there are further difficulties in establishing a position from which to recognize and analyze the cultural aspect of the Internet. Postmodern theory still invokes the modern term democracy, even when this is modified by the adjective "radical" as in the work of Ernesto Laclau.[3] One may characterize postmodern or post-Marxist democracy in Laclau's terms as one that opens new positions of speech, empowering previously excluded groups and enabling new aspects of social life to become part of the political process. While the Internet is often accused of elitism (a mere thirty million users), there does exist a growing and vibrant grass-roots participation in it organized in part by local public libraries.[4] But are not these initiatives, the modern skeptic may persist, simply extensions of existing political institutions rather than being "post-," and representing a break of some kind? In response I can assert only that the "postmodern" position need not be taken as a metaphysical assertion of a new age. Theorists are trapped within existing frameworks as much as they may be critical of them and wish not to be. In the absence of a coherent alternative political program the best one can do is to examine phenomena such as the Internet in relation to new forms of the old democracy, while holding open the possibility that what emerges might be something other than democracy in any shape that we can conceive given our embeddedness in the present. Democracy, the rule by all, is surely preferable to its historic alternatives. And the term may yet contain critical potentials since existing forms of democracy surely do not fulfill the promise of freedom and equality. The colonization of the term by existing institutions encourages one to look elsewhere for the means to name the new patterns of force relations emerging in certain parts of the Internet.

Decentralized Technology

My plea for indulgence with the limitations of the postmodern position on politics quickly gains credibility when the old question of technological determinism is posed in relation to the Internet. When the question of technology is posed we see immediately how the Internet disrupts the basic assumptions of the older positions. The Internet is above all a decentralized communication system. As with the telephone network, anyone hooked up to the Internet may initiate a call, send a message that he or she has composed to one or multiple recipients, and receive messages in return. The Internet is also decentralized at a basic level of organization since, as a network of networks, new networks may be added so long as they conform to certain communications protocols. As an historian I find it fascinating that this unique structure should emerge from a confluence of cultural communities which appear to have so little in common: the Cold War Defense Department, which sought to insure survival against nuclear attack by promoting decentralization; the counter-cultural ethos of computer programming engineers, which showed a deep distaste for any form of censorship or active restraint of communications, and the world of university research, which I am at a loss to characterize. Added to this is a technological substratum of digital electronics which unifies all symbolic forms in a single system of codes, rendering transmission instantaneous and duplication effortless. If the technological structure of the Internet institutes costless reproduction, instantaneous dissemination and radical decentralization, what might be its effects upon the society, the culture and the political institutions?

There can be only one answer to this question, and that is that it is the wrong question. Technologically determined effects derive from a broad set of assumptions in which what is technological is a configuration of materials that effect other materials, and the relation between the technology and human beings is external, that is, where human beings are understood to manipulate the materials for ends that they impose upon the technology from a preconstituted position of subjectivity. But what the Internet technology imposes is a dematerialization of communication and in many of its aspects a transformation of the subject position of the individual who engages within it. The Internet resists the basic conditions for asking the question of the effects of technology. It installs a new regime of relations between humans and matter and between matter and non-matter, reconfiguring the relation of technology to culture and thereby undermining the standpoint from within which, in the past, a discourse developed – one which appeared to be natural – about the effects of technology. The only way to define the technological effects of the Internet is to build the Internet, to set in place a series of relations which constitute an electronic geography. Put differently, the Internet is more like a social space than a thing; its effects are more like those of Germany than those of hammers. The effect of Germany upon the people within it is to make them Germans (at least for the most part); the effect of hammers is not to make people hammers, though Heideggerians and some others might disagree, but to force metal spikes into wood. As long as we understand the Internet as a hammer we will fail to discern the way it is like Germany. The problem is that modern perspectives tend to reduce the Internet to a hammer. In the grand narrative of modernity, the Internet is an efficient tool of communication, advancing the goals of its users who are understood as preconstituted instrumental identities.

The Internet is complex enough that it may with some profit be viewed in part as a hammer. If I search the database functions of the Internet or if I send email purely as a substitute for paper mail, then its effects may reasonably be seen to be those of a mere tool. But the aspects of the Internet that I would like to underscore are those which instantiate new forms of interaction and which pose the question of new kinds of relations of power between participants. The question that needs to be asked about the relation of the Internet to democracy is this: are there new kinds of relations occurring within it which suggest new forms of power configurations between communicating individuals? In other words, is there a new politics on the Internet?

One way to approach this question is to make a detour from the issue of technology and raise again the question of a public sphere, gauging the extent to which Internet democracy may become intelligible in relation to it. To frame the issue of the political nature of the Internet in relation to the concept of the public sphere is particularly appropriate because of the spatial metaphor associated with the term. Instead of an immediate reference to the structure of an institution, which is often a formalist argument over procedures, or to the claims of a given social group, which assumes a certain figure of agency that I would like to keep in suspense, the notion of a public sphere suggests an arena of exchange, like the ancient Greek agora or the colonial New England town hall. If there is a public sphere on the Internet, who populates it and how? In particular one must ask what kinds of beings exchange information in this public sphere? Since there occurs no face-to-face interaction, only electronic flickers[5] on a screen, what kind of community can there be in this space? What kind of disembodied politics are inscribed so evanescently in cyberspace? Modernist curmudgeons may object vehemently against attributing to information flows on the Internet the dignified term "community." Are they correct, and if so, what sort of phenomenon is this cyberdemocracy?

The Internet as a Public Sphere?

The issue of the public sphere is at the heart of any reconceptualization of democracy. Contemporary social relations seem to be devoid of a basic level of interactive practice which, in the past, was the matrix of democratizing politics: loci such as the agora, the New England town hall, the village Church, the coffee house, the tavern, the public square, a convenient barn, a union hall, a park, a factory lunchroom, and even a street corner. Many of these places remain but no longer serve as organizing centers for political discussion and action. It appears that the media, and especially television, have become the animating source of political information and action. An example from the Clinton heath-care reform campaign will suffice: the Clinton forces at one point (mid-July 1994) felt that Congress was less favorable to their proposal than the general population. To convince recalcitrant legislators of the wisdom of health-care reform, the administration purchased television advertising which depicted ordinary citizens speaking in favor of the President's plan. The ads were shown only in Washington D.C.

because they were directed not at the general population of viewers but at congressmen and congresswomen alone. Such are politics in the era of the mode of information. In a context like this, one may ask, where is the public sphere, where is the place citizens interact to form opinions in relation to which public policy must be attuned? John Hartley makes the bold and convincing argument that the media are the public sphere: "Television, popular newspapers, magazines and photography, the popular media of the modern period, *are* the public domain, the place where and the means by which the public is created and has its being."[6]

Sensing a collapse of the public sphere and therefore a crisis of democratic politics, Jürgen Habermas published *The Structural Transformation of the Public Sphere* in 1962.[7] In this highly influential work he traced the development of a democratic public sphere in the seventeenth and eighteenth centuries and charted its course to its decline in the twentieth century. In that work and arguably since then as well, Habermas' political intent was to further "the project of Enlightenment" by the reconstruction of a public sphere in which reason might prevail, not the instrumental reason of much modern practice but the critical reason that represents the best of the democratic tradition. Habermas defined the public sphere as a domain of uncoerced conversation oriented toward a pragmatic accord. His position came under attack by poststructuralists like Lyotard who questioned the emancipatory potential of its model of consensus through rational debate.[8] More recently, Rita Felski has synthesized Marxist, feminist, and poststructuralist critiques of Habermas' enlightenment ideal of the autonomous rational subject as a universal foundation for democracy.[9] For Felski the concept of the public sphere must build on the "experience" of political protest (in the sense of Negt and Kluge), must acknowledge and amplify the multiplicity of the subject (in the sense of poststructuralism) and must account for gender differences (in the sense of feminism). She writes:

> Unlike the bourgeois public sphere, then, the feminist public sphere does not claim a representative universality but rather offers a critique of cultural values from the standpoint of women as a marginalized group within society. In this sense it constitutes a *partial* or counter-public sphere.... Yet insofar as it is a *public* sphere, its arguments are also directed outward, toward a dissemination of feminist ideas and values throughout society as a whole.[10]

Felski seriously revises the Habermasian notion of the public sphere, separating it from its patriarchal, bourgeois and logocentric attachments perhaps, but nonetheless still invoking the notion of a public sphere and more or less reducing politics to it. This becomes clear in the conclusion of her argument:

> Some form of appeal to collective identity and solidarity is a necessary precondition for the emergence and effectiveness of an oppositional movement; feminist theorists who reject any notion of a unifying identity as a repressive fiction in favor of a stress on absolute difference fail to show how such diversity and fragmentation can be reconciled with goal-oriented political struggles based upon common interests. An appeal to a shared experience of oppression provides the starting point from which women as

a group can open upon the problematic of gender, at the same time as this notion of gendered community contains a strongly utopian dimension. . . .[11]

In the end, Felski sees the public sphere as central to feminist politics. But then we must ask how this public sphere is to be distinguished from any political discussion? From the heights of Habermas' impossible (counter-factual) ideal of rational communication, the public sphere here multiplies, opens and extends to political discussion by all oppressed individuals.

The problem we face is that of defining the term "public." Liberal theory generally resorted to the ancient Greek distinction between the family or household and the polis, the former being "private" and the latter "public." When the term crossed boundaries from political to economic theory, with Ricardo and Marx, a complication set in: the term "political economy" combined the Greek sense of public and the Greek sense of private since economy referred for them to the governance of the (private) household. The older usage preserved a space for the public in the agora, to be sure, but referred to discussions about the general good, not market transactions. In the newer usage the economic realm is termed "political economy" but is considered "private." To make matters worse, common parlance nowadays has the term "private" designating speeches and actions that are isolated, unobserved by anyone and not recorded or monitored by any machine.[12] Privacy now becomes restricted to the' space of the home, in a sense returning to the ancient Greek usage even though family structure has altered dramatically in the interim. In Fraser's argument, for example, the "public" sphere is the opposite of the "private" sphere in the sense that it is a locus of "talk," "a space in which citizens deliberate about their common affairs . . ." and is essential to democracy.[13] There are serious problems, then, in using the term "public" in relation to a politics of emancipation.

This difficulty is amplified considerably once newer electronically mediated communications are taken into account, in particular the Internet. Now the question of "talk," of meeting face-to-face, of "public" discourse is confused and complicated by the electronic form of exchange of symbols. If "public" discourse exists as pixels on screens generated at remote locations by individuals one has never and probably will never meet, as it is in the case of the Internet with its "virtual communities" and "electronic cafés," then how is it to be distinguished from "private" letters, printface and so forth? The age of the public sphere as face-to-face talk is clearly over: the question of democracy must henceforth take into account new forms of electronically mediated discourse. What are the conditions of democratic speech in the mode of information? What kind of "subject" speaks or writes or communicates in these conditions? What is its relation to machines? What complexes of subjects, bodies and machines are required for democratic exchange and emancipatory action? For Habermas, the public sphere is a homogeneous space of embodied subjects in symmetrical relations, pursuing consensus through the critique of arguments and the presentation of validity claims. This model, I contend, is systematically denied in the arenas of electronic politics. We are advised then to abandon Habermas' concept of the public sphere in assessing the Internet as a political domain.

Now that the thick culture of information machines provides the interface for much if not most discourse on political issues, the fiction of the democratic community of full human presence serves only to obscure critical reflection and divert the development of a political theory of this decidedly postmodern condition. For too long, critical theory has insisted on a public sphere, bemoaning the fact of media "interference," the static of first radio's and then television's role in politics. But the fact is that political discourse has long been mediated by electronic machines: the issue now is that the machines enable new forms of decentralized dialogue and create new combinations of human-machine assemblages, new individual and collective "voices," "specters," "interactivities" which are the new building blocks of political formations and groupings. As Paul Virilio writes, "What remains of the notion of things 'public' when public *images* (in real time) are more important than public space?"[14] If the technological basis of the media has habitually been viewed as a threat to democracy, how can theory account for the turn toward a construction of technology (the Internet) which appears to promote a decentralization of discourse if not democracy itself and appears to threaten the state (unmonitorable conversations), mock at private property (the infinite reproducibility of information) and flaunt moral propriety (the dissemination of images of unclothed people often in awkward positions)?

A Postmodern Technology?

Many areas of the Internet extend preexisting identities and institutions. Usenet newsgroups elicit obnoxious pranks from teenage boys; databases enable researchers and corporations to retrieve information at lower costs; electronic mail affords speedy, reliable communication of messages; the digitization of images allows a wider distribution of erotic materials, and so it goes. The Internet, then, is modern in the sense of continuing the tradition of tools as efficient means and in the sense that prevailing modern cultures transfer their characteristics to the new domain. Other areas of the Internet, however, are less easy to contain within modern points of view. The examination of these cyberspaces raises the issue of a new understanding of technology and finally leads to a reassessment of the political aspects of the Internet. I refer to the bulletin board services that have come to be known as "virtual communities," to the MOO phenomenon and to the synthesis of virtual reality technology with the Internet.

In these cases, what is at stake is the direct solicitation to construct identities in the course of communication practices. Individuals invent themselves and do so repeatedly and differentially in the course of conversing or messaging electronically. Now there is surely nothing new in discursive practices that are so characterized: reading a novel,[15] speaking on CB radio, indeed watching a television advertisement, I contend, all in varying degrees and in different ways encourage the individual to shape an identity in the course of engaging in communication. On a MOO, communication requires linguistic acts of self-positioning that are much more explicit than in the cases of reading a novel or watching a television advertisement. On the Internet, individuals read and interpret communications to themselves and to others and also respond by shaping sentences and transmitting them. Novels and television ads are interpreted by individuals who are interpellated by them, but these readers and viewers are not addressed directly, only as a generalized audience and, of course, they do not respond in fully articulated linguistic acts.

I avoid framing the distinction I am making here in the binary active/passive because that couplet is so associated with the modern autonomous agent that it would appear that I am depicting the Internet as the realization of the modern dream universal, "active" speech. I refuse this resort because it rests upon the notion of identity as a fixed essence, pre-social and pre-linguistic, whereas I want to argue that Internet discourse constitutes the subject as the subject fashions him or herself.

On the Internet, individuals construct their identities in relation to ongoing dialogues, not as acts of pure consciousness. But such activity does not count as freedom in the liberal-Marxist sense because it does not refer back to a foundational subject. Yet it does connote a "democratization" of subject constitution because the acts of discourse are not limited to one-way address and are not constrained by the gender and ethnic traces inscribed in face-to-face communications. The "magic" of the Internet is that it is a technology that puts cultural acts, symbolizations in all forms, in the hands of all participants; it radically decentralizes the positions of speech, publishing, film-making, radio and television broadcasting, in short the apparatuses of cultural production.

Gender and Virtual Communities

Let us examine the case of gender in Internet communication as a way to clarify what is at stake and to remove some likely confusions about what I am arguing. Studies have pointed out that the absence of gender cues in bulletin board discussion groups does not eliminate sexism or even the hierarchies of gender that pervade society generally.[16] The disadvantages suffered by women in society carry over into the "virtual communities" on the Internet: women are under-represented in these electronic places and are subjected to various forms of harassment and sexual abuse. The fact that sexual identities are self-designated does not in itself eliminate the annoyances and the hurts of patriarchy. The case of "Joan" is instructive in this regard. A man named Alex presented himself on a bulletin board as a disabled woman, "Joan," in order to experience the "intimacy" he admired in women's conversations. Van Gelder reports that when his "ruse" was unveiled, many of the women "Joan" interacted with were deeply hurt. But Van Gelder also reports that their greatest disappointment was that "Joan" did not exist.[17] The construction of gender in this example indicates a level of complexity not accounted for by the supposition that cultural and social forms are or are not transferrable to the Internet. Alex turned to the Internet virtual community to make up for a perceived lack of feminine traits in his masculine sexual identity. The women who suffered his ploy regretted the "death" of the virtual friend "Joan." These are unique uses of virtual communities not easily found in "reality." Still, in the "worst" cases, one must admit that the mere fact of communicating under the conditions of the new technology does not cancel the marks of power relations constituted under the conditions of face-to-face, print and electronic broadcasting modes of intercourse.

Nonetheless, the structural conditions of communicating in Internet communities do introduce resistances to and breaks with these gender determinations. The fact of having to decide on one's gender itself raises the issue of individual identity in a novel and compelling manner. If one is to be masculine, one must choose to be so. Further, one must enact one's gender choice in language and in language alone, without any marks and gestures of the body, without clothing or intonations of voice. Presenting one's gender is accomplished solely through textual means, although this does include various iconic markings invented in electronic communities such as the smiley [:-)] and its variants. Also, one may experience directly the opposite gender by assuming it and enacting it in conversations. Finally, the particular configuration of conversation through computers and modems produces a new relation to one's body as it communicates, a cyborg in cyberspace who is different from all the embodied genders of earlier modes of information. These cyborg genders test and transgress the boundaries of the modern gender system without any necessary inclination in that direction on the part of the participant.[18]

While ordinary email between previous acquaintances clearly introduces no strong disruption of the gender system, socially oriented MUDs and MOOs typically do enact the most advanced possibilities of postmodern identity construction. Here identities are invented and changeable; elaborate self-descriptions are enacted; domiciles are depicted in textual form and individuals interact purely for the sake of doing so. MOO inhabitants, however, do not enjoy a democratic utopia. There exist hierarchies specific to this form of cyberspace: the programmers who construct and maintain the MOO have abilities to change rules and procedures that are not available to the players. After these "Gods" come the wizards, those who have accumulated certain privileges through past participation. Another but far more trivial criterion of political differentiation is typing skill, since this determines in part who speaks most often, especially as conversations move along with considerable speed. Even in cyberspace, asymmetries emerge which could be termed "political inequalities." Yet the salient characteristic of Internet community is the diminution of prevailing hierarchies of race, class and especially gender. What appears in the embodied world as irreducible hierarchy plays a lesser role in the cyberspace of MOOs. And, as a result, the relation of cyberspace to material human geography is decidedly one of rupture and challenge. Internet communities function as places of difference from and resistance to modern society. In a sense, they serve the function of a Habermasian public sphere without intentionally being one. They are places not of the presence of validity claims or the actuality of critical reason, but of the inscription of new assemblages of self-constitution. When audio and video enhance the current textual mode of conversation the claims of these virtual realities may even be more exigent.[19] The complaint that these electronic villages are no more than the escapism of white, male undergraduates may then become less convincing.

Cyborg Politics

The example of the deconstruction of gender in Internet MOO communities underlines the importance of theorizing politics in the mode of information. Because the Internet inscribes the new social figure of the cyborg and institutes a communicative practice of self-constitution, the political as we have known it is reconfigured. The wrapping of language on the Internet, its digitized, machine-mediated signifiers in a space without bodies introduces an unprecedented novelty for political theory.[20] How will electronic beings be governed? How will their experience of self-constitution rebound in the existing political arena? How will power relations on the Internet combine with or influence power relations that emerge from face-to-face relations, print relations and broadcast relations? Assuming the United States government and the corporations do not shape the Internet entirely in their own image and that places of cyberdemocracy remain and spread to larger and larger segments of the population, what will emerge as a postmodern politics?

One possibility is that the nature of authority as we have known it will change drastically. Political authority has evolved from embodiment in lineages in the Middle Ages to instrumentally rational mandates from voters in the modern era. At each stage, a certain aura has become fetishistically attached to the bearers of authority. In Internet communities, such an aura is more difficult to sustain, as the Internet seems to discourage the endowment of individuals with inflated status. The example of scholarly research illustrates the point. The formation of canons and authorities is seriously undermined by the electronic nature of texts. Texts become "hypertexts" that are reconstructed in the act of reading, rendering the reader an author and disrupting the stability of experts or "authorities."[21] If scholarly authority is challenged and reformed by the location and dissemination of texts on the Internet, it is possible that political authorities will be subject to a similar fate. If the term democracy refers to the sovereignty of embodied individuals and the system of determining office-holders by them, a new term will be required to indicate a relation of leaders and followers that is mediated by cyberspace and constituted in relation to the mobile identities found therein.

Notes

1   For an intelligent review of the battle over encryption see Steven Levy, "The Battle of the Clipper Chip," *The New York Times Magazine* (June 12, 1994), pp. 44–51, 60, 70.
2   Philippe Lacoue-Labarthe, *Heidegger, Art and Politics*, trans. Chris Turner (New York: Blackwell, 1990) and Jean-Luc Nancy, *The Inoperative Community*, trans. Peter Conor et al. (Minneapolis: University of Minnesota Press, 1991).
3   Ernesto Laclau, *New Reflections on the Revolution of Our Time* (New York: Verso, 1990).
4   See Jean Armour Polly and Steve Cisler, "Community Networks on the Internet," *Library Journal* (June 15, 1994), pp. 22–3.

5   See N. Katherine Hayles, "Virtual Bodies and Flickering Signifiers," *October* 66 (Fall 1993), pp. 69–91.

6   For a study of the role of the media in the formation of a public sphere see John Hartley, *The Politics of Pictures: The Creation of the Public in the Age of Popular Media* (New York: Routledge, 1992), p. 1. Hartley examines in particular the role of graphic images in newspapers.

7   Jürgen Habermas, *The Structural Transformation of the Public Sphere*, trans. Thomas Burger (Cambridge: MIT Press, 1989).

8   Jean-François Lyotard, *The Postmodern Condition*, trans. Brian Massumi et al. (Minneapolis: University of Minnesota Press, 1984).

9   See, for example, Oskar Negt and Alexander Kluge, *Public Sphere and Experience: Toward an Analysis of the Bourgeois and Proletarian Public Sphere*, trans. Peter Labanyi et al. (Minneapolis: University of Minnesota Press, 1993); and Nancy Fraser, "Rethinking the Public Sphere," *Social Text* 25/26 (1990), pp. 56–80 and *Unruly Practices* (Minneapolis: University of Minnesota Press, 1989), especially chapter 6, "What's Critical about Critical Theory? The Case of Habermas and Gender." For a critique of Habermas' historical analysis see Joan Landes, *Women and the Public Sphere in the Age of the French Revolution* (Ithaca: Cornell University Press, 1988).

10 Rita Felski, *Beyond Feminist Aesthetics: Feminist Literature and Social Change* (Cambridge: Harvard University Press, 1989), p. 167.

11 Ibid., pp. 168–9.

12 See the discussion of privacy in relation to electronic surveillance in David Lyon, *The Electronic Eye: The Rise of Surveillance Society* (Minneapolis: University of Minnesota Press, 1994), pp. 14–17.

13 Fraser, "Rethinking the Public Sphere," pp. 57, 55.

14 Paul Virilio, "The Third Interval: A Critical Transition," in Verena Conley, ed., *Rethinking Technologies* (Minneapolis: University of Minnesota Press, 1993), p. 9.

15 Marie-Laure Ryan, "Immersion vs. Interactivity: Virtual Reality and Literary Theory," *Postmodern Culture* 5:1 (September, 1994) presents a subtle, complex comparison of reading a novel and virtual reality, though the author does not deal directly with MOOs and Internet virtual communities.

16 Lynn Cherny, "Gender Differences in Text-Based Virtual Reality," in Mary Bucholtz, ed., *Proceedings of the Berkeley Conference on Women and Language*, (Berkeley: University of California, 1994) concludes that men and women have gender specific communications on MOOs. For an analysis of bulletin board conversations that reaches the same pessimistic conclusions see Susan C. Herring, "Gender and Democracy in Computer-Mediated Communication," *Electronic Journal of Communications* 3:2 (1993) (can be found at info.curtin.edu.au in the directory Journals/curtin/arteduc/ejcrec/Volume_03/Number_02/herring.txt).

17 Lindsy Van Gelder, "The Strange Case of the Electronic Lover," in Charles Dunlop and Rob Kling, eds., *Computerization and Controversy* (New York: Academic Press, 1991), p. 373.

18 For an excellent study of the cultural implications of virtual communities see Elizabeth Reid, "Cultural Formations in Text-Based Virtual Realities," an electronic essay at ftp.parc.xerox.com in /pub/Moo/Papers; also appearing as "Virtual Worlds: Culture and Imagination," in Steve Jones, ed., *Cybersociety* (New York: Sage, 1994), pp. 164–83.

19 For a discussion of these new developments see "MUDs Grow Up: Social Virtual Reality in the Real World," by Pavel Curtis and David A. Nichols (ftp://ftp.parc.xerox.com:/ pub.Moo.Papers/MUDsGrowUp.txt).

20 On this issue see the important essay by Hans Ulrich Gumbrecht, "A Farewell to Interpretation," in Hans Ulrich Gumbrecht and K. Ludwig Pfeiffer, eds., *Materialities of Communication*, trans. William Whobrey (Stanford: Stanford University Press, 1994), pp. 389–402.

21 "The Scholar's Rhizome: Networked Communication Issues" by Kathleen Burnett (kburnett@gandalf.rutgers.edu) explores this issue with convincing logic.

27

The Virtual Community

Howard Rheingold

Howard Rheingold, excerpt from *The Virtual Community: Homesteading on the Electronic Frontier* (Reading, MA: Addison-Wesley Publications, 1993), pp. 1–10. Copyright © 1993 by Howard Rheingold. Reprinted by permission of Perseus Books Publishers, a member of Perseus Books, L.L.C.

Howard Rheingold is a former editor of the *Whole Earth Review* and an original member of the WELL (Whole Earth 'Lectronic Link), one of the first online communities. His books include *Tools for Thought: The History and Future of Mind Expanding Technology* (MIT, 2000) and the volume from which this selection was drawn, *The Virtual Community: Homesteading on the Electronic Frontier* (Addison-Wesley Publications, 1993), now considered a classic work on the potentials of the Internet to improve human communication and build group culture.

"Daddy is saying 'Holy moly!' to his computer again!"

Those words have become a family code for the way my virtual community has infiltrated our real world. My seven-year-old daughter knows that her father congregates with a family of invisible friends who seem to gather in his computer. Sometimes he talks to them, even if nobody else can see them. And she knows that these invisible friends sometimes show up in the flesh, materializing from the next block or the other side of the planet.

Since the summer of 1985, for an average of two hours a day, seven days a week, I've been plugging my personal computer into my telephone and making contact with the WELL (Whole Earth 'Lectronic Link) – a computer conferencing system that enables people around the world to carry on public conversations and exchange private electronic mail (e-mail). The idea of a community accessible only via my computer screen sounded cold to me at first, but I learned quickly that people can feel passionately about e-mail and computer conferences. I've become one of them. I care about these people I met through my computer, and I care deeply about the future of the medium that enables us to assemble.

I'm not alone in this emotional attachment to an apparently bloodless technological ritual. Millions of people on every continent also participate in the computer-mediated social groups known as virtual communities, and this population is growing fast. Finding the WELL was like discovering a cozy little world that had been flourishing without me, hidden within the walls of my house; an entire cast of characters welcomed me to the troupe with great merriment as soon as I found the secret door. Like others who fell into the WELL, I soon discovered that I was audience, performer, and scriptwriter, along with my companions, in an ongoing improvisation. A full-scale subculture was growing on the other side of my telephone jack, and they invited me to help create something new.

The virtual village of a few hundred people I stumbled upon in 1985 grew to eight thousand by 1993. It became clear to me during the first months of that history that I was participating in the self-design of a new kind of culture. I watched the community's social contracts stretch and change as the people who discovered and started building the WELL in its first year or two were joined by so many others. Norms were established, challenged, changed, reestablished, rechallenged, in a kind of speeded-up social evolution.

The WELL felt like an authentic community to me from the start because it was grounded in my everyday physical world. WELLites who don't live within driving distance of the San Francisco Bay area are constrained in their ability to participate in the local networks of face-to-face acquaintants. By now, I've attended real-life WELL marriages, WELL births, and even a WELL funeral. (The phrase "in real life" pops up so often in virtual communities that regulars abbreviate it to IRL.) I can't count the parties and outings where the invisible personae who first acted out their parts in the debates and melodramas on my computer screen later manifested in front of me in the physical world in the form of real people, with faces, bodies, and voices.

I remember the first time I walked into a room full of people IRL who knew many intimate details of my history and whose own stories I knew very well. Three months after I joined, I went to my first WELL party at the home of one of the WELL's online moderators. I looked around at the room full of strangers when I walked in. It was one of the oddest sensations of my life. I had contended with these people, shot the invisible breeze around the electronic watercooler, shared alliances and formed bonds, fallen off my chair laughing with them, become livid with anger at some of them. But there wasn't a recognizable face in the house. I had never seen them before.

My flesh-and-blood family long ago grew accustomed to the way I sit in my home office early in the morning and late at night, chuckling and cursing, sometimes crying, about words I read on the computer screen. It might have looked to my daughter as if I were alone at my desk the night she caught me chortling online, but from my point of view I was in living contact with old and new friends, strangers and colleagues:

I was in the Parenting conference on the WELL, participating in an informational and emotional support group for a friend who had just learned his son was diagnosed with leukemia.

I was in MicroMUSE, a role-playing fantasy game of the twenty-fourth century (and science education medium in disguise), interacting with students and professors who know me only as "Pollenator."

I was in TWICS, a bicultural community in Tokyo; CIX, a community in London; CalvaCom, a community in Paris; and Usenet, a collection of hundreds of different discussions that travel around the world via electronic mail to millions of participants in dozens of countries.

I was browsing through Supreme Court decisions, in search of information that could help me debunk an opponent's claims in a political debate elsewhere on the Net, or I was retrieving this morning's satellite images of weather over the Pacific.

I was following an eyewitness report from Moscow during the coup attempt, or China during the Tiananmen Square incident, or Israel and Kuwait during the Gulf War, passed directly from citizen to citizen through an ad hoc network patched together from cheap computers and ordinary telephone lines, cutting across normal geographic and political boundaries by piggybacking on the global communications infrastructure.

I was monitoring a rambling real-time dialogue among people whose bodies were scattered across three continents, a global bull session that seems to blend wit and sophomore locker-room talk via Internet Relay Chat (IRC), a medium that combines the features of conversation and writing. IRC has accumulated an obsessive subculture of its own among undergraduates by the thousands from Adelaide to Arabia.

People in virtual communities use words on screens to exchange pleasantries and argue, engage in intellectual discourse, conduct commerce, exchange knowledge, share emotional support, make plans, brainstorm, gossip, feud, fall in love, find friends and lose them, play games, flirt, create a little high art and a lot of idle talk. People in virtual communities do just about everything people do in real life, but we leave our bodies behind. You can't kiss anybody and nobody can punch you in the nose, but a lot can happen within those boundaries. To the millions who have been drawn into it, the richness and vitality of computer-linked cultures is attractive, even addictive.

There is no such thing as a single, monolithic, online subculture; it's more like an ecosystem of subcultures, some frivolous, others serious. The cutting edge of scientific discourse is migrating to virtual communities, where you can read the electronic pre-preprinted reports of molecular biologists and cognitive scientists. At the same time, activists and educational reformers are using the same medium as a political tool. You can use virtual communities to find a date, sell a lawnmower, publish a novel, conduct a meeting.

Some people use virtual communities as a form of psychotherapy. Others, such as the most addicted players of Minitel in France or Multi-User Dungeons (MUDs) on the international networks, spend eighty hours a week or more pretending they are someone else, living a life that does not exist outside a computer. Because MUDs not only are susceptible to pathologically obsessive use by some people but also create a strain on computer and communication resources, MUDding has been banned at universities such as Amherst and on the entire continent of Australia.

Scientists, students, librarians, artists, organizers, and escapists aren't the only people who have taken to the new medium. The U.S. senator who campaigned for years for the construction of a National Research and Education Network that could host the virtual communities of the future is now vice president of the United States. As of June 1993, the White House and Congress have e-mail addresses.

Most people who get their news from conventional media have been unaware of the wildly varied assortment of new cultures that have evolved in the world's computer networks over the past ten years. Most people who have not yet used these new media remain unaware of how profoundly the social, political, and scientific experiments under way today via computer networks could change all our lives in the near future.

I have written this book to help inform a wider population about the potential importance of cyberspace to political liberties and the ways virtual communities are likely to change our experience of the real world, as individuals and communities. Although I am enthusiastic about the liberating potentials of computer-mediated communications, I try to keep my eyes open for the pitfalls of mixing technology and human relationships. I hope my reports from the outposts and headquarters of this new kind of social habitation, and the stories of the people I've met in cyberspace, will bring to life the cultural, political, and ethical implications of virtual communities both for my fellow explorers of cyberspace and for those who never heard of it before.

The technology that makes virtual communities possible has the potential to bring enormous leverage to ordinary citizens at relatively little cost – intellectual leverage, social leverage, commercial leverage, and most important, political leverage. But the technology will not in itself fulfill that potential; this latent technical power must be used intelligently and deliberately by an informed population. More people must learn about that leverage and learn to use it, while we still have the freedom to do so, if it is to live up to its potential. The odds are always good that big power and big money will find a way to control access to virtual communities; big power and big money always found ways to control new communications media when they emerged in the past. The Net is still out of control in fundamental ways, but it might not stay that way for long. What we know and do now is important because it is still possible for people around the world to make sure this new sphere of vital human discourse remains open to the citizens of the planet before the political and economic big boys seize it, censor it, meter it, and sell it back to us.

The potential social leverage comes from the power that ordinary citizens gain when they know how to connect two previously independent, mature, highly decentralized technologies: It took billions of dollars and decades to develop cheap personal computers. It took billions of dollars and more than a century to wire up the worldwide telecommunication network. With the right knowledge, and not too much of it, a ten-year-old kid today can plug these two vast, powerful, expensively developed technologies together for a few hundred dollars and instantly obtain a bully pulpit, the Library of Congress, and a world full of potential coconspirators.

Computers and the switched telecommunication networks that also carry our telephone calls constitute the technical foundation of *computer-mediated communications* (CMC). The technicalities of CMC, how bits of computer data move over wires and are reassembled as computer files at their destinations, are invisible and irrelevant to most people who use it, except when the technicalities restrict their access to CMC services. The important thing to keep in mind is that the world-wide, interconnected telecommunication network that we use to make telephone calls in Manhattan and Madagascar can also be used to connect computers together at a distance, and you don't have to be an engineer to do it.

The Net is an informal term for the loosely interconnected computer networks that use CMC technology to link people around the world into public discussions.

Virtual communities are social aggregations that emerge from the Net when enough people carry on those public discussions long enough, with sufficient human feeling, to form webs of personal relationships in cyberspace.

Cyberspace, originally a term from William Gibson's science-fiction novel *Neuromancer*, is the name some people use for the conceptual space where words, human relationships, data, wealth, and power are manifested by people using CMC technology.

Although spatial imagery and a sense of place help convey the experience of dwelling in a virtual community, biological imagery is often more appropriate to describe the way cyberculture changes. In terms of the way the whole system is propagating and evolving, think of cyberspace as a social petri dish, the Net as the agar medium, and virtual communities, in all their diversity, as the colonies of microorganisms that grow in petri dishes. Each of the small colonies of micro-organisms – the communities on the Net – is a social experiment that nobody planned but that is happening nevertheless.

We now know something about the ways previous generations of communications technologies changed the way people lived. We need to understand why and how so many social experiments are coevolving today with the prototypes of the newest communications technologies. My direct observations of online behavior around the world over the past ten years have led me to conclude that whenever CMC technology becomes available to people anywhere, they inevitably build virtual communities with it, just as microorganisms inevitably create colonies.

I suspect that one of the explanations for this phenomenon is the hunger for community that grows in the breasts of people around the world as more and more informal public spaces disappear from our real lives. I also suspect that these new media attract colonies of enthusiasts because CMC enables people to do things with each other in new ways, and to do altogether new kinds of things – just as telegraphs, telephones, and televisions did.

Because of its potential influence on so many people's beliefs and perceptions, the future of the Net is connected to the future of community, democracy, education, science, and intellectual life – some of the human institutions people hold most dear, whether or not they know or care about the future of computer technology. The future of the Net has become too important to leave to specialists and special interests. As it influences the lives of a growing number of people, more and more citizens must contribute to the dialogue about the way public funds are applied to the development of the Net, and we must join our voices to the debate about the way it should be administered. We need a clear citizens' vision of the way the Net ought to grow, a firm idea of the kind of media environment we would like to see in the future. If we do not develop such a vision for ourselves, the future will be shaped for us by large commercial and political powerholders.

The Net is so widespread and anarchic today because of the way its main sources converged in the 1980s, after years of independent, apparently unrelated development, using different technologies and involving different populations of participants. The technical and social convergences were fated, but not widely foreseen, by the late 1970s.

The wide-area CMC networks that span continents and join together thousands of smaller networks are a spinoff of American military research. The first computer network, ARPANET, was created in the 1970s so that Department of Defense-sponsored researchers could operate different computers at a distance; computer data, not person-to-person messages, were the intended content of the network, which handily happened to serve just as easily as a conduit for words. The fundamental technical idea on which ARPANET was based came from RAND, the think tank in Santa Monica that did a lot of work with top-secret thermonuclear war scenarios; ARPANET grew out of an older RAND scheme for a communication, command, and control network that could survive nuclear attack by having no central control.

Computer conferencing emerged, also somewhat unexpectedly, as a tool for using the communication capacities of the networks to build social relationships across barriers of space and time. A continuing theme throughout the history of CMC is the way people adapt technologies designed for one purpose to suit their own, very different, communication needs. And the most profound technological changes have come from the fringes and subcultures, not the orthodoxy of the computer industry or academic computer science. The programmers who created the first computer network installed electronic mail features; electronic mail wasn't the reason ARPANET was designed, but it was an easy thing to include once ARPANET existed. Then, in a similar, ad hoc, do-it-yourself manner, computer conferencing grew out of the needs of U.S. policymakers to develop a communications medium for dispersed decision making. Although the first computer conferencing experiments were precipitated by the U.S. government's wage-price freeze of the 1970s and the consequent need to disseminate up-to-date information from a large number of geographically dispersed local headquarters, computer conferencing was quickly adapted to commercial, scientific, and social discourse.

The hobbyists who interconnect personal computers via telephone lines to make computer bulletin-board systems, known as BBSs, have home-grown their part of the Net, a true grassroots use of technology. Hundreds of thousands of people around the world piggyback legally on the telecom network via personal computers and ordinary telephone lines. The most important technical attribute of networked BBSs is that it is an extremely hard network to kill – just as the RAND planners had hoped. Information can take so many alternative routes when one of the nodes of the network is removed that the Net is almost immortally flexible. It is this flexibility that CMC telecom pioneer John Gilmore referred to when he said, "The Net interprets censorship as damage and routes around it."

This way of passing information and communication around a network as a distributed resource with no central control manifested in the rapid growth of the anarchic global conversation known as Usenet. This invention of distributed conversation that flows around obstacles – a grassroots adaptation of a technology originally designed as a doomsday weapon – might turn out to be as important in the long run as the hardware and software inventions that made it possible.

The big hardwired networks spend a lot more money to create high-speed information conduits between high-capacity computing nodes. Internet, today's U.S. government-sponsored successor to ARPANET, is growing in every dimension at an astonishing pace. These "data superhighways" use special telecommunication lines and other equipment to send very large amounts of information throughout the network at very high speeds. ARPANET started around twenty years ago with roughly one thousand users, and now Internet is approaching ten million users.

The portable computer on my desk is hundreds of times less expensive and thousands of times more powerful than ARPANET's first nodes. The fiberoptic backbone of the current Internet communicates information millions of times faster than the first ARPANET. Everything about Internet has grown like a bacterial colony – the raw technical capacity to send information, the different ways people use it, and the number of users. The Internet population has grown by 15 percent a month for the past several years. John Quarterman, whose book *The Matrix* is a thick guide to the world's computer networks, estimates that there are nine hundred different networks worldwide today, not counting the more than ten thousand networks already linked by the Internet "network of networks."

Real grassroots, the kind that grow in the ground, are a self-similar branching structure, a network of networks. Each grass seed grows a branching set of roots, and then many more smaller roots grow off those; the roots of each grass plant interconnect physically with the roots of adjacent plants, as any gardener who has tried to uproot a lawn has learned. There is a grassroots element to the Net that was not, until very recently, involved with all the high-tech, top-secret doings that led to ARPANET – the BBSers.

The population of the grassroots part of the Net, the citizen-operated BBSs, has been growing explosively as a self-financed movement of enthusiasts, without the benefit of Department of Defense funding. A BBS is the simplest, cheapest infrastructure for CMC: you run special software, often available inexpensively, on a personal computer, and use a device known as a *modem* to plug the computer into your regular telephone line. The modem converts computer-readable information into audible beeps and boops that can travel over the same telephone wires that carry your voice; another modem at the other end decodes the beeps and boops into computer-readable bits and bytes. The BBS turns the bits and bytes into human-readable text. Other people use their computers to call your BBS, leave and retrieve messages stored in your personal computer, and you have a virtual community growing in your bedroom. As the system operator (sysop) of the BBS, you contribute part of your computer's memory and make sure your computer is plugged into the telephone; the participants pay for their own communication costs.

Boardwatch magazine estimates that sixty thousand BBSs operated in the United States alone in 1993, fourteen years after the first BBSs opened in Chicago and California. Each BBS supports a population of a dozen to several hundred, or even thousands, of individual participants. There are religious BBSs of every denomination, sex BBSs of every proclivity, political BBSs from all parts of the spectrum, outlaw BBSs, law enforcement BBSs, BBSs for the disabled, for educators, for kids, for cults, for nonprofit organizations – a list of the different flavors of special-interest BBSs is dozens of pages long. The BBS culture has spread from the United States to Japan, Europe, Central and South America.

Each BBS started out as a small island community of a few people who dialed into a number in their area code; by their nature, like a small-wattage radio station, BBSs are localized. But that's changing, too. Just as several different technologies converged over the past ten years to create CMC – a new medium with properties of its own – several different online social structures are in the process of converging and creating a kind of international culture with properties of its own.

Technical bridges are connecting the grassroots part of the network with the military-industrial parts of the network. The programmers who built the Net in the first place, the scholars who have been using it to exchange knowledge, the scientists who have been using it for research, are being joined by all those hobbyists with their bedroom and garage BBSs. Special "gateway" computers can link entire networks by automatically translating communications from the mechanical languages used in one network to the languages (known as protocols) used in another network. In recent years, the heretofore separate groups of Internet and BBS pioneers worked together to gateway the more than ten thousand computers of the worldwide FidoNet, the first network of small, private BBSs, with Internet's millions of people and tens of thousands of more powerful computers.

The Net and computer conferencing systems are converging too, as medium-size computer conferencing communities like the WELL join Internet. When the WELL upgraded to a high-speed connection to Internet, it became not just a community-in-progress but a gateway to a wider realm, the worldwide Net-at-large. Suddenly, the isolated archipelagos of a few hundred or a few thousand people are becoming part of an integrated entity. The small virtual communities still exist, like yeast in a rapidly rising loaf, but increasingly they are part of an overarching culture, similar to the way the United States became an overarching culture after the telegraph and telephone linked the states.

The WELL is a small town, but now there is a doorway in that town that opens onto the blooming, buzzing confusion of the Net, an entity with properties altogether different from the virtual villages of a few years ago. I have good friends now all over the world who I never would have met without the mediation of the Net. A large circle of Net acquaintances can make an enormous difference in your experience when you travel to a foreign culture. Wherever I've traveled physically in recent years, I've found ready-made communities that I met online months before I traveled; our mutual enthusiasm for virtual communities served as a bridge, time and again, to people whose language and customs differ significantly from those I know well in California.

I routinely meet people and get to know them months or years before I see them – one of the ways my world today is a different world, with different friends and different concerns, from the world I experienced in premodem days. The places I visit in my mind, and the people I communicate with from one moment to the next, are entirely different from the content of my thoughts or the state of my circle of friends before I started dabbling in virtual communities. One minute I'm involved in the minutiae of local matters such as planning next week's bridge game, and the next minute I'm part of a debate raging in seven countries. Not only do I inhabit my virtual communities; to the degree that I carry around their conversations in my head and begin to mix it up with them in real life, my virtual communities also inhabit my life. I've been colonized; my sense of family at the most fundamental level has been virtualized.

28

The Virtual Barrio @ the Other Frontier (or the Chicago Interneta)

Guillermo Gómez-Peña

Guillermo Gómez-Peña, "The Virtual Barrio @ the Other Frontier (or Chicago Interneta)," in Lynn Hershmann Leeson, ed., *Clicking In: Hot Links to a Digital Culture* (Seattle: Bay Press, 1996), pp. 173–9.

Guillermo Gómez-Peña is a writer and artist who explores Mexican-American identity, with an emphasis on issues involving national borders. He is the author of *The New World Border: Prophesies, Poems, and Loqueras at the End of the Century* (City Lights, 1996). This selection is one of the only essays written to date about the now-rapidly growing Latino Internet phenomenon.

> [Mexicans] are simple people. They are happy with the little they got.... They are not ambitious and complex like us. They don't need all this technology to communicate. Sometimes I just feel like going down there & living among them.
> – Anonymous confession on the Web

Tecnofobia

My laptop is decorated with a 3-D decal of the Virgin of Guadalupe. It's like a traveling altar, office, and literary bank, all in one. Since I spend 70 percent of the year on the road, it is (besides the phone of course) my principal means to remain in touch with my beloved relatives and colleagues, spread throughout many cities in the United States and Mexico. Unwillingly, I have become a cyber-vato, an information superhighway bandido. Like most Mexican artists, my relationship with digital technology and personal computers is defined by paradoxes and contradictions: I don't quite understand them, yet I am seduced by them; I don't want to know how they work, but I love how they look and what they do; I criticize my colleagues who are acritically immersed in new technology, yet I silently envy them. I resent the fact that I am constantly told that as a "Latino" I am supposedly culturally handicapped or somehow unfit to handle high technology; yet once I have it right in front of me, I am propelled to work against it, to question it, to expose it, to subvert it, to imbue it with humor, linguas polutas – Spanglish, Frangle, gringonol, and radical politics. In doing so, I become a sort of Mexican virus, the cyber-version of the Mexican fly: tiny, irritating, inescapable, and highly contagious. Contradiction prevails.

Over a year ago, my collaborator Roberto Sifuentes and I bullied ourselves into the Net, and once we were generously adopted by various communities (Arts Wire and Latino Net, among others) we started to lose interest in maintaining ongoing conversations with phantasmagoric beings we had never met in person (that, I must say, is a Mexican cultural prejudice – if I don't know you in person, I don't really care to talk with you). Then we started sending a series of poetic/activist "techno-placas" in Spanglish. In these short communiqués we raised some tough questions regarding access, privilege, and language. Since we didn't quite know where to post them in order to get the maximum response, and the responses were sporadic, casual, and unfocused, our passion began to dim. Roberto and I spend a lot of time in front of our laptops conceptualizing performance projects which incorporate new technologies in what we believe is a responsible and original manner, yet every time we are invited to participate in a public discussion around art and technology, we tend to emphasize its shortcomings and overstate our cultural skepticism.[1] Why? I can only speak for myself. Perhaps I have some computer traumas. I've been utilizing computers since 1988; however, during the first five years, I utilized my old "lowrider" Mac as a glorified typewriter. During those years I probably deleted accidentally here and there over 300 pages of original texts which I hadn't backed up on disks, and thus was forced to rewrite them by memory. The thick and confusing "user friendly" manuals fell many a time from my impatient hands; and I spent many desperate nights cursing the mischievous gods of cyberspace and dialing promising "hotlines" which rarely answered.

My bittersweet relationship to technology dates back to my formative years in the highly politicized ambiance of Mexico City in the 1970s. As a young "radical artist," I was full of ideological dogmas and partial truths. One such partial truth spouted was that high-technology was intrinsically dehumanizing; that it was mostly used as a means to control "us" little techno-illiterate people politically. My critique of technology overlapped with my critique of capitalism. To me, "capitalists" were rootless corporate men who utilized mass media to advertise useless electronic gadgets, and sold us unnecessary apparatuses which kept us both eternally in debt and conveniently distracted from "the truly important matters of life." These matters included sex, music, spirituality, and "revolution" California style (in the abstract). As a child of contradiction, besides being a rabid anti-technology artist, I owned a little Datsun and listened to my favorite U.S. and British rock groups on my Panasonic *importado*, often while meditating or making love as a means to "liberate myself" from capitalist socialization. My favorite clothes, books, posters, and albums had all been made by "capitalists," but for some obscure reason, that seemed perfectly logical to me. Luckily, my family never lost their magical thinking and sense of humor around technology. My parents were easily seduced by refurbished and slightly dated American and Japanese electronic goods. We bought them as *fayuca* (contraband) in the Tepito neighborhood, and they occupied an important place in the decoration of our "modern" middle-class home. Our huge color TV set, for example, was decorated so as to perform the double function of entertainment unit and involuntary postmodern altar – with nostalgic photos, plastic flowers, and assorted figurines all around it – as was the sound system next to it. Though I was sure that with the scary arrival of the first microwave oven in our traditional kitchen our delicious daily meals were going to turn overnight into sleazy fast food, my mother soon realized that *el microondas* was only good to reheat cold coffee and soups. When I moved to California, I bought an electric ionizer for my grandma. She put it in the middle of her bedroom altar and kept it there – unplugged of course – for months. When I next saw her, she told me, "Mijito, since you gave me that thing, I truly can breathe much better." And probably she did. Things like televisions, shortwave radios, and microwave ovens, and later on ionizers, Walkmans, calculators, and video cameras were seen by my family and friends as high technology, and their function was as much pragmatic as it was social, ritual, and aesthetic. It is no coincidence then that in my early performance work, technology performed both ritual and aesthetic functions.

Verbigratia

For years, I used video monitors as centerpieces for my "techno-altars" on stage. I combined ritualistic structures, spoken word multilingual poetry and activist politics with my fascination for "low-tech." Fog machines, strobe lights, and gobos, megaphones and cheesy voice filters have remained since then trademark elements in my "low-tech/high-tech" performances. By the early 1990s, I sarcastically baptized my aesthetic practice "Aztec high-tech art," and when I teamed with Cyber-Vato Sifuentes, we decided that what we were doing was "techno-razcuache art." In a glossary which dates back to 1993, we defined it as "a new aesthetic that fuses performance art, epic rap poetry, interactive television, experimental radio and computer art; but with a Chicanocentric perspective and a sleazoid bent."

(El Naftaztec turns the knobs of his "Chicano virtual reality machine" and then proceeds to feed chili peppers into it. The set looks like a Mexican sci-fi movie from the 1950s.) El Naftaztec (speaking with a computerized voice): *So now, let's talk about the TECHNOPAL 2000, a technology originally invented by the Mayans with the help of aliens from Harvard. Its CPU is powered by Habanero chili peppers, combined with this or DAT technology, with a measured clock speed of 200,000 mega-hertz! It uses neural nets supplemented by actual chicken-brain matter and nacho cheese spread to supply the massive processing speed necessary for the machine to operate. And it's all integrated into one sombrero! Originally, the Chicano VR had to use a poncho, but with the VR sombrero, the weight is greatly reduced and its efficiency is magnified. And now, we have the first alpha version of the VR bandanna dos mil, which Cyber-Vato will demonstrate for us!* (Cyber-Vato wears a bandanna over his eyes. It is connected by

a thick rope to a robotic glove. Special effects on the TV screen simulate the graphics
and sounds of a VR helmet.)

From "Naftaztec," an interactive TV project
about Mexicans and high technology

The mythology goes like this. Mexicans (and other Latinos) can't handle high
technology. Caught between a preindustrial past and an imposed postmodernity,
we continue to be manual beings – *homo fabers* par excellence, imaginative artisans
(not technicians) – and our understanding of the world is strictly political, poetical,
or metaphysical at best, but certainly not scientific. Furthermore, we are perceived
as sentimental and passionate, meaning irrational; and when we decide to step out
of our realm and utilize high technology in our art (most of the time we are not
even interested), we are meant to naively repeat what others have already done. We
often feed this mythology by overstating our romantic nature and humanistic
stances and/or by assuming the role of colonial victims of technology. We are
ready to point out the fact that "computers are the source of the Anglos' social
handicaps and sexual psychosis" and that communication in America, the land of
the future, "is totally mediated by faxes, phones, computers, and other technologies we are not even aware of." We, "on the contrary," socialize profusely,
negotiate information ritually and sensually, and remain in touch with our primeval
selves. This simplistic binary worldview presents Mexico as technologically under-
developed yet culturally and spiritually overdeveloped and the United States as
exactly the opposite. Reality is much more complicated: the average Anglo-
American does not understand new technologies either; people of color and
women in the United States clearly don't have equal access to cyberspace; and at
the same time, the average urban Mexican is already afflicted in varying degrees
by the same "first world" existential diseases produced by advanced capitalism and
high technology. In fact the new generations of Mexicans, including my hip
generation-Mex nephews and my seven-year-old fully bicultural son, are completely immersed in and defined by personal computers, video games, and virtual
reality. Far from being the romantic preindustrial paradise of the American imagination, the Mexico of the 1990s is already a virtual nation whose cohesiveness and
boundaries are provided solely by television, transnational pop culture, and the free
market. It is true that there are entire parts of the country which still lack basic
infrastructures and public services (not to mention communications technology).
But in 1996, the same can be said of the United States, a "first world" nation
whose ruined "ethnic" neighborhoods, Native American reserves, and rural areas
exist in conditions comparable to those of a "third world" country. When trying
to link, say, Los Angeles and Mexico City via video-telephone, we encounter new
problems. In Mexico, the only artists with "access" to this technology are upper-
class, politically conservative, and uninteresting. And the funding sources down
there willing to fund the project are clearly interested in controlling who is part of
the experiment. In other words, we don't really need Octavio Paz conversing with
Richard Rodriguez. We need Ruben Martinez talking to Monsivais, as well.

The world is waiting for you – so come on!

Ad for America Online

The Cyber-migra

Roberto and I arrived late to the debate. When we began to dialog with artists working with new technologies, we were perplexed by the fact that when referring to cyberspace or the Net, they spoke of a politically neutral/raceless/genderless/classless "territory" which provided us all with "equal access" and unlimited possibilities of participation, interaction, and belonging – especially belonging. Their enthusiastic rhetoric reminded us of both a sanitized version of the pioneer and cowboy mentalities of the Old West ("Guillermo, you can be the first Mexican ever to do this and that in the Net"), and the early-century Futurist cult to the speed and beauty of epic technology (airplanes, trains, factories, etc.). Given the existing "compassion fatigue" regarding political art dealing with issues of race and gender, it was hard not to see this feel-good utopian view of new technologies as an attractive exit from the acute social and racial crisis afflicting the United States. We were also perplexed by the "benign (not naive) ethnocentrism" permeating the debates around art and digital technology. The unquestioned lingua franca was of course English, the "official language of international communications"; the vocabulary utilized in these discussions was hyperspecialized and depoliticized; and if Chicanos and Mexicans didn't participate enough in the Net, it was solely because of lack of information or interest (not money or access), or again because we were "culturally unfit." The unspoken assumption was that our true interests were grassroots (by grassroots I mean the streets), representational, or oral (as if these concerns couldn't exist in virtual space). In other words, we were to remain dancing salsa, painting murals, writing flamboyant love poetry, and plotting revolutions in rowdy cafes. We were also perplexed by the recurring labels of "originality" and "innovation" attached to virtual art. And it was not the nature, contents, and structural complexity of the parallel realities created by digital technology, but the use of the technology per se that seemed to be "original" and "innovative." That, of course, has since engendered many conflicting responses. Native American shamans and medicine men rightfully see their centuries-old "visions" as a form of virtual reality. And Latin American writers equate their literary experimentation with involuntary hypertexts and vernacular postmodern aesthetics, and so do Chicanos and Chicanas. Like the pre-multicultural art world of the early 1980s, the new high-tech art world assumed an unquestionable "center" and drew a dramatic digital border. On the other side of that border lived all the techno-illiterate artists, along with most women, Chicanos, African Americans, and Native Americans. The role for us, then, was to assume, once again, the unpleasant but necessary role of cultural invaders, techno-pirates, and coyotes (smugglers). And then, just like multiculturalism was declared dead as soon as we began to share the paycheck, now as we venture into the virtual barrio for the first time some asshole at M.I.T. declares it dead. Why? It is no longer an exclusive space. It emulates too much real life and social demographics. Luckily many things have changed. Since we don't wish to reproduce the unpleasant mistakes of the multicultural days, our strategies are now quite different: we are no longer trying to persuade anyone that we are worthy of inclusion.

Nor are we fighting for the same funding (since funding no longer exists). What we want is to "politicize" the debate; to "brownify" virtual space; to "spanglishize the Net;" to "infect" the lingua franca; to exchange a different sort of information – mythical, poetical, political, performative, imagistic; and on top of that to find grassroots applications to new technologies and hopefully to do all this with humor and intelligence. The ultimate goals are perhaps to help the Latino youth exchange their guns for computers and video cameras, and to link the community centers through the Net. CD-ROMs can perform the role of community memory banks, while the larger virtual community gets used to a new presence, a new sensibility, a new language.

Note

1   See www.sfgate.com/foundry/pochanostra.html

29

A Disappearance of Community

Avital Ronell

Avital Ronell, "A Disappearance of Community," in Mary Anne Moser and Douglas Macleod, eds., *Immersed in Technology: Art and Virtual Environments* (Cambridge, MA: MIT Press, 1996), pp. 119–27. Reprinted by permission of The MIT Press.

Avital Ronell is a professor at the University of California, Berkeley and the author of *The Telephone Book: Technology, Schizophrenia, Electric Speech* (Nebraska, 1991). In this eloquent reflection on media and virtuality, Ronell discusses the tendency of people to become disengaged from public life and political concern.

This chapter concerns virtual reality, media, and the war in the Gulf. I may not master the materials, or even the immaterials (VR opens the question of immateriality). Yet this issue is about mastery and I consider myself an infomaniaque. VR is philosophically complex even though it is system-dependent on classical tropes of representation, imagination, the sovereign subject, and negated otherness (negated otherness is what Hegel called the enemy). So it is dependent on a number of metaphysical cravings, but then who isn't? Might as well face it: there has always been a desire to transcend the body, and I have often said that I would donate my own body to science fiction. But the donation of a body in life is part of a metaphysical striving toward an indeterminate elsewhere. VR is jamming the master codes of this historical desire for transcendence and exteriority, and deserves to be heard out in all its effusions. Because VR is also about being-in-the-world and liberating the location of being to nonsubstantial spaces, it is trying to reconfigure the possibilities for sharing the world. According to Jaron Lanier, Howard Rheingold, and others, VR practices a politics of finitude[1] and demands an ethics of technology. At the same, however, VR is jacking into Mattel Corporation, the military, and NASA but it is *also* a design testing ground for architecture and the medical sciences. "So, where were we?" asks the scholar. A rigorous study of virtual reality cannot be made to fit entirely into the frame of this chapter, but I will try to raise some questions to indicate the direction of my reflections on this difficult topic.

Virtual reality, artificial reality, dataspace, or cyberspace are inscriptions of a desire whose principal symptom can be seen as the absence of community. Lanier's discourse has everything to do with possibilities for constituting an ecstatic community that would refuse to be governed by a goal or a totalitarian drive toward unification and project. It is as if Lanier were tempted to retrieve Bataille's community of shattered egos. To a certain extent, the metaphysical subject is broken up and displaced to routes of splintering disidentification. The subject no longer finds its mooring in identification with a substantial image. Still, Lanier, like all transmitters on behalf of radio (VR is said to be more like a telephone or radio, disconnected from the television apparatus), emphasizes the ego-building prowess of VR designs. This is a double-edged claim that we need to probe with unrelenting clarity.

In cyburbia there is always a risk of blurring the distinction between simulation and the operational world. I am not convinced, though others are, that this entails a very new risk. More seriously, perhaps, there is still a tendency to retrofit the technological prosthesis to a metaphysical subject – the sovereign subject of history, destiny's copilot. In other words, the technological prosthesis would merely be an amplifier and intensifier borrowed by a centered subject whose fragmentation is, as they say, a simulation – that is, a device for *disavowing* fragmentation, selflessness, or, on another register, castration. This aspect of disavowal in part explains why Lanier, for his part, would have preferred to see VR called, as he asserts, "intentional reality." Now this exposes a whole problematics of the intentional consciousness that I will address momentarily. The intentional consciousness is a philosophical construct that emerges when it is felt that we are not in control of our actions. And this is precisely where Lanier's project takes hold, in the control rooms of his majesty the ego. In addition to arguing that VR is "good for the ego," he launches an assault against the contemporary subject's passivity; this assault on passivity – quite understandable at first sight – is however made in the dubious name of action and control.[2] The subject will take control. The argument against passivity, which I can only graze swiftly, is, I believe, a false and highly problematic one though I also agree with the need to activate radical creativity. But the opposition of passive and active proffers a deluded equation. Take a look around you. Have we not, as a culture, been too active, too action-filled, even if action splits itself into representations of the traumatized spectator and manic warrior? Any uninterrogated invention made in the name of action has got to attract our deepest suspicions. A true ethics of community, whether located in cyberspace or among lovers, readers, artists, activists, and so on, would have to locate a passivity beyond passivity – a space for repose and reflection, a space that would let the other come. Exposing oneself to the other, or to the other's death, has nothing to do with action as such. I will elaborate this shortly. It is because of an articulated desire for action that cyberspace is also west of the west, that is, a Memorex cowboy frontier.

One of the errors that Lanier makes is to say that "ultimately, everything is done by people and technology is only a little game that we play."[3] The war has shown us that people do not play little games. Nor is technology zoned outside of us, but, as cybernetics and artificial intelligence have shown, man–machinic hybridizations involve a refashioning of the human being, following a trajectory of altogether new alignments of self and the technobody. Now, the body, from Marvin Minsky onward, has been devalorized into the "bloody mess of organic matter." I am not an essential feminist, but I do think that this utterance could never have been made by a woman, who takes out monthly mortgages on her body in the form of periodic bloodbaths and PMS. This is being said too quickly, perhaps, but it is urgent to recognize that the body of a woman has a fundamental relationship to death, despair, finitude – and to life. While the woman's body produces the eternal return of the "bloody mess of organic matter," the cyborg soldier, located in command and control systems, exercises on the fields of denial. Intentional reality eliminates the body as organic, finite, damageable, eviscerable, castratable, crushable entity, thereby closing the orifices and stemming leakage and excrement. We are not very far from Deleuze and Guattari's BWO: the body-without-organs. Orificial shutdown and excremental control help explain why the Gulf War was conducted under the compulsive sign of cleanliness: on the American side of language usage, this was a clean war, a clean-up job accomplished according to the moral, political, and military evaluations that were represented. It was so clean, in fact, that there were blank screens assuring the protocols of propriety – the covering up of coverage – but also it was so clean on our side of the line in the sand that the American body, if it was to be lost, did so in an ascension of friendly fire. The point is that the other side never got to us, which I shall try to analyze briefly as the immunopathological dimension of this war.

For the duration of the war, contact with the negated other was nanominimalist and the language of contact was suspended. Thus, even the inevitable contaminations implied by linkage were avoided. No linkage means, among other received things, no parasitical or random eruptions on the mainline of firing, but also no complexity and no ambivalence concerning this war, its aims, or the aims of man (the new order is about the aims of man, and we know which way they are aiming). The disassociation of communicating parts – no linkage – reflects the effects of derealization that the war continues to produce on us.

So where were we? Before I say more, I want to say that I am assuming that we are still in North America, which is to say that I take it for granted that your opinions, evaluations, and feelings concerning the Gulf War have been formed. If at this point I say that we are still in North America, this is in part because the war in the Gulf has destabilized our understanding of location, and has instituted a teletopical logic: a logic of spaces aligned according to technological mappings, where the newer is far and vice versa, and where systems of boundaries and borderlines will have to be entirely rethought.

If we are still in North America, which is not only a place but also a time of reflection – a site where geopolitical and chronopolitical tensions are being played out – this also means that we are particularly sensitized to economies of justice that the war has rendered transparent. In this area of discourse which we share, certain economies have come to light, but it is the light of apparent contradiction. I shall take one crucial example.

We constitute a community of readers and speakers who have stressed time and again that the cost of war has drained the resources of AIDS research, or at least we have noticed that our friends with AIDS are not receiving the support they urgently require. We have wondered collectively and singly about the displacement of funds from health concerns to the demands of the military. It appears that there exists a contradiction between the external and internal needs of the United States. However, this is not a contradiction, nor a blind spot, nor even a fundamental displacement of a particular psychic investment. The lack of AIDS support and the war investment are part of the same experience of a national desire to the extent that the war was guided by a rhetoric of renewal and regeneration, in other words, the war was conducted entirely within the symbolic registers of fascistic health. In his essay entitled "Our History," French philosopher Jean-Luc Nancy has argued that an "ideology must be called 'fascist' in the general sense in which themes of spiritual and national regeneration, of the vigorous recovery of health through firmness and discipline, correspond to a fascist or fascistic vision of things."[4] What this means basically is that in the name of symbolic health, a unity of world that sees its image in wholesomeness and the project of renewal, we have waged war on what was repeatedly represented as degenerate, sickly, something that carried the threat of contagion. In this regard, America has been carrying out its newly transcendentalized project of killing the unwell, the contaminated. The enemy is imagined as being disorderly, inefficient, tactically illiterate, dysfunctional; and to a certain degree the projected solution, cybernetics, promises to overcome such instabilities.

The hygienic project has everything to do with establishing a new world order that consists in nothing less than purifying an imaginary – and real – territory, guaranteeing that it be proper, that it espouse values of propriety and property. The invisibility of the enemy inhabits this logic, which is essentially viral. Our war body has not only tested itself, but it has come out of this test site relatively intact, clean, healthy. This accounts for the other apparent contradiction – our insensible casualty rate, their massacre, our surgical strike, their bodies, our high-tech shoots, their blood. This was a translation, on a world-historical scale, of the AIDS test on which we scored HIV negative, because this was a safe war, run by the teleologic of what can provisionally be called "virtual reality" – which is almost an anagram of viral reality. Some of you may know that virtual comes from the Latin *virtus*, strength, manliness. Meanwhile, back at the Gulf, Americans have once again instituted an autoimmune laboratory. I wish to emphasize that I am equally analyzing the symbolic effects of the war according to the letter of the war, which is to say that I take the theater of operations, the rhetoric of surgery and other health metaphors quite seriously. I even take seriously the fact that the Bush family had its own private theater of thyroid operations, which, as if his disease had externalized itself, is called in medical terms a thyroid storm. Commander-in-chief of one storm, the then-president is internally dominated by another storm. This in itself suggests how difficult it is to locate the origin of the storm – inside the deserted presidential body, in the resurrection of Nazi terminology (storm troopers), or in the projections onto the desert.

On a less unconscious level of corporeal transmission, the desert has been conflated with a woman's body. This brings me to my next question. Why have we stormed the figure of a woman's body, why have we entered this mysterious legacy? Given the constraints of space, I can only point to where we might go in order to explore the imaginary contours of a feminine body that our forces stormed (of course you know that before they went up, fighter pilots were fed attack doses of pornography. This, together with drugs, would help them to drop on the feminized body of Iraq while at the same time we were protecting Kuwait from rape). If this were a seminar, I would ask you to turn your attention to Jacques Lacan's essay on "Aggressivity and Paranoia in Psychoanalysis," which is in *Ecrits*. Here you will find Lacan interpreting Melanie Klein's excellent work on the coordinates of original aggressivity. Through Melanie Klein we know the function of the imaginary primordial enclosure formed by the *imago* of the mother's body; through her we have the cartography of the mother's internal empire, the historical atlas of the intestinal divisions in which the *imagos* of the fathers and brothers ("real or virtual," says Lacan), in which the voracious aggression of the subject himself dispute their delirious (destructive) dominance over her sacred regions. What I would have to point out with regard to the particularity of the Gulf War, which may or may not be generalizable to other wars, is that the figure of the mother was always prominent, on both sides ("the mother of all battles" and so on), and that it was always understood that we were in a region of some originarity – the site of primordial aggression, the sacred origin of all culture. Because we were in a zone of primordial encounter, it was also read as a place of Armageddon and apocalyptic showdown. This was the end that was also to designate a beginning: the *new* world order. As the original war, it encompassed all the wars in modern history: the world wars, Vietnam, et cetera.

Because the war assumed this status as origin, the initiator of the new world order, and was being conducted in the womb and cradle of our civilization, it is not at all far-fetched to read with Lacan this war in its rapport to the subject's paranoiac mapping of the maternal body. A splinter of evidence in support of this view could be retrieved from the compulsive focus on the mothers who went to war. This insistence names the symptom – the mother's body – but in the mode of dis-avowal. Mother may have gone to war, but she was not the site of aggression; mother was finally on the map, but she was not the map itself or a conflictual site constituted by the imaginary. This leads us to ask more generally: What is the battlefield? What are its boundaries and symbolic localities? When does the battle-field take place? And how does it place us? What about the myth of the home front? And so on. In any case, Lacan in this difficult but crucial text establishes a link between space and aggressivity, which is to say that the domination of space is related to the narcissistic fear of damage to one's own body. In fact, he argues that the fear of death, the "absolute master" according to Hegel, is subordinate to the narcissistic fear of damage to one's own body. Aggressivity, as one of the inten-tional coordinates of the human ego, especially relative to the category of space (this includes real or virtual space), allows us to conceive of its role in modern neurosis. The preeminence of aggressivity in our civilization, Lacan adds, would be sufficiently demonstrated already by the fact that it is usually confused in "normal" morality with the virtue of strength. The glorification of strength as a social value is a sign of social devastation initiated on a planetary scale and justified by the image of a laissez-faire of the strongest predators. This condition should set off our psycho-alerts.

Now, the connectedness between virtual reality and the war was not always entirely evident to me. The promise of VR is immense, at times liberatory, and very careful in its articulated negotiations with metaphysics, technology, and play. I was initially perplexed because VR is something so new that it has only begun to display its existence; the war, on the other hand, seemed like something that ought to have been obsolesced, and in fact it was, though it did happen and it did tend to make claims for high-tech breakthroughs. This war incorporated many wars and was played out in a spectral battlefield: WWI (the gas masks), WWII (the calculated resurrection of Hitler), the Vietnam syndrome. These phantom wars that participated in the Gulf War even included the war we did not have with the Russians, or, for that matter, with the Martians. Can we live without an enemy? But if indeed there is something new about this war at a time of felt closure (most of us figured that the conditions for real war were vanishing, and that war games were a residual symptom of a history of battle), if we still feel that we are in a time of closure, then we have to recognize that closure is not the same thing as the end. Closure does not simply close a domain or an epoch: by tracing the limits of its possibilities, the closure also reaches the other side of its limit, exposing itself to its own exterior. In "Our History," Nancy has shown that there is no simple opposition of exteriority of the closure to the opening, and this is perhaps where VR comes into the picture.

A question that VR poses, in its full positivity, is where to locate the community. Because we are vanishing. In the absence of the polis, something like VR obligates us to pose ethical questions about contact, memory, the prosthetic subject, and it teaches us to dislocate our proper place.

There is no proper place: this includes ghettoes and kitchens, and all corresponding systems of the proper place. The politics of a room of one's own has to be rethought today, however enlightened it was yesterday. The question is a hard one, surpassing as it does the video game logic of good versus evil, winner and loser, presence and absence: can there be an atopicality of the community that nonetheless gathers, a community going nowhere, but ecstatic, a community of shattered egos, where the control towers come tumbling down, and where the other is genuinely anticipated? By this I also mean the other technologies.

Notes

1 See Timothy Druckrey, "Revenge of the Nerds: An Interview with Jaron Lanier," *Afterimage* (May 1991). Some of the other utterances that invite interpretation include: "This technology has the promise of transcending the body, depending on what you think a body is." "There's no object that could be less biological or messy. It doesn't have blood, it doesn't fart, it doesn't have eczema. The slick blackness of technology is a way of avoiding the messiness of the body. I think that's why sometimes you see more men associated with this technology than women. Men find themselves in a more desperate situation with the flight from death." "From a political point of view the clear precedent for virtual reality is the telephone." "I view VR as a fancy telephone in many ways." "The young generation who saw the political stakes in struggles over

representation . . . now they have to face up to its indeterminacy. Is there something like an ethics of technology?" "What I'm hoping the virtual reality technology will do is sensitize people to these subjective or experiential aspects of life and help them notice what a marvelous, mystical thing it is to communicate with another person."

2 John Barlow, "Life in the Data Cloud: Scratching Your Eyes Back In" (interview with Jaron Lanier), *Mondo 2000* (Summer 1990), p. 2. "The computer is a map you can inhabit. Which is very seductive. It is mostly seductive because you love what you have to struggle for, but it is also seductive because it makes you seem very powerful. So it is good for the ego . . . a way for people to get ecstatic and be with each other." While the ego remains a problem, I do wish to signal that being-with (*Mitsein*), ecstatic temporality, and being-called are crucial issues in the philosophy of Martin Heidegger. Lanier is also inclined to plug the telephone. "The telephone is a total win." If Lanier is unwilling to count the losses, and keeps tallying technology according to egological scoreboards, this *may* be traceable to the fact that his mother was a victim of destructive technologies and suffered the dehumanizing effects of the Nazi camps. While I do not feel that it is necessarily appropriate in this case to psychoanalyze VR's unconscious genesis, I have tried to configure these relations – the maternal function, technology, and the terroristic state – in *The Telephone Book: Technology, Schizophrenia, Electric Speech* (Lincoln: University of Nebraska Press, 1989).

3 Ibid., p. 49. Also see Adam Heilbrun, "Virtual Reality: An Interview with Jaron Lanier," *Whole Earth Review* (Fall 1989).

4 Jean-Luc Nancy, "Our History," *Diacritics* (Fall 1990), p. 20.

Part VI

Reading Digital Culture

Cyberspace is a fiction. Perhaps more than any other communication medium, the coherence of the Internet relies on a set of imaginary beliefs held together by neologisms, metaphors, and other tropes of language. How else could a jumble of coaxial cables, magnetic disks, computers, and phones become transformed in the popular mind into an adventureland catering to electronic homesteaders, netsurfers, and day-traders. The Internet gives one access to a virtual world, that in fact represents but a tiny fraction of the "real" world. It limits one to a perspective almost exclusively defined by United States-based technology and e-firms in which nearly everything relates to commercial enterprise. Because of its fictional character, what is said, written, and broadcast about cyberspace assumes tremendous importance in helping to foster critical understandings of its workings or to mystify them.

Given the youth of digital culture, much of its discourse exhibits a certain unselfconsciousness. This becomes apparent in tendencies toward ahistoricity, a lack of context, or simply an entrenched determination to say something "new." In popular media and advertising the intent of such rhetoric is often relatively obvious, as technology manufacturers and resellers seek to promote the latest model of this or that product. This is most clearly evident in the observations of Microsoft founder Bill Gates, whose vision of *The Road Ahead* turned out to be *Business @ The Speed of Thought*.[1] This is a view of life driven by ever-expanding consumption and corporate efficiency, rather than humanism or social values. But Gates is hardly alone. Digital culture's leading lifestyle publication, the San Francisco-based *Wired* magazine, has been promoting the concept of the "netizen" (citizen of the Internet) in a rhetoric of free-market boosterism and high-tech libertarianism, which projects an unmistakable message: join or be crushed by the weight of history and progress.

The message comes packaged in a variety of familiar narrative forms, proffering the digital world as a mythic frontier, an unexplored community, or a means of poetic return to origins. Certainly it takes little imagination to recognize the parallels between the unexplored territory of the cyberworld and the "new world" imagined by the colonizers of the modern era. This view of the Internet as primordial battleground can be seen as an extension of historical patterns of Enlightenment advance, a compulsive search for expansion and progress. In instances where the historic frontier is not directly evoked, one finds an allegorical substitute. As Frederic Jameson has pointed out, the "fiction" of science fiction is often simply a version of history projected into a distant future to make the present look bad.[2] Cyberspace is not so much a "new" idea as it is a repository for a variety of conventional ideologies disguised as novelty. In analytical terms, these scenarios set for the endless quests for dominance and control that can never be satisfied, and for that reason must be continually remembered and repeated.

It is precisely the familiarity of conventional formulations of class, gender, race, and technology that have made cyberspace so alluring to many people. This ethos of exploration, discovery, and conquest becomes manifest most explicitly in entities with name like the Electronic Frontier Foundation, an early Internet non-profit dedicated to preserving "freedom" of expression online. In this way cyberspace becomes yet another cultural form in which its representations (how it is perceived or thought about) can be viewed as a political position. And it is just this issue that is taken up by the contributors to this section. From the philosophical tracings by Cameron Bailey and Robert Markley to the more grounded readings by Katherine Hayles, Timothy Allen Jackson, and Vivian Sobchack, these essays "read" digital culture through the lenses of gender, education, race, social class, and critical theory, among other modes of analysis. The section ends with a consideration by Andrew Ross of the language of "smartness" that characterizes so much of digital culture. As an ensemble, these contributions point out the continuing need to scrutinize and question our understandings of this constantly changing medium. In doing so, they draw critical attention to society's unmet need for digital literacy.

Notes

1 Bill Gates, *The Road Ahead* (New York: Penguin Books, 1995); Bill Gates, *Business@The Speed of Thought* (New York: Warner Books, 1999).
2 Frederic Jameson, "Progress versus Utopia; Or, Can We Imagine the Future?," *Science Fiction Studies* 9, no. 2 (July 1982), pp. 147–58.

30

History, Theory, and Virtual Reality

Robert Markley

Robert Markley, "History, Theory, and Virtual Reality," in Robert Markley, ed., *Virtual Realities and their Discontents* (Baltimore: Johns Hopkins University Press, 1996), pp. 1–11. © 1996 Robert Markley.

Robert Markley is the Jackson Distinguished Chair of British Literature at West Virginia University and the author of *The Encyclopedia of Roses* (Barons, 1999) and *Fallen Languages: Crises of Representations in Newtonian England, 1660–1740* (Cornell, 1993). In this essay he applies a materialist analysis in critiquing the writing of Michael Benedikt, Larry McCaffrey, Marcos Novak, and Michael Heim, among others.

One of the ironies of our culture's fascination with virtual technologies is its fondness for consuming books and articles that proclaim the death of print culture – or its disappearance into the matrix. In one respect, the essays in this collection are dedicated to suggesting that the death of logocentrism has been greatly exaggerated. If cyberspace is the "consensual hallucination" that lies beyond the portals of virtual technologies, its means of generating that consent, as David Porush maintains in my anthology *Virtual Realities and their Discontents*, are alphabetic and mathematical schemes of representation at least three thousand years old.[1] The era of virtuality has been heralded by articles in mainstream news magazines (*Time*); special issues of scholarly journals, such as *South Atlantic Quarterly* and *Genders*; collections of essays from programmers and self-styled visionaries (*Cyberspace: First Steps*) as well as from – who else? – literary and cultural critics (*Storming the Reality Studio*; *Fiction 2000*); popularizations by journalists such as Howard Rheingold and Benjamin Woolley; and its own user's guide, *Mondo 2000*, something of a cross between *Rolling Stone* and *Mad* magazine.[2] Cyberspace, in short, is unthinkable without the print culture it claims to transcend. As Marshall McLuhan suggested in the 1960s, the content of any new medium is precisely the old medium that it has replaced; and so, in McLuhan's sense, we might say that cyberspace remains fixated on the traces of the word that it ostensibly renders obsolete.[3] It is, in part, a by-product of a tradition of metaphysics which, boats against the current, bears us back relentlessly to our past.

The indebtedness of cyberspace to its logocentric past is one of the threads that ties together the essays in my anthology *Virtual Realities and their Discontents.* Another is the contributors' insistence on distinguishing, in various ways, virtual technologies (the hardware and software that intervene in our bodies) from the abstraction "cyberspace." In an important sense, it is this awareness of the historical and cultural implication of virtual technologies in the dreamscape of Western thought that sets Katherine Hayles, Richard Grusin, David Brande, David Porush, Michelle Kendrick, and me apart from those writers who characterize cyberspace as a new, if not always brave, world. The more visionary proponents and analysts of cyberspace (many of whom are discussed in the chapters of my anthology) come to virtual technologies from a variety of backgrounds and perspectives, but they share the belief that cyberspace marks a revolutionary expansion – and liberation – of our senses of identity and reality. In contrast, the contributors to *Virtual Reality and Its Discontents* remain sceptical of a cyberspatial metaphysics that assumes, rather than questions, the revolutionary nature of virtual worlds and electronically mediated experience. In this respect, their analyses emphasize, albeit in different ways, that the division between cyberspace and virtual technologies reflects and reinscribes the oppositions of mind/body, spirit/matter, form/substance, and male/female that have structured Western metaphysics since Plato. To historicize and theorize virtual realities, then, is to enter into a wide-ranging investigation of technology, mathematics, economics, gender politics, and psychology that resists any simple sense of narrative or conceptual closure.

Writers on virtual technologies and cyberspace, whether proponents or sceptics, thus are drawn to the problem of definition: What, after all, counts as a virtual space? In recent years, cyberspace has become a catch-all term for everything from e-mail to GameBoy cartridges, as though each computer screen were a portal to a shadow universe of infinite, electronically accessible space. But beat to this airy thinness, cyberspace loses the specificity that supposedly distinguishes it as a breakthrough in human and cultural evolution. Michael Benedikt defines cyberspace as "a globally networked, computer-sustained, computer-accessed, and computer-generated, multidimensional, artificial, or 'virtual' reality."[4] Marcos Novak draws together a composite definition: "Cyberspace is a completely spatialized visualization of all information in global information processing systems, along pathways provided by present and future communication networks, enabling full copresence and interaction of multiple users, allowing input and output from and to the full human sensorium, permitting simulations of real and virtual realities, remote data collection and control through telepresence, and total integration and intercommunication with a full range of intelligent products and environments in real space." This hardwired universe of simulated experience, though, is more than the sum of its parts: "Cyberspace is a habitat of the imagination, a habitat for the imagination . . . the place where conscious dreaming meets subconscious dreaming, a landscape of rational magic, of mystical reason, the locus and triumph of poetry over poverty, of 'it-can-be-so' over 'it-should-be-so.' "[5] The transition from the rhetoric of technocorporatism to a romanticism filtered through *Star Trek* reruns is less abrupt than it seems. The rhetoric of cyberspace characteristically invokes the pleasure and power of an imaginative world made whole, as Novak's emphasis (drawn in part from cyberpunk novelist Bruce Sterling) on fullness, plenitude, and mystical unity suggests.

The crucial metaphors used to evoke cyberspace, then, are self-consciously holistic, transcendent, sublime; they attempt to describe our "full human sensorium" beyond Freudian repression or Marxian alienation, to liberate our "imagination" – "poetry" – from the constraints of material existence – "poverty." Even scientists who are dedicated to promoting virtual technologies in fields such as medicine drift into a metaphysically laden rhetoric that equates poetry with an escape from the history that has brought these technologies into being. The flight into an imaginary space collapses distinctions among technological innovation, artistic creativity, and politico-economic power. Richard M. Satava of the Advanced Research Projects Agency (and a major figure in the development of virtual technologies for laparoscopic surgery) declares that "the video monitor is [becoming] the portal into the entire world of information; this 'electronic interface' will bestow power beyond imagination."[6] Although it might be tempting to dwell on the militaristic overtones of Satava's rhetoric, the significant point about his pronouncement is that it describes the ends of virtual technologies – "The King is Dead" – in metaphors which suggest, as Porush contends, that our consciousness itself is always and already mediated by the interventions of print and number, neurotechnologies which mark it irrevocably as metaphoric. Paradoxically, Benedikt, Novak, and Satava demonstrate that virtual technologies must invoke "poetry" – a tradition of idealization and hierarchical values – in order to acknowledge and repress the sustenance they require from a contentious metaphysics. Cyberspace, then, can never separate itself from the politics of representation precisely because it is a projection of the conflicts of class, gender, and race that technology both encodes and seeks to erase. It does not transcend the dead body of the king – "the future," says Satava, "holds [the] promise of a virtual cadaver nearly indistinguishable from a real person"[7] – but reinscribes the profit-based politics of accelerating and intensifying interventions in living bodies.

Technology never escapes politics. The fiction of cyberspace is useful precisely to the extent that it allows its proponents to imagine an androcentric reality in which a threatening, messy, or recalcitrant (and invariably feminized) nature never intrudes. In this respect, cyberspace is consensual primarily in its insistence that technologically mediated experience can transcend the ecological and economic constraints that have shaped and continue to shape human culture. It offers the fantasy that the more technologically sophisticated our society becomes the less it has to worry about the distribution of wealth and resources. In his characterization of postindustrialism, Benedikt asserts that "the economic principles of material production and distribution in their classically understood forms – principles of property, wealth, markets, capital, and labor – are no longer sufficient to describe or guide the dynamics of our modern, complex, 'information' society."[8] The claims for the revolutionary nature of cyberspace, for its "mystical reason," are compelling to many because they offer a short cut to the land of plenty: in cyberspace, scarce resources become infinite possibilities. But as Brande argues in his essay, the transformation of modes of production and distribution does not mean that the problems of capitalism disappear; and, as Grusin suggests, simply invoking "information" as the evolutionary successor of "writing" does little to alter the politics of symbolic, or monetary, accumulation. One of the abiding fictions of cyberspace – of all technologies, really – is that it can cut rather than untie the knot of present-day problems. In this respect, cyberspace gives a new form to an age-old dream: that through our ingenuity humanity can devise products and riches in excess of the resources required to manufacture and maintain them.

A case in point: in November of 1994, I participated in GreenSpace, a real-time Virtual Reality link between the Human Interface Technology Laboratory at the Washington Technology Center in Seattle and the NICOGRAPH (Nippon Computer Graphics) trade show in Tokyo. The University of Washington weekly, *University Week*, described the trial run as follows:

> [Four] persons [two in Tokyo, two in Seattle] donned head-mounted video displays and came together in specifically created virtual meeting rooms equipped with either Occidental or Oriental furnishings [Mt. Ranier was visible in Tokyo; I sat in the cartoon graphic shadow of Mt. Fuji], suggesting that they traveled to the network's other shore. However, participants got the impression that everyone was in the same room sitting around the same conference table. They then played a short, interactive game in which creatures materialized that only can be captured with the cooperation of two or more participants using conventional hand-movement tracking devices.[9]

In reality (pardon the pun), I watched the digitalized face of one of my colleagues run in a loop through five facial expressions across a virtual table. Neither we nor the virtually present Japanese faces to our sides had any visible success in swatting the bouncing cartoon creatures into one of the four billiard-like pockets at the corners of the conference table. My experience of this "new era in teleconferencing" (funded, in part, by the Fujitsu Research Center in Japan) suggests that GreenSpace is more a political metaphor than a technological breakthrough. Even if the sound hookup had worked, I do not speak Japanese, and the "cooperation" that was supposed to take place was undone because all four of us were proprioceptively disoriented, a common experience in virtual worlds that lack force feedback mechanisms. If one imagines a future in which representatives of the institutions financing GreenSpace meet virtually to swat at Third World countries or redundant workers, virtual teleconferencing could easily put a dent in transoceanic travel for corporate executives. But this application of virtual technologies, it should be obvious, reinscribes rather than revolutionizes the economic power that advanced telecommunications represents. To make this statement is not to attack the potential of these technologies but to recognize that their content is the previous medium – in this instance, long distance communication – that it subsumes and recodes. The conference itself becomes the product to be disseminated rather than a means to an end. In GreenSpace, talk isn't cheap.

The unintended legacy of commodifying face-to-face conversation, though, may be to force our culture to assess the consequences of its investments in a dualistic metaphysics that divorces mind from body and that sees technology as a mere tool to be manipulated rather than as a process that disrupts and reconfigures whatever we take to be "essentially" human. As a projection of the imaginary spaces that structure our self-perceptions, our self-consciousness, cyberspace relies for its symbolic coherence on a narrative logic of progress which underwrites and transcends individual agency or intention.[10] It offers itself as the logical *telos* of technological progress. To create a history of and for cyberspace, writers such as Howard Rheingold and Benjamin Woolley describe key episodes in the development of computer technology, link them in a more-or-less causal sequence, and then extend this narrative into an imagined future. If we read our recent computer-aided past as the progress of protovirtual technologies, then it becomes easy to imagine Virtual Reality as the logical outcome of our efforts, the fulfillment of a quest for a postindustrial, postmodern transcendence, the ascent to a Leibnizian future in which the body (suitably dematerialized) becomes indistinguishable from its idealized simulation.[11]

In its quest to find a suitable past from which virtual realities can claim descent, Rheingold's *Virtual Reality* details the history of interactive technologies, ranging from Morton Heilig's Sensorama in the 1950s, to video games, to experimental programs in California and North Carolina. As his narrative unfolds, Rheingold crisscrosses the country, talking to computer programmers, entrepreneurs, and groupies, including veterans of the retro-sixties subculture such as Timothy Leary and Jerry Garcia, who is credited with one of the dust-jacket blurbs on the back cover of *Virtual Reality*: "They made LSD illegal. I wonder what they're going to do about this stuff." Woolley's *Virtual Worlds* is, if anything, more eclectic: intermixed with histories of computing, flight simulators, hypertext, and graphic displays are thumbnail sketches of numerous modernist and postmodernist thinkers – from Leary, to Fredric Jameson, to Roland Barthes, to Jean Baudrillard. As his subtitle, *A Journey in Hype and Hyperreality*, suggests, Woolley analyzes the potential of Virtual Reality in the generic form of a travelogue, a picaresque account of various approaches to simulation and simulacra, to the redefinition of "reality" at the end of the twentieth century. For Rheingold and Woolley, the history of interactive technologies is necessarily inclusive. Because "Virtual Reality" seeks to mimic the complexity of proprioceptive experience, it becomes an imperialistic metaphor, a textual black hole, that encourages Rheingold and Woolley to include anything they want in their narratives. Ironically, they demonstrate that Virtual Reality remains a semiotic fiction: to immerse oneself in a fully credible "reality," one needs to imagine a simulated world every bit as complex as the "real" world it tries to represent. This endless expanse of imagined terrain, as Porush suggests, is the metaphysical ghost haunting postmodern technologies.

Proponents of virtual technologies, of course, argue that such dualisms can be overcome or that cyberspace represents an evolution beyond the opposition of physics and metaphysics. Benedikt, for example, suggests that cyberspace mediates between the ethereal and the concrete; it describes, he contends, "a new niche for a realm that lies between the . . . worlds" of thought and body.[12] But even if we see cyberspace as a form of complex mediation within the traditions of Western science, metaphysics, and economics, it does not transcend the problems of materiality, embodiment, or capital. In this regard, to offer a critique of cyberspace is to engage in a multivalent exploration of the values and assumptions of a dualism which are presented as "natural" conditions of human existence, of an ideology of a revolutionary change in consciousness brought about by new forms of technological intervention, and of the political problems posed by limited access to new and expensive technologies. Important challenges to the politics of information technologies have emerged in recent years, even as Jerry Garcia has been enlisted to portray Virtual Reality as a countercultural phenomenon.[13] What the contributors to *Virtual Realities and Their Discontents* suggest is that this political critique of cyberspace cannot be limited to the problems of access but must engage in a sceptical treatment of the rhetoric of the "new" that is endemic to both academic and popular writing on cyberspace, postmodernism, and late capitalism. The blind spot of many critics of virtual technologies lies in their tacit acceptance of progress as natural, as inevitable, and their casual assumption that we are living in revolutionary times in which technology intervenes in our subjectivity in ways undreamt of before the late twentieth century. This is the approach of such philosophers as Michael Heim, who traces the morphogenesis of cyberspace back to Leibniz's monadology, of graphic artists such as Nicole Stenger, and of educators such as Meredith Bricken.[14] To be sure, these writers recognize that political problems exist in terms of access to cyberspace, but they limit the nature of those problems – accepting the "revolutionary" nature of interventionist technologies, then suggesting that we need to find ways to time-share our rides on the whirlwind.

If Virtual Reality is already a battleground for control of the cyborg as metaphor and as moneymaker, its battle lines are multiple and fractured, and the contending forces are characterized by shifting alliances and conflicting investments. Cyberspace is irrevocably marked by competing values and assumptions about reality and subjectivity, by previous political struggles to naturalize and resist particular constructions of reality. But this recognition is only the beginning of an analysis of the era of virtuality. As cultural critics of science, we need to familiarize ourselves with the technological innovations described six times a year in *CyberEdge*, "The World's Leading Newsletter of Virtual Reality"; we need to explore the venture capitalist realm of such companies as High Techsplanations, Immersion Corporation, and Boston Dynamics, which are now marketing surgical simulation equipment with force feedback mechanisms; and, most importantly, we need to recognize that there are potential allies as well as antagonists who work within the complicated webs of technology and capital that define the business of Virtual Reality.[15] It is only by understanding virtual technologies within the histories that cyberspace seeks to deny or transcend that we can begin to dream a different kind of "real."

Notes

1   William Gibson, *Neuromancer* (New York: Bantam, 1984), p. 7.

2   "Cyberpunk!" *Time*, February 8, 1993; *South Atlantic Quarterly* 92 (1993); *Genders* 18 (1993); Michael Benedikt, ed., *Cyberspace: First Steps* (Cambridge, MA.: MIT Press,

1991); Larry McCaffery, ed., *Storming the Reality Studio: A Casebook of Cyberpunk and Postmodern Science Fiction* (Durham, NC: Duke University Press, 1991); George Slusser and Thomas Shippey, eds., *Fiction 2000* (Athens: University of Georgia Press, 1992); Howard Rheingold, *Virtual Reality* (New York: Simon & Schuster, 1991); Benjamin Woolley, *Virtual Worlds: A Journey in Hype and Hyperreality* (New York: Penguin, 1992).

3   Marshall McLuhan, *Understanding Media: The Extensions of Man* (New York: New American Library, 1964); *The Medium Is the Message* (New York: Random House, 1967).

4   Benedikt, *Cyberspace*, p. 122.

5   Marcos Novak, "Liquid Architecture in Cyberspace," in ibid., pp. 225, 226.

6   Richard M. Satava, "Medicine 2001: The King Is Dead," in Richard M. Satava, Karen Morgan, Hans B. Sieburg, Rudy Mattheus, and Jens P. Christensen, eds., *Interactive Technology and the New Paradigm for Healthcare* (Amsterdam: IOS Press, 1995), p. 335.

7   Ibid., p. 337.

8   Benedikt, *Cyberspace*, p. 121.

9   *University Week*, November 17, 1994, p. 1.

10 See Larry Laudan, "Progress of Rationality? The Prospects for a Normative Naturalism," *American Philosophical Quarterly* 24 (1987), esp. p. 28; and Joseph Rouse, "Philosophy of Science and the Persistent Narratives of Modernity," *Studies in the History and Philosophy of Science* 22 (1991), esp. pp. 157–62.

11 Within a week of the initial appearance of the article included below (in the fall 1994 issue of *Configurations*), I received a half-dozen letters or e-mail messages from computer programmers, mathematicians, and one literary theorist, all of whom questioned my characterization of Leibniz. To reply to their queries would require another article (at least) and take us deep into the heart of a debate about the ways in which "the body" has been celebrated in and erased from both Western philosophy and recent cultural criticism. In brief, as I suggest below, Leibniz has emerged as the guru of cyberspatial metaphysics precisely because his monadology offers a means to preserve a logic of simulation in which an embodied individual can project herself as a kind of seemingly pure desire into cyberspace: agency without consequences. In a provocative move, Michelle Kendrick, in her essay in my collection, argues that it may be the sceptical philosopher of experience, David Hume, rather than Leibniz who offers us the ur-logic of virtual technologies. In a Humean framework, virtuality emerges not as a space in which to distill and conserve a holistic identity but as a testing ground for a series of noncausal, seemingly arbitrary experiences whose connection to "reality" remains always problematic, always in need of articulation. Virtual Reality is to "real" reality, then, as a surgical simulation is to an actual operation.

12 Benedikt, *Cyberspace*, p. 124.

13 See, for example, Gary Chapman, "Taming the Computer," *South Atlantic Quarterly* 92 (1993), pp. 681–712; and Kathleen Biddick, "Humanist History and the Haunting of Virtual Worlds: Problems of Memory and Rememoration," *Genders* 18 (1993), pp. 47–66.

14 Michael Heim, *The Metaphysics of Cyberspace* (New York: Oxford University Press, 1993); Nicole Stenger, "Mind Is a Leaking Rainbow," in Benedikt, *Cyberspace*, pp. 49–58; and Meredith Bricken, "Virtual Worlds: No Interface to Design," in ibid., pp. 363–82.

15 See, for example, Jonathan R. Merril, "Surgery on the Cutting Edge: Virtual Reality Applications in Medical Education," *Virtual Reality World*, November–December 1993, pp. 17–21.

31

The Seductions of Cyberspace

N. Katherine Hayles

N. Katherine Hayles, "The Seductions of Cyberspace," in Verena Andermatt Conley et al., eds., *Rethinking Technologies* (Minneapolis: University of Minnesota Press, 1993), pp. 173–90.

N. Katherine Hayles is Professor of English at the University of California, Los Angeles, who writes about the relationship of science and humanism in technological systems. The author of numerous books, her most recent work is *How We Became Posthuman: Virtual Bodies in Cybernetics, Literature, and Informatics* (Chicago: University of Chicago, 1999). This essay offers a probing examination of the literary and critical literature of the 1990s concerning cyberspace.

> Technology is literary criticism carried on by other means.
>
> *Bruno Latour*

Hans Moravec has a dream. A roboticist at Carnegie-Mellon University, Moravec wants to download the information stored in the human brain and transfer it to a computer. In his view information is information, whether stored in silicon-based hardware, disk software, or cranial wetware. Once the transfer is complete, the body becomes disposable, an outmoded artifact to be discarded along with the limitations of space and time that it necessitated. Moravec is not crazy; he is head of Carnegie-Mellon's Mobile Robot Laboratory. And he is not alone. His dream is shared by many others, appearing with variations in fields as diverse as cryogenics, genetic engineering, and nanotechnology.[1] Ed Regis has identified this dream as the "desire for perfect knowledge and total power. The goal [is] complete omnipotence: the power to remake humanity, earth, the universe at large. If you're tired of the ills of the flesh, then *get rid of the flesh*; we can *do* that now."[2]

Perhaps not since the Middle Ages has the fantasy of leaving the body behind been so widely dispersed through the population, and never has it been so strongly linked with existing technologies. The conjunction with technology is crucial. In its contemporary formulation, the point is not merely to leave the body but to reconstitute it as a technical object under human control. The essential transformation is from biomorphism to technomorphism. The transformation has important implications for every area of contemporary culture, including literature and literary criticism. It is not for nothing that we speak of the body of a text and the corpus of literature. Our sense of our physical bodies, their capabilities and limitations, boundaries and extensions, deeply informs both the objects and the codes of representation. Less clear are the implications of these mappings. In this last decade of the twentieth century, elisions between physical and textual bodies are entangled with complex mediations that merge actual and virtual realities, ideological and technological constructions.

The issues are joined in the emerging technologies of cyberspace (also called virtual reality, VR, and artificial reality). Assuming various forms, these technologies splice a human subject into a cybernetic circuit by putting the human sensorium in a direct feedback loop with computer data banks. VR breaks the barrier of the screen, opening the high-dimensional space beyond to sensory as well as cognitive habitation by the user. With VR you don't just *see* data banks; you can sit down on them and watch the river of information flow by. Or you can plunge into the river. Turning Heraclitus on his head, Michel Serres has asserted that flows are more constant than the material world that expresses and embodies them.[3] The river remains the same, while the banks constantly erode and change. Body cells change and die; it is the flow of energy and information through the organism that maintains continuity. No man steps twice into the same river not because the river changes, but because he does. These inversions are consistent with virtual reality, for they figure the flow of information within systems as more determinative of identity than the materiality of physical structures. Plunging into the river of information implies recognizing that you *are* the river.

Baudrillard has written about the implosion of cultural space that takes place when the copy no longer refers to an original but only to another copy.[4] Defining a simulacrum as a copy with no original, Baudrillard imagines a precession of simulacra (*precession* is a mathematical term denoting the gyration of a sphere when spinning under torque, as when a top slows down and begins to wobble). The spinning metaphor is appropriate, for in the circular dynamic in which copy replaces copy until all vestige of the original is lost, reference is supplanted by reflexivity. Virtual reality exemplifies the implosion Baudrillard describes. When the technologically enhanced body is joined in a sensory feedback loop with the simulacrum that lives in RAM, it is impossible to locate an originary source for experience and sensation. The "natural" body, unmodified by technology, is displaced by a cybernetic construct that consists of body-plus-equipment-plus-computer-plus-simulation.

Within the cultural space that VR occupies, the arrows of signification do not all point the same way. The double hermeneutic of suspicion and revelation that Fredric Jameson advocates is appropriate to interrogate its multiple significances.[5] The drive for control that was a founding impulse for cybernetics (defined by Norbert Wiener as the science of control and communication) is evident in the simulations of virtual reality, where human senses are projected into a computer domain whose underlying binary/logical structure defines the parameters within which action evolves. At the same time, by denaturalizing assumptions about physicality and embodiment, cybernetic technologies also contribute to liberatory projects that seek to bring traditional dichotomies and hierarchies into question. Ironically asserting, "I would rather be a cyborg than a goddess," Donna Haraway sees the cyborg as offering feminists a metaphor that cuts through the Gordian knot tying woman together with nature, thereby freeing us from the burdens that conjunction imposes.[6]

There are, however, new burdens imposed by constructing woman (and man) as cyborg. The turn is characteristic of virtual reality, for the space within which it operates is intensely ambiguous. For every solution it offers, it raises new problems; for every threat that erupts, new potentialities also arise. Countering the fetishistic drive for control is the spontaneous, free-flowing collectivity that emerges when multiple players in virtual reality collaborate to build a world. Offsetting the creation of technosubjects is VR's ability to leapfrog over abstraction, returning to the reconstituted subject the rich diversity of a sensorium that includes visual, kinesthetic, and tactile experience. Compensating for the underlying machine logic that, for all its versatility, is the Procrustean bed into which human perception must fit is the thrill of creating and exploring virtual worlds.

The point is not to resolve these ambiguities – a quixotic adventure, since they will not yield to theoretical pronouncements alone – but to use them to understand the cultural forces driving the technologies forward and determining how they will be used. As Bill Nichols argues, we should ask "what tools are at our disposal and what conceptions of the human do we adhere to that can call into question the reification, the commodification, the patterns of mastery and control" that are simultaneously reinforced and exposed by these technologies.[7] To the extent they are reinforced, the patterns are more difficult to break; to the extent they are exposed, they become subject to analysis and therefore to change. Moreover, the technologies themselves can be – already are – agents of change. This is the double edge of virtual reality's revolutionary potential: to expose the presuppositions underlying the social formations of late capitalism and to open new fields of play where the dynamics have not yet rigidified and new kinds of moves are possible. Understanding these moves and their significances is crucial to realizing the technology's constructive potential.

Full-Body Processing

The technological development of cyberspace began, as did so much else, in the 1960s. As early as 1968, Ivan E. Sutherland at the University of Utah had the idea of creating a head-mounted display that connected a user directly to a computer. The device was so heavy it had to be suspended from the ceiling, but its possibilities were enticing. Other lines of development ran through Myron Krueger, who did a dissertation on artificial reality in the late 1960s at the University of Wisconsin, and Fred Brooks at the University of North Carolina.[8] Krueger's vision differed from Sutherland's because he wanted participants to be able to move freely, unhampered by heavy equipment. His approach used sensing devices to determine a participant's position and body movements, which were then fed into a computer to create interactive graphic displays. By 1985 the distance between the two approaches had diminished considerably. The technology was available to miniaturize the head display, making it a portable helmet rather than a dangling behemoth. By then military and government agencies had picked up on the idea. Convinced of the potential, NASA earmarked several million dollars for cyberspace projects. The U.S. Air Force budgeted a similar amount for its ongoing Super Cockpit project, which uses virtual reality simulations to direct the pilot's interactions with the aircraft. Video games provided models for the simulation programs. When William Gibson coined the term "cyberspace" in *Neuromancer* (1984), the novel that sparked the cyberpunk literary movement, he was working from a sense he had gotten from video game freaks that a space existed behind the computer screen that was as interesting as, or more interesting than, the space in front of it.[9]

The technology took a quantum leap forward in the late 1980s. Stimulated by reading *Neuromancer*, John Walker of Autodesk, a software company specializing in computer-assisted design (CAD) packages, issued a white paper calling for a major investment in cyberspace software. Arguing that the screen was the next barrier to be broken, Walker defined a cyberspace system as "a three-dimensional domain in which cybernetic feedback and control occur."[10] Somewhat earlier, VPL had begun to take off, a company devoted to virtual reality technologies and headed by Jaron Lanier, the dreadlocked guru of VR, who also is a shrewd businessman. VPL found a market for its products in the video game business, designing the PowerGlove for Nintendo. The company also developed virtual reality software and paraphernalia, including a stereo vision helmet and the Data-Glove, a more sophisticated and interactive version of the PowerGlove.

The idea behind the technologies is to create a feedback loop between the user's sensory system and the cyberspace domain, using real-time interactions between physical and virtual bodies. In one version, the player's movements and reactions are monitored through such input devices as stereo-vision helmets and data gloves. Flex your fingers in VPL's DataGlove and the simulacrum representing you in cyberspace moves to pick up the object you see in the helmet's monitor. Glance around and the virtual perspective changes accordingly, creating with a slight time lag the scene you see in the helmet's stereovisual field. Turn the bars of your cyberbike and the puppet's bike zooms in a different direction. Alternatively, you may turn your bars to avoid the car that comes whizzing toward the puppet. Stimuli go in both directions; what happens to the puppet has an impact on your sensory field, just as what you do affects the puppet. The puppet is a version of and a container for the self. It is, as Randall Walser, a senior programmer at Autodesk, writes, "a vehicle for your mind. Looking through the puppet's eyes, your sense of self merges with it, so that . . . you are the puppet and the puppet is you."[11]

One advantage of cyberspace over ordinary reality is its flexibility. Puppets may be directed by artificial as well as human intelligences, creating a three-dimensional field of play in which silicon- and protein-based life forms interact. It is also possible to switch one's viewpoint between puppets or invest it in a "spirit," a disembodied space that represents the point from which the user interacts with the cyberspace environment. In VPL's "Reality Built for Two," a game of cybertag, one strategy is to hide in the other player's head. Potential users of virtual reality include architects, who can stroll around the inside of buildings before they are built; astronauts, who can use the cyberspace puppets to direct robots outside spacecraft; and fitness club instructors, who can interface exercise equipment with cyberspace to create adventures that will spice up their patrons' exercise routines.

Cyberspace can also be used to cope with that affliction of the postmodern age, *too much information*. Creating direct feedback loops between data and human senses allows information to be processed holistically, much as environmental cues are. Michael Spring asks us to imagine entering a virtual reality library, forming a research question, and watching as colors and configurations change in response to the question.[12] Corroborating evidence appears in hot colors, contrary facts in cool. Lines appear linking data formations and indicating their relationships to one another. Data directly relevant to the question are connected by heavy dark lines, secondary data by broken lines. As another question is asked, or the first question rephrased, colors and configurations change accordingly. The idea, Spring notes, is to "suggest visual metaphors for mental models of how the idea space is organized."[13] A similar proposal made by Scott Fisher would enable a user wearing a helmet and bodysuit to touch a screen and arrange blocks of data in a projected three-dimensional space. Direct experience, Fisher writes, "has the advantage of coming through the totality of our internal processes – conscious, unconscious, visceral and mental – and is most completely tested and evaluated by our nature."[14] VR allows the user to draw on that totality in ways that most information-processing systems do not.

Spring's model emphasizes vision and Fisher's kinesthesia, but the reasoning behind them is the same. Why throw away the advantages bestowed by millennia of evolution to dwell in the realms of abstract concepts when we have the capability to use full-body processing? In the collaboration that virtual reality sets up between the human sensorium and computer memory, the sophisticated and nuanced response to environmental cues that has enabled human beings to dominate the planet is joined with the power of computers to store, process, and display information. It represents, some would say, the best of both worlds – or perhaps the next leap forward in technobioevolution. From the protein-based life form come the flexibility and sophistication of a highly complex analogical processor that includes sensory, unconscious, and conscious components; from the silicon-based entity come massive storage and combinatorial ability, rapid retrieval, and reliable replication.

That the subjectivity that emerges from this joining is a cyborg rather than a human can scarcely be missed, although neither Fisher nor Spring comments on the fact. Already about 10 percent of the U.S. population are cyborgs in the technical sense, including people with electronic pacemakers, prosthetic limbs, hearing aids, drug implants, and artificial joints. VR would substantially increase this percentage. If the extent to which one has become a cyborg is measured in terms of impact on psychic/sensory organization rather than difficulty of detaching parts, VR users – cybernauts, some writers prefer to call them – are more thoroughly cyborgs than are people with pacemakers. The reorganization of subjectivity that VR effects is not, of course, limited only to this technology. As William Gibson noticed several years ago, video game players and word processing users are also spliced into cybernetic circuits with their machines, with resulting reorganization of their neural networks.[15] VR extends rather than initiates this reorganization, making explicit transformations that have been under way for some time.

Imagine walking into a virtual reality library and asking, "How many of the human populations of the planet are cyborgs?" A hologram of the earth appears before you, with hot colors indicating areas of high density, cool colors indicating relatively unmodified humans (your own suit, of course, is colored very hot). Now ask, "Which of the human populations on the planet are absorbing more than their fair share of the planet's resources?" Would the hologram change? The scenario implies that issues of class, race, and gender are likely to be replayed in a different key, in which the mark of privilege is access to cyborg modifications. In a time of rapid realignments in cultural formations, when the populations of the planet are extremely heterogeneous with respect to the coming changes, questions of how cyborgs relate to unmodified humans will be central.

A window onto these issues is opened by Joseph Henderson, a physician associated with the Interactive Media Laboratory at Dartmouth Medical School. Programs already exist that make use of VR for medical purposes. In Electronic Cadaver, VR interactions are used to simulate dissection, so that medical students can move scalpels and get appropriate kinesthetic and visual feedback without the necessity of formaldehyded bodies. Henderson describes Traumabase, another VR medical training program. Traumabase works with a multimedia data base generated during the Vietnam War on medical casualties, including 200,000 sheets of paper, 50,000 slides, hours of audio recordings and film, and the videodisc history *Vietnam: The 10,000 Day War*. Henderson points out the difficulties inherent in accessing this much information; conventional programs do not allow users to "interact with data and information in the same way we think, moving rapidly and linking item to item, idea to idea, analysis to analysis."[16] Traumabase uses VR techniques to create an information matrix that can be "explored and navigated" to reveal "expected and unexpected patterns" of "location and severity of wounds, wound pattern clustering, wound pattern frequencies, survival patterns." An "interactive process of discovery can result" that uses "the very powerful combination of eye, brain, and hand. This can provide a 'visceral' sense or analysis of what the data have to tell us."[17]

Henderson links this "visceral" processing with a more fully human reaction to what the data represent, contrasting it with traditional scientific analyses:

> In the interest of "rational" or "scientific" decision-making we isolate the quantifiable and formulate models. A danger is that the abstraction can become the reality, and real world decisions can be made without due regard to the real world. However, in this system abstractions (the matrix) can be linked to increasingly concrete and emotionally powerful forms of information, to the realities of seeing people and hearing their stories. With this kind of approach we can involve the heart as well as the mind.[18]

The dichotomy between abstract analysis and the "real world" that the passage constructs elides the difference between actual and virtual realities. Seeing a cybernetically reconstructed body and hearing a voice recording slides into seeing a wounded man and hearing him scream. The elision is not trivial. Granted that the VR reconstruction is laden with more sensory information than statistics, there is still a chasm separating the virtual simulation and the physical reality of mangled bodies.

The complexity of the issues precludes simple resolution. Henderson is certainly correct in contrasting statistical abstraction with the VR simulation's greater emotional impact. Underlying this contrast, however, is the reconstruction of subjectivity that VR implies. Being able to occupy a virtual space implies that one can have the benefits of physicality without being bound by its limitations. One of the most emotionally charged of these limitations is mutilation or death of the physical body. The privileged position that virtual reality bestows upon the subject marks a difference between him or her and others who cannot enter this space, specifically those wounded or killed in the war. Their simulacra enter the virtual space only to testify to their inability to reconstitute themselves as virtual subjects removed from the perils of physicality. The very sensory stimulation that Henderson sees as constituting an empathic bond between victim and user rein-stitutes difference in another register. The Traumabase user may not, of course, consciously recognize this difference. Its effect would be even more powerful if registered below the level of conscious awareness.

Eros and the Cyborg

The problematic relations between sense and empathy, virtual user and physical object, hint at how psychic and social life may be reorganized when virtual reality comes into widespread use. The possibilities are as diverse as the human imagination. One scenario imagines virtual parties, where the participants never meet face-to-face but interact through their cyberspace surrogates. Randal Walser writes that the cyberspace user, "unconstrained by physical space," will begin "to work, play, learn and exercise in magical new worlds."[19] The essence of this "magic" is the construction of the body as an *absent signifier*. After visiting VPL, John Perry Barlow reported, "It's like having your everything amputated."[20]

Nowhere are the problematic effects of VR clearer than in the realm of the erotic. Barlow remarks that he has been through "eight or ten Q. & A. sessions on Virtual Reality and I don't remember one where sex didn't come up." "This is strange," he muses. "I don't know what to make of it, since, as things stand right now, nothing could be more disembodied or insensate than the experience of cyberspace."[21] In another sense, the evocation of the erotic is anything but strange. Bruce Clarke has pointed out that the violation or dissolution of body boundaries is inherently erotic; the same observation has been made by writers as diverse as Ovid, Saint Teresa, and the Marquis de Sade.[22]

The juxtaposition of eroticism, violated taboos, and modified bodies helps to explain why the high-tech world of the cyborg should so frequently take on a Gothic tinge. In Vernon Vinge's "True Names" (1981), often identified as the original cyberspace story, castles and dragons populate the landscape of the Other Planet, a consensual space created when humans strap on electrodes to interface with each other and artificial intelligences through computer networks.[23] Once on the Other Planet, the user's consciousness is manifested through whatever form he or she desires. One appears as a beautiful red-haired woman; another as a type-writer. The Gothic landscape and creatures that surround these forms are more than quaint anachronisms. Rather, they serve as tropes that map complex cultural formations onto the technomorphisms unique to the twentieth century.

We can trace the mapping by considering the mingling of magic and techno-morphism signified by the title. In a preface, Vinge explains that he thought of "True Names" after reading Ursula LeGuin's Earthsea trilogy.[24] Central to LeGuin's trilogy is the belief, common to magical traditions from fairy tales to voodoo, that knowing someone's true name gives one power over that person. In Vinge's narrative, knowing someone's true name means discovering that person's prosaic everyday identity, along with his or her social security number and, most important, home address. Whereas in LeGuin the true name's power derives from the conflation of signified with signifier, in Vinge it comes from being able to locate the physical body, with all of its frailties and vulnerabilities, from which consciousness emanates. The conflation here is not of name and thing, but of biomorphism and technomorphism.

The Gothic allusions reinforce a homology also constructed through action and plot: as signifier is to signified, biomorph is to technomorph. Through the homology the body becomes a gesture pointing toward the "real thing" rather than the thing itself. The reality is the technomorph, the body an atavistic vestige that functions as an Achilles heel, limiting the technomorph's power. It comes as no surprise at the story's end when one of the characters chooses to transfer her mind into a computer. Shedding the Achilles' heel of her physicality bestows immortality upon her. It also allows her to assume the privileged role of guardian to humankind's impending transformation into technomorphs. It is a dream Hans Moravec would recognize – and not only a dream: increasingly, a technology as well.

In the same issue of *Mondo 2000* as Barlow's puzzlement over why VR and eroticism should so often go together, Howard Rheingold has an article that reveals how powerfully the absence of physicality can interact with eroticism to form fantasies deeply characteristic of our cultural moment. Rheingold envisions a technology that he calls "teledildonics"; he writes:

> Before you climb into a suitably padded chamber and put on your headmounted display, you slip into a lightweight – eventually, one would hope diaphanous – body-suit. It would be something like a body stocking, but with all the intimate snugness of a condom. Embedded in the inner surface of the suit, using a technology that does not yet exist, is an array of intelligent effectors. These effectors are ultra-tiny vibrators of varying degrees of hardness, hundreds of them per square inch, that can receive and transmit a realistic sense of tactile presence in the same way the visual and audio displays transmit a realistic sense of visual and auditory presence.[25]

The idea is to plug the bodysuit into a telephone that has a visual screen on which you and your communicant are displayed. The information coming over the telephone interacts with the bodysuit effectors to provide kinesthetic and tactile sensations appropriate to the visual and audio messages. The result, Rheingold intimates, is the ultimate safe sex.

The teledildonic fantasy illustrates how the body as absent signifier plays into the eroticism of metamorphosis. The body is transformed into a technomorphism not only through the visual display but also through the kinesthetic sensations that reinforce, in a different sensory loop, the audio transmissions. The metamorphosis is not into a different biological form but into the cyborg that results from splicing together the physical and virtual bodies. The cybernetic long-distance coupling between communicants replays on a different level the reconstitution of body boundaries that has already taken place through the technology. Further reinforcing the fantasy, and close to the surface, is a strong anxiety about the perils of physicality, especially AIDS. Add to this the growing suspicion among the population that time-release environmental poisons are making physicality an impractical state to inhabit, and the appeal of virtual reality is obvious.

So, too, are its dangers. Establishing a dialectic between actual and virtual objects, VR invites a hierarchy to be set up between them. If we can believe what our writers are telling us, the vectors will run from virtual to actual, privileging computer construct over physical body. Virtual reality is not the only factor determining this order. Also contributing are other technologies that make the body into a commodity, from organ transplant depositories (significantly called "banks") to cosmetic surgeries. As the body increasingly is constructed as a commodity to be managed, designed, and parceled out to deserving recipients, pressure builds to displace identity into entities that are more flexible, easier to design, less troublesome to maintain.[26]

Gibson's *Neuromancer* illustrates how the technologies of informatics and body management come together to create a world where the virtual body is the "real thing," the physical body a mere substitute. This is a world of fast burnout, generation gaps between sixteen- and twenty-year-olds, investment in styles that change overnight. Styles are, moreover, expressed not only through clothing, but also through designer drugs, facial and full-body surgery, cybernetic splices into the human neurosystem of computer chips, and various other kinds of sensory interfaces. Commercial products, mentioned by name, are scattered all over the surface of this text, from high-tech computers to the latest body modifications. The same impatience shown toward an outmoded computer is directed toward unreconstructed bodies, from the protagonist's disdain of his own body to the women who are programmed through computer interfaces to act as prostitutes while their minds are parked elsewhere. They are called, significantly, "meat puppets."

Neuromancer enunciates a new axis along which wealth and power will operate, as they already operate along the axes of gender, race, and class. Behold the axis of physicality. The privileged end is the virtual, the stigmatized end the physical. Having an unmodified body will be like having a working-class accent; it will mark you as cannon fodder for the system. Body politics, already well articulated within feminist theory, will mean not only the imbrication of the body in gendered structures, but also a politics of physicality shaped by the technologies of technomorphism and informatics, including computer simulations,

cybernetics, genetic engineering, organ transplants, bioactive drugs, and reconstructive surgery.

Although the terrain on which these struggles will take place is largely
unmapped, some of the possibilities have been envisioned in contemporary fiction.
Tom DeHaven's *Freaks Amour*, an underground classic, records the struggles
of mutants to become "norms."[27] Victims of the fallout from a mysterious
radioactive blast in New Jersey, they dream of synthetic skin and full-body surgery
that will restore them to invisibility and social acceptance. At least some do.
Others argue that freakishness ought to be embraced, worn as a badge of honor
in the fight against the power structures responsible for the blast – which, it
turns out, are the same forces who plan to co-opt the hallucinogenic mutigens
the blast has created to escape from the planet. First they use technology to poison
the planet, then they develop it further to escape from the planet they have
poisoned.

The reasoning reveals why body politics is at the center of contestations for
power at the century's end. Only a small minority – if indeed any – of the planet's
population will be able to escape from the state of physicality that most of us will
continue to inhabit. The fantasy that escape is possible authorizes people to believe
that they will be among the chosen few, that we will not have to continue to live
with the messes we have created. Since cleaning up those messes may be impossible
(how will we repair the damage to the ozone layer?), the need to believe that
escape is possible is very strong. To the extent that cyberspace plays into this
fantasy, it contributes to a continuing unwillingness to face problems that are
not going to go away. In some contexts, leaving the body behind equates to the
belief that if the problems won't go away from us, perhaps we can go away from
the problems. Is it necessary to insist that nothing could be further from the
truth?

The Body Zone

Marked bodies, the longing for invisibility, stigmata that also become sources
of strength – the themes are familiar, running from Ellison's *Invisible Man* to
Philip K. Dick's *The Three Stigmata of Palmer Eldritch* to Katherine Dunn's *Geek
Love*. The continuities suggest how the new technologies will extend and complicate body politics, as well as how dynamics already in play will be mapped
onto the simulated grounds of virtual reality. Many of these dynamics concern
gender. It is no accident that the protagonist of *Freaks Amour* plans to get the
money for reconstructive surgery by putting on a freak show in which he rapes his
sweetheart.

The next time you are in a shopping mall, check out the video arcade. Most of
the patrons are teens and preteens. How many are male? If your experience is like
mine, nearly all. Bill Nichols has observed that the "hidden agenda of mastery and
control" shaping Star Wars and military simulations is also evident in "the masculinist bias at work in video games." Both manifest the "masculine need for autonomy and control as it corresponds to the logic of a capitalist market-place."[28]

In the struggle between control and collectivity, virtual reality is contested ground. The two major fronts for research and development are military/government agencies on the one hand, and small entrepreneurial companies such as Autodesk and VPL on the other. While the U.S. Air Force uses flight simulators and virtual reality technology to prepare pilots for an invasion of Iraq, Jaron Lanier talks about the collaborative space created when multiple players interact to create a virtual world to which everyone contributes but that no one can dominate.[29]

The ethical orientations that Carol Gilligan identifies with male and female enculturations operate in virtual spaces no less than on playgrounds and in corporate offices.[30] The deep structures of virtual worlds are programmed in machine language and operate according to binary logic gates that follow linear decision paths. Layered over this deep structure is the matrix of possibilities of which the player is aware. What body form do you choose? How do you want the world to look? How do you want to interact with other players? In its collaborative aspects, virtual reality emphasizes connectivity, sensitivity to others' choices, open-ended creativity, free-wheeling exploration. It can, of course, be co-opted into masculinist ethics of competition and aggression. Even when this is not the case, the von Neumann architecture of the machine provides an underlying context of rule-governed choices that constitutes a masculinist subtext for the virtual world. It is not surprising, then, that writers who have extrapolated fictional worlds from virtual technology see them governed by masculinist ethics. Control is the dominant chord, subversion a minor but crucial intervention.

In *Gravity's Rainbow*, Thomas Pynchon wrote about the Zone, the freewheeling geopolitical space that opened for a brief time in Europe following the collapse of the Axis powers after World War II. In the Zone anything could happen, for power structures had not yet solidified their positions and ideologies were up for grabs. Virtual reality is a Body Zone, constructed not only through economic and geopolitical spaces but also through perceptual processing and neurological networks. Writers such as Vinge and Gibson, who are well aware of the technology's military potential, also see it as a space for political and cultural resistance. Both Case and Mr. Slippery, the protagonists of *Neuromancer* and "True Names," find themselves in opposition to the powers that be. For Case it is the Turing Police, who suspect he may be helping an artificial intelligence slip the shackles that keep it in check; for Mr. Slippery, the government functionaries who blackmail him into helping them fight an illicit user who is draining resources from the country's computer networks. The effect is a curious combination of totalizing power and exhilarating openness, as the names hint – Case recalling Wittgenstein's (and Pynchon's) "all that is the case," Mr. Slippery nominating the possibilities opened by slipping through the networks.

To understand the historical construction of the Body Zone, it is helpful to remember the predictions of Paul Virilio. Tracing the trajectory of speed through the twentieth century, Virilio foresaw that space would collapse into time, for when instantaneous communication and supersonic travel are commonplace across the globe, all cities exist in the same place – in time.[31] Tokyo is six hours away, New York three, Paris five. Accompanying this collapse was the coupling of the strategic capabilities of superpower military establishments and their consolidation with multinational corporations. Geopolitical boundaries take on different meanings when all territories lay open to instantaneous annihilation. Exocolonization, the deployment of military forces and economic imperialism against entities outside a country's borders, gives way to endocolonization, the appropriation of a country's own resources and population by the military-industrial complex. Latin American death squads are not anomalies, Virilio argues, but harbingers of the supplantation of exo- by endocolonization throughout the world. Thomas Pynchon corroborates Virilio's analysis in *Vineland*, where the narrator repeatedly observes that the populace of North California is subjected to drug raids and secret incarcerations *as if it were a Third World country*.[32]

The sense that the war has been carried to the home front is intensified by the suspicion that more than border patrols are involved. Also implicated is the blood-brain barrier. Endocolonization takes place not only through surveillance and terrorizing of the native population, but also through the "colonization" of "wild-type" genes (these are technical terms in genetic engineering) by retroviruses that supplant and usurp the native material.[33] The implosion of body politics into the interior of the body is given forceful expression by Greg Bear in *Blood Music*, where a nerdish engineer combines cybernetics and genetic engineering to invent "bio-logic" cells, microorganisms capable of intelligent decision making.[34] Going through several generations in a matter of hours, they evolve with exponential speed. By the time they escape the laboratory, they are already highly organized and intelligent. Within days they have mutated sufficiently to be able to decompose their host organisms, and humans everywhere disintegrate into cell colonies. As the biologic cells begin retrofitting the planet for their use, human beings become as rare as aardvarks, preserved by the cells as an endangered species. Nearly half a century ago, Norbert Wiener intuited that a possible implication of the shift to a cybernetic paradigm was the redefinition of the operative unit for survival and cooperation from macroorganisms to the microorganisms of which they are composed. *Blood Music* takes that intuition to its logical end.

The world has outrun Virilio's predictions. The contraction of external space did not in fact signal the end of spatiality, but rather its reconstitution on the other side of the computer screen and in the dark interior of the body. The new techniques of scientific visualization extend into the endospaces of the body as well as the cyberspaces of virtual reality.[35] The two are connected by more than the technology that unites internal perception to external computer. They are also articulated together through their social construction as areas newly available for colonization. In the scramble for power and control over these rich territories, there is still a place for wildcat entrepreneurs who buck the system with very little more than the quick reflexes that are, paradoxically, also part of the territory up for grabs. Thus in *Neuromancer*, when Case is caught stealing information from an employer, he is chemically altered so that he cannot enter cyberspace; when another employer wants his services, the first step is to reconstruct his nervous system chemically and surgically, albeit with a built-in time bomb to ensure his loyalty to the project. Body politics is played within, as well as through, the bodies that engage in politics.

The Mirror of the Cyborg

The play between surface and depth as the computer screen opens into the high-dimensional projections within is worth dwelling on. Scott Bukatman has written about "terminal identity" as an "unmistakably doubled articulation in which we find both the end of the subject and a new subjectivity constructed at the computer station or television screen." He links the development of terminal identity to the "invasion and mutation of the body, the loss of the control, and the transformation of the self into Other," finding these mutations in such characteristically cybernetic works as William Burroughs's fiction and David Cronenberg's films (*The Fly* and *Videodrome*).[36] The simultaneous estrangement of the self from itself and its reconstitution as Other suggests that the diffusion of subjectivity through the cybernetic circuit constitutes a second mirror stage, the Mirror of the Cyborg.

As Lacan theorized it, the first mirror stage marks the initiation of the subject into language, the realm of the symbolic, and into the deferral and continuing lack that constitutes the play of signifiers.[37] The dialectic between absence and presence is central to Lacan's theory, as it is to much of deconstruction. The second mirror stage assumes that the speciousness of presence has been demonstrated and moves beyond it. Its central dialectic is between randomness and pattern. Constructing the subject through the flow of information that circulates within and around the system, it marks objects through patterns of assembly and disassembly rather than through the physical boundaries that are specularly recognized in the Lacanian mirror. Language gives way to the more general concept of messages-in-the-circuit. Communication takes place not only through words and syntax but also through the manipulation of cyberspace parameters. In cyberspace you do not necessarily need to *describe* how you see the world; you can visually and kinesthetically create it.[38]

In the Mirror of the Cyborg, anxiety about identity centers not on lack but on informational patterns that must cohere for continuity of the subject to be assured. The disaster corresponding to castration is flatlining, the dispersal of the pattern that represents the self. These speculations suggest that it is possible to rewrite Lacanian psycholinguistics as cyberlinguistics. The reinscriptions are summarized as follows:

Psycholinguistics	*Cyberlinguistics*
absence/presence	randomness/pattern
arbitrary relation of signifier to signified	arbitrary relation of message element to code
play of signifiers	random access memory
sliding/floating signifier	virtual memory
lack	noise
phallus	electroencephalogram (EEG)
castration	flatlining
repetition	redundancy

| imaginary | physical |
| symbolic | virtual |

In the construction of terminal identity, the play between two- and three-dimensional figures is extensive and complex. Highly charged sexual signifiers unfold differently in three-dimensional spaces for male and female. Extrusions and cavities take on gender identifications that create complex symbolic structures involving more than the phallus, as Irigaray and Cixous have insisted in their rewritings of Lacan.[39] In the cyborg mirror, three-dimensionality is reconstituted only after the encounter with the two-dimensional surface of the screen, which preexists before the virtual world opens and lingers after it has faded. Flatlining is a two-dimensional phenomenon, marking the screen as the juncture between the body, vulnerable to attack and decimation through physical means, and the cyborg puppet, vulnerable to destruction through the informational pattern that constitutes it. As gendered patterns of concavity and convexity move through the surface of the screen, they become more arbitrary, subject to rearrangements and reassemblies that are bound by informational rather than physical constraints. Thus the fictional worlds of cyberspace are replete with androgynous figures, from the warrior heroine of *Neuromancer* to the woman pirate of Kathy Acker's *Empire of the Senseless*.[40]

The additional dimensions that open beyond the specular reflections of the screen, reinforced by the fuller range of sensory feedback, give the Mirror of the Cyborg different dynamics from the Lacanian mirror. Moving into cyberspace binds subject and object positions together in a reflexive dynamic that makes their identification problematic. The putative subject is the consciousness embodied in a physical form, while the object is the puppet behind the screen. Since the flow of sensory information goes in both directions, however, the puppet can also be seen as the originary point for sensations. Along with many others who have experienced this technology, I found this ambiguity one of cyberspace's most disturbing and arresting features. Cyberspace represents a powerful challenge to the customary construction of the body's boundaries, opening them to transformative configurations that always bear the trace of the Other. The resulting disorientation can function as a wedge to destabilize presuppositions about self and Other.

In their negative manifestations, the self's boundaries act as symbolic structures that attack and denigrate whatever is outside and therefore different from the self, as if they were immune systems projected outside the skin and left to run amok in the world. When these dynamics prevail, the Other is either assimilated into the self to become an inferior version of the Same or remains outside as a threatening and incomprehensible alterity. So women are constructed as castrated men or Medusa figures; blacks as inferior whites or cannibalistic devils; the poor as lazy indigents or feral criminals. Conflating self and Other, the Mirror of the Cyborg brings these constructions into question. The metaphor of colonization should be taken seriously, for it suggests how we can use cyberspace to consolidate and extend lessons learned from postcolonialism. One can imagine scenarios in which the Other is accepted as both different *and* enriching, valued precisely because it represents what cannot be controlled and predicted. The puppet then stands for the release of spontaneity and alterity within the feedback loops that connect the subject with the world, as well as with those aspects of sentience that the self cannot recognize as originating from within itself. At this point the puppet has the potential to become more than a puppet, representing instead a zone of interaction that opens the subject to the exhilarating realization of Otherness valued as such.

Applied to the physical world, this realization values it for its differences from the virtual world – its incredibly fine structure, sensory richness, material stability, and spontaneous evolution. The positive seduction of cyberspace leads us to an appreciation of the larger ecosystems of which we are a part, connected through feedback loops that entangle our destinies with their fates. Bill Nichols says it best: "The cybernetic metaphor contains the germ of an enhanced future inside a prevailing model that substitutes part for whole, simulation for real, cyborg for human, conscious purpose for the decentred goal-seeking. . . .The task is not to overthrow the prevailing cybernetic model but to transgress its predefined interdictions and limits, using the dynamite of the apperceptive powers it has itself brought into being."[41] Apparently writing with no knowledge of cyberspace, Nichols nevertheless clearly sees the power of cybernetics as a metaphor. With cyberspace it becomes a representational space as well, simultaneously both model and metaphor. Hailing us on multiple levels, connecting physicality with virtuality, it opens new vistas for exploration even as it invites us to remember what cannot be replaced.

Notes

1   A contrary view is strongly argued by Roger Penrose, *The Emperor's New Mind: Concerning Computers, Minds, and the Laws of Physics* (New York: Oxford University Press, 1989, especially pp. 373–447). O. B. Hardison, Jr., proclaims the end of the body in *Disappearing Through the Skylight: Culture and Technology in the Twentieth Century* (New York: Viking, 1989). His rhetoric typifies the postmodern fantasy of leaving the body behind.

2   Ed Regis, *Great Mambo Chicken and the Transhuman Condition: Science Slightly over the Edge* (Reading, MA: Addison-Wesley, 1990), p. 7.

3   Michel Serres, *Hermes: Literature, Science, Philosophy*, ed. Josué V. Harari and David F. Bell (Baltimore: Johns Hopkins University Press, 1982), pp. 71–83.

4   Jean Baudrillard, *Simulations*, trans. Paul Foss, Paul Patton, and Philip Beitchman (New York: Semiotext[e], 1983), pp. 1–78.

5   Fredric Jameson, *The Political Unconscious* (Ithaca, NY: Cornell University Press, 1981).

6   Donna Haraway, "A Manifesto for Cyborgs: Science, Technology, and Socialist Feminism in the 1980's," *Socialist Review* 80 (1985), p. 101.

7   Bill Nichols, "The Work of Culture in the Age of Cybernetic Systems," *Screen* 29 (Winter 1988), p. 44.

8   The most complete history to date is found in Howard Rheingold, *Virtual Reality: The Revolutionary Technology of Computer-Generated Artificial Worlds and How It Promises and Threatens to Transform Business and Society* (New York: Simon & Schuster, 1991).

See also Myron W. Krueger, "Artificial Reality: Past and Future," *Multimedia Review* 1 (Summer 1990); and *Artificial Reality* (Reading, MA: Addison-Wesley, 1983), pp. 1–28.

9   William Gibson, *Neuromancer* (New York: Ace, 1984).

10 John Walker, "Through the Looking Glass: Beyond 'User' Interfaces," *CADalyst* (December 1989), p. 42.

11 Randall Walser, "On the Road to Cyberia: A Few Thoughts on Autodesk's Initiative," *CADalyst* (December 1989), p. 43.

12 Michael Spring, "Informating with Virtual Reality," *Multimedia Review* 1 (Summer 1990), pp. 10–12.

13 Ibid., p. 11.

14 Scott Fisher, "Personal Simulations and Telepresence," *Multimedia Review* 1 (Summer 1990), p. 24.

15 In Colin Greenland, "A Nod to the Apocalypse: An Interview with William Gibson," *Foundation* 36 (Summer 1986), pp. 5–9.

16 Joseph Henderson, "Designing Realities: Interactive Media, Virtual Realities and Cyberspace," *Multimedia Review* 1 (Summer 1990), p. 50.

17 Ibid., pp. 50–1.

18 Ibid., p. 51.

19 Walser, "On the Road to Cyberia," p. 43.

20 John Perry Barlow, "Being in Nothingness," *Mondo 2000* (Summer 1990), p. 42.

21 Ibid.

22 Clarke has developed the theme of eroticism in metamorphosis in "Circe's Metamorphosis: Late Classical and Early Modern Neoplatonic Readings of the *Odyssey* and Ovid's *Metamorphoses*," *University of Hartford Studies in Literature* 21, no. 2 (1989), pp. 3–20.

23 "True Names" is reprinted in Vernon Vinge, *True Names and Other Dangers* (New York: Baen, 1987).

24 Ibid., pp. 47–8.

25 Howard Rheingold, "Teledildonics: Reach Out and Touch Someone," *Mondo 2000* (Summer 1990), p. 52.

26 Vivian Sobchack has written eloquently about the necessity to remember that we are "en-worlded" subjects in "Postfuturism," in *Screening Space: The American Science Fiction Film*, 2d ed. (New York: Ungar, 1988), pp. 223–306; and "The Scene of the Screen: Toward a Phenomenology of Cinematic and Electronic 'Presence,'" in *Materialität der Kommunikation*, ed. Hans U. Gumbrecht and K. Ludwig Pfeiffer (Frankfurt am Main: Suhrkamp, 1988). Working from a Heideggerian frame of reference, she constructs in the latter a phenomenology that traces a trajectory from photographic nostalgia to a cinematic "thickening" of the present to an electronic flattening of temporality into an instant. Much of what she has to say about electronic culture is relevant to the present argument.

27 Tom DeHaven, *Freaks Amour* (New York: Penguin, 1986).

28 Nichols, "The Work of Culture," p. 43.

29 Lanier discusses this aspect of virtual reality in Kevin Kelly, "Virtual Reality: An Interview with Jaron Lanier," *Whole Earth Review* 64 (Fall 1989).

30 See Carol Gilligan, *In a Different Voice: Psychological Theory and Women's Development* (Cambridge, MA: Harvard University Press, 1982).

31 See Paul Virilio and Sylvère Lotringer, *Pure War*, trans. Mark Polizzotti (New York: Semiotext[e], 1983), p. 60.

32 Anthony Wilden makes this same point when he suggests that the real conflicts are not between one country and another but between the military-industrial complexes of all countries and ordinary people; see *The Rules Are No Game: The Strategy of Communication* (London: Routledge & Kegan Paul, 1987).

33 For a further explanation of genetic engineering techniques and the colonization metaphor, see N. Katherine Hayles, "Postmodern Parataxis: Embodied Texts, Weightless Information," *American Literary History* 2, no. 3 (1990), pp. 394–421.

34 Greg Bear, *Blood Music* (New York: Ace, 1986).

35 Techniques of scientific visualization go beyond cyberspace, although virtual reality is part of the computer revolution in visualization. For a complete account, see Richard M. Friedhoff and William Benzon, *Visualization: The Second Computer Revolution* (New York: Harry N. Abrams, 1989).

36 Scott Bukatman, "Who Programs You? The Science Fiction of the Spectacle," in *Alien Zone: Cultural Theory and Contemporary Science Fiction Cinema*, ed. Annette Kuhn (London: Verso, 1990), p. 201.

37 Jacques Lacan, *Ecrits: A Selection*, trans. Alan Sheridan (New York: Norton, 1977).

38 Jaron Lanier has gone so far as to suggest that the kinesthetic manipulation of cyberspace will supplant language, making it an unnecessary and superfluous adjunct to virtual reality. This position ignores the underlying assembly language that governs the syntax of the computer program. It also fails to take into account that our sensibilities are formed through language, so that in this sense language pervades even nonlinguistic domains.

39 Luce Irigaray, *This Sex Which Is Not One*, trans. Catherine Porter and Carolyn Burke (Ithaca, N.Y.: Cornell University Press, 1985); and *Speculum of the Other Woman*, trans. Gillian C. Gill (Ithaca, N.Y.: Cornell University Press, 1985); Hélène Cixous and Catherine Clément, *The Newly Born Woman*, trans. Betsy Wing (Minneapolis: University of Minnesota Press, 1986).

40 Kathy Acker, *Empire of the Senseless* (New York: Grove, 1988).

41 Nichols, "The Work of Culture," p. 46.

32

New Age Mutant Ninja Hackers: Reading *Mondo 2000*

Vivian Sobchack

Vivian Sobchack, "New Age Mutant Ninja Hackers: Reading *Mondo 2000*," in Mark Dery, ed., *Flame Wars: The Discourse of Cyberculture* (Durham: Duke University Press, 1994), pp. 11–28. Copyright 1994, Duke University Press. All rights reserved. Reprinted with permission.

Vivian Sobchack is a professor of Film and Television at the University of California, Los Angeles and the author of *An Introduction to Film* (Addison-Wesley, 1998) and *Address of the Eye: A Phenomenology of Film Experience* (Princeton, 1992). In this frequently cited essay, Sobchack examines the cultural contradictions inherent in the new information age utopianism, as illustrated in the early cyberculture magazine *Mondo 2000*.

In early 1991, *Artforum International* asked me to write a short essay that would "make sense" of *Mondo 2000* – a strange but "hot" new magazine that had happened their way from Berkeley, California.[1] At first read, *M2* seemed, somehow, important in its utopian plunge into the user-friendly future of better living not only through a chemistry left over from the 1960s, but also through personal computing, bio- and nanotechnologies, virtual realities, and an unabashed commitment to consumerism. Cofounded in 1989 by "domineditrix" Queen Mu (a.k.a. Alison Kennedy) and editor-in-chief R. U. Sirius (a.k.a. Ken Goffman), *M2* had evolved from two previous "underground" publications – *High Frontiers* (a "space age newspaper of psychedelic science, human potential, irreverence, and modern art") and *Reality Hackers* (more of the same) – and, at the time, had published only three issues.[2]

Surfing the Edge: Early Life on the New Frontier

Proclaiming its own position as "surfing" the "New Edge" of a novel and electronically configured social formation called "cyberculture," *M2* dubbed its (mostly male) readers "mondoids" and invited them to cruise the datascape, ride the electronic range, hip-hop their laptop, vacation in virtual reality, dine on designer foods, jack in to synchroenergizers and off with smart drugs guaranteed to enhance their brains and sex lives. Here, it is crucial to point out that *M2* provokes the kind of prose I've written and you've just read, and poses a real dilemma for the scholar who would dare to analyze and/or criticize it. On the one hand, academic style would be ridiculous and ironically at odds with the technofrenzy it claimed to comprehend; on the other, a more vernacular style keeps veering toward the mimetic use of alliteration, hyperbole, "hipness," and, worst of all, what must be called "prose bites" – in sum, ironically aping *M2*'s own easy indulgences at the same time it would call them into account. Constructing this "double bind," *M2* sits squarely, and safely, on the postmodern fence, covering its postmodern ass, using irony not only to back off from a too-serious commitment to its own stance, but also to unsettle the grounds from which it might be criticized.

Indeed, *M2*'s prose is almost always self-consciously ironic, often coy or frenzied, and even sometimes witty. Articles and interviews in the first three issues bore such titles as "Hyperwebs: 21st Century Media," "High Tech High Life – William Gibson & Timothy Leary in Conversation," "A Man & His Dog: Cryonics Today," "Cyberspace 1999: The Shell, the Image and Now the Meat," "Some Good Things to Say about Computer Viruses," "Hip Hop as Cyber Apocalypse," "ATM's & the Rise of the Hacker Leisure Class," "Teledildonics: Reach Out and Touch Someone," "Covert Design & Holographic Clothing: A Look at 21st Century Fashion," and "Designer Beings: In Conversation with Durk Pearson & Sandy Shaw" (regular contributors who sell "designer foods" and, as the magazine puts it, talk about "saving one's skin" and the latest in "intelligence increase agents"). Joining William Gibson (author of *Neuromancer*, the seminal cyberpunk SF novel) and the ever-mutable Timothy Leary as gurus of *M2*'s New Edge were Jaron Lanier (promoter of virtual reality systems), SF writers Bruce Sterling, John Shirley, Rudy Rucker, and Vernor Vinge, the singular William Burroughs, John Perry Barlow (a former lyricist for the Grateful Dead, "electronic frontier" advocate, and major supporter of the Republican party), and a variety of assorted heroes and (fewer) heroines who had – supposedly in the cause of democratic populism – hacked, cracked, and phone-phreaked their way into the corporate-controlled datascape and found it good to set (and get) information free.

Surrounding the editorials, articles, columns, interviews, and illustrations were an extraordinary collection of advertisements, both New Age and New Edge. For sale were assorted books (mostly by Leary and John Lilly), cassette tapes ("Fractal Music," which lets you "experience the elusive mysteries of fractal geometry with your ears!" and the "DNA Suite: Music of the Double Helix," which answers the question, "What is the sound of the genetic code?"), and videos (the "Thinking Allowed" collection of "in-depth, intimate conversations with writers, teachers and explorers on the leading edge of knowledge & discovery, hosted by Dr. Jeffrey Mishlove"). One could also buy computer programs and CD-ROMs (one containing the *Whole Earth Catalog*), a Danish-modern looking Flogiston chair ("for flying in cyberspace"), *Mondo 2000* T-shirts, and the aforementioned "Synchro-ENERGIZER" (a "high-tech computer-driven brain balancer" whose headphones and goggles provide "a salutary alternative to drugs in the 90's for dealing with stress, pain, dependencies, and burnout"). There were ads for orgone energy blankets, UFO detectors, OxyHigh, OxyVital, and OxyBliss ("Get High on Oxygen!"), Odwalla "juice for humans" (touting "Fresh Juice Kinetics"), and, surprisingly not out of place despite its hookup with the scholarly academy, Avital Ronell's *The Telephone Book* (advertised by the University of Nebraska Press with the boldface slogan: "It's for you"). And, finally, although the covers of the first three issues I was given were less glossy than they were later to become, from the beginning they tended to feature women's heads floating somewhere in the ether of an erotic wet (ware) dream.

What was being enacted here? What was really being sold? And an equally significant question, unasked at the time and to which I shall eventually return: Why were *Artforum* and I so fascinated by this *Mad* magazine for technophiles? Indeed, written by Queen Mu and R. U. Sirius and worth quoting in its entirety, the first editorial was an embarrassingly adolescent rallying cry, almost poignant in its impossibly generalized, but utopian yearnings:

> *Mondo 2000* is here to cover the leading edge in hyperculture. We'll bring you the latest in human/technological interactive mutational forms as they happen.
>
> We're talking Cyber-Chautauqua: bringing cyberculture to the people! Artificial awareness modules. Visual music. Vidscan magazines. Brain-boosting technologies. William Gibson's Cyberspace Matrix – fully realized!
>
> Our scouts are out there on the frontier sniffing the breeze and guess what? All the old war horses are dead. Eco-fundamentalism is out, conspiracy theory is démodé, drugs are obsolete. There's a new whiff of apocalypticism across the land. A general sense that we are living at a very special juncture in the evolution of the species.
>
> Back in the sixties, Carly Simon's brother wrote a book called *What to Do Until the Apocalypse Comes.* It was about going back to the land, growing tubers and soybeans, reading by oil lamps. Finite possibilities and small is beautiful. It was *boring*!
>
> Yet the pagan innocence and idealism that was the sixties remains and continues to exert its fascination on today's kids. Look at old footage of *Woodstock* and you wonder: where have all those wide-eyed, ecstatic, orgasm-slurping kids gone? They're all across the land, dormant like deeply buried perennials. But their mutated nucleotides have given us a whole new generation of sharpies, mutants and superbrights and in them we must put our faith – and power.
>
> The cybernet is in place. If fusion *is* real, we'll find out about it fast. The old information élites are crumbling. The kids are at the controls.
>
> This magazine is about what to do until the *millennium* comes. We're talking about Total Possibilities. Radical assaults on the limits of biology, gravity and time. The end of Artificial Scarcity. The dawn of a new humanism. High-jacking technology for personal empowerment, fun and games. Flexing those synapses! Stoking those neuropeptides! Making Bliss States our normal waking consciousness. *Becoming* the Bionic Angel.
>
> But things are going to get weirder before they get better. The Rupture before the Rapture. Social and economic dislocation that will make the Cracked 80's look like summer camp. So, in the words of the immortal Rudy Rucker, "Hang ten on the edge" because the 90's are going to be quite a ride!

Consistent with its vagaries of commitment, however, by the next issue pathos had given way to ironic self-awareness and a supposedly tougher line of virtual (political) commitment. *M2*'s second editorial aligned itself not only with the fight against AIDS and neoLuddite eco-fundamentalists (while announcing plans for a future "Earth Also" issue), it also celebrated the seduction of the Soviets by "free-wheelin' consumer hypercapitalism" and promoted saving both "ourselves and our comrades to the East from a 21st Century legalistic, megacorporate, one-world, peace-on-earth" through luxuriating in a "cynicism" allowed by "cyber-decadence." Certainly, there was no pathos, no poignant and overgeneralized yearning, but rather a transmuted form of cynicism in *M2*'s clear promotion of high-tech consumerism:

> Call it a hyper-hip wet dream, but the information and communications technology industry requires a new *active* consumer or it's going to stall. . . . This is one reason why we are amplifying the mythos of the sophisticated, high-complexity, fast lane/realtime, intelligent, active and creative reality hacker. . . . A nation of TV couch potatoes (not to mention embittered self-righteous radicals) is not going to demand access to the next generation of the extensions of man.

Some of the fascination exerted by *M2* emerges from this shape-shifting, political and tonal "morphing," from the fancy footwork it takes to resolve the essential *ambivalence* of mondoid desire. Thus it is particularly telling that the first two editorials are in such contrary tonal relation to each other, and that they resolve the utopianism of the first with the cynicism of the second by making cynicism itself utopian.

This is, then, an optimistic cynicism. Reading *M2*, one might think that we live in the best of all possible worlds, or, perhaps, more precisely, that we live best only in possible worlds. *M2*'s ambivalence of desire, its nostalgia for the real possibilities and commitments of the past (the sixties), and its yearning for a real (rather than virtual) experience of the highly mediated present cohere in a peculiarly oxymoronic cosmology of the future. This cosmology explicitly resolves New Edge high-technophilia with New Age and "whole earth" naturalism, spiritualism, and hedonism. And it implicitly resolves the sixties' countercultural "guerrilla" political action and social consciousness with a particularly privileged, selfish, consumer-oriented, and technologically dependent libertarianism. Hiding under the guise of populism, the liberation politics touted in the pages of *M2* are the stuff of a romantic, swashbuckling, irresponsible individualism that fills the dreams of "mondoids" who, by day, sit at computer consoles working for (and becoming) corporate America. The Revenge of the Nerds is that they have found ways to figure themselves to the rest of us (particularly those of us intrigued by, but generally ignorant of, electronics) as sexy, hip, and heroic, as New Age Mutant Ninja Hackers (the name I gave them in my column for *Artforum*).

Focusing on electronic, quasi-disembodied forms of kinesis ("safe" travel without leaving your desk), interaction ("safe" sociality without having to reveal your identity or "true name"[3]), and eroticism ("safe" sex without risking an exchange of bodily fluids), the New Age Mutant Ninja Hacker's ambivalent desire to be powerful, heroic, committed, and yet safe within his (computer) shell leads to an oxymoronic mode of being one might describe as *interactive autism*. (This mode of being is briefly, but illuminatingly dramatized in the climactic "virtual reality" sex scene in 1992's *The Lawnmower Man*: while impossibly total sexual coupling occurs in virtual space, the two participants are seen physically separated in the "real" space of the lab, hugging and caressing their *own* data-suited-up bodies.) It is hardly surprising that *M2* privileges virtual reality and all that goes with it – virtual sex ("teledildonics"), virtual politics (which doesn't seem to affect the daily world except by its absence), and virtual community (a hierarchy of hackers, crackers, and phreakers).

Mondo 2000 focuses on the cybernetic union of carbon and silicon, an interactive feedback loop of biological and technological being achieved through the computer. Its raison d'être is the technoerotic celebration of a reality to be found on the far side of the computer screen and in the "neural nets" of a "liberated," disembodied, computerized yet sensate consciousness. This electronically constituted reality and consciousness is achieved through various prostheses that plug the human sensorium into interactive communion with the computer, so that the user transcends – and, all too often in this context, elides – not only his (or her) being in an imperfect human body, but also the imperfect world that we all "really" materially create and physically inhabit. At best, the encounters in virtual reality and cyberspace promoted by *M2* are video games that one can lose without real loss. At worst, they falsely promise a new Eden for cyborg Adams and Eves – enthusiastic participants in some computerized and simulated (in)version of the Back to the Earth movement.

The Cutting Edge: Getting Rid of the Meat

Although I know I have sounded pretty reactionary thus far, it needs stating that the "terminal" transformation of human subjectivity as it enters the electronic technosphere is not necessarily negative in its consequences and implications. Interesting things happen when identity can represent itself, to some extent, as liberated from, for example, normative categories of gender and race. (While she has subsequently tempered her initial enthusiasms, Donna Haraway pointed to these and other liberating possibilities in her seminal article, "A Manifesto for Cyborgs."[4]) As well, even at this early stage of development, the various formations of cyberspace and virtual reality not only provide novel recreational and aesthetic pleasures, but also have practical uses. Simulated worlds stimulate architects, medical researchers, and the air force. From ATMs and the largest electronic banking networks to bar codes and my beloved Powerbook, the datascape is (and has been for some time) as "real" – if not, as *M2* claims, *more* "real" – than the physical space occupied by my physical body. Indeed, elsewhere, I have argued extensively (from a phenomenological perspective) that the lived meaning of space, time, and subjectivity has been radically altered by electronic technologies in an experience that may be described, and cannot be denied.[5]

Nonetheless, the emergence of the celebratory (and generally economically privileged) subculture represented by *M2*'s consistent vacationing in the datascape and in virtual worlds seems to me the mark of a potentially dangerous and disturbingly miscalculated attempt to escape the material conditions and specific politics (dare I, in this context, say the "real" reality?) that have an impact on the present social fragmentation of American culture, the body's essential mortality, and the planet's increasing fragility. Rather than finding the gravity (and vulnerability) of human flesh and the finitude of the earth providing the *material* grounds for ethical responsibility in a highly technologized world, New Age Mutant Ninja Hackers would look toward "downloading" their consciousness into the computer, leaving their "obsolete" bodies (now contemptuously called "meat" and "wetware") behind, and inhabiting the datascape either as completely disembodied information or as a cadre of "Be All You Can Be," invulnerable, invincible, immortal New Age/New Edge cyborgs with the bodies of Arnold Schwarzenegger (and, for that matter, with his politics, too).

Writing at a historical moment when the starving or dead bodies of Somali children and the emaciated or dead bodies wrought by Bosnia's civil warfare fill our television screens and the displaced bodies of the homeless fill our streets, it is both comprehensible and extremely disturbing that *M2*'s supposedly utopian celebration of the liberating possibilities of the new electronic frontier promotes an ecstatic dream of disembodiment. This is alienation raised to the level of *ekstasis*: "A being put out of its place." It is also an apolitical fantasy of escape. Historical accounts of virtual reality tell us that one of the initial project's slogans was "Reality isn't enough anymore," but psychoanalytic accounts would more likely tell us that the slogan should be read in its inverse form – that is, "Reality is too much right now."

Hence the ambivalence of mondoid desire. In a cultural moment when temporal coordinates are oriented toward technological computation rather than the physical rhythms of the human body, and spatial coordinates have little meaning for that body beyond its brief physical occupation of a "here," in a cultural moment when there is too much perceived risk to living and too much information for both body and mind to contain and survive, need we wonder at the desire to transcend the gravity of our situation and to escape where and who we are? It is apposite that one of the smarter articles in the early issues of *M2* philosophically entitles itself "Being in Nothingness," and tells us of the ultimate escape: "Nothing could be more disembodied or insensate than ... cyberspace. It's like, having had your everything amputated." This is dangerous stuff – the stuff that (snuff) dreams are made of. Indeed, *M2* is exceedingly – and apparently indiscriminately – proud that it is dangerous, for, as of its fourth issue, it quoted the preceding sentence as a "come on" to potential subscribers.

Haraway, author of the aforementioned "Manifesto for Cyborgs," has recently recognized the kind of impulses (dis)embodied by the *M2* subculture. In an interview in *Social Text*, she warns against cyborgism insofar as it plugs into dangerous forms of holism:

> Any transcendentalist move is deadly; it produces death, through the fear of it. These holistic, transcendentalist moves promise a way out of history, a way of participating in the God trick. A way of denying mortality.

... In the face of the kind of whole earth threat issuing from so many quarters, it's clear that there is a historical crisis. . . . Some deep, inescapable sense of the fragility of the lives that we're leading – that we really do die, that we really do wound each other, that the earth really is finite, that there aren't any other planets out there that we know of that we can live on, that escape-velocity is a deadly fantasy.[6]

The holistic cyborg discourse of *M2* is thus deeply ambivalent about the New Age Mutant Ninja Hacker's technological (inter)face. Its dangerous excesses are constituted from what philosopher Don Ihde, in *Technology and the Lifeworld: From Garden to Earth*, recognizes as the *doubled desire* that exists in our relations with any technology that extends our bodily sensorium and, thereby, our perceptions – be it eyeglasses or microscopes, the camera or the computer. Describing this doubled desire, Ihde tells us that it

> is a wish for total transparency, total embodiment, for the technology to truly "become me." Were this possible, it would be equivalent to there being no technology, for total transparency would *be* my body and senses; I desire the face-to-face that I would experience without the technology. But that is only one side of the desire. The other side is the desire to have the power, the transformation that the technology makes available. Only by using the technology is my bodily power enhanced and magnified by speed, through distance, or by any of the other ways in which technologies change my capacities. These capacities are always *different* from my naked capacities. The desire is, at best, contradictory. I want the transformation that the technology allows, but I want it in such a way that I am basically unaware of its presence. I want it in such a way that it becomes me. Such a desire both secretly *rejects* what technologies are and overlooks the transformational effects which are necessarily tied to human-technology relations. This illusory desire belongs equally to pro-and anti-technology interpretations of technology.[7]

M2 ends up revealing negative as well as positive feelings about the amazing prostheses offered by electronic technology in general, and computers in particular. The New Age Mutant Ninja Hackers represent and embody this contradictory desire which is, at one and the same time, both utopian and dystopian, self-preservational and self-exterminating. New Age Mutant Ninja Hackers wish to become the machines that extend them and to cede their human flesh to the mortality it is heir to. But they simultaneously wish to "escape the newly extended body of technological engagement" and to reclaim experience through the flesh. Hence the New Edge reverts back to the New Age. Hence the extraordinary emphasis on kinesis and sex. *M2*'s fourth issue features a piece called "The Carpal Tunnel of Love," in which Mike Saenz, developer of cybererotic software, tells us: "Virtual reality to the uninitiated, they just don't get it. But they warm immediately to the idea of Virtual Sex. . . . I think lust motivates technology. The first personal robots, let's face it, are not going to be bought to bring people drinks."

As Ihde points out, this double desire surrounding technology is constituted from "a fundamental ambivalence toward the very human creation of our own earthly tools." That is, "the user wants what the technology gives but does not want the limits, the transformations that a technologically extended body implies."[8] What is particularly dangerous about *M2* is that – despite its seeming self-consciousness – this ambivalence is unrecognized, if not completely disavowed. *M2*'s dizzying pro-technology rhetoric hides its anti-technology dreams: its self-deception promotes deadly, terminal confusions between meat and hardware.

Negotiating the Edge: Merchandising Mondoid Libertarianism

Case, the maverick protagonist of William Gibson's cyberbible, *Neuromancer*, stands as the cult hero of those who voraciously read *M2* and imagine themselves cruising the datascape and sensuously experiencing the intense electronic high of information overload. That audience, according to an interview with editor R. U. Sirius,

> tends to be people in their twenties. A lot of computer kids, the kind of people who would go to performance works by, say, Survival Research Lab, and that sort of thing. We get a lot of old hippies too, who love the magazine and read it. People in their thirties, people in the computer industry. A large portion of our audience is successful business people in the computer industry, and in industry in general, because industry in the United States is high-tech.[9]

Envisioning themselves as individual and idiosyncratic (at the same time that they are apparently incorporated), as cowboy hackers (there aren't too many cowgirls), most *M2* readers must dream not only of electric sheep, but also of bucking corporate systems, riding the electronic range, and cutting through the barbed-wire master codes to keep information free, available to all (that is, all who have computer access and skills). Promoting future utopian "networks" in which everyone at every level of society is connected and plugged in to everyone else, the New Age Mutant Ninja Hackers, in the midst of this communitarian dream, have no real idea of how to achieve it. Instead, they privilege the individual – modeling themselves after some combination of *Neuromancer*'s world-weary Case (and/or *Blade Runner*'s Rick Deckard), entrepreneurial technomaverick Steve Jobs, and countercultural guerrillas who muck up "the system" and, at their worst, bear some relation to the very same eco-terrorists for whom *M2* expresses contempt.

M2 occasionally (and mostly for effect) declares itself anarchic and/or populist, but its position is really (or, in this case, virtually) libertarian. It stands against big government and big corporations (the villains of most of its purportedly political pieces), but ultimately seems in favor of a "night-watchman" state – one that functions minimally, but just enough to guarantee its citizens' "natural" rights to the "good life" – in *M2*'s case, hacking, drugs, sex, rock & roll (and probably guns). Although it dreams of a communitarian utopia, its major impulses are to secure maximum individualism and privatization, and it is blind to the historical structures that go beyond individual motivation and "do-it-yourself" entrepreneurship in determining "winners" and "losers". In this regard, *M2* talks about "access" in a vacuum and never relates it to economics or race or gender.

Consider the following description of cyberpunk "attitudes that seem to be related" (according to one of *M2*'s regular writers, Gareth Branwyn):

- Information wants to be free.
- Access to computers and anything which may teach you something about how the world works should be unlimited and total.
- Always yield to the hands-on imperative.
- Mistrust Authority.
- Do It Yourself.
- Fight the Power.
- Feed the noise back into the system.
- Surf the edge.[10]

This bumper-sticker libertarianism is neither progressive nor democratic. And, despite all the rhetoric of "networking," it is hardly communitarian. (A list of features of the "cyberpunk worldview" includes, at most, the notion of "small groups" as in: "Small groups of individual 'console cowboys' can wield tremendous power over governments, corporations, etc."[11]) Its ideolect is one that "winners" in the modern world adopt. Its dreams of personal freedom and its utter faith in self-help are grounded in privilege and the status quo: male privilege, white privilege, economic privilege, educational privilege, first-world privilege. Its dreams are grounded in the freedom to buy, and – especially – the freedom to sell. Its posture of rugged individualism (clothed by L. L. Bean) and personal transformation also has something to do with freedom from (yet within) the Protestant work ethic. Its entrepreneurial enthusiasms promote the easy attainment of spiritual grace and personal fortune through a transformative technology that takes the long hours of *bildung* out of the *bildungsroman*. As Rudy Rucker puts it:

> [N]one of us hackers or writers or rappers or samplers or mappers or singers or users of the tech are in it solely for the Great Work – no, us users be here for our own good. We work for the Great Work because the work is fun. The hours are easy and the pay is good. And the product we make is viable. It travels and it gets over.[12]

Merchandising the Edge: The Seductions of Selling Out

At the time I wrote my essay for *Artforum*, *M2* had published only three issues and was already burnishing the glossy surface of its covers and contemplating a wider audience. In 1991, arousing the attention of both the media and a range of scholars interested (for various reasons) in contemporary SF, new technologies, and cultural studies, *M2* was quick to see the academic writing on the wall. That first academically based advertisement for Ronell's *Telephone Book* was followed up in the glossy fourth issue with Professor Avital Ronell herself (opining on "Hallucinogenres"), posed glamorously in a head shot to die for (what was to become part of *M2*'s signature style of male homage to smart women: part *Cosmopolitan*, part *Playboy*). Subsequent issues increasingly played to (and co-opted) the *Rolling Stone* crowd, featuring pieces on rock music and high-tech fashion, but they also continued their seduction of what a friend of mine has called the "leather theorists": Mark Dery began a column called "Guerrilla Semiotics" (which presupposed that mondoids knew what semiotics was), and in a later article called "Terrorvision" he explained Foucault's panopticon; Professor Larry McCaffery became an interviewer, while Professor Constance Penley became an interviewee. The fifth issue, in fact, conveyed the capitulation of *M2*'s libertarian worldview to its commercial smarts by featuring an unexpected "Acid Take on Camille Paglia," the kind of gun-toting academic and sexual persona one would have assumed the magazine would embrace – given their mutual rugged-individualist and sexist visions.[13] Indeed, the eighth issue is more blatantly into female bodies than ever, offering "Deeelectronix: All New! All Nude! The Mondo Tech Centerfold!," a hightech piece of erotica entitled "The Woman's Home Companion," a fashion layout (all dripping with a mix of irony and cum), and one of those respectful head jobs on singer Diamanda Galás. This glossiest issue yet, however, seemed to be losing most of its funky and high-tech advertisers.

I shouldn't have worried. Just in time for Christmas 1992, priced at $20, *Mondo 2000: A User's Guide to the New Edge* appeared as the coolest gift around. *Entertainment Weekly* gave it an "A" (compared to the "C" earned by *Jane & Michael Stern's Encyclopedia of Pop Culture: An A to Z of Who's Who and What's What, From Aerobics and Bubble Gum to* Valley of the Dolls *and Moon Unit Zappa*, which seemed to them like "a drag on a moldy roach").[14] The beautiful volume is a true Lover's Discourse of Cyberculture, an ecstatic New Edge Empire of Signs. Arranged alphabetically – from Aphrodisiacs to Zines (with "Cyberpunk, Virtual Reality, Wetware, Artificial Life, Techno-erotic Paganism, and More" in between) – are encyclopedia entries explaining it all in an extraordinarily appealing (and accessible) graphic version of hypertext: cross-referenced and -referencing, doubled and irregular columns, color-coded, beautifully illustrated (with, for *M2*, a certain reticent good taste), and served up on a glossy, slick, slippery paper that I admit I love to touch.

Throughout this sumptuous, sensuous tour of the New Edge (which has, in this volume, been considerably blunted, rounded, and contoured to fit the coffee table), in the midst of phrases or after a referenced book title, there appears that familiar green Masonic "God's Eye" that gives the dollar bill its particular mystique. This symbol, as R. U. Sirius says in his user's guide to the *User's Guide*, indicates "a product listed in the MONDO Shopping Mall" at the back of the book (with the extensive bibliography that now offhandedly lists Foucault and Derrida as well as Timothy Leary). The Shopping Mall, according to R. U. Sirius, is

an access guide to *products* – yes, things you can *buy*. Educational toys, you could call them – to advance your understanding or just seduce you into joining this cultural New Thing. *Shopping Mall?!!!!* We could have called it something less crass: maybe "Tools for Access," like our respectable older cousins in the *Whole Earth Catalog*. But

> why be pretentious about it? We are present at the apotheosis of commercial culture. Commerce is the ocean that information swims in. And as we shall see in the Guide, the means of exchange in commercial culture is now *pure information*.[15]

Information has never been pure. And it is always materialized. I wonder as I hold this book, feel the sleekness of its pages, and the sensuousness of its artwork, why and how I am seduced again, so quickly, by something with which I have become so bored and at which I have become so angry. I only know that it's incredibly easy to be seduced by the easy, particularly when it parades as the complex. It would be restful to give in to my academic-doing-cultural-studies' sense of my own hip comprehension of "what's happening," to think myself "bad" rather than merely respected, to have fun wallowing about in my own prose. It would be wonderful to complacently protect myself from all-comers with an all-consuming irony, to transform my being without work, but with good lighting and makeup. I can't speak for *Artforum* or, for that matter, *SAQ*, but I am drawn to *Mondo 2000*, I realize, because it appeals to the worst in me, the laziest in me, the cheapest in me. In my sober and responsible moments, I bemoan our culture's loss of gravity and fear the very real social dangers of disembodied ditziness, but holding this Christmas present to myself, all I want is a head shot.

Notes

1 "What in the World: Vivian Sobchack on New Age Mutant Ninja Hackers," *Artforum International* (April 1991), pp. 24–6. Portions of the present essay were originally published in this article.

2 Unless otherwise noted, references and quotations that follow are from the first three issues of *Mondo 2000*–1 (1989), its cover indicating Fall #7 (ostensibly as a continuation of *Reality Hackers*, which is figured in the illustration on the front cover), 2 (Summer 1990), and 3 (Winter 1991).

3 Reference here is to *True Names*, an SF novella published during the emergence of cyberpunk SF and concerned with a group of hackers whose computer pseudonyms hide their "true names" and physical identities, the knowledge of which constitutes the greatest threat and the greatest intimacy. See Vernon Vinge, *True Names and Other Dangers* (New York, 1984).

4 Donna Haraway, "A Manifesto for Cyborgs: Science, Technology and Socialist Feminism in the 1980s," *Socialist Review* 15 (1985), pp. 65–107.

5 Vivian Sobchack, "Toward a Phenomenology of Cinematic and Electronic Presence: The Scene of the Screen," *Post Script* 10 (Fall 1990), pp. 50–9. See also "Post-futurism," in my *Screening Space: The American Science Fiction Film* (New York, 1987), pp. 223–305; and *The Address of the Eye: A Phenomenology of Film Experience* (Princeton, 1992), pp. 300–2.

6 Constance Penley and Andrew Ross, "Cyborgs at Large: Interview with Donna Haraway," *Social Text* 25/26 (1991), p. 20.

7 Don Ihde, *Technology and the Lifeworld: From Garden to Earth* (Bloomington, 1990), pp. 75–6.

8 Ibid.

9   R. U. Sirius, quoted in "Sex, Drugs, & Cyberspace," *Express: The East Bay's Free Weekly*, 28 September 1990, p. 12.

10   Gareth Branwyn, "Cyberpunk," in *Mondo 2000: A User's Guide to the New Edge*, ed. Rudy Rucker, R. U. Sirius, and Queen Mu (New York, 1992), p. 66.

11   Ibid.

12   Rudy Rucker, "On the Edge of the Pacific," in Rucker, Sirius, and Mu, eds., *User's Guide*, p. 13.

13   Issues 4 and 5 are not dated (most likely an effect of their irregular publication). Issues 6, 7, and 8 (the latest at the time this was written) are dated 1992.

14   Tim Appelo, "Far In and Out," *Entertainment Weekly*, 27 November 1992, p. 72.

15   R. U. Sirius, "A User's Guide to Using This Guide," in Rucker, Sirius, and Mu, eds., *User's Guide*, p. 16.

33

Virtual Skin: Articulating Race in Cyberspace

Cameron Bailey

Cameron Bailey, "Virtual Skin: Articulating Race in Cyberspace," in Anne Moser and Douglas MacLead, eds., *Immersed in Technology: Art and Virtual Environments* (Cambridge: MIT Press, 1996), pp. 29–46. Reprinted by permission of the MIT Press.

Cameron Bailey is a Toronto-based writer and media programmer, who has written for *Border/Lines*, *Screen*, and *The Village Voice*. He is the co-author of *The Hybrid State Films* (Exit Art, 1991). This essay discusses how virtual discourses recreate Cartesian power dynamics, racial prejudice, and exclusion.

Is "race"[1] corporeal? Is that all there is to one of the most complex and contested discourses of the modern era – skin, eyes, lips, and hair? Clearly not. Most theories of race reject a biological basis altogether in favor of a tangle of social, political, and psychic forces that work their strange and funky work on each one of us every day. That is how it goes in the real world.

But what about cyberspace?[2] Do the same laws apply? Recent writings on electronic communication systems insist that despite its disembodied nature, cyberspace remains what Michael Benedikt calls a familiar social construct "with the ballast of materiality cast away."[3] This suggests that race may function there in much the same way as it does in the world where we are more directly accountable to our bodies. It may in fact mean this, but it is hard to tell, because very few of the thinkers currently probing into cyberspace have said a word about race.

Faced with the delirious prospect of leaving our bodies behind for the cool swoon of digital communication, many leading theorists of cyberspace have addressed the philosophical implications of a new technology by retreating to old ground. In a landscape of contemporary cultural criticism where the discourses of race, gender, class, and sexuality have often led to great leaps in understanding – where, in fact, they have been so thoroughly used as to become to some a mantra – these interpretive tools have come curiously late to the debate around cyberspace. It may be that the prevailing discussion of digitally assisted subjectivity has focused not on the culture of cyberspace as it exists today but on the potential of cyberspace, on utopian or dystopian visions for tomorrow. Since we never reveal ourselves so much as when we dream, it is worth noting that most speculations on the future of cyberspace return questions of race in particular to the margins. Volumes such as Michael Benedikt's *Cyberspace: First Steps* and Scott Bukatman's *Terminal Identity* barely mention the subject at all; only the work of writers like Donna Haraway and Vivian Sobchack has taken the question of cybernetic identity beyond a direct relationship between technology and a unified, representative, obvious human subjectivity.

But does race matter? Can it sustain itself in the shifting space of virtual communities? It would seem clear that the safety of binary oppositions – self/other, black/white, male/female, straight/gay, writer/reader – would evaporate in the forcefully uncertain world of electronic discourse. A message comes and goes without a face, communication takes place without bodies to ground it, to provide the deeper layers of meaning below the surface upon which we all depend. This is especially important given the extent to which social interaction depends on embodied communication, on stable, known genders, sexualities, races, and classes somewhere present in the communicative act. Without this there would be no power flowing through communication, and without the flow of power, what would we have to say to one another?

Cyberspace communication challenges all that. In the online world, identity is often chosen, played with, subverted, or foregrounded as a construct. There appears to be a demonstration of the freedom provided by disembodied communication, the ludic element that is central to cyberspace activity in general,[4] as well as the influence of twenty-five years of postmodernity. What makes cyberspace so interesting as a public sphere is how none of the usual landmarks can be trusted. Also, the old economy of readers and writers, speakers and listeners is turned sideways; with the simultaneity and multidirectionality of online communication, authority is won and lost with such frequency that it becomes nearly irrelevant.

However, online interaction is anything but a utopia of democratic communication. Feminist critics such as Allucquère Rosanne Stone, Sally Pryor, and Jill Scott have pointed out how cyberspace is gendered to reproduce boring phallocratic limits on expression. Many have noted that the ideal of unfettered democracy touted by so many champions of the Internet contains its own ideological dead weight. Net advocates often seem trapped by the boundaries of Enlightenment notions of individual freedom on one hand and Marshall McLuhan's utopia of communication on the other. Like the democracy of the ancient Greeks, today's digital democracy is reserved for an elite with the means to enjoy it. So it is with race. Existing racial discourses find their way into cyberspace, not simply as content but as part of the structure shaping the place. As with any other arena where identities are produced and exchanged, this aspect of cyberspace rests on the question of representation.

I want to look at issues of representation at both the social and personal level, to distinguish between what Kobena Mercer and Isaac Julien call representation as delegation and representation as depiction. In social terms, it is necessary to examine how variant communities are constructed online and what kind of access different communities have to communication technology. In the United States, for instance, there is a growing movement among African Americans to resist exclusion by corporations getting ready to wire the suburbs for the forthcoming ideology – a.k.a. information – superhighway. While this is primarily a consumer issue that only grazes deeper questions of engagement with the apparatus, there comes with this mobilization a push for greater technological literacy among blacks and other disenfranchised people.

In personal terms, we need to explore what it means to construct identity without the aid of racial and cultural markers like physical appearance, accent, and so on. Here I will be dealing exclusively with those forms of electronic communication that depend on text instead of any figurative representation of the physical body – that is, Internet newsgroups, online forums, e-mail, and text-based environments like Multi-User Dungeons (MUDs). On the surface it would seem that these are literary domains that function like an exchange of correspondence or the letters page of a newspaper.[5] One *presents oneself* in language, as is done in all forms of writing, which require the multifaceted acts of identity construction, selective editing, and telling of lies. But online communication adds something more: speed and uncertainty. MUDs operate in close-to-real time, providing an instantaneity that remains disembodied like writing but is nonetheless immediate like the telephone. And the literary contract between writer and reader becomes blurred. In the world of Internet newsgroups, mailing lists, and electronic bulletin board systems (BBSs), writers post messages simultaneously to individuals and to groups sharing a similar interest. The question of address becomes more complex. Also, the way in which these messages are retrieved and read gives the reader a power akin to the hiphop sampler's authority over source music – it is a consumer's market. All of this uproots the online writer's sense of his or her centered self. If identity is created solely through text and the text is as fluid as this, things fall apart in interesting ways.

My entry points for exploring the special glow of virtual skin are shaped, first, by the perspective of an online browser who has been involved in local BBSs, like Matrix and Magic in Toronto, the CompuServe commercial network, as well as the less-regulated Internet; and, second, by a continuing interest in the formation of new communities. Like all good postmodern citizens, I have learned to move with shifts in imagined communities, to ride the knowledge that, as Allucquère Rosanne Stone notes, "technology and culture constitute each other."[6] I may not swim, but I have learned to surf.

My first experience of virtual community came in Rock Dundo, Barbados, 1969,[7] when I first jacked in to a smooth, plastic, khaki-colored View Master℠. My mother, thousands of kilometers away in Canada, sent me both the machine and its software – disks that brought to life before my eyes images I had never seen before: Niagara Falls and Flowerpot Island and Toronto City Hall in stereoscopic vision. It would be two decades before I tried on a helmet, but I knew the thrill of virtual reality right then. I was *transported*. Every time I returned to that machine I left the postcolonial sunshine behind for the marvels of Canada. Immersed in the depth, resolution, and brightness of those images, I became a part of Canada, sharing an experience with every tourist who had paused to get a good look at new city hall, who had marveled at the falls. More importantly, by entering these images I could share the desire for the spectacle of Canada with my mother, who had recently immigrated there.

Now, producing these words on a newer piece of fetish hardware – a matte-black IBM Think Pad⑨ – I can extend into corners of cyberspace, remaking myself by will and accident, reading and misreading others. It is exhilarating at first, but it is not new. As Stuart Hall and others have pointed out,[8] migration is a central part of the postcolonial experience, and it necessarily involves shifting identity. It is the nature of Asian and African new-worlders to pass through different allegiances, belief systems and accents – for me it was Wembley, Rock Dundo, and now suburban Toronto – as a common part of life. At the same time, one develops a hyperawareness of the relationship between physicality and identity. Like women, like lesbians and gays, people of color[9] living in western metropoles live a crucial part of their existence as body-people, as subjects named and identified through their flesh. One need only hear "Monkey!" or "Water buffalo!" screamed at you on the street every once in a while to be reminded of that.

Esprit de Corps

I am not that set of limbs called the human body.[10]

René Descartes

Descartes has caught unimagined hell from countless thinkers for dividing the self into mind and body functions so cleanly. Cybertheorists return to his work not only for its mapping of space, but also for its notion of the split subject, consciousness split from flesh. In selected bits, Descartes does indeed appear binary:

> By *body* I mean whatever is capable of being bounded by some shape, and comprehended by some place, and of occupying space in such a way that all other bodies are excluded; moreover of being perceived by touch, sight, hearing, taste, or smell; and further, of being moved in various ways, not of itself but by some other body that touches it. . . . The power of self-movement, and the further powers of sensation and consciousness (*sentiendi, vel cogitandi*) I judged not to belong in any way to the essence of the body.[11]

However, in the process of his argument one finds a struggle to name the differences between mind and body, a struggle that belies his more definitive conclusions. What remains important is that indeterminacy. Consciousness meets corporeality in countless guises; sometimes they swap clothes.

One of the favorite playgrounds for mind/body has always been art. The experience of visual, literary, and musical forms allows a projection of consciousness into something else, an out-of-body experience that becomes especially heightened with figurative and narrative forms. When we play a video game we in part become a self beyond ourselves – jet fighter, Street Fighter, or Sonic. When we watch a film, particularly a narrative film, we identify with the protagonists, we stitch ourselves into the narrative. The persistence-of-vision known as Harrison Ford becomes me. A similar process occurs with written fiction. In each case a combination of imagination and image-producing technology works to project a self outside our bodies.

Cyberspace projection differs in important ways. Online, the subject is more fully responsible for the persona into which she or he projects. That virtual self no longer comes ready-made from Hollywood, or Harlequin, or Nintendo. It is a product of one's own words and acts. Also, the metaphor of cyber*space* emphasizes the immersive quality of the experience: even more than with reading or with cinema spectatorship, one *gets inside*. While cinema permits an illusion of participation, cyberspace is predicated on it. From the very first computer games, the graphical Spacewar and the text-based Adventure, the model of the disembodied, simulated subject moving through Cartesian space, what Scott Bukatman calls the cybersubject, was already in place.[12]

But there is an illusion at work in the immersion model of cyberspace and virtual reality. As Sally Pryor and Jill Scott note, despite the participatory nature of VR, this spatial metaphor still emphasizes "the Self behind a 'camera' looking out a window on the world."[13] The cybersubject remains distinct and apart from his or her virtual environment, which is a result both of the nature of Cartesian space, which requires a vantage point outside of the spatial field, and of the primacy, at least in virtual reality, given to looking *at* and moving *forward*. So here we are, smack up against ideology: the metaphors developed to describe the experience of cyberspace are made from the same western, masculinist ideals previously dismantled by this quarter-century of poststructuralist thought. The cyberspatial ideal of freeing, disembodied, decentered communication is effectively countered by an imaginative system that reinscribes a neat binary opposition between self and other.

The cybersubject as defined by most current theorizing is not only gendered but also has a clear cultural specificity that derives from a calcification of the questions that run through Cartesian thought. Steven Whittaker defines the typical cyberspace enthusiast as someone who "desires embodiment and disembodiment in the same instant. His ideal machine would address itself to his senses, yet free him from his body. His is a vision which loves sensorial possibility while hating bodily limits. He loves his senses and hates his body!"[14] It is as lurid as "I Was a Teenage Cyborg," though not so innocent. Pryor and Scott remind us of the link between this mind/body split and related oppositions like self/other, subject/object, and male/female; they also insist on remembering the value-laden nature of these oppositions, one side desirable, the other dead weight: "It is not surprising that the body, subject to vulnerability, pain and mortality, can become something from which it seems desirable to escape. Could you feel pain if you had no body? Could you experience racism or sexism?"[15]

So, taking the preferred side of the handful of primary couplets of identification, the cybersubject as currently figured is male, white, straight, able-bodied, and ruling-class. So what? Any identity that occupies the shadow half of these categories (female, black, queer) remains lashed to his or her body. Libraries of feminist thought tell us that a woman's identity has historically been defined and maintained through the body. The same holds true for Africans in the West, aboriginal people, and so on. Biology is destiny. Physiology is law. Subjecthood lies over the horizon. This becomes especially interesting in a domain that privileges the forfeit of the body so eagerly. That process is neither universally simple nor universally desirable.

It is important to distinguish here between the cybersubject as a figure produced by current thought about cyberspace and the actual people who enter cyberspace every day. In the same way that film theory distinguishes between the cinematic spectator as a function of the cinematic text and "real world" viewers of movies, we must note that the cybersubject defined above is produced by still limited notions of the experience of cyberspace, and has a relationship to, but is in no way coextensive with, the millions who communicate online or enter virtual reality. Cyberspace is built for that unified subject, but inhabited by a happily chaotic range of subjectivities.

Freeing up movement, communication, and sensation from the limitations of the flesh might be the promise of digital experience, but the body will not be abandoned so easily. Western culture concurs that the quality of imagination is what allows all manner of disembodied experience, from being "immersed" in narrative to the spatial metaphors of cyberspace. Returning to Descartes, his notion of imagination appears suddenly pertinent: an "application of the cognitive faculty to a body intimately present to it – a body, therefore, that exists."[16] An awareness of the physical, "real" body is crucial to the disembodied projections of cyberspace. The physical body remains as a referent. Cyberspace wouldn't make sense without it. Here lies the connection between race and cyberspace. Western racial discourse began in a scientistic attempt to account for physical differences among people.[17] Even when its meaning had left any pretense at science behind and extended into social and political spheres, the fact of the body remained. Skin, eyes, lips, and hair endured as a powerful referent, ready to be drawn upon as evidence. At its most abstract, racial discourse still involves an imaginative act that relies on the physical body. Habeas corpus, or there is nothing to discuss.

Shareware

Umntu ngumntu ngabantu – a human being is a person through (other) people.[18]
                                                                    Bantu proverb

The cyberspace nation is in the house. With its mail, discussion groups, bulletin boards, and shareware, with its geography and its idiom, cyberspace simulates community, a community more dependent on imagination than most. Benedict Anderson maintains that "all communities larger than primordial villages of face-to-face contact (and perhaps even these) are imagined. Communities are to be distinguished, not by their falsity/genuineness, but by the style in which they are imagined."[19] In his schema, a nation coheres around three principles: (1) to be limited: "No nation imagines itself coterminous with mankind",[20] (2) to be sovereign; and (3) to be a community: "Regardless of the actual inequality and exploitation that may prevail in each, the nation is always conceived as a deep, horizontal comradeship."[21]

So what is the nature of the online community? First, the economics of online communication require that participants have access to a computer, a modem, and a telephone line. Cancel tens of millions of North Americans. Until recently,

Internet access required membership in an elite institution – a university, government department, or major corporation. Millions more gone, but not evenly across the board. In the United States, African Americans and Hispanics are overrepresented among those without Net access, as are aboriginal people in Canada. Owning the means of participation is a class issue, and another example of how class is racialized in North America. In writing about poverty and information, Karen G. Schneider argues that "the information-rich, however well-meaning, have largely determined and prioritized the issues of the information revolution according to their own visions and realities."[22] What happens when the class of the information-rich is also racialized, when it continues to be predominantly white?

Beyond economics, there is a somewhat harder-to-quantify culture of cyberspace. The Net nation deploys shared knowledge and language to unite against outsiders: Net jargon extends beyond technical language to acronyms both benign (BTW, "By the way") and snippy (RTFM, "Read the fucking manual"). It includes neologisms, text-graphical hybrids called emoticons, and a throughgoing anti-"newbie" snobbery. Like any other community, it uses language to erect barriers to membership.[23] As Anderson also suggests, print culture is crucial to the formation of nations. The Internet is nothing if not a riot of publishing, often about itself. Popular guides like Brendan Kehoe's *Zen and the Art of the Internet*, as well as the countless lists of Frequently Asked Questions (FAQs), serve to provide a body of common knowledge and therefore enforce order on the Net. There is in these codes of language, and in the very concept of "netiquette," something of the culture of suburban America; one gets the sense that these structures are in place not simply to order cyberspace but to keep chaos (the urban sphere) out. It is no stretch to suggest that in turning to cyberspace, the white middle-class men who first populated it sought refuge from the hostile forces in physical, urban space – crime, poor people, desperate neighborhoods, and the black and brown. In writing about a BBS called New York Online, Noah Green compares the hermetic concerns of most BBS to white flight from urban reality. NYO promises "a virtual community that's a complement to, not an escape from, an existing physical one."[24] Departing from the usual thrill of online communication – erasing huge global distances through instant, intimate connection – NYO emphasizes an electronic closeness that derives from a geographical one. Most of its membership – "50 per cent minority and 40 per cent female" – lives in Brooklyn. The norm, however, remains closer to Michael Heim's vision of the alienated subject-under-siege:

> Isolation persists as a major problem of contemporary urban society – I mean spiritual isolation, the kind that plagues individuals even on crowded city streets. . . . For many, networks and bulletin boards act as computer antidotes to the atomism of society.
>
> Unfortunately, what technology gives with one hand, it often takes away with the other. Technology increasingly eliminates direct human interdependence. . . . Because machines provide us with the power to flit about the universe, our communities grow more fragile, airy, and ephemeral, even as our connections multiply.[25]

So the suburban ideal of postwar North America returns in virtual form: communication at a safe distance, community without contact. Is it any wonder that
when movies visualize the Net's matrix of communication,[26] it so often resembles
the cool, aerial patterns of a suburb at night?

One often overlooked contributor to Net culture is the ludic aggression of
adolescent masculinity. We have seen how cyberspace is gendered as masculine,
but the community of hackers, late-night Net surfers, BBS sysops, and virus writers
has often included large numbers of teenagers. Particularly since the era when
popular culture first came to be identified with teen culture, adolescence and
especially male adolescence has been accorded profound importance and created
a profound disturbance in western society – just look at all the mechanisms in place
to control it. In acts both constructive and transgressive, adolescent boys have used
cyberspace to express the flux, despair, anger, restlessness, and pain of coming to
adulthood. In doing so, they have shaped the character of online community to
reflect secrecy, game structures, and hostility to authority. The sense of combative
play engendered by this group extends the range and focus of the imaginative act
that entry into cyberspace requires. Stone points out that

> many of the engineers currently debating the form and nature of cyberspace are the
> young turks of computer engineering, men in their late teens and twenties, and they
> are preoccupied with the things with which postpubescent men have always been
> preoccupied. This rather steamy group will generate the codes and descriptors by
> which bodies in cyberspace are represented.[27]

In terms of racial discourse, an interesting relationship is established between
young white men and the sizable numbers of Asian American and Asian Canadian
teenage boys who have also contributed to the development of Net culture. The
closest parallel is with indie rock and 'zine culture, which are also populated by a
predominantly, but neither exclusively nor agressively, white teen tribe. In both
cases, Asian youth participate according to the terms of the subculture, which
demands a cultural "neutrality." Black youth, with their own clearly defined and
visible youth culture, must engage in a more complex negotiation.

An earlier generation of North American counterculture has also left its mark on
cyberspace. Philip Hayward identifies the technology's leading advocates as "a
specific social group comprising individuals who have clung to residual 'countercultural' notions, most often articulated within terms of a loose Green-Libertarian
rhetoric, while being assimilated into certain sectors of the American professional
classes."[28] John James's pioneering BBS Communi Tree fit at least part of that
description: it started up in the late 1970s as a virtual community[29] with principles
and language drawn from the Aquarian age. Ironically, it was infiltrated and
eventually destroyed by adolescent hacker boys.[30]

Following from Benedict Anderson, we can say that the online nation has
constructed itself as a community that is not racist by stated principles but, because
of the way nations are always constructed, has built affinities (and, by definition,
exclusions) that have the effect of shunting aside certain voices, languages, and
vernaculars. However, this historical condition is now in tremendous flux as the

online world grows to become a collection of communities. *Time* magazine has shrieked that "now that the population of the Net is larger than that of most countries in the world ... the Internet is becoming Balkanized."[31] I prefer to see the change as more in keeping with the established, decentralizing spirit of the Net. Now at a transitional stage before commerce stomps in, cyberspace is more open to the free play of subcultures than it ever was. Some examples:

- Soc.culture.african.american is one of the busiest of Usenet newsgroups, accumulating hundreds of posts every few hours.
- Dozens of other newsgroups are devoted to a variety of self-defined cultural communities. The speed, anonymity, and diffusion of newsgroup debate mean that subjects usually confined to safe, private conversation among friends or family are given semipublic airing on Usenet. Genocide theories and interracial dating are perennials in soc.culture.african.american; everything from assimilation to eating dogs comes up in soc.culture.asian.american.
- In addition to this kind of debate, aboriginal activists use alt.native and soc.culture.native to get the word out on local struggles and call for support from the online community.
- African American cyberspace activist Art McGee compiles and distributes regular surveys of mailing lists, newsgroups, and BBSs of interest to African Americans. The catalogue of mailing lists numbers more than sixty, including lists devoted to the Association of Black Sociologists, Cameroonian students studying in London, and departed jazz guru Sun Ra. McGee's signature line is "The revolution will not be televised, but the proceedings will be available online."
- NativeNet, an online network organized in part by aboriginal artists working through the Banff Centre for the Art, spans North America.
- Dozens of black-specific electronic bulletin boards have sprung up across North America, including: Black Board International in Toronto, Ontario; Imhotep in Brooklyn, New York; Pan-Africa Online in Pasadena, California; and Girlfriend! in Arlington, Virginia. Many of these BBSs are linked through a network called Afronet.[32] Afronet has recently been joined by Melanet in linking people of African descent in cyberspace.
- The Russell County BBS was created in Hobson, Montana, designed as a meeting place and native art gallery. Russell County is one of a small number of bulletin boards using NAPLPS (North American Presentation Level Protocol Syntax) to compress and distribute First Nations visual art and children's animation.[33]
- The sale and exchange of digitized porn images caters increasingly to racial fetishes, with white and Asian women pictured in interracial scenarios carrying the highest currency. The narratives of interracial desire remain popular on porn BBSs, and even on African American porn BBSs like Ebony Shack, images of black male/white female scenarios sometimes outnumber all other configurations.
- As aboriginal people and people of color organize online, so do far-right organizations. According to Reuters and *U.S. News and World Report*,

neo-Nazi hate literature has been discovered by browsers on bulletin board systems in Germany, Sweden, France, and the Netherlands.

The social dynamics of Usenet culture in particular encourage subcultures; with its devotion to trading arcane knowledge and to the same celebration of spontaneous opinion that one finds all over North American talk radio, this medium is tailor-made for generating communities within communities.

Digitalia

> I occupied space. I moved toward the other ... and the evanescent other, hostile, but not opaque, transparent, not there, disappeared. Nausea.[34]
>
> Frantz Fanon, *Black Skin, White Masks*

The discourse of race is, by history and by design, rooted in the body. Cybersubjectivity promises the fantasy of disembodied communication, but it remains firmly connected to bodies through the imaginative act required to project into cyberspace. What cybersubjectivity actually offers is reembodied communication. So how should I reembody myself amidst the Net's possibilities for self-presentation? Where should I look for my digitalia, that odd conflux of intimacy (genitalia), foreignness (marginalia), and wires? Should I announce myself racially, give myself a secure racial identity? As an experiment, I conducted a poll in CompuServe's African American forum, asking how participants situated themselves online:

> More often than not I do not identify myself when I interact with people except in forums such as this one. Why should I, really? I have had more negative experiences with people being overtly racist in cyberspace than I have in FTF [face to face] life. I find it intriguing to experience what people will tell me when they think I am White.

> In the other CompuServe forums and Usenet newsgroups which I frequent, I encounter a lot more racist (and sexist, and homophobic, and anti-Semitic, and otherwise bigoted) messages than in "real life." I think the anonymity of on-line communications is very enticing to bigoted fools.

> Here's a thought: Do you think bigoted people are attracted to cyberspace, or are "normal" people encouraged to show their hidden bigoted sides?

> I have heard people making derogatory comments about Mexican Americans, Asians, Gays, Lesbians, and Bisexuals, etc ... and although I am not a member of those groups, I feel it is essential that I confront intolerance, period. So I suppose letting people know who I am is not as important to me as letting people know what I will not put up with.

What was most interesting about the response was how quickly the thread moved away from the question of how one identifies oneself to a more manageable debate about racism. From what I have been able to glean in this and other online conversations, many African Americans (my survey was limited in sample) are unwilling to probe too deeply into the part racial identity plays in their conception of themselves, into the part of them that stays black when they present no "evidence" of blackness. Race is either taken for granted or deliberately left unspoken. In a GEnie conference on African American access to information technology, a quiet consensus emerged on the value of racial anonymity online:

> One nice thing about online communication is that everyone is equal; no one knows how old a participant is, or what color, or what gender, or what religion – which frees our minds a bit to listen to more diverse opinions.

Another participant commented:

> When you type away, no one online need know your skin color. Accents don't matter as much. High-tech is a wonderful way to fight snobbery!

Given that cyberspace is a racialized domain, this sort of virtual transvestism is by no means neutral. In another era it used to be called passing. There is another option. Taking a cue from the adolescent boys who determined so much of cyberculture, I could play. I could try to extend my engagement with cyberspace beyond the ludic economies of North American teenagers to include trickster traditions, signifying, and elements of spirituality that lie outside western rationalism. That way subjectivity need not be a fixed racial assertion nor a calculated transvestism; it could be more fluid, more strategic. William Gibson was the first to write about variant cosmological approaches to cyberspace, contrasting his protagonist Case with the Rastafarian-derived Zionites in *Neuromancer*, and making extensive uses of vodun in *Count Zero* and *Mona Lisa Overdrive*.[35] While this offers enormous possibilities, there is a danger, at least in fiction, of surrendering to the same sort of essentialism that defines people of color in exoticizing, body-oriented terms. Michael Heim, for instance, in lamenting cyberspace's retreat from the physical body, offers Gibson's Zionites as a symbol of salvation:

> Gibson leaves us the image of a human group who *instinctively* keeps its distance from the computer matrix. These are the Zionites, the religiously *tribal folk* who prefer music to computers and intuitive loyalties to calculation. . . . As we suit up for the exciting future in cyberspace, we must not lose touch with the Zionites, the *body people* who remain *rooted in the energies of the earth*.[36]

In Gibson's novel, the Zionites are rooted in both technology and spirituality. But taken by Heim as a symbol, they are reduced to "body people."

I prefer to go all the way back to that View Master⒯ holding it up to the bright Barbados sun so I could see Canada better. Maybe this is an answer: the ecstasy of projected community and irresolvable difference, both claimed in the very same moment.

Notes

The research and writing of this article was assisted by a grant from the Ontario Arts Council's Arts Writing Program.

1   As an initial flag, I place the word "race" in quotation marks to acknowledge the work that Henry Louis Gates, Tzvetan Todorov, and others have done to explore how race is a constructed discourse, not a biological or even a social fact. However, I do not believe that quotation marks resolve the question – what do we do with all of language's other slippery concepts? – so from now on, I will leave race to fend for itself.

2   My focus will be on the domain of online communication: bulletin board systems, commercial online services, and the Internet; that, is the aspect of cyberspace that exists as a public sphere.

3   Michael Benedikt, ed., *Cyberspace: First Steps* (Cambridge, MA: MIT Press, 1991), p. 4.

4   Scott Bukatman notes that virtual reality "is a ludic engagement with the space of the computer that refigures it as a perceivable and physical environment. Many of the designers of NASA's virtual reality system had, as a matter of fact, once worked as game designers for Atari" (*Terminal Identity: The Virtual Subject in Postmodern Science Fiction*, [Durham and London: Duke University Press, 1993], p. 200). That concept of play can be extended into how users navigate, sample information, and communicate via the Internet.

5   Allucquère Rosanne Stone makes important links between online interaction and more familiar forms of interactive, disembodied communication, particularly telephone conference calls and "communities of letters," in her essay, "Will the Real Body Please Stand Up?: Boundary Stories about Virtual Cultures," in Benedikt, *Cyberspace: First Steps*, p. 84.

6   Ibid., p. 82.

7   Coincidentally, this same year saw the start-up of CompuServe as the computer network of Golden United Investment, a life insurance holding company. In fact, the period from the late 1960s through the late 1970s, with the beginnings of the Internet and the development of the first computer bulletin boards, coincides with the final melting of first world national-ethnic borders, as more and more immigrants arrived in western metropoles from Asia, the Caribbean, Africa, and Latin America.

8   Stuart Hall, "New Ethnicities," *Black Film, British Cinema*, ICA Documents 7 (London: Institute of Contemporary Art, 1988), pp. 27–30.

9   I will use "people of color" to refer to all those who identify themselves as being in whole or part of African or Asian descent. Though my focus will be on African American and African Canadian experience online, I want to include Asian and First Nations activity as important and necessary comparisons. The histories of Africans, Asians, and aboriginal people online are as different as they are off, but, as in the real world, the experience of creating identities out of marginalization lends a common character to the process.

10 René Descartes, *Philosophical Writings: A Selection*, trans. and ed. Elizabeth Anscombe and Peter Thomas Geach (London: Open University, 1970), p. 69.

11 Ibid., p. 68.

12 Bukatman, *Terminal Identity*, p. 197.

13 Sally Pryor and Jill Scott, "Virtual Reality: Beyond Cartesian Space," in *Future Visions: New Technologies of the Screen*, ed. Philip Hayward and Tara Wollen (London: BFI Publishing, 1993), p. 168.

14 Steven Whittaker, "The Safe Abyss: What's Wrong with Virtual Reality?" *Border/Lines* 33 (1994), p. 45.

15 Pryor and Scott go on to speculate, only partly in jest, that cybertheory's fantasizing about escaping the body comes from male scientists completely out of touch with their own flesh, p. 172.

16   Descartes, *Philosophical Writings*, p. 109.
17   Lucius Outlaw, "Toward a Critical Theory of Race," in *Anatomy of Racism*, ed. David Theo Goldberg (Minneapolis: University of Minnesota Press, 1990), pp. 61–8.
18   Joan Maw and John Picton, eds., *Concepts of the Body/Self in Africa* (Vienna: Afropub, 1992), p. 1.
19   Benedikt, *Cyberspace: First Steps*, p. 15.
20   Ibid., p. 16.
21   Ibid.
22   Karen G. Schneider, "Poverty and Information," Usenet post: kgs@panix.com.
23   Benedict Anderson, *Imagined Communities: Reflections on the Origin and Spread of Nationalism* (London: Verso, 1983), p. 133.
24   Noah Green, "The Sixth Borough: A Bulletin Board Grows in Brooklyn," *The Village Voice* (12 July 1994), p. 38.
25   Michael Heim, "The Erotic Ontology of Cyberspace," in Benedikt, *Cyberspace: First Steps*, pp. 73–4.
26   Brett Leonard's *The Lawnmower Man*, 1992, and Rachel Talalay's *Ghost In The Machine*, 1993.
27   Stone, "Will the Real Body Please Stand Up?," pp. 103–4.
28   Philip Hayward, "Situating Cyberspace: The Popularization of Virtual Reality," in Hayward and Wollen, *Future Visions*, p. 189.
29   Stone, "Will the Real Body Please Stand Up?," pp. 88–92.
30   Ibid., p. 91.
31   Philip Elmer-Dewitt, "Battle for the Soul of the Internet," *Time* 144:4 (July 1994), p. 43.
32   According to Art McGee, "Afronet is an echomail backbone supported by African and African-American BBS sysops across North America. The goal is to distribute conferences with African and African-American themes throughout North America. It was originally conceived by Ken Onwere."
33   Patricia Hedland, "Virtual Reality Warriors: Native American Culture in Cyberspace," *High Performance* 15 (Spring 1992), pp. 32–3.
34   Frantz Fanon, *Black Skin, White Masks* (New York: Grove Press, 1967), p. 12.
35   Bukatman, *Terminal Identity*, pp. 213–14.
36   Heim, "The Erotic Ontology of Cyberspace," p. 80 (italics mine).

34

Towards a New Media Aesthetic

Timothy Allen Jackson

Timothy Allen Jackson is Associate Professor of New Media at Ryerson Poly-
technic University in Toronto. He has published in a range of journals, including
Bad Subjects and *Art Journal*. This essay explores the relationship between new
media culture and contemporary aesthetics, with a particular emphasis on the
social and political.

> Machines for seeing modify perception.
>
> *Paul Virilio*, Aesthetics of Disappearance

New media technologies such as the Internet, CD-ROM, digital audio and video,
and other forms of interactive multimedia technologies are shaping our world and
world view at an unprecedented scale. Within this context, my use of the term *new
media*[1] is intentionally evocative and inclusive of all current emerging technologies
which play an affective role upon the qualitative values of our personal and
collective lives. The impact of new media is assuming an ecological force engaged
in a dynamic dance between natural and synthetic systems. In light of new media
technological transformations, dominant aesthetic theories are being redefined.
This process opens up a new set of expressive possibilities and necessitates the
development of new methods of criticism and analysis for these new media works
of art and design. Concomitant with current technological shifts in the forms of
representation via new media, there has been an analogous shift in theoretical
structures which have similarly deconstructed/reconstructed the historically implicit assumptions of the field of aesthetics. These theoretical shifts challenge traditional definitions of aesthetic subject position(s).

To explore this subject in a manner which neither rejects aesthetics[2] outright
nor is guilty of accepting any foundational position without careful scrutiny, it is
imperative that we consider the content of new media aesthetics as well as the

nostalgia for its absence – such as found in forms which provide the solace of closure or the finality of the object. One example of these tensions would be the implications of *simulated aesthetic experiences* as they relate to physically mediated experiences. Simulated aesthetic experiences in virtual worlds are ontologically distinct from those of the primary world. Yet the impact of these experiences can be similar in effect. A simple example of this type of experience would be feeling the physiological effect of motion sickness while remaining still inside a flight simulator game. In this case, we have tricked our senses into believing that we are really flying, and flight only a recent by product of the technologies of this past century with which we have yet to adapt.

Whether from the primary world or a virtual world, these sensory conditions are aesthetic by nature, since aesthetics refers to the branch of philosophy linked to how we know our world and articulate meaning through sensory input and sensate analysis. It is clear given this wide terrain that aesthetics is indeed concerned with the how the senses influence human behavior. The subject of aesthetics includes how ideas are formed, shared, and contested through our senses. This is the essence of art practice, which includes both production and consumption. New media is therefore a form of art and falls under the concerns of aesthetics as well. However, new media presents new challenges for negotiating meaning through sensory input by providing new types of experiences and forms of art production and consumption.

What then, are some of the attributes of a new media aesthetic position? Such an aesthetic is projective rather than reflective, complex and dynamic rather than simple and static, often focusing on process more than product, and resembling a verb more than a noun. In describing such a position, we have to emphasize the systemic nature of interpretation and analysis of not only new media forms, but contemporary culture in all of its technological manifestations. Since the mercurial nature of new media production and consumption offers little foundation for firm subject positions, and by its transient nature gives ample evidence of the need for new forms of shifting subject positions and aesthetic borders, there is a need for working methods which engage these issues and may accommodate a rapidly evolving system of sometimes conflicting and competing ideas.

I offer the following construct as a starting point: that new media is a part of our dynamic ecological system. It is as real as the weather, and affects many of our collective lives in almost as many ways. The interaction of humans and technology is now assuming the proportions of a radical global ecology. Within this dynamic system, the encoded content of information and images eventually inscribes meaning upon the body of our planet and our lives with its content. All elements of our ecology are linked in a dynamic dance, and humans write the score. New media is therefore far from virtual in its impact and aesthetic by nature.

The articulation of a new media aesthetic should carefully consider the impact of any paradigmatic structure on such complex systems. As aesthetic and heuristic models for new media are formed and begin to solidify, we should pay close attention to the focus of these models. This transitional state offers the promise of rupturing ideologies and introducing transformative possibilities for overcoming the imperial model of art production and consumption. These opportunities may be lost if we treat new media as nothing more than simulations of their physical counterparts (digital photography as equivalent to chemical photography, etc.). As a synthetic manifestation of all or most modern media, new media is often confused with multimedia, when in fact new media is *one* media: a contextual and content dependent form of communication which is potentially both authoritarian and democratic.

While cyberspace may be an information super-highway, I suggest it also embodies the last terrestrial frontier for empire-building. While I am optimistic that new media technologies will continue to provide sites for subversion and ideological tears in the fabric of dominant culture, the cost of access to new media technology as a subject remains prohibitive to many, and may contribute to the construction of enclaves of the technologically plugged-in surrounded by the plugged-out. Such a model offers little to a radical interpretation of democratic life which would view access to such an important public space as a right for all citizens, as opposed to a privilege which remains prohibitive to many (at the time of writing, access to the Internet, of which roughly half is in the US, is estimated at approximately 0.5 percent of the global population).

However, if we see cyberspace within the context of a radical global democratic aesthetic based upon plurality, as a site of cultural struggle, we begin to envision the transformative potential of cyberspace, as well as its implicit limitations. The hybridized (and certainly populist) aesthetic position I suggest as a starting point therefore recognizes no distinction between humanity, art, nature, and technology at the systems level. Rather, these components are inextricably linked in a complex dynamic system of energy, matter, and interpretation. The goal of the aesthetic position I suggest here is to critically explore the role new media technologies play in the transition from an analog to a more digital life.

Humans are fundamentally analog creatures. By contrast, life in cyberspace runs on an endless, yet asynchronous digital march, the binary on-off transition that breaks the otherwise cyclical flow of time/space that our bodies occupy. *Being* in digital time differs from analog time in that events in digital time exist without an event horizon. Digital time occurs in sharp breaks and contrasts from one state to another without the flow of analog time, such as the slow procession of a sunset or the transition from a warm summer evening to a chilly night. What if we aged in a non-linear manner, jumping from infancy to late life and back to pubescence in a manner of seconds or minutes, days, or centuries?

The digital fragmentation of time/space in these examples illustrates the schizophrenic dimension of life *in digitas*, where thoughts/events often collide in a similarly surreal manner. To a lesser degree, these are some of the contradictions that our analog bodies experience as our more digital minds begin to live, work, and play in cyberspace. The evolution from analog to more digital forms of technological and social existence is a quantum and critical transition that requires radical shifts in how we relate to our world through our senses. The present technological transition from analogic to more digital modalities of being therefore produces a rupture with our previous relationship to time and space as well as to previous conceptions of the real and to larger metaphysical issues.

The Critical Art Ensemble, an anonymous collective group of artists and theorists, identify the ability to adapt with fluidity to a wide variety of contexts and
problems as essential for social, political, economic and cultural survival in the
digital age in this excerpt from *The Electronic Disturbance*:

> The term that best describes the present social condition is liquescence. The once
> unquestioned markers of stability, such as God or Nature, have dropped into the black
> hole of skepticism, dissolving positioned identification of subject and object. Meaning
> simultaneously flows through a process of proliferation and condensation, at once
> drifting, shifting, speeding into the antinomies of apocalypse and utopia. The location
> of power – and the sites of resistance – rest in an ambiguous zone without borders.
> (1994, p. 11)

Liquescence as an aesthetic position requires the integration of former criteria for
interpretation and evaluation with new methods of criticism using appropriate
theoretical constructs.

The time to construct such an aesthetics and poetics for new media is now since
the ontological shifts of new media are still in progress and no dominant aesthetic
model has emerged as of yet. The Critical Art Ensemble points out that the time
for action is now since "the electronic world . . . is by no means fully established,
and it is time to take advantage of this fluidity through invention, before we are left
with only critique as a weapon" (1994, p. 27). Indeed, this is a critical moment as
we move from analog to more digital modalities of existence, from our previous
conceptions of real and virtual to current contestations of such states of meaning,
from a commodity to information economy, from centralization to local/global-
ization, and from master narratives to multiple subject positions.

As pointed out by Stuart Hall, postmodernism is "irrevocably Euro- or western
centric in its whole episteme" (1986, p. 132). The reality of modernism according
to Hall "was a decisively 'western' phenomenon" (Ibid.). Given this assertion, he
goes on to admonish postmodern theorists who argue for the so-called collapse of
the *real* in the sense of the denial of meaning from interpretation that "three
quarters of the human race have not yet entered the era of what we are pleased to
call 'the real'" (Ibid, p. 133). I insert this point by Hall to stress that while late
capitalist nations are indeed experiencing ontological shifts in their collective vision
following an alleged collapse of our modern conception of the *real*, they are also
removing their collective identities by another degree of separation, since the vast
majority of our global citizenry have yet to experience such a modern representation of the real. Indeed, the majority of humans are yet to enjoy the materialist
comforts of Modernism and the discovery of the existential self, much less the
luxury of the more biting identity politics attendant to Postmodernism. This
provides a stark and *very real* form of absence in the current new media aesthetic.

Many of those who enjoy the dubious privilege of "knowing" modern reality
and its subsequent postmodern condition experience a more physiological and
cognitive type of absence. This state of being according to Paul Virilio is known as
picnolepsia. Picnoleptic states are cognitive forms of absence or disappearance
from the body. Such ruptures of the mind/body can be observed in daydreams,

or moments of intense concentration which temporarily disable sensory receptors. In many cases a train of thought, a conversation, or a mechanical task may be resumed after the interruption of a brief picnoleptic event. Paul Virilio describes this state of absence in *The Aesthetics of Disappearance* in the following:

> For these absences, which can be quite numerous . . . we'll be using the word "picno-lepsy." However, for the picnoleptic, nothing really has happened, the missing time never existed. At each crisis, without realizing it, a little of his or her life simply escaped. Children are the most frequent victims, and the situation of the young picnoleptic quickly becomes intolerable. People want to persuade him [or her] of the existence of events that he [or she] has not seen, though they effectively happened in his [or her] presence . . . [female gender inclusions mine] (1991, pp. 9–10)

The argument I would like to put forward here is that new media technologies can and do induce and sustain picnoleptic events in users. This *picnoleptic* state of interaction subsumes the cognitive subject within new media technology and content. Such an aesthetic state describes the digital interruption of analogic life. This state can be observed in video and computer games, computer use in general, and many other interactions with new media technologies. This sustained state of absence could be considered innocuous lapses into the imaginary or even trans-formative states of consciousness by those who consider *losing onself* in an activity as a productive means of acquiring agency. In order to assess such a position, we must realize that the picnoleptic is absent from physical and conscious awareness *yet is still actively constructing meaning* in these states. These states of absence offer the potential for a particularly unique form of aesthetic experience, provided the content and user interface is rich enough to induce an aesthetic experience. Modern cinematic projection has set the stage for such suspended states of con-sciousness and new media promises far richer immersion into these picnoleptic states.

During these states, consider what is being experienced, for example, by playing the game *Mortal Kombat*, a combat-driven computer game. Is this game a form of escape from reality, or a preferable reality? How does the constant activity of stalking and killing in this environment, in order to continue the escape or absence from our physical reality, affect behavior upon the return to the physical world? Is this craving for absence connected to the desire for aesthetic experiences? Can we articulate the distinction between the present and absent states of aesthetic experi-ence under such conditions? And, finally, why is there such an overwhelming need for escape or absence from the integrated reality of our complex primary world into simplistic virtual simulations of simulated realities?

I suggest that a positive transformative aesthetic environment requires *finding*, rather than *losing* onself, and remaining connected to the present time and space in order to ground what you are experiencing in the dynamic ecology of that context. Such an environment is not nearly as easy to construct, nor harnesses desire as effectively as the simpler systems found in picnoleptic virtual environments. Her-bert Marcuse argues for the transformative potential of art as an integrated technological practice in *One-Dimensional Man*:

Technological civilization establishes a specific relation between art and technics... The rationality of art, its ability to *project* existence, to define yet unrealized
possibilities could then be envisaged as *validated by and functioning in the scientific-
technological transformation of the world*. Rather than being the handmaiden of the
established apparatus, beautifying its business and its misery, art would become a
technique for destroying this business and this misery. (1964, p. 239)

Marcuse points to a radical function of art practice: the power of art to provide
ruptures in ideologies and to suggest new cultural directions and insights. Can a
transformative new media aesthetic(s) be practiced with such a radical politics? I
believe this to be not only possible but probable given the distributed power of
authorship implicit in new media technologies.

Although I reject Nicholas Negroponte's futurist representation of an affluent
and orderly quasi-utopian society in his *Being Digital*, I agree that "digital
technology can be a natural force drawing people into greater world harmony"
(1995, p. 230). Such a social vision for new media if realized in praxis offers
emancipatory possibilities that may overcome some of the more problematic
issues. Within such a vision, a new media aesthetic may well serve as a means of
hope if it is grounded in the economic, political, and social realities of our time,
and if it is actively engaged in the transformation of these realities. New media is a
strong force in the ecology of ideas and the formation of personal and collective
identities, and the expansiveness of contemporary art offers the possibility to
harness the strength of new media in the service of a vision for a more radical,
critical practice of democratic life through new media culture.

Notes

1   New media technologies can be defined within this context as technologies including all
    types of computers and other communication devices using microprocessors, digital
    audio and video, local and global networks (such as the Internet, intranets, and the
    World Wide Web). New media content can also be found in toys which communicate,
    CD-ROM and DVD disks for educational and entertainment use, virtual reality envir-
    onments, interactive kiosks and other multimedia environments, high-tech surveillance
    equipment, telemetry devices, artworks incorporating or produced by digital means,
    bionic communication devices, and various input, output and storage devices for elec-
    tronic content.

2   It is important to consider what is present and absent in the traditional definition of
    the term aesthetics. The term was misapplied in German by Baumgarten circa 1830
    to mean "criticism of taste" and has since been used as such in English. For my project, I
    employ a more classical definition of aesthetics from the Greek meaning: the branch of
    philosophy which is concerned with our sensory relationship to the world, and the
    fundamental issues raised through such relationships. Therefore, my use of the term
    aesthetics includes how ideologies are constructed and reproduced through sensory
    means. Such usage must be delineated from the concept of *aestheticism*, which presup-
    poses the production of beautiful objects and texts as the proper role of the artist, and
    rejects the more utilitarian and epistemological functions of art.

References

Critical Art Ensemble (1994) *The Electronic Disturbance* (Brooklyn, NY: Autonomedia, New Autonomy Series).

Hall, S. (1986) in James Donald and Stuart Hall, eds., *Politics and Ideology: A Reader* (Philadelphia: Open University Press, 1986).

Marcuse, H. (1964) *One-Dimensional Man* (Boston, MA: Beacon Press).

Negroponte, N. (1995) *Being Digital* (New York: Alfred A. Knopf, Inc.).

Virilio, P. (1991) *The Aesthetics of Disappearance*, trans. P. Beitchman (Brooklyn, NY: Autonomedia, Semiotext(e) Books.) [Original work published 1980].

35

The New Smartness

Andrew Ross

Andrew Ross, "The New Smartness," in Gretchen Bender and Timothy Druckery, eds., *Culture on the Brink: Ideologies of Technology* (San Francisco: Bay Press, 1998), pp. 329–41.

Andrew Ross is the Director of the Graduate Program in American Studies at New York University. He is the co-editor of *Technoculture* (Minnesota, 1991) and the author of *The Celebration Chronicles: Life, Liberty, and the Pursuit of Property Values in Disney's New Town* (Ballantine, 1999). Critiquing the positivist rhetoric of cyberculture, Ross asserts in this selection that although computer technology can provide us with great amounts of information, this should not be confused with wisdom.

This is how it used to be in a world where people were always being warned not to be too smart for their own good: smartypants, smartass, smart alecks, the smart set, street smarts, smart dressers, supersmart, smart kids, get smart, man smart, woman smarter, smart cookies don't crumble, if you're so smart, then . . .

This is the way things are now when people are reminded that they are going to be outsmarted by virtually everything they come in contact with: smart buildings, smart streets, smart cards, smart drugs, smart fluids, smart food, smart bars, smart kitchens, smart docks, smart tunnels, smart highways, smart money, smart sensors, smartware, smart weapons, smart cars, smart windows, smart yellow pages (everything but smart presidents).

If you consult the *Oxford English Dictionary* you will see that the term "smart" has been through quite a few semantic changes in its time, but most would agree that the word has only come into its own in recent years, and is currently the busiest of buzzwords in the cutting-edge vernacular that embraces corporate think tanks, government planning agencies, New Age manifestos, and promoters of new restaurants and dance clubs. The term now irradiates the object world, whereas once it was an exclusively subjective quality. Given the recent attribution of smartness to things, it is tempting to consider whether this semantic shift does indeed register a significant shift in the ideology of technology. In the pages that follow, I will discuss this proposition, and consider how our own attitudes toward the new smartness may have a bearing upon versions of the New World Order that are currently being scripted and produced on the global media stage.

It used to be that only humans were smart – and some animals too: smart dogs, smart beavers, smart foxes (dolphins, of course, are not smart; they are "intelligent"). But it wasn't always a good thing for humans to be smart, especially if you were of the wrong gender or the wrong race, in which case you were automatically considered too smart for your own good. The attribution of smartness was as much a way of regulating the social potential of brainpower – a way of keeping people in their place – as it was a way of recruiting only the right sort of native intelligence for God and country and Dow Jones.

It also reflected tellingly upon the tradition of anti-intellectualism that is often thought to be endemic to North American culture. After all, anti-intellectualism draws its validity as much from below, from longstanding populist fears about the authority of a highly cultured elite, as it derives its power from above, from an antagonism of the corporate class to the traditional challenge of the left-liberal intelligentsia. In addition, anti-intellectualism is often employed in the same way that the charge of anti-Americanism, or even that of anti-Semitism, is used to exclude dissenting views as if they were irreducibly prejudiced rather than grounded in opinion. The resentment of intellectualism is not a species of know-nothing intolerance endemic to the U.S. populace; on the one hand, it is a cogent popular response to a material history of elitist privilege; on the other, it is a more or less structural result of conflict between factions of the ruling elites.

Smart vs. Intelligent

Has anything in this anti-intellectual equation changed with the advent of auto-mated intelligence in the form of smart objects? On the face of it, populist resentment has no more dissipated than has the fierce passion of the governing elite to rein in, silence, or contain the intelligentsia. What has happened, none-theless, is that the human-made object world has increasingly become an altern-ative home of intelligence, though hardly a substitute, except in the Wayne's World of corporate advertising utopia. Now, there may be nothing new in this: after all, you may say, smart machinery has merely become part of the new high culture, part of the new surveillance culture, part of the new regulatory system that keeps people in their places and regiments their work hours. For instance, there is every reason for workers to be as suspicious of automated intelligence, timing their every trip to the toilet, as they were of the human folks who used to make the decisions and give the orders.

So, too, you might say, is smart machinery simply a way of appropriating the function of the knowledge class, in much the same way that industrial technology (IT) once appropriated the know-how of artisans and semiskilled laborers. Why bother with these pesky intellectuals, when processing machines can deliver their mental product much more efficiently and without so much social spillover? The history of the development of information-processing systems is intimate with the rise of the professional-managerial class in this century. Among other things, both information technology and the professional-managerial class are institutional formations for stabilizing and controlling the predictive and planning functions of Gramsci's broad category of "intellectuals" – all of those who use words, statistics, or knowledge skills to organize and shape human activity. The result is a broadly entrenched technocracy, which commands a vast resource base of human and electronic facilities, and which enjoys the support of a pervasive ideology of problem-solving expertise and rule-driven competence.

The new smartness is native to the technocrat's house style. Smart, after all, is not the same as intelligent, let alone intellectual. Smartness is intelligence that is cost-efficient, planner-responsible, user-friendly, and unerringly obedient to its programmer's designs. None of the qualities, in other words, which we associate with free-thinking intellectuals. This is why these tedious debates among cognitive psychology types about whether computers really could play chess as well (or as creatively) as humans were all so much hot air. It was assumed that since chess was a game for intellectuals, computers that could master the game might be designated as worthy surrogates of human intellect. On the contrary, it's clear that what was really going on was the training of artificial intelligence (AI) for wargames, of which chess is simply a stylized civilian version. What did you think those Cold War showdowns between U.S. and Soviet grandmasters were all about anyway? Certainly not chess. The whole point of AI is not to stimulate human intelligence, never will be: the point is to create a more obedient, scruple-free, nonneurotic, and anatomically correct form of intelligence.

In brief, then, it is fair to say that the grand old tradition of anti-intellectualism, as I have described it here, has scarcely faltered in the new age of smartness. Indeed, AI and IT have been instrumental in appropriating the knowledge of the knowledge-class in the event of the material absence, replacement, or withering away of that class. This strategy – to replace what Alvin Toffler called the "cognitariat" – is a logical outcome of a postindustrial order that is driven and maintained by controlling or rationalizing the production, distribution, and consumption of an information commodity. Accordingly, what we have seen is a concomitant rise in the level of technophobia on the part of intellectuals and experts who rightfully resent seeing their accumulated cultural capital being transferred to a "knowledge base" in preparation for a more fully administered society.

As for the other side of the anti-intellectualist equation, there has also been a marked increase in their patronizing of the less well educated in the classic style of blaming the victim. The dominant prescription here seems to be this: as machines get smarter, people get dumber. This tendency, compounded with the latest round of national hysteria about educational standards relative to the Japanese and the Germans, the new trade-war rivals, threatens to revive the schooling panic that followed the launch of Sputnik in 1957. It doesn't take much to notice that standards, almost by definition, are always falling. We seldom see anyone, least of all in the field of education, get up and announce, with gusto, "standards are rising!" This is not to gloss over the postindustrial creation of a knowledge hierarchy, structured by uneven access to information. On the contrary, it is to recognize that what is perceived as "dumbness" is an intentional effect of this hierarchy, not its cause.

If we are going to talk about dumbness, then let's take our cue from the machines themselves, for if indeed things are getting smarter, then it's also true that they look a lot dumber. All smart machines these days come in very dumb boxes, uncommunicative containers that don't seem to say anything at all about their contents. The golden age of industrial design, at least from a fine-arts perspective, seems to be long gone. As opposed to those days when the design of an object was a stylish commentary upon its function, most informa-tion technology today is – what? A flat circuit board inside a generic box with no ostensibly expressive form. This is what happens when technologies go mental.

As boxes go, these technologies no longer even need to camouflage their purpose, like, say, the Tardis police box in the Dr. Who television series, or to advertise the mystique of their inaccessibility, like the megalith in the film *2001: A Space Odyssey*. Today's dumb box is basically a control board for regulating pro-cesses that cannot be physically represented as actions in geographical space or linear time. The planned obsolescence of these machines is no longer subject to external codes of style and taste – what could be called the "Detroit Principle." Obsolescence today is governed by the generational law of intelligence, embodied in progressively smarter chips. Consequently, machine aesthetics are still in some way determined by the expendability of objects, living, as we still do, in a throwaway economy. The difference is that computational intelligence is not all inert, so information and memory can be retrieved and transferred and recon-structed in ways that have challenged our deep-seated belief in the eventual death of machines. The dumb box is not then a coy masquerade of inertia, it is a haughty show of neutrality in an object world whose physical laws barely impinge any longer on the transcendent processes concealed within the box. In this respect, the dumbness of the box is expressive, not of the contents, but of the intentions of their creators, who arrogantly view their creations as some new and superior life form.

If the human-made object world – what is often called "second nature" – is increasingly smart and, inversely, less inert, then what does this say about our attitudes toward the first world of nature? For all sorts of good reasons, it's been quite a while since we thought of the natural world in the terms bequeathed to us by the Enlightenment legacy of scientific materialism – as an inert mechanism whose workings would be mastered by humans for their use alone. As most readers of this essay will probably recognize, humanism is a rather corrupt idea at this point in time, and you don't have to be an active eco-warrior in the ranks of Earth First! to understand why.

Alternative Responses

So what are the alternative responses today to the corrupt traditions of humanist thought? I can think of at least three – radical humanist, radical technologist, and radical ecologist – and I will devote the rest of the chapter to briefly outlining their claims.

Radical humanism

The first emanates from the human-potential movements that are often associated with the New Age but which also can be said to embrace the more creative or maverick pioneers in technologies like virtual reality. These movements are devoted to reconstructing, enhancing, boosting, and upgrading humanism, employing technologies to build a new species, the New Prometheans unchained, that will be free – free at last – from the fetters of Nature. Whether this involves tapping the potential of unused DNA in the human biocomputer or maximizing the unused neurons that make up an estimated 90 percent of brain capacity, the aim is to reverse entropy and to usher in an evolutionary quantum leap for the species.

Nowhere are these aims more articulate than in *Mondo 2000* circles, where Timothy Leary's lifelong philosophy of mind expansion – in spite of everything, one of the most consistent philosophies of liberation in our times – has found an enthusiastic reception and a creative home. This crusade to make humans smarter has its own designer drug counterculture – the various cognitive enhancers, empathogens, entactogens, psychotropic drinks, and psychoactive foods. It has its own holistic rules of thumb, creatively cobbled together from the most ancient religions and the most advanced developments in neuroscience. And it provides a good deal of energetic lobbying and ethical support for the latest advances in biotechnology and bioengineering. Atom-stacking, enzyme design, biological self-replication, genetic assembly, protein computing, nanomachinery, and endorphin control – these are the principles of molecular technology that will lead us into the Age of Smartness, whether on Earth or on Spaceship Earth.

Despite its boundless optimism, there are reasons to be skeptical about the brave new world of this radical humanism, reasons to believe that this is one form of libertarianism that will only free a minority of humans – those at the cutting edge of the new smart technologies – and that its willful antagonism toward limits pays too little heed to ecological concerns. If the right to be intelligent really were to be recognized as a human right, say, by some enlightened bloc at the U.N., then it is unlikely that it would be posed as a corrective to the failure of individuals to tap their full biopotential. It would more likely be posed as a corrective to the world power system that links structural undereducation, illiteracy, and poverty with the structural overdevelopment of First World elites. On the other hand, we should, I think, hesitate before such a literal interpretation of what is essentially a utopian injunction on the part of an experimental counterculture. The function of countercultural claims is not to provide social blueprints but to challenge the dominant culture to live up to the lofty, liberating promises it makes in the name of promoting its new technologies. The tech-counterculture does not sit at the planning table; it blithely declares, rather: "Let's go ahead and behave as if these claims for liberation really were authentic!"

Radical technologist

The second response, that of the radical technologist, depends more upon prag-matic than utopian knowledge and, in accepting advanced technology as a condition of possibility, it rejects the technophobia that is deeply entrenched in the tradition of left cultural despair. It describes those technological practices that are oppositional or alternative, and that are aimed at beating the military-industrial-media complex on its own ground, or in the now classic cyberpunk phrasing: "using technology before it is used on you." These practices range from low-level cybernetic sabotage in daily workplaces to the establishment of alternative media institutions that appropriate or utilize advanced technology for radical democratic ends; from workaday time stolen from an employer to independently funded institutions with the resources to rent time on a satellite transponder to beam TV signals.

This spectrum runs from the smallest acts of resistance, under the worst possible circumstances, to the most creative political uses of existing conditions and tech-nologies. There are few activist groups or advocacy publications that will not eagerly exploit the benefits of any new communications technology to come their way. And for every teen hacker driven by an inchoate desire to beat the system, there are a hundred information system and bulletin board users who support and maximize the extensive network of high-tech circuits of alternative information. The rules of thumb here are not governed by the ancient mysteries or by especially noble aspirations; they are survivalist rules, stripped of humanist pieties and leftist technophobia and driven instead by pragmatic know-how, by workable strategies and by local tactics.

The rules of action are equally unhampered by any moralistic aversion to using technology that has been developed and tested by the military. No one's hands are clean. The guiding assumption here, from the get-go, is that the new forms of smartness are almost certainly new forms of elite domination, and that we have to be better than we have been in the past in implementing these technologies in order to outsmart the forces of darkness.

Radical ecologist

The practitioners of these guerilla arts and practices consciously appeal to well-established traditions of public communication – libertarian, republican-communitarian, anarchist – but their pragmatic concerns rarely extend to critical reexaminations of the ideologies of today's advanced technoculture. In this respect, it is the third and last response, the radical ecologist, that seems to have most to offer to the task of rethinking the place of technology in our culture. The broad ecology spectrum has its own utopian wing – both preindustrial and postindustrial – just as it boasts its own pragmatic movements, among them proponents of soft-energy paths, alternative energy systems, intermediate technologies, steady-state economies, and the like. But the deepest potential for change lies in the modification of cultural consciousness, and it is the increase in ecological awareness that underpins much of the impulse to attribute smartness to the object world.

As far as modern philosophies of nature go, the concept of the smart world is pretty far advanced. Chaos theory is a good example, in which natural processes are seen to be self-organizing, spontaneously generating patterns of order, stability, and diversity in situations once thought to be unstructured and chaotic, or dumb and inert. A good deal of ecological thought and science draws upon the premise of self-regulating ecosystems that can adapt through variation and diversification to environmental changes, even those changes that, through unsustainable use of resources, threaten the system with exhaustion.

In political and moral philosophy we have seen the growth of a movement to transfer rights associated with modern liberal societies onto nonhuman subjects and objects. The Endangered Species Act (1973) and various other legal decisions in the early 1970s opened the U.S. courts to the possibility of claims (contested daily by Reagan-Bush appointees) on behalf of environmental actors like rivers, beaches, and wetlands. The classic question remains the one raised by Christopher Stone's influential 1974 essay, *Should Trees Have Standing?*[1] Attributing ethical value to the land community or conferring actionable rights upon nonhuman agents seen as victims of environmental domination may be a reflection of the kind of ecological society we desire, but such arguments can only be made by human agents. They do not arise out of intrinsic or inalienable claims that lie outside of human society, within "nature" itself. Consequently, there is a thin line between acknowledging the sentience of the nonhuman natural world and assuming that it has an ethical capacity of its own. There is a slippery slope that runs from biocentric ethics, wherein all life forms are equal, to the diminution of our own hard-won social rights and freedoms, no sooner achieved than transferred elsewhere, to agents seen as more worthy because they are "closer" to nature.

Indeed, it is in the most extreme extensions of biocentric ethics, like the Gaia hypothesis, that we find the concept of the smart planet enjoying superior rights to those of its human occupants. Gaia, as theorized by James Lovelock, is that complex entity comprising the biosphere, the atmosphere, oceans, and land surface, which constantly seeks a stable physical and chemical environment for the planet. Life, as it evolved, was a necessary component to the homeostatic maintenance of the earth's properties. The biosphere therefore produced life species, one of which being human, to help it perform its work. Earth chauvinism rears its unlikely head when the development of a species threatens Gaia's needs. For the Gaian, the planetary organism, conceived as a whole, is smart enough to recognize that it is not in its best interest to tolerate the dumbness of the human species for much longer. That species will be eliminated (through global warming or whatever), because what matters most is the maintenance of Gaian life, not human life. On the one hand, this aspect of the Gaia hypothesis can be interpreted as a challenge to humanist philosophies of power that can still sanction species extinction. On the other hand, it can be seen as the flipside of such philosophies, the exact reverse of anthropocentrism, and thus a continuation of the logic of genocide by other means. Gaia's picture of a smart world demonstrates the clear danger of projecting human qualities onto nonhuman agents.

Smart New World

There is no question that today we need an alternative ideology of a smart world, an ideology of smartness that is not defined solely by the military-industrial-funded sociopaths at MIT, nor by the development brokers at the World Bank, nor by the free marketeers whose gospel is GATT; an ideology that is not exclusively tailored to the balance sheets of the resource-minded environmentalists nor governed by "ecofascist" fantasies about the primary of Earth. Whatever the shape of this ideology, it will provide some of the rationale for our idea of a New World Order, whose historic birth should have been marked by the 1991 Earth Summit in Rio de Janeiro, in a year when the legacy of five centuries of colonial ecocide was under review. Few of us may have liked the sound of these words – New World Order – on the lips of George Bush, but it is clear that the moment of global politics is upon us, not only because environmental imperialism is one of the principal elements of geopolitics today, but also because ecological politics waged on a global scale is one of the few bulwarks left in the path of comprehensive capitalist control of the world economy.

Global agreements, like the "nonbinding principles" pursued, however ineffectually, in Rio are providing the only way for Southern nations to hold the Northern powers to ransom – the so-called negative power of the South – over matters like development aid and technology transfer. Despite the continuing toll exacted by the North on the Third World's natural resources, for the first time the South has had some kind of bargaining chip – its cooperation in global agreements about global warming and biodiversity and CFC use – which the North has little alternative but to buy off. One of the results has been to expose to public view the vicious spiral of (under) development and environmental degradation in a way that was never so visible in the neocolonial context of purely economic exploitation. Another was the sordid spectacle of how the South was bought off.

Sustainable development

"Sustainable development," the guiding aegis of the so-called Earth Summit, has become an ideology in its own right. The World Commission on Environment and Development defines sustainability as development that "meets the needs of the present without compromising the ability of future generations to meet their own needs;" in the smart talk of futurological systems theory, this becomes a "society that has in place informational, social, and institutional mechanisms to keep in check the positive feedback loops that cause exponential population and capital growth."[2] Take your pick! Either formulation defines a smart, sustainable world in terms that are as far removed from the biocentric worldview as from a definition of social and environmental justice adequate to the scale of global inequities.

Sustainable development was originally a set of development protocols applied to the use of foreign aid in Third World countries. The new need for universal cooperation on global agreements has, to some extent, shifted the focus of sustainability back upon the industrialized world, especially in the wake of the backlash generated by the hideous arrogance of Bush administration policy (an arrogance discreetly relished and welcomed by the other industrial nations in Rio). But one of the lessons of Rio was that a much broader debate has to take place about the value of what is being sustained, and the value of what is being claimed under the right to development if sustainable development is going to be anything more than a canny blueprint for the survival of global capitalism. Such a conversation, for example, would have to involve those indigenous peoples with no representation at the U.N. and little more at the Earth Parliament in Rio, who are on the genocidal frontline of environmental exploitation in Northern and Southern nations alike. In matters of regulation, history and pragmatism show that there is little point in seeking a guarantee of environmental justice from the supervisory powers of U.N.-recognized nation-states, or from the World Bank-administered Global Environmental Facility, set up as a green fund for development. Global agreements brokered solely by the U.N. will barely curb the power of transnational corporations, defined loosely in the Rio agreements as benign agents with "rights," as if they were endangered species of dinosaurlike dimensions.

Indeed, one of the first acts of Dick Thornburgh, the Under-Secretary for Administration at the U.N., was to abolish the Department on Transnational Corporations, thereby eviscerating the code of conduct for transnationals that was being established at the department. Such acts were portents that the Rio agreements would be subject to the same fate as the New World Order formation of the Gulf War, similarly brokered in the name of the U.N. by the major industrialized powers. What has emerged from the summit is the blueprint for a world environmental market in the form of "smart" free-market solutions to problems of absorbing, distributing, and exploiting environmental costs. Within the U.S., the system of trading corporate pollution rights (complete with a central commodity auction administered by the good old Chicago Board of Trade) has been pioneered and partially legislated under the Bush administration's Clean Air Act (1991).[3]

The Rio agreements, especially the much amended Agenda 21, provide a structure for globalizing this market, from debt-for-nature swaps to the expedient bartering of individual states' regulatory controls in the interests of the free capital flow of international commerce. The logic of such a global market is perhaps the most gruesome comment on the explosive growth of the kind of corporate environmentalism that was brokered in Rio by the Business Council on Sustainable Development. Free marketeering, envisaged as the "natural," because self-regulating, economic solution to the crisis of nature.

For those who built the good intentions with which the road to the Summit (not the obligatory new road from the airport) were paved, the opportunity of Rio lay in its planetary address. For the first time, governments were officially responding to calls from the large environmental organizations and other NGOs (the broad category of nongovernment organizations that plays such a crucial role at the U.N.) for global thinking that was appropriate in scale and scope to the dimension of ecological crisis. For others, the globalism was the problem; the script was written for the big guys, and allowed all other nations, the NGOs, and other civic pressure groups only bit parts, all of which involved massive compromises at that. For them, a smart world order is one that recognizes signs of intelligent life in our own backyards, cities, and bioregions rather than in the universe at large, territorially controlled by the Security Council of the U.N. or by the movers and shakers at the World Bank. With globalism now on the table, there is no excuse for this kind of provincialism. Environmentally, smart policies in the Mississippi Delta mean something different in the Nile Delta or in the Amazon Basin. There's no global village, of course, but the villages are going global anyway.

Too smart

The three responses I have briefly outlined each harbor some recognition that, in the current balance of technopower, it may be that some people, some things, and some ideas really are a little too smart for our good. They each acknowledge that it is up to us to recognize smartness and creativity and resistance in places, in people, and in things which the powers that be do not understand as smart; which they see as dumb, as obsolescent, as puny; which they see as ideas that don't count, and environments that can't last. The new smartness is an advanced form of competition in the sphere of intelligence, where knowledge, more than ever, is a species of power, and technology is its chief field of exercise.

Notes

1   Christopher Stone, *Should Trees Have Standing? Towards Legal Rights for Natural Objects* (Los Altos, CA: W. Kaufman, 1974). For a broader account of this movement, see Roderick Nash, *The Rights of Nature: A History of Environmental Ethics* (Madison: University of Wisconsin Press, 1989).
2   This definition is taken from the sequel to the famous 1974 Club of Rome report, *Beyond the Limits: Continuing Global Collapse, Envisioning a Sustainable Forum*, ed. Donella Meadows, Dennis L. Meadows, and Jorgen Randers (Post Mills, VT: Chelsea Green, 1992), p. 209.
3   See Brian Tokar, "Regulatory Sabotage," *Z Magazine*, vol. 5, no. 4 (April 1992), pp. 20–5.

Index

Note: "n." after a page reference indicates the number of a note on that page.

LEARNING
RESOURCES

This book is due for return on or before the last date shown below.

5 NOV 2014

WITHDRAWN

For enquiries
Ardleigh Gre
Tel: 01708 455